HUMAN RIGHTS RESPONSIBILITIES IN THE DIGITAL AGE

This book examines the tangled responsibilities of states, companies and individuals surrounding human rights in the digital age. Digital technologies have a huge impact – for better and worse – on human lives; while they can clearly enhance some human rights, they also facilitate a wide range of violations.

States are expected to implement efficient measures against powerful private companies, but, at the same time, they are drawn to technologies that extend their own control over citizens. Tech companies are increasingly asked to prevent violations committed online by their users, but their own business models depend on the accumulation and exploitation of users' personal data. Meanwhile, where civil society has a crucial part to play in upholding human rights, it is also the case that individuals harm other individuals online. All three stakeholders (states, companies and individuals) need to ensure that technology does not provoke the disintegration of human rights.

Bringing together experts from a range of disciplines, including law, international relations and journalism, this book provides a detailed analysis of the impact of digital technologies on human rights that will be of interest to academics, research students and professionals concerned by this issue.

Human Rights Responsibilities in the Digital Age

States, Companies and Individuals

Edited by
Jonathan Andrew
and
Frédéric Bernard

·HART·
OXFORD · LONDON · NEW YORK · NEW DELHI · SYDNEY

HART PUBLISHING

Bloomsbury Publishing Plc

Kemp House, Chawley Park, Cumnor Hill, Oxford, OX2 9PH, UK

1385 Broadway, New York, NY 10018, USA

29 Earlsfort Terrace, Dublin 2, Ireland

HART PUBLISHING, the Hart/Stag logo, BLOOMSBURY and the Diana logo are trademarks of Bloomsbury Publishing Plc

First published in Great Britain 2021

Copyright © The editors and contributors severally 2021

The editors and contributors have asserted their right under the Copyright, Designs and Patents Act 1988 to be identified as Authors of this work.

All rights reserved. No part of this publication may be reproduced or transmitted in any form or by any means, electronic or mechanical, including photocopying, recording, or any information storage or retrieval system, without prior permission in writing from the publishers.

While every care has been taken to ensure the accuracy of this work, no responsibility for loss or damage occasioned to any person acting or refraining from action as a result of any statement in it can be accepted by the authors, editors or publishers.

All UK Government legislation and other public sector information used in the work is Crown Copyright ©. All House of Lords and House of Commons information used in the work is Parliamentary Copyright ©. This information is reused under the terms of the Open Government Licence v3.0 (http://www.nationalarchives.gov.uk/doc/open-government-licence/version/3) except where otherwise stated.

All Eur-lex material used in the work is © European Union, http://eur-lex.europa.eu/, 1998–2021.

A catalogue record for this book is available from the British Library.

Library of Congress Cataloging-in-Publication data

Names: Andrew, Jonathan, editor. | Bernard, Frédéric, 1979- editor.
Title: Human rights responsibilities in the digital age : states, companies, and individuals / edited by Jonathan Andrew and Frédéric Bernard.
Description: Gordonsville : Hart Publishing, an imprint of Bloomsbury Publishing, 2021. | Includes bibliographical references and index.
Identifiers: LCCN 2021020329 (print) | LCCN 2021020330 (ebook) | ISBN 9781509938834 (hardback) | ISBN 9781509952700 (paperback) | ISBN 9781509938841 (pdf) | ISBN 9781509938858 (Epub)
Subjects: LCSH: Human rights—21st century. | Human rights—Effect of technological innovations on. | Social responsibility of business—Law and legislation. | International law and human rights. | Privacy, Right of.
Classification: LCC K3240 .H8625 2021 (print) | LCC K3240 (ebook) | DDC 323—dc23

LC record available at https://lccn.loc.gov/2021020329

LC ebook record available at https://lccn.loc.gov/2021020330

ISBN:	HB:	978-1-50993-883-4
	ePDF:	978-1-50993-884-1
	ePub:	978-1-50993-885-8

Typeset by Compuscript Ltd, Shannon

To find out more about our authors and books visit www.hartpublishing.co.uk. Here you will find extracts, author information, details of forthcoming events and the option to sign up for our newsletters.

This book was made possible through the generous support of the Swiss Federal Department of Foreign Affairs and of the University of Geneva.

The editors wish to express their utmost gratitude to Alice Breathe, *Adjointe scientifique*, for her tireless commitment, dedication and diligence in the realisation of this publication.

The opinions expressed in it are those of the authors and do not necessarily reflect the views of any particular organisation.

TABLE OF CONTENTS

Contributors .... *xiii*

1. *Introduction* *1*
   Jonathan Andrew

   I. The Evolution of Human Rights in the Digital Age 1
   II. State Obligations to Respect, Protect and Fulfil Human Rights
       in the Digital Sphere 5
   III. Corporate Responsibilities in the Digital Sphere 9
   IV. Apportioning Responsibilities Fairly 12
   V. Civic Duties in the Digital Sphere 15
   VI. Dialogue, Cooperation and Regulation 16

2. *Cybersecurity and Human Rights: Understanding the Connection* *19*
   Vivek Krishnamurthy, Devony Schmidt and Amy Lehr

   I. Defining Cybersecurity 20
      A. The Contested Definition of Security 24
      B. Lessons Learned 25
      C. A Parsimonious Definition of Cybersecurity 26
   II. The Relationship between Cybersecurity and
       Human Rights 27
      A. (Cyber-)Security and Human Rights Trade-Offs 27
      B. Implications 32
   III. Conclusion 35

3. *Perils of Data-Intensive Systems in the Philippines and Asia* *37*
   Jamael Jacob

   I. A Digital and Data-Driven World 38
   II. Shifting to the East 41
   III. Impact of Data-Intensive Systems 45
   IV. The Philippines: A Case Study 50
   V. Conclusion 57

4. *Freedom of Peaceful Assembly and Association in an Age of Online Networks and Mobile Sensing* 61
   Jonathan Andrew

   I. Introduction 61
   II. The Limits of Surveillance in European and US Jurisprudence 63
   III. From Labour Relations and Political Representation to Interactive Gaming: The Evolution of Assembly and Association 66
   IV. Ubiquitous Sensing Networks: A Paradigm Shift for Monitoring Capabilities 71
   V. Conclusion 74

5. *Algorithms of Occupation: Use of Artificial Intelligence in Israel and Palestine* 75
   Marwa Fatafta

   I. Introduction 75
   II. Artificial Intelligence and Human Rights 78
   III. Predictive Policing in Israel and Palestine 81
   IV. Conclusion 89

6. *The Facebook Oversight Board and the UN Guiding Principles on Business and Human Rights: A Missed Opportunity for Alignment?* 93
   Stefania Di Stefano

   I. Introduction 93
   II. Private Norms Governing the Digital Public Sphere 95
      A. Content Moderation: The 'Essence' of Platforms 95
      B. How Facebook Governs Speech 98
   III. An Independent Mechanism to Adjudicate Content Disputes 101
   IV. The Facebook Oversight Board and the UN Guiding Principles on Business and Human Rights 107
      A. The UN Guiding Principles on Business and Human Rights and the Corporate Responsibility to Respect and Remedy 107
      B. A Missed Opportunity for Alignment? 110
   V. Conclusion 115

7. *Privacy in the Workplace: A Human Rights Due Diligence Approach* 117
   Isabel Ebert and Isabelle Wildhaber

   I. Introduction 117
   II. Data-Driven Workplace Monitoring and Privacy 119
      A. Opacity of Governance Structures 120
      B. Limitations of Relying on Design-Based Protection and the Data Literacy of Supervisors 121

		C.	Low Bargaining Power of Employees to Challenge the Use of Certain Tools in the Workplace 122

        C. Low Bargaining Power of Employees to Challenge the Use of Certain Tools in the Workplace 122
        D. Risks Arising from a Combinatory Logic of Monitoring Tools 123
        E. Heightened Risks for Marginalised Groups, People of Colour and Women...124
   III. Addressing Systemic Challenges for Privacy from a Business and Human Rights Perspective 126
        A. Assessing Impacts..128
        B. 'Techno-social' Stakeholder Engagement 130
        C. Grievance Mechanisms and Remedy..131
        D. Oversight and Accountability...132
   IV. Conclusion..133

8. *Freedom to Think and to Hold a Political Opinion: Digital Threats to Political Participation in Liberal Democracies*..135
Jérôme Duberry

   I. Introduction 135
   II. Freedom of Expression, Freedom of Thought and Freedom of Opinion 136
   III. Political Participation in Liberal Democracies 138
   IV. Towards New Forms of Political Participation 140
   V. Digital and Data-Driven Political Communication Tools..............144
   VI. Assessing the Veracity of News 147
   VII. Conclusion...150

9. *Is There a Human Rights Obligation to Protect Democratic Discourse in Cyberspace?*...151
Nula Frei

   I. Introduction 151
   II. The 'Public Space' in Democratic Theory...152
   III. A Human Rights Obligation to Protect Democratic Discourse in the 'Offline' World 154
        A. The Negative Obligation to Abstain from Interfering in Political Speech...155
        B. The Positive Obligation to Protect Democratic Discourse 155
   IV. Democratic Discourse in Cyberspace 160
        A. Another Structural Transformation of the Public Sphere?...160
        B. Case Law of the Court 161
        C. Protecting Democratic Discourse in Cyberspace?..................164
   V. Conclusion..165

x   Table of Contents

10. *The European Approach to Governing Harmful Speech Online* 167
    Frédéric Bernard and Viera Pejchal

    I.   Hate Speech, Harm and the Threat to Democracy 169
    II. The European Court of Human Rights' Case Law on
         Hate Speech 171
         A. The Main Tenets of the European Court of Human Rights'
            Case Law on Freedom of Expression 172
         B. Hate Speech's Degree of Illegitimacy 174
         C. Online Hate Speech 178
    III. Assessment 180
         A. The Three-Pronged Approach 180
         B. The Role of Companies 181

11. *Hate Speech and Journalism: Challenges and Strategies* 185
    Guido Keel

    I.   Introduction 185
    II. Journalism Under Pressure 186
    III. The Concept of Hate Speech from a Journalist's Perspective 188
    IV. Journalists Writing about, Witnessing and Receiving Hate Speech 192
         A. Journalistic Routines: Writing about Hate Speech 192
         B. Dealing with User-Generated Hate Speech 194
         C. Journalists as Victims of Hate Speech 201
    V.   Conclusion 203

12. *Digital Technologies for Sustainable Development* 205
    Claudia Abreu Lopes and Marcus Erridge

    I.   Introduction 205
    II. The Role of ICTs for Achieving the SDGs 206
    III. The Role of ICTs for Monitoring the SDGs 210
    IV. The Inequality Threats Posed by ICTs 216
    V.   Conclusion 218

13. *Digital Technologies and the Rights of Children in Europe* 221
    Rezvan Kaseb and Elizabeth Milovidov

    I.   Children and Young People in the Digital Environment 221
    II. The European Legal Framework on Children's Rights in
         the Digital Environment 223
         A. United Nations Convention on the Rights of the Child 223
         B. The Treaty on European Union, the Charter of Fundamental
            Rights and the European Convention on Human Rights 224
         C. General Data Protection Regulation 225

	III.	The European Policy Framework on Children's Rights in the Digital Environment...226	
		A.	European Union Guidelines 227
		B.	Council of Europe Recommendations 227
		C.	Organisation for Economic Co-operation and Development Recommendations...229
		D.	Committee on the Rights of the Child General Comments........230
		E.	European Courts' Jurisprudence.....................................231
	IV.	Responsibilities Towards Children in the Digital Environment..........233	
		A.	Parents and Caregivers 233
		B.	Educators..235
		C.	Industry 236
		D.	Government 237
		E.	Children and Young People 239
	V.	Conclusion...240	

14. *Conclusion*..*241*
    Frédéric Bernard

Index *247*

CONTRIBUTORS

Claudia Abreu Lopes is a Research Fellow at the United Nations University International Institute for Global Health.

Jonathan Andrew is a Research Fellow at the Geneva Academy of International Humanitarian Law and Human Rights.

Frédéric Bernard is a Professor of Public Law at the University of Geneva.

Stefania Di Stefano is a PhD candidate at the Graduate Institute of International and Development Studies in Geneva.

Jérôme Duberry is a Research Fellow at the Dusan Sidjanski Centre of Excellence in European Studies, Global Studies Institute, University of Geneva, and a Research Associate at the Albert Hirschman Centre on Democracy, Graduate Institute of International and Development Studies in Geneva.

Isabel Ebert is a Senior Research Fellow at the Institute of Business Ethics, University of St. Gallen, and Adviser at the UN Human Rights B-Tech Project.

Marcus Erridge is a PhD candidate on the Human Rights in Contemporary Societies programme at the Centre for Social Studies of the University of Coimbra.

Marwa Fatafta is a Policy Analyst at Al-Shabaka and the Middle East and North Africa Policy Manager at Access Now.

Nula Frei is a Senior Research Fellow at the University of Fribourg and a Lecturer at the Global Studies Institute of the University of Geneva.

Jamael Jacob is the Director of the University Data Protection Office at Ateneo de Manila University, as well as the Policy and Legal Advisor of the Foundation for Media Alternatives (FMA).

Rezvan Kaseb is a PhD candidate at the University of Zurich.

Guido Keel is the Director of the Institute of Applied Media Studies at the Zurich University of Applied Sciences.

Vivek Krishnamurthy is Samuelson-Glushko Professor of Law at the University of Ottawa and a Fellow of the Carr Center for Human Rights Policy at the Harvard Kennedy School.

Amy Lehr is a Senior Associate of the Center for Strategic and International Studies (CSIS), Washington, DC, and a Lecturer at the University of Virginia School of Law.

Elizabeth Milovidov is a member of the Working Group of experts on Digital Citizenship Education and an independent expert on Digital Parenting and Children and Internet for the Children's Rights Division of the Council of Europe.

Viera Pejchal is a Human Rights Officer at the United Nations. The views expressed here are her own and do not necessarily reflect the views of the United Nations.

Devony Schmidt is an Associate at Freshfields Bruckhaus Deringer US LLP, New York.

Isabelle Wildhaber is a Professor of Private Law and Business Law at the University of St. Gallen and Director at the Institute for Work and Employment Research at the University of St. Gallen.

1

Introduction

JONATHAN ANDREW

I. The Evolution of Human Rights in the Digital Age

The value of existing human rights to both individuals and groups extends beyond their immediately apparent benefits: the enjoyment of interdependent rights, whether conscious or not, enables citizens to develop their own autonomy and identity. How does the shift of so many of our activities into the 'cyber sphere' influence our fundamental rights and thus our sense of identity?

It is almost two decades since 180 governments affirmed the applicability of the Universal Declaration of Human Rights to the online sphere at the first World Summit on the Information Society in 2003.[1] The United Nations Human Rights Council and General Assembly have frequently reiterated that the 'same rights that people have offline must also be protected online'.[2] This approach reflects the expectation, ever since international human rights instruments were first formulated, that standards and fundamental principles will always apply regardless of advances in technology, and that, rather than seek to institute new rights for cyberspace, existing human rights should be extended to the online sphere. Nevertheless, due to the persistent lack of access to the internet in certain countries, often stemming from poverty or poor infrastructure, though also from both targeted and blanket shutdowns and other suppressive tactics by certain governments, the Human Rights Council has also repeatedly affirmed the importance of applying 'a comprehensive human rights-based approach when providing and expanding access to the Internet'.[3] The question as to whether there exist 'digital rights', borne of the evolving interactions exhibited in the digital sphere, remains open to discussion.[4]

---

[1] See World Summit on the Information Society (WSIS), Declaration of principles, WSIS-03/GENEVA/DOC/4-E (12 December 2003) 1.

[2] Most recently in the Resolution adopted by the General Assembly on 16 December 2020 (see UN Doc A/RES/75/176, 4 and 6).

[3] See, eg, A/HRC/RES/75/176, 2.

[4] See, eg, R Jørgensen, 'What Platforms Mean When They Talk About Human Rights' (2017) 9 *Policy & Internet* 280; M Zalnieriute, 'From Human Rights Aspirations to Enforceable Obligations by Non-State Actors in the Digital Age: The Case of Internet Governance and ICANN' (2019) 21 *Yale Journal*

It is apparent, however, that digital technologies are contributing towards shifts in the perceptions of fundamental rights such as freedom of expression and the right to privacy. On one hand, the functionality that digital communication channels provide has heightened the role of freedom of expression in enhancing the realisation of other interdependent fundamental rights. On the other, the widespread sharing of thoughts and opinions online would suggest that attitudes towards privacy and data protection are being recalibrated. Vast differences in the perceptions of privacy among citizens of different cultures and backgrounds might imply that the concept remains intrinsically nebulous.[5] A key concern in this context is that privacy and data protection are critical to the wider impact of evolving digital technologies on other interdependent human rights. Citizens will likely press for revision or implementation of new legislation when they are able to apprehend the risk of interference in their fundamental rights. If the threat is difficult to conceive of, the call for specific or more extensive regulatory oversight is likely to be weakened. A re-evaluation of the proportionality of the data collection and processing taking place, for example, will take time, since many of the impacts of this monitoring may be imperceptible to the layperson.

The evolving nature of the interpretation of the principal instruments that safeguard fundamental rights is critical in this context. According to the European Court of Human Rights (ECtHR), for example, the European Convention on Human Rights (ECHR) is a living instrument anchored to the reality of the Member States in which it applies,[6] a principle that is immediately relevant to the impacts of technological change on society. The Court has accordingly determined that the notion of 'private life' is a broad one, not susceptible to exhaustive definition;[7] that 'personal data' is defined as 'any information relating to an identified or identifiable individual';[8] and that 'public information can fall within the scope of private life where it is systematically collected and stored in files held by the authorities'.[9] These affirmations demonstrate the shifting scope of a human right in conjunction with technological change. For the courts, interpreting precepts anew for the situations that digital technologies present and reconciling those interpretations with precedent is a complex task.

---

of Law & Technology 278; N Jansen Reventlow and J McCully, 'Digital Rights Are *All* Human Rights, Not Just Civil and Political' (*Medium*, 27 February 2019). See also earlier discussion of this topic in P De Hert and D Kloza, 'Internet (Access) as a New Fundamental Right. Inflating the Current Rights Framework?' (2012) 3 *European Journal of Law and Technology*.

[5] See, eg, RC Post, 'Three Concepts of Privacy' (2001) 89 *The Georgetown Law Journal* 2087; DJ Solove, *Understanding Privacy* (Cambridge MA, Harvard University Press, 2008); S Fischer-Hübner et al, 'Online Privacy: Towards Informational Self-Determination on the Internet' (2011) 1 *Dagstuhl Manifestos* 1; F Jutand, 'The Challenges of Privacy' in C Dartiguepeyrou (ed), *The Futures of Privacy* (Paris, Fondation Télécom, 2014) 7; R Lipman, 'Online Privacy and the Invisible Market for Our Data' (2016) 120 *Penn State Law Review* 777.

[6] See, eg, *Tyrer v UK*, no 5856/72 (25 April 1978) 31; *Marckx v Belgium*, no 6833/74 (13 June 1979) 41.

[7] *Niemietz v Germany*, no 13710/88 (16 December 1992) 29.

[8] *S and Marper v UK*, nos 30562/04 and 30566/04 (4 December 2008) 41.

[9] *Rotaru v Romania*, no 28341/95 (4 May 2000) 43.

It has been particularly interesting therefore to see how precedent has been applied to new and evolving situations, for example with regard to the appreciation of the chilling effect that mass surveillance may have on the individual and on populations as a whole. The case of *Rotaru v Romania* illustrates this point, where the ECtHR reiterated its finding from earlier cases that mass surveillance of populations could have a grave impact on the rights to privacy and family life, even when citizens are unable to substantiate whether they had indeed been subject to a form of monitoring.[10]

Subsequently, in the *Smirnova v Russia* case, the ECtHR elaborated the scope of protections pertaining to our consciousness, reflecting an evolving appreciation of the need to recognise less tangible aspects of the human personality. The notion of 'private life' encompasses the protection of

> the moral and physical integrity of the individual, including the right to *live privately, away from unwanted attention*. It also secures to the individual *a sphere within which he or she can freely pursue the development and fulfilment of his personality* (emphasis added).[11]

The Court has increasingly taken the opportunity in its deliberations to underscore how uninvited and intrusive attention inhibits a person's capacity to form their own identity.

Courts have also been keen to review the necessity of measures, regulations and exemptions that governments have put in place in response to new technological capabilities – and exercised their powers to limit overly broad dispensations that effectively sidestep the safeguards for privacy and other dependent rights in the online sphere. In the *Ryneš* case, the Court of Justice of the European Union stated that the protection of the fundamental right to private life requires that 'derogations and limitations in relation to the protection of personal data must *apply only in so far as is strictly necessary*' (emphasis added).[12]

Also of importance in the context of our online interactions has been the elucidation of a less immediately palpable aspect of the intrinsic core of privacy, which is the value of the social dimension of human interactions to other interdependent human rights and to our own personal development. This was recognised in the *Biriuk v Lithuania* case, where the ECtHR's judgment emphasised the intrinsic value of the protection of a person's private life in allowing for their personal development, noting that its scope also encompasses a social dimension:

> As to respect for the individual's private life, the Court reiterates the fundamental importance of its protection in order to ensure the development of every human being's

---

[10] ibid 35. See also *Weber and Saravia v Germany*, no 54934/00 (29 June 2006); *Liberty and Other Organisations v UK*, no 58243/00 (1 July 2008); *Kennedy v UK*, no 26839/05 (18 May 2010); *Big Brother Watch and Others v UK*, nos 58170/13, 62322/14 and 24960/15 (13 September 2018).
[11] *Smirnova v Russia*, nos 46133/99 and 48183/99 (24 July 2003) 95.
[12] Judgment in C-212/13, *Ryneš* (11 December 2014) 28.

personality. That protection extends beyond the private family circle to include a social dimension.[13]

Moreover, in *Mikulić v Croatia*, the Strasbourg Court held that private life 'includes a person's physical and psychological integrity and can sometimes embrace aspects of an individual's physical and social identity'.[14] The Court's affirmation as to the scope of the protection given to a person's private life, particularly as regards their psychological integrity, needs contextualising in respect of the consequences of surveillance and monitoring. In this regard the Court's reaffirmation that respect for private life 'must also comprise to a certain degree the right to establish relationships with other human beings' is also relevant.[15] Inherent to both points is the notion that the formation and development of a human's personal integrity requires that a degree of shelter be given to the personal sphere from the pernicious effects of surveillance.

Notions of privacy are evolving in part as a result of our increasing reliance on connectivity and online services to enable and facilitate many aspects of our daily lives. This also raises questions as to whether the notion of the 'right of access to the internet' can be proven tenable and indeed whether it would further influence the scope of other associated and interdependent rights such as, inter alia, privacy and the right to data protection, freedom of peaceful assembly and association, and the right to freedom of expression.

Certain scholars have argued that the existing international human rights framework is no longer adapted to the scenarios we face in the online world.[16] Given the huge shifts in power observed over the past decade as the largest technology corporations expand their global dominance and amass even greater influence, such a proposition merits due consideration. Modern digital technologies also challenge assumptions about jurisdiction and territoriality which are based, first, on the notion that location in itself matters and should determine the application of the law and, second, that the entities in question have an identifiable and stable spatial location, either inside or outside a determined territory.[17] Technology gives rise to novel situations that continually challenge the application of legal precedent.

The chapters that follow illustrate how the extant legislative framework has addressed challenges brought about by technological innovation, but also expose areas in which the regulatory environment has lacked the necessary capacity for responsive and effective enforcement. They highlight the importance of the notion of 'technological neutrality' in laws that intend to regulate an open-ended

---

[13] *Biriuk v Lithuania*, no 23373/03 (25 November 2008) 38.
[14] *Mikulić v Croatia*, no 53176/99 (7 February 2002) 53.
[15] ibid.
[16] See, eg, A Deeks, 'An International Legal Framework for Surveillance' (2015) 55 *Virginia Journal of International Law* 291.
[17] See, eg, JC Daskal, 'The Un-Territoriality of Data' (2015) 125 *Yale Law Journal* 326.

process,[18] where their provisions must necessarily incorporate sufficient resolution, clarity and distinction, while also allowing the scope for unanticipated advances in digital technologies.

As much of human activity continues to shift online, affording significant scope for the enjoyment of human rights, the capacity of different actors to infringe those rights is also considerable. Digital innovation is reshaping relationships between government, businesses and civil society, as well as the interdependencies between stakeholder obligations, responsibilities and duties.[19]

II. State Obligations to Respect, Protect and Fulfil Human Rights in the Digital Sphere

Human rights have been conceived, interpreted and have evolved primarily in terms of states' obligations – and indeed of states' capacity to effect control over their citizens. States are obliged to act so as to respect human rights in the digital realm: to refrain from violating the human rights that an individual or group may exercise online and also to abstain from employing digital technologies to violate those rights. In the digital age, the capabilities and methods through which oppressive measures can be enacted are significant.

As early as 1984, the ECtHR provided guidance on the principles governing interception and more general programmes of surveillance in relation to evolving monitoring capabilities:

> In particular, the requirement of foreseeability cannot mean that an individual should be enabled to foresee *when* the authorities are likely to intercept his communications so that he can adapt his conduct accordingly. Nevertheless, the law must be sufficiently clear in its terms to give citizens an adequate indication as to the *circumstances* in which and the *conditions* on which public authorities are empowered to resort to this secret and potentially dangerous interference with the right to respect for private life and correspondence (emphases added).[20]

This judgment is particularly valuable for its articulation of the criteria by which the notion of foreseeability is to be construed: foreseeability is primarily dependent on the provision of an adequate indication as to the circumstances and conditions under which monitoring may be lawfully employed. The Court's statement does

---

[18] See, eg, B-J Koops, 'Should ICT Regulation Be Technology-Neutral?' in B-J Koops et al (eds), *Starting Points for ICT Regulation: Deconstructing Prevalent Policy One-Liners* (The Hague, TMC Asser Press, 2006); L Bennett Moses, 'Recurring Dilemmas: The Law's Race to Keep Up with Technological Change' (2007) UNSW Law Research Paper no 2007-21; M Birnhack, 'Reverse Engineering Informational Privacy Law' (2013) 15 *Yale Journal of Law and Technology* 24.

[19] This introduction distinguishes between obligations (for states), responsibilities (for businesses) and duties (for individuals) but uses the more general term 'responsibilities' when applied to several categories of duty-bearer.

[20] *Malone v UK*, no 8691/79 (2 August 1984) 67.

not address the measure deployed. This begs the question whether, with modern technological advances, a citizen can comprehend the possibility of an interference in her rights where she is wholly unaware as to the means at the disposal of public authorities.

The integration of large-scale data mining and artificial intelligence facilitates mass surveillance and predictive policing, and unduly influences behaviours and life choices. It can serve to generate statistical norms that are then used to categorise behaviours according to these standards. If monitoring of this nature encourages individuals to adopt behaviours perceived as 'more normal' and refrain from abnormal or 'non-usual' behaviours, it is highly intrusive to a person's private life and severely inhibits intimacy and aspects of an individual's identity linked to self-expression.[21]

Successive UN Special Rapporteurs on freedom of opinion and expression, as well as the Office of the High Commissioner for Human Rights, have underscored the importance of encryption to online communications and to the protection of the enjoyment of interdependent rights including the right to peaceful assembly and association, and freedom of movement.[22] States that interfere with individuals' secure or anonymous communications may therefore also infringe upon other human rights, as is highlighted in chapter two by Vivek Krishnamurthy, Devony Schmidt and Amy Lehr in their discussion of the nexus of cybersecurity with the safeguard of privacy through the use of encryption and other measures to secure transmissions from covert surveillance. Moreover, as demonstrated by Marwa Fatafta, in chapter five, even the knowledge of monitoring or interference in the ability to communicate securely can constitute a chilling effect on these rights.

States are also required to take positive measures to protect an individual's rights in the online sphere from arbitrary interference by third parties by enacting legislation. Guidance from the former Special Rapporteur on freedom of opinion and expression, David Kaye, has outlined an obligation on the state to 'provide such safety in law and policy that will allow individuals to secure themselves online'.[23] At the same time, any restrictions that states enact must respect human rights standards vis-à-vis a potential limitation or restriction of other rights. In the

---

[21] See DJ Phillips, 'Ubiquitous Computing, Spatiality, and the Construction of Identity: Directions for Policy Response' in I Kerr (ed), *Lessons from the Identity Trail: Anonymity, Privacy and Identity in a Networked Society* (New York, Oxford University Press, 2009) 308.

[22] See UNHRC, 'Report of the Special Rapporteur on the Promotion and Protection of the Right to Freedom of Opinion and Expression' (17 April 2013) UN Doc A/HRC/23/40, 89; 'Report of the Special Rapporteur on the Promotion and Protection of the Right to Freedom of Opinion and Expression' (22 May 2015) UN Doc A/HRC/29/32, 17; 'Report of the Office of the United Nations High Commissioner for Human Rights, The Right to Privacy in the Digital Age' (14 June 2014) UN Doc A/HRC/27/37, 34. See also Council Declaration of 28 May 2003 on freedom of communication on the Internet, principle 7.

[23] UNHRC, 'Report of the UN Special Rapporteur on the Promotion and Protection of the Right to Freedom of Opinion and Expression, David Kaye' (22 May 2015) UN Doc A/HRC/29/32, 11.

online sphere, we need to consider how the provision of social media platforms by business enterprises engages the state's broader responsibilities to ensure the necessary conditions for citizens' enjoyment of rights such as freedom of expression.

There is an inherent tension between business and government, the latter of course being reliant on the former for providing both opportunities for economic growth (nowadays an unfaltering expectation of the electorate) and tax revenues to finance public spending. This point is particularly contentious in many jurisdictions where the nebulous, indefinite nature of the online sphere has afforded major tech companies the leeway to reduce their tax liabilities.[24] Questions arise as to the appropriate balance of competing interests, especially as businesses seek to develop a competitive advantage, while bodies charged with providing oversight and regulation must ensure that citizens are not obliged to use a certain product or service based on its pervasiveness, so-called 'technological inevitability'.

States must also ensure that individuals can meaningfully realise their rights, including through the availability of appropriate remedies for violations of these rights.

States' responsibilities extend to the educational needs of their citizens to learn the necessary skills to embrace the opportunities for civic engagement and employment that the digital transformation can offer. Rezvan Kaseb and Elizabeth Milovidov, in chapter thirteen, underscore that governments must galvanise efforts to augment digital literacy in young people. Such initiatives might also be extended and made accessible to others in our communities needing information and skills development, including the marginalised and disenfranchised. To date, there has been too little discussion as to how governments (and industry) can better furnish individuals and communities with the knowledge and resources to empower them to more effectively and proactively shape the implementation and evolution of digital technologies in society. Rather, citizens, despite being conscious that such innovations may adversely impact their enjoyment of fundamental rights, are insufficiently equipped to evaluate and articulate concerns. Policymakers should note that attempts to address deprivation by simply widening access to online services could in fact prove harmful to economically marginalised individuals and groups and further diminish their life choices by furnishing businesses with data insights that are leveraged in ways that exacerbate division and further limit social mobility. Jamael Jacob indeed discusses in chapter three how government-backed technology solutions to social welfare issues have in certain cases only aggravated the problems they were intended to address: leading in the longer term to wider societal distrust of the digitisation of public services.

In sum, states must respect, protect and fulfil human rights, and are obliged to ensure that they employ 'judicial, administrative, educative and other appropriate

---

[24] See, eg, GR Dowling, 'The Curious Case of Corporate Tax Avoidance: Is It Socially Irresponsible?' (2014) 124 *Journal of Business Ethics* 173.

measures in order to fulfil their legal obligations'.²⁵ More than ever, states must engage proactively to play a positive role in shaping the digital transformation of societies.

The obligation of the state to provide for the security of its citizens within its jurisdiction also engages it to adequately enforce both international and domestic legal provisions vis-à-vis human rights. As Jamael Jacob shows, a framework of legal, constitutional, and institutional safeguards is insufficient to ensure rights-holders are shielded from harm. Rather, his analysis underscores the essential need for enforcement as a means to deter breaches of the law and their resultant impact on the enjoyment of rights. Similarly, Marwa Fatafta's appraisal of the use of AI systems in public security highlights that the context in which they are deployed directly influences their initial development and implantation, in effect skewing them towards disproportionately harming marginalised communities. Without sufficient oversight, particularly in the initial phases of development of these technologies, we risk a further expansion of systems of monitoring and surveillance that constitute grave interferences to the core enjoyment of many interdependent human rights, including the right to privacy, freedom of peaceful assembly and association (see in particular chapter four), freedom of religion, and freedom of movement.

Vivek Krishnamurthy, Devony Schmidt and Amy Lehr, in chapter two, also consider the challenges of providing security for citizens, but from the angle of cybersecurity. As the authors note, the Human Rights Committee has affirmed in its General Comment No 35 that 'security of the person' refers to 'freedom from injury to the body and the mind, or bodily and mental integrity'. The General Comment also articulates how the state is required 'to take appropriate measures [...] to protect individuals from foreseeable threats to life or bodily integrity', including from 'individual criminals or irregular groups, including armed or terrorist groups, operating within their territory'.²⁶ The authors' analysis grapples with the very real concerns regarding interferences by states and other actors that seek to undermine faith in democratic processes and considers different approaches towards proportionate responses in asking what the responsibilities of internet intermediaries might be. These issues are particularly topical where we observe that states, terrorist groups, organised crime, and other private actors are increasingly engaging in sophisticated disinformation campaigns on social media platforms to undermine their adversaries.

---

[25] UN Human Rights Committee, General Comment No 31, 'The Nature of the General Legal Obligations Imposed on States Parties to the Covenant' (26 May 2004) UN Doc CCPR/C/21/Rev.1/Add.13, 7. See also 6: 'The legal obligation under article 2, paragraph 1 [of the ICCPR], is both negative and positive in nature'.

[26] UN Human Rights Committee, General Comment No 35, 'Article 9 (Liberty and Security of Person)' (16 December 2014) UN Doc CCPR/C/GC/35, 3, 7, 9.

III. Corporate Responsibilities in the Digital Sphere

Businesses and investors, particularly as regards the tech sector, are being called upon by both governments and civil society to acknowledge that they have specific responsibilities towards society as they develop or use technologies with the potential to interfere with the enjoyment of human rights.[27]

Especially relevant in this context is the degree of control that tech companies exercise in so many areas of citizens' lives. Individuals may feel inhibited, coerced or even manipulated in day-to-day transactions that immediately affect their life choices and social welfare, and thus their social and economic rights. The apprehension among some citizens that they may be unable to opt out of using certain platforms, for example, for communicating with members of their community, is perturbing. A further concern is whether platforms should be allowed to exercise their discretion over citizens' conversations and interactions, and act as the first line of defence of moral standards. A pivotal ruling with respect to this shift in responsibilities was the judgment of the European Court of Justice in the *Google Spain* case.[28] The approach risks shifting the responsibility of protecting the right to freedom of expression to parties largely unanswerable for their actions in this regard, and to invite censorship.[29] Concerns that the ruling provides only cursory guidance to business enterprises in how to adjudicate complaints brought by citizens have proven well founded.[30] In chapter six, Stefania Di Stefano questions whether Facebook's recent creation of an Oversight Board to review content moderation decisions represents a meaningful reorientation of its practices towards greater compliance with the United Nations Guiding Principles on Business and Human Rights.

Issues relating to agency are also of immediate concern where digital technologies may furnish other actors, such as employers or law enforcement, with capabilities that extend to monitoring, surveillance and predictive policing. Isabel Ebert and Isabelle Wildhaber's and Marwa Fatafta's chapters highlight the scope of possible interferences.

---

[27] See, eg, UN Human Rights Committee, General Comment No 34, 'Article 19: Freedoms of Opinion and Expression', UN Doc CCPR/C/GC/34 (12 September 2011) 7; Council of Europe, Committee of Ministers, 'Recommendation CM/Rec(2012)4 on the Protection of Human Rights with Regard to Social Networking Services' (4 April 2012); European Commission, 'Recommendation (EU) 2018/334 on Measures to Effectively Tackle Illegal Content Online' (1 March 2018); OECD, *An Introduction to Online Platforms and Their Role in the Digital Transformation* (Paris, OECD Publishing, 2019).

[28] *Google Spain SL and Google Inc v Agencia Española de Protección de Datos (AEPD) and Mario Costeja González* (2013) C-131/12. See also *Google LLC, successor in law to Google Inc v Commission nationale de l'informatique et des libertés (CNIL)* (2019) C-507/17.

[29] See, eg, JE Cohen, 'The Regulatory State in the Information Age' (2016) 17 *Theoretical Inquiries in Law* 369; RF Jørgensen and L Zuleta, 'Private Governance of Freedom of Expression on Social Media Platforms: EU Content Regulation Through the Lens of Human Rights Standards' (2020) 41 *Nordicom Review* 51.

[30] See, eg, B-J Koops, 'Forgetting Footprints, Shunning Shadows: A Critical Analysis of the "Right to Be Forgotten" in Big Data Practice' (2011) 8 *SCRIPTed* 229; J Lee, 'What the Right to Be Forgotten Means to Companies: Threat or Opportunity?' (2016) 91 *Procedia Computer Science* 542.

A further complaint frequently directed towards the intermediaries of the internet relates to their inconsistent exercise of largely unchecked powers, based in part on a dominance achieved by scaling operations to edge out competition and diminish opportunities for emergent rivals, so that smaller entities are effectively operating at the mercy of dominant global players that exercise far too much control over livelihoods. Steadily more of the smaller businesses and workers that interface with and rely on digital platforms provided by large tech companies (such as Uber, Airbnb, Amazon, Facebook and others) are seeking the intervention of policymakers and legislators to loosen the grip of dominant enterprises over the marketplaces in which they operate. Achieving a compromise that is acceptable to the respective parties requires understanding that the provision of products and services through digital channels can directly implicate critical interests such as a person's ability to secure their own livelihood.

The success of businesses engaged in vast data-harvesting operations belies the enormous damage that aspects of their activities have inflicted on vital features of democratic societies (see in particular the chapters by Nula Frei and Jérôme Duberry). Guido Keel, in chapter eleven, describes how the dependence of citizens in many jurisdictions on social media platforms for news stories has severely undermined the financial viability and therefore the 'watchdog' role of the Fourth Estate. Since a critical, well-established mission of the press and media in many countries has been to expose and report on violations of human rights, the continued weakening of this function puts fundamental rights at risk.

The incumbents in the tech sector are increasingly seen by different stakeholders, including governments and regional commissions, as undermining protective frameworks that have been put in place over generations to ensure that hard-won rights are secured and defended from possible abuse, particularly by actors with considerable leverage to cow and subdue complainants.

When John Ruggie took on the role of Special Representative of the Secretary-General on human rights and transnational corporations and other business enterprises in 2005, deliberations on developing human rights standards for companies had only had a limited impact, with businesses little incentivised to engage in the discussion and contribute towards the fulfilment of this objective. The adoption in 2011 by the Human Rights Council of the 'Guiding Principles on Business and Human Rights', with their comprehensive and coherent framework for stakeholders, represented a major milestone in the ongoing process of elaborating the responsibilities of companies towards ensuring the safeguard of human rights.[31] The Guiding Principles specify the respective responsibilities of both governments and businesses in preventing and mitigating businesses' adverse impacts on the enjoyment of human rights. A particularly important innovation was their comprehensive articulation of the scope of due diligence that

---

[31] UN OHCHR, 'Guiding Principles on Business and Human Rights: Implementing the United Nations "Protect, Respect and Remedy" Framework' (2011) UN Doc HR/PUB/11/04.

businesses are expected to undertake in pursuit of their operations and activities. Furthermore, the adoption of the Guiding Principles forced business enterprises at the global level to reconsider their provision of remedial mechanisms to address grievances relating to the violation of human rights. Stefania Di Stefano's evaluation of Facebook's Oversight Board in chapter six and Isabel Ebert and Isabelle Wildhaber's examination of workplace monitoring in chapter seven highlight the need for remedial mechanisms that meet the standards set by the Guiding Principles.

However, the scale of digital transformation is such that the decade since the adoption of the Guiding Principles may be considered a lengthy time span. The challenges of applying them to the tech sector are not insignificant though various initiatives have been proposed to facilitate this adjustment.[32] While the Guiding Principles remain a cornerstone for assessing compliance with human rights standards, the lack of prior cases that can serve as relevant examples for new technologies and new fields of operation in the tech sector (in particular in fast-developing areas of innovation such as artificial intelligence and biometrics) create barriers to their immediate application.[33]

Efforts to address interferences in the rights to privacy, freedom of expression, freedom of religion, freedom of association and other interdependent rights resulting from online activities have so far been mostly retroactive.[34] Human Rights Impact Assessments have largely been conducted by parties attempting to alleviate or mitigate the negative effects of existing technologies, the possible effects of which were insufficiently reviewed ahead of delivery.[35] A pressing problem is how to improve the engagement of relevant actors in working together to model new

---

[32] See, eg, European Parliament, Directorate-general for external policies policy department, 'Implementation of the UN Guiding Principles on Business and Human Rights' (February 2017) EP/EXPO/B/COMMITTEE/FWC/2013-08/Lot8/09; BSR, 'Human Rights Review: Facebook Oversight Board' (December 2019) available at www.bsr.org/reports/BSR_Facebook_Oversight_Board.pdf. For a pertinent example of the complexities of evaluating human rights impacts in-country, see the review of Norwegian telecommunications company Telia, 'Human Rights Impact Assessments and Responsible Divestment Plan for Business Region Eurasia: Summary Project Report for Telia Company' (October 2016) available at www.teliacompany.com/globalassets/telia-company/documents/about-telia-company/bsr-telia-company-hria-summary.pdf.

[33] BSR, 'Human Rights Assessments in the Decisive Decade: Applying UNGPs in the Technology Sector' (11 February 2020) available at www.bsr.org/en/our-insights/blog-view/human-rights-assessments-in-the-decisive-decade-ungp-challenges-technology.

[34] See, eg, the criticisms voiced in the 2018 report by the Independent International Fact-Finding Mission on Myanmar as to the foreseeability of the adverse impacts of the weaponisation of social media and its adverse human rights impacts: UNHRC, 'Report of the detailed findings of the Independent International Fact-Finding Mission on Myanmar' (17 September 2018) UN Doc A/HRC/39/CRP.2, 256.

[35] P Dave, 'Facebook Says Human Rights Report Shows It Should Do More In Myanmar' (*Reuters*, 6 November 2018); S Stecklow, 'Why Facebook is losing the war on hate speech in Myanmar' (*Reuters*, 15 August 2018). The more recent civil rights audit of Facebook's operations highlighted concerns that the social network's policies continue to undermine progress in safeguarding human rights: see LW Murphy et al, 'Facebook's Civil Rights Audit – Final Report' (8 July 2020) available at https://about.fb.com/wp-content/uploads/2020/07/Civil-Rights-Audit-Final-Report.pdf.

products and services in the online sphere and discover possible threats to human rights before implementation.[36] The existing methodologies of due diligence have simply been adapted from other industries. The tech sphere requires new tools, as the current instruments for analysis lack the capability for both hardware and software developers, and indeed civil society activists, to effectively analyse, foresee and mitigate risks to human rights.[37] In the context of artificial intelligence, for example, we might consider the value of prototypes and scenario-planning exercises, engaging the respective stakeholders, to model potential harms in the early phases of the technology development lifecycle.[38] One possibility is to leverage the threat-modelling methodologies that already exist within industry for identifying possible vulnerabilities in products and services in order to ascertain how human rights violations could be avoided, but there is certainly a need to develop more coherent methodologies to prevent human rights infringements in the digital sphere. Companies' engagement at the early stages of the development lifecycle is critical in order to assess potential liabilities without unnecessary delay. The tech industry also needs to determine how to achieve a longer-term engagement with governments and international organisations that is more effective in delivering solutions, particularly on pressing human rights issues such as facial recognition, artificial intelligence, cybersecurity and the leveraging of social media networks and online discussion platforms against vulnerable individuals and groups, as described in Marwa Fatafta's chapter, Vivek Krishnamurthy, Devony Schmidt and Amy Lehr's chapter, and my own.

IV. Apportioning Responsibilities Fairly

An important advance in elaborating the human rights obligations and responsibilities of states and businesses operating on the internet took place in 2018, when the Council of Europe adopted its 'Recommendation on the Roles and Responsibilities of Internet Intermediaries'.[39] As has proven the case with previous instruments instituted by the Council of Europe (for example the Convention

---

[36] See Article 19's analysis of the deficiencies in existing practices: Article 19, 'Public Interest, Private Infrastructure' (2018) available at www.article19.org/wp-content/uploads/2018/06/HRIA-report-UNGP_5.6.pdf, 15–20.

[37] The 'Human Rights Impact Assessment Guidance and Toolbox' (2020) developed by the Danish Institute for Human Rights outlines only a cursory approach to the challenge of analysing impacts. See also the approach to human rights impact assessments developed by BSR, and the absence of scenario-planning activities: BSR, 'Conducting an Effective Human Rights Impact Assessment Guidelines, Steps, and Examples' (2013) available at www.bsr.org/reports/BSR_Human_Rights_Impact_Assessments.pdf, 11–17.

[38] See CR Sunstein, 'Hazardous Heuristics' (2002), John M Olin Program in Law and Economics Working Paper no 165, 14.

[39] Council of Europe, 'Recommendation CM/Rec(2018)2 on the Roles and Responsibilities of Internet Intermediaries' (7 March 2018).

for the Protection of Individuals with regard to Automatic Processing of Personal Data), this accomplishment of Europe's most influential human rights body could also, in the long term, have an impact globally. With the introduction of the Recommendation, the Committee of Ministers, the executive body of the organisation, called on states to enhance efforts within their respective jurisdictions to provide a framework, based on human rights and the rule of law, that comprehensibly articulates the principal obligations of the state towards the protection and promotion of human rights in the digital environment, and also the respective responsibilities of intermediaries.[40]

The key provisions of the Recommendation for governments include, inter alia:

- Public authorities should only make a 'request, demand or other action [...] addressed to internet intermediaries that interferes with human rights and fundamental freedoms' when prescribed by law (para 1.1.1);
- Legislation giving powers to public authorities to interfere with internet content should clearly define the scope of those powers and available discretion, to protect against arbitrary application (para 1.2.2);
- 'When intermediaries remove content based on their own terms and conditions of service, this should not be considered a form of control that makes them liable for the third-party content for which they provide access' (para 1.3.3; see also Frédéric Bernard and Viera Pejchal's chapter ten on the scope of internet intermediaries' responsibilities);
- 'When internet intermediaries restrict access to third-party content based on a State order, State authorities should ensure that effective redress mechanisms are made available and adhere to applicable procedural safeguards' (para 1.3.3).

In addition, the Recommendation requests of states that they heighten efforts to develop an online environment that is safe and enabling (Preamble, para 6),[41] and afford sufficient scope for intermediaries, users and all affected parties to clearly understand both their rights and responsibilities. States should:

engage in a regular, inclusive and transparent dialogue with all relevant stakeholders, including from the private sector, public service media, civil society, education

---

[40] See also Council of Europe, Committee of experts on Internet Intermediaries (MSI-NET), 'Study on Human Rights Dimensions of Automated Data Processing Techniques (in Particular Algorithms) and Possible Regulatory Implications', MSI-NET(2016)06rev6 (2016) available at rm.coe.int/study-on-algorithmes-final-version/1680770cbc.

[41] cf the ECtHR's advisory statement following the case *Dink v Turkey* which noted that 'States had positive obligations in relation to freedom of expression: they must not just refrain from any interference but must sometimes take protective measures even in the sphere of the relations of individuals between themselves. They were also required to create a favourable environment for participation in public debate by all the persons concerned, enabling them to express their opinions and ideas without fear.' See Information Note on the Court's case-law no 133 (August–September 2010). See also EPRA (European Platform of Regulatory Authorities) Secretariat, 'Creating a Safe and Enabling Online Environment Where Stakeholders Know Their Rights and Obligations is the Key to a Better Content Moderation' (20 March 2018) available at www.epra.org/news_items/coe-recommendation-on-the-

establishments and academia, with a view to sharing and discussing information and promoting the responsible use of emerging technological developments related to internet intermediaries that impact the exercise and enjoyment of human rights and related legal and policy issues (Preamble, para 12).

The Recommendation anticipates effective collaboration between the parties so as to ensure the development of appropriate self-regulation and co-regulatory frameworks (para 1.3.10), and provides for the establishing of mechanisms for redress for claims made in respect of violations of human rights in the digital sphere (paras 1.1.3, 1.5.2). It calls for educational literacy and media programmes to be implemented and promoted that help users to benefit from the online environment, while minimising their exposure to the risk of harm or interference in the fundamental rights (Preamble, para 8; para 1.5.4).

For service providers in the digital environment, the Recommendation's provisions include, inter alia:

- Plain language and accessible formats requirement for terms of service (para 2.2.1);
- A call to include outside stakeholders in the process of drafting terms of service (para 2.2.2);
- Transparency on how restrictions on content are applied (para 2.2.1) and detailed information on how algorithmic and automated means are used (para 2.2.3);
- Any measures taken to remove or block content as a result of a state order should be implemented using the least restrictive means (para 2.3.1).

The efforts to provide a Recommendation on the specific subject of internet intermediaries reflect the importance the Council of Europe ascribes to articulating the expectations of governments vis-à-vis political engagement and the participation of industry on matters concerning fundamental freedoms in the digital sphere, as well as to ensuring that human rights such as privacy and freedom of expression are upheld online.

The Recommendation also aims to articulate the necessary conditions for the online sphere to contribute to human rights protections that in turn foster open debate and a plurality of opinions, while ensuring all stakeholders know their rights and obligations: the centrality of ensuring that further transparency is introduced to all processes of content moderation is underscored (Preamble, para 6; paras 1.3.9, 2.3.2). The Recommendation is especially pertinent in light of the challenges for citizens in foreseeing how oversight, political interference or the actions of courts or regulatory bodies may determine how companies react to pressure to

---

roles-and-responsibilities-of-internet-intermediaries; JS Pielemeier, 'Disentangling Disinformation: What Makes Regulating Disinformation So Difficult?' [2020] *Utah Law Review* 917; F Fagan, 'Optimal Social Media Content Moderation and Platform Immunities' (2020) 50 *European Journal of Law and Economics* 437.

block or filter content. These restrictions undermine the protection of rights in the digital sphere and thus the Recommendation represents a timely intervention by the Council of Europe to articulate a clear, cogent and comprehensive elucidation of the applicable legal framework by which such decisions should be reached. It must be recalled, however, that the Recommendation is a relatively recent development. Time will tell how effective its guidance will prove when faced with further technological innovation. Moreover, we need also consider that the work of the Council of Europe on these critical issues is ongoing.

V. Civic Duties in the Digital Sphere

Despite their impact on fundamental rights, digital technologies are becoming integrated into our daily lives without sufficient reflection. Certain observers perceive their adoption as inevitable, the unavoidable consequence of scientific advancement and human progress. Indeed, it is arguable that the proliferation of devices and sensing capabilities, the ubiquity of computing in our environment, has already fashioned a degree of acquiescence that tacitly accepts digital transformation as inexorable. Weiser observed that 'the most profound technologies are those that disappear. They weave themselves into the fabric of everyday life until they are indistinguishable from it'.[42] As individuals, we must recognise the importance of appraising which interests are being served when we select digital tools.

Furthermore, we need also consider how human rights have traditionally emphasised the individual's interests rather than those of groups or associations. Ongoing development of intrusive surveillance has significant consequences for individuals and communities alike. The reality of the implementation of emerging digital technologies is that interferences and harm increasingly have a societal interest and broader structural implications. Stakeholders must consider the inherent capability of such technologies to directly effect measures of social engineering that would risk widespread and prolonged impacts on communities and the development of communities in society as a whole, particularly as regards ensuring the necessary cohesion and harmony among citizens required of a stable, functioning democracy. Jérôme Duberry, in chapter eight, calls attention to the role of social media platforms and messaging applications in the proliferation of disinformation and 'fake news', the effect of echo chambers on discourse and exposure to a plurality of opinions (including those which may diverge considerably from one's own) and the use of profiling techniques to target individuals with specific content that may exclude the possibility of exposure to broader, more diverse positions and interpretations.

The Human Rights Committee's recent General Comment No 37 highlights a certain tension in respect of obligations that may entail the implementation of

---

[42] M Weiser, 'The Computer for the 21st Century' (1991) 265 *Scientific American* 94.

restrictions to protect the rights and freedoms of others: measures may be enacted for the protection of human rights of people not participating in an assembly online.[43] The discussion in the General Comment is particularly apt in the context of the debate over the legitimacy of methods such as distributed denial-of-service (DDoS) attacks as a form of protest in the online sphere. This issue has proven contentious, especially where one considers the impact of such activities on public authorities, where the externalities may include disruption to, or even closure, of essential public services.[44]

The relationship between individual rights and public interest goals is significant for the development of technologies such as artificial intelligence. Although the relationship between the two may be multi-dimensional, central to our understanding of judicially protected human rights is the notion that they protect an individual's interests from being overridden by collective utility.[45] Yet the premise that an individual should be protected against the will of the collective appears almost counter-intuitive to the principle of *majoritarianism* on which democracy is largely based. Claudia Abreu Lopes and Marcus Erridge's chapter twelve on responsible use of data by researchers adds weight to the argument that the effective safeguard of human rights in the online sphere requires coordination and a collective response in order to prove effective. They also draw attention to the need to ensure transparency in the dialogue between stakeholders, particularly with regard to developing coherent and workable frameworks for open-source data while protecting privacy and ensuring data protection.

VI. Dialogue, Cooperation and Regulation

Generating workable solutions to the human rights impacts of technologies requires meaningful engagement and action on the part of stakeholders. This process must take into account that practices and methodologies within the tech industry differ considerably from those of national governments, the wider public sector, civil society and intergovernmental organisations. Further efforts are required to equip stakeholders with the information and understanding needed to appreciate the nuances of decision-making processes in areas outside their specialisation. The digital age necessitates that human rights advocates continually

---

[43] UN Human Rights Committee, General Comment No 37, 'Article 21 (Right of peaceful assembly)' (23 July 2020) UN Doc CCPR/C/GC/37, 47.

[44] See, eg, E Zuckerman et al, '2010 Report on Distributed Denial of Service (DDos) Attacks', Berkman Center Research Publication No 2010-16 (2020); S Li, 'When Does Internet Denial Trigger the Right of Armed Self-Defense?' (2013) 38 *Yale Journal of International Law* 179; S Aaronson, 'What Are We Talking About When We Discuss Digital Protectionism?' (2017) Working Paper for the Economic Research Institute of Asia (Eria).

[45] See SM Noveck, 'Is Judicial Review Compatible with Democracy?' (2008) 6 *Cardozo Public Law, Policy & Ethics Journal* 401. See also M Walzer, 'Philosophy and Democracy' (1981) 9 *Political Theory* 379.

develop their knowledge of how digital technologies are developed and function. Often, it would appear that different parties struggle to develop a common language and framework through which to explore critical issues. A key concern is whether the tech industry, which has so far opted for ethics standards and moral commitments over human rights, is in fact inclined to purposefully acknowledge its human rights responsibilities. If not, how should reform be set in motion? Questions immediately arise as to which inducements would prove most efficacious and whether a more punitive regulatory approach might deter innovation in the sector. In liberal western democracies, the regulatory approach has largely been 'soft-touch' and market-led, empowering businesses to innovate in order to realise the economic benefits of digitisation. In weighing up possible responses, stakeholders need to take into account the gains in welfare and job opportunities created through the delivery of technologies. Society places a lot of faith in technology to deliver solutions to emergent needs, as is apparent in chapter twelve on the use of digital technologies for advancing the right to the health and freedom from discrimination. Regulation must tread a careful path: affording the necessary oversight, appraisal and enforcement of legislation, while allowing the necessary freedom for digital technologies that benefit society. Stifling the vigour and drive that extend the boundaries of human achievement and deliver positive results for humanity would prove counterproductive. This quandary illustrates the difficulty of balancing competing interests in protecting, promoting and realising the enjoyment of human rights.

2

Cybersecurity and Human Rights: Understanding the Connection

VIVEK KRISHNAMURTHY, DEVONY SCHMIDT AND AMY LEHR

This chapter seeks to conceptualise the relationship between cybersecurity and human rights. This relationship, which remains largely unexplored,[1] is important to consider given the prominence of cybersecurity issues on the global public policy agenda.

We advance three claims in this chapter. First, the goal of cybersecurity policy should be to protect human rights and thus people. Second, the trade-offs that are inherent in any cybersecurity measure can and should be reconceptualised in terms of human rights, in view of what we believe to be the proper goal of cybersecurity (ie, the promotion of human rights and protection of people). Third, such trade-offs can then be evaluated by using existing legal mechanisms to evaluate whether the human rights impacts of any policy measure are justifiable. Doing so can help ensure that cybersecurity policy measures are consistent with the overarching legal duty of states to protect human rights, and of non-state actors to respect them.

In Part I, we probe the nature and definition of cybersecurity. We challenge the idea that cyberspace and the physical world remain meaningfully distinct, and develop a parsimonious definition of cybersecurity with reference to historic debates around the meaning of security.

In Part II, we use our definition of cybersecurity to consider the kinds of trade-offs policymakers must weigh when evaluating cybersecurity measures. By challenging the idea that cybersecurity involves a trade-off between 'security' and 'privacy' in the specific case of the encryption policy debate, we show how 'both sides' of such cybersecurity policy debates can be recast in terms of human rights. Doing so permits us to assess the trade-offs inherent in cybersecurity

---

[1] As one leading scholar notes, 'the connection between cybersecurity and human rights has been underappreciated in the literature to date'. SJ Shackelford, 'Should Cybersecurity be a Human Right: Exploring the Shared Responsibility of Cyber Peace' (2019) 55 *Stanford Journal of International Law* 155, 157.

policy-making on a 'like-for-like' basis, and facilitates the use of mechanisms such as the human rights doctrines of legality, necessity, and proportionality to evaluate whether limitations on certain rights are permissible.[2]

I. Defining Cybersecurity

Cybersecurity has been aptly described as a 'capacious concept, susceptible to varying definitions'.[3] Notwithstanding this imprecision, entire fields of activity have emerged that use the term 'cybersecurity' in their name. There are cybersecurity laws and policies,[4] cybersecurity courses and degrees,[5] and cybersecurity products and services.[6]

One could seek to deduce the meaning of cybersecurity from the varied uses of this term in common parlance. Several years ago, researchers at New America compiled a list of existing definitions of key information security-related terms.[7] This report's section on 'cyber-security' lists 47 distinct definitions that run to seven, single-spaced pages and illustrate the range of topics that are encompassed by this 'capacious concept'.[8] For example, the US National Institute of Science and Technology (NIST) defines cybersecurity as 'the ability to protect or defend the use of cyberspace from cyber attacks',[9] whereas the European Union's Cybersecurity Strategy states that its namesake term 'refers to the safeguards and actions that can be used to protect the cyber domain, both in the civilian and military fields, from those threats that are associated with or that may harm its

---

[2] United Nations Human Rights Committee, General Comment No 34, 'Article 19: Freedoms of opinion and expression' (12 September 2011) UN Doc CCPR/C/GC/34. As discussed in Section II.B, below, only some rights can be subjected to limitations. Among those that can be are the rights to free expression and privacy, which are often pertinent to cybersecurity debates.

[3] K Eichensehr, 'Public-Private Cybersecurity' (2017) 95 *Texas Law Review* 467, 474 fn 18.

[4] See, eg, US Department of Homeland Security, Cybersecurity Strategy (15 May 2018) available at www.dhs.gov/sites/default/files/publications/DHS-Cybersecurity-Strategy_0.pdf; Zhonghua Renmin Gongheguo Wanglao Anquan Fa [Cybersecurity Law] (promulgated by the Standing Committee of the National People's Congress, 7 November 2016, effective 1 June 2017) available at https://web.archive.org/web/20161029174914/http://www.npc.gov.cn/npc/xinwen/lfgz/flca/2015-07/06/content_1940614.htm (unofficial English translation available at www.newamerica.org/cybersecurity-initiative/digichina/blog/translation-cybersecurity-law-peoples-republic-china).

[5] Eg, the University of California, Berkeley offers an online Master's degree course in 'Information and Cybersecurity' (see https://requestinfo.cybersecurity.berkeley.edu), while the Harvard University Extension School offers a Graduate Certificate in Cybersecurity (see www.extension.harvard.edu/academics/professional-graduate-certificates/cybersecurity-certificate).

[6] Eg, RSA, a leading cybersecurity company, organises a series of annual conferences attended by thousands of cybersecurity professionals selling the wares of hundreds of cybersecurity companies. See www.rsaconference.com.

[7] T Maurer and R Morgus, 'Compilation of Existing Cybersecurity and Information Security Related Definitions' (*New America*, October 2014) available at https://newamerica.org/documents/1569/compilation-of-existing-cybersecurity-and-information-security-related-definitions.pdf.

[8] Maurer and Morgus, 'Compilation' 25–32.

[9] ibid 26.

interdependent networks and information infrastructure'.[10] The International Organization for Standardization defines the term as the 'preservation of confidentiality, integrity and availability of information in the [sic] Cyberspace',[11] whereas the International Telecommunications Union describes cybersecurity as: 'the collection of tools, policies, security concepts, security safeguards, guidelines, risk management approaches, actions, training, best practices, assurance and technologies that can be used to protect the cyber environment and organization and user's assets'.[12] While this range of definitions can be fairly characterised as 'frighteningly inexact',[13] there are some common threads. First and foremost, all of these definitions include the notion of 'cybersecurity' as protection against threats or attacks. This is sensible, given a dictionary definition of 'security' as 'freedom from danger'.[14] More significantly, 31 of the 47 definitions captured by New America refer to cybersecurity with respect to the protection of 'cyberspace' or of a separate 'cyber domain', in distinction to the physical world.

In so doing, these definitions reflect a strain of thinking going back to the early days of the internet that views cyberspace as a separate domain from physical, corporeal reality. As John Perry Barlow, the author of the famous 'Declaration of the Independence of Cyberspace', put it in 1996:

> Cyberspace consists of transactions, relationships, and thought itself, arrayed like a standing wave in the web of our communications. Ours is a world that is both everywhere and nowhere, but it is not where bodies live. [...]
>
> Your legal concepts of property, expression, identity, movement, and context do not apply to us. They are all based on matter, and there is no matter here.[15]

This view of cyberspace as a separate, transcendent, and non-corporeal domain has always been controversial. In the very same year that Barlow declared the independence of cyberspace, Judge Frank Easterbrook penned a famous article entitled 'Cyberspace and the Law of the Horse'.[16] Easterbrook's argument is that there is no coherent subfield of law that is worthy of being deemed 'cyberlaw', but that the rise of technology simply raises problems surrounding the application of existing bodies of law to new circumstances.

Easterbrook's critique of cyberlaw applies *mutatis mutandis* to conventional definitions of cybersecurity, inasmuch as they presume that the concept applies only to a separate 'cyber domain'. Several of the definitions collected by

---

[10] ibid 31.
[11] ibid 32.
[12] ibid 31.
[13] ibid 32, citing K O'Donoghue, 'Some Perspectives on Cybersecurity: 2012' (*Internet Society*, 12 November 2012).
[14] 'Security', *Merriam-Webster Dictionary* (online ed) available at www.merriam-webster.com/dictionary/security.
[15] JP Barlow, 'A Declaration of the Independence of Cyberspace' (8 February 1996) available at www.eff.org/cyberspace-independence.
[16] F Easterbrook, 'Cyberspace and the Law of the Horse' [1996] *University of Chicago Legal Forum* 207.

New America recognise that the boundaries between cyberspace and physical space are blurry at best. For example, several of the definitions encompass the protection of all devices connected to the internet,[17] while others include the protection of critical infrastructure systems containing networked components.[18]

The illusion that there exists a separate 'cyber domain', whose protection is the rightful province of cybersecurity, has been shattered by two developments. The first is the rise of the Internet of Things (IoT). Ours is an age where internet-connected computers are becoming part and parcel of most 'things' in our lives. As computing devices become ever faster, cheaper, and smaller, we have internet-connected watches and microwaves, toys and thermostats, pacemakers, parking meters, and of course, phones. This makes it increasingly difficult to conceptualise cybersecurity as pertaining to the protection of a separate 'cyber domain', when 'cyberspace' and 'physical space' have merged in the form of mundane objects we interact with all the time.

The second stems from the response of the big social media companies (especially Facebook) to revelations that various actors (including Cambridge Analytica and Russia's 'Internet Research Agency') leveraged their platforms to tilt the outcome of the 2016 US presidential elections in Donald Trump's favour. What is particularly interesting about the former is that Cambridge Analytica's manipulations of Facebook did not involve the breach of any of the electronic security measures that the company had put into place to prevent unauthorised access to its systems.[19] Nor can the impacts of these activities be said to be limited to a distinct 'cyber domain'. Consider the following statement by Facebook's Deputy General Counsel in the immediate aftermath of the Cambridge Analytica revelations:

> *The claim that this is a data breach is completely false.* Aleksandr Kogan requested and gained access to information from users who chose to sign up to his app, and everyone involved gave their consent. People knowingly provided their information, *no systems were infiltrated, and no passwords or sensitive pieces of information were stolen or hacked.* (Emphases added)[20]

Nothing we have encountered contradicts Grewal's statement that 'no [Facebook] systems were infiltrated' by Cambridge Analytica or by any of the campaigns of disinformation and manipulation that targeted the 2016 US elections.[21] Rather, the evidence suggests that these malevolent actors gained access to Facebook's

---

[17] Maurer and Morgus, 'Compilation' 31.
[18] ibid.
[19] JC Wong, 'The Cambridge Analytica Scandal Changed the World – But It Didn't Change Facebook' *The Guardian* (18 March 2019).
[20] P Grewal, 'Suspending Cambridge Analytica and SCL Group from Facebook' (*Facebook Newsroom*, 16 March 2018) available at https://newsroom.fb.com/news/2018/03/suspending-cambridge-analytica.
[21] L Franceschi-Bicchierai, 'Why We're Not Calling the Cambridge Analytica Story a "Data Breach"' (*Vice*, 19 March 2018) available at www.vice.com/en_us/article/3kjzvk/facebook-cambridge-analytica-not-a-data-breach.

'walled garden' through the garden gate: they created Facebook accounts through the usual process, and took advantage of the platform's affordances (such as its targeted advertising service, and its architecture that permits app developers to access vast quantities of user data) to wreak havoc during the 2016 election.[22]

While the actions of Cambridge Analytica and others violated numerous elements of Facebook's Platform Policy,[23] neither these violations nor Facebook's measures in response seem to fit well into the conventional definitions of 'cybersecurity' – given that the objectives of the Russians and of the other merchants of disinformation[24] cannot fairly be said to have been in the 'cyber domain'. Rather, they were to get inside the minds of voters to change their beliefs and perceptions and impact their behaviour at the ballot box.

Even so, Facebook's head of cybersecurity policy said the following about the company's response to both foreign and domestic misinformation campaigns ahead of the 2018 US midterm elections: 'Information operations, what we're talking about here – *it's a security challenge*, which means that you have sophisticated adversaries that are continually trying to figure out new ways to cause harm and to manipulate your platform' (emphasis added).[25]

In offline terms, the manipulation of Facebook and other social media platforms is more analogous to a miscreant submitting a misleading ad to a newspaper which it proceeds to print, than it is to the miscreant breaking into the newspaper's offices to get the ad printed by forcible means. The latter would strike most people as a security problem, whereas the former probably does not. Nonetheless, if efforts to define a term should be informed by how it is used in the field, the fact that Facebook's head of cybersecurity policy views the manipulations described above as a 'security challenge' should be consequential.

In view of these trends, how do we appropriately define cybersecurity? Can a meaningful distinction be drawn between security and cybersecurity, in an age where everything is digitised and computerised? Is there any such thing as a distinct cyber domain anymore, or does the appropriate subject of cybersecurity include protecting the integrity of our mental processes against attempts to manipulate them online?

---

[22] K Wagner, 'Here's How Facebook Allowed Cambridge Analytica to Get Data for 50 Million Users' (*Vox*, 17 March 2018) available at www.vox.com/2018/3/17/17134072/facebook-cambridge-analytica-trump-explained-user-data.

[23] Letter from Damian Collins, MP to Sir Nick Clegg (17 July 2019) available at www.parliament.uk/documents/commons-committees/culture-media-and-sport/190717-Chair-to-Sir-Nick-Clegg-Facebook-re-clarification-regarding-oral-evidence%20.pdf.

[24] S Frenkel, 'Facebook Tackles Rising Threat: Americans Aping Russian Schemes to Deceive' *The New York Times* (11 October 2018); M Isaac and S Frenkel, 'Facebook Removes Iranian Network That Was Spreading Disinformation' *The New York Times* (26 October 2018).

[25] T Mak, 'As Midterms Approach, Facebook Ramps Up Disinformation Fight' (*NPR Morning Edition*, 18 October 2018) available at www.npr.org/2018/10/18/658376619/as-midterms-approach-facebook-ramps-up-disinformation-fight.

A. The Contested Definition of Security

The debates that raged at the end of the Cold War regarding the proper definition of the term 'security' are instructive in defining cybersecurity with greater clarity. During the Cold War, the field of 'security studies' emerged in the US to study the dangerous nuclear competition with the Soviet Union.[26] For those involved in this field, the definition of 'security' was simple: 'security' referred to the 'ability of states to defend themselves against encroachments on their territorial integrity and political sovereignty'.[27]

This view of 'security' as referring to the security of the nation-state against external armed threats remained dominant throughout the Cold War, but once the Berlin Wall fell, 'redefining "security" [became] something of a cottage industry'.[28] Scholars and policymakers suggested that the definition of security should be broadened to include new threats, such as poverty, environmental degradation, and even cultural preservation. Inherent in these arguments was the claim that the *referent* of security should be redefined from the state in favour of individual human beings.[29] In the view of what became known as the 'human security' movement, the aim of 'security' ought to be to protect individuals from threats to their survival and well-being – even if those threats emanate from the state itself. In the words of the International Commission on Intervention and State Sovereignty's 2001 report:

> The fundamental components of human security – the security of people against threats to life, health, livelihood, personal safety and human dignity – can be put at risk by external aggression, but also by factors within a country, including 'security' forces. [...]
>
> The traditional, narrow perception of security leaves out the most elementary and legitimate concerns of ordinary people regarding security in their daily lives. It also diverts enormous amounts of national wealth and human resources into armaments and armed forces, while countries fail to protect their citizens from chronic insecurities of hunger, disease, inadequate shelter, crime, unemployment, social conflict and environmental hazard. [...] The concept of human security can and does embrace such diverse circumstances.[30]

Each of this definition's components of human security correspond to human rights that are protected by international law, ranging from civil and political rights (eg, the rights to life and personal safety) to economic, social, and cultural

---

[26] P Williams, *Security Studies: An Introduction*, 2nd edn (London, Routledge, 2012) 2–4.
[27] YF Khong, 'Human Security: A Shotgun Approach to Alleviating Human Misery' (2001) 7 *Global Governance* 231, 231.
[28] D Baldwin, 'The Concept of Security' (1997) 23 *Review of International Studies* 5, 5.
[29] I Atack, 'Human Security, Human Rights and Human Development' in *The Ethics of Peace and War: From State Security to World Community* (Edinburgh, Edinburgh University Press, 2005).
[30] International Commission on Intervention and State Sovereignty, 'The Responsibility to Protect' (December 2001) 15 available at http://responsibilitytoprotect.org/ICISS%20Report.pdf.

rights (eg, the rights to health and livelihood).[31] This is no accident, as 'the litmus test for human security' has been described as 'success in delivering basic rights'.[32]

By contrast, critics of human security theory contend that its purpose is nothing more than to raise the profile of certain issues. Issues that are anointed as 'security' issues have long received top billing on both the domestic and international political agendas, hence: '[o]nce an issue like drug trafficking is securitised, its status in the policy hierarchy changes. It becomes an urgent issue, worthy of special attention, resources, and fast-track or immediate amelioration or resolution, perhaps even by military means.'[33] Correspondingly, critics contend that making 'the security of each and every individual on the planet the object of our concern' results in '(total) paralysis of our ability to prioritise'.[34] If everything is a security issue, of what use is the term? This critique of human security led, in turn, to one leading scholar of the era declaring security to be an 'essentially contested concept',[35] meaning that the term is 'so value-laden that no amount of argument or evidence can ever lead to agreement on a single version as the "correct or standard use"'.[36]

B. Lessons Learned

The relevance of the foregoing to current debates about the definition of cybersecurity is that, now as then, there is a great deal of instrumentalism in the crafting of definitions. Just as the human security movement of the 1990s sought to elevate issues on the public policy agenda by deeming them to be security issues, capacious definitions of cybersecurity may promote the prioritisation of the goals, priorities, and ambitions that they encompass on the public policy agenda by 'cyber-securitising' them.

Fortunately, the debates of the 1990s also offer us a pathway to devising a parsimonious and analytically useful definition of cybersecurity. One of the most useful works of this era is a review essay by Baldwin, who defines security quite simply as a state where there exists 'a low probability of damage to acquired values'.[37] 'Acquired values' are the things (both material objects and conceptual notions) that we value and therefore want to protect against threats. Hence, a rigorous building code provides security for the acquired value in buildings against the threat of an earthquake, just as a policy of deterrence provides a state with security against the threat

---

[31] T Dunne and NJ Wheeler, '"We the Peoples": Contending Discourses of Security in Human Rights Theory and Practice' (2004) 18(1) *International Relations* 9, 18.
[32] ibid 18.
[33] Khong, 'Human Security' 231.
[34] ibid 232.
[35] B Buzan, *People, States and Fear: An Agenda for International Security Studies in the Post Cold-War Era* (New York, Harvester Wheatsheaf, 1991) 7.
[36] Baldwin, 'The Concept of Security' 10 (quoting WB Gallie, 'Essentially Contested Concepts' (1956) 56 *Proceedings of the Aristotelian Society*, ns 167, 168).
[37] Baldwin, 'The Concept of Security' 13.

posed by a neighbour's military build-up. 'Security' in Baldwin's definition has no referent; rather, it is a value-neutral concept that is analytically useful in evaluating whether measures to promote the security of an 'acquired value' are worthwhile.

What is most interesting about Baldwin's definition is how similar it is to a definition of security posited by Schneier, one of the world's leading 'security technologists', at about the same time. Schneier defines security as the prevention of 'adverse consequences from the intentional and unwarranted actions of others'.[38] These 'unwarranted actions', which Schneier calls 'attacks', are directed towards 'assets' – which can be as small as an individual diamond or as large as a state's entire infrastructure. Security against such 'attacks' is provided by 'countermeasures' employed by 'defenders', which can range from locks on doors (providing security against burglars) to a firewall (providing security against cyber-intruders).[39]

There is much common ground between Schneier and Baldwin. What Baldwin calls an 'acquired value' accords with Schneier's idea of an 'asset' that security protects. The two only really part company when it comes to protection against unintentional adverse consequences. 'Security concerns itself with intentional actions' according to Schneier, whereas 'protecting assets from unintentional actions is safety, not security'.[40] Hence Schneier would view a building code that protects against the adverse consequences of an earthquake as a safety measure, rather than a security measure.

C. A Parsimonious Definition of Cybersecurity

How can we use the relative agreement between Baldwin and Schneier regarding the definition of security, to come up with a rigorous and analytically useful definition of cybersecurity? Our goal in so doing is to have a definition of cybersecurity that we can use to interrogate the relationship of this concept with human rights, though doing so also facilitates rigorous analysis of problems that are deemed to be cybersecurity issues.

If simplicity and parsimony are virtues, we propose no longer 'loading' the definition of cybersecurity with the specific objectives that different actors seek to achieve by means of various policy measures. Instead, following Baldwin and Schneier, we propose defining cybersecurity very simply as the 'prevention of adverse consequences caused by the intentional and unwarranted actions of others through the use of electronic systems'. In the next section, we will use this definition to help us probe the relationship between cybersecurity and human rights, and understand why human rights should be the standard against which the costs and benefits of cybersecurity measures are weighed.

---

[38] B Schneier, *Beyond Fear: Thinking Sensibly About Security in an Uncertain World* (New York, Copernicus, 2003) ch 1.
[39] ibid.
[40] ibid.

II. The Relationship between Cybersecurity and Human Rights

As Part I demonstrates, the term 'security' has little commonly understood meaning on its own. It must be defined vis-à-vis what is being protected. Security is the state where some 'asset' or 'acquired value' faces a 'low probability of damage' from 'attack', but the term has no analytical utility unless we specify what 'acquired values' or 'assets' we are trying to protect.

The question then arises as to what assets cybersecurity measures should protect, given our definition of cybersecurity as the 'prevention of adverse consequences caused by the intentional and unwarranted actions of others through the use of electronic systems'. At first glance, cybersecurity measures appear to be directed at protecting assets such as electronic devices and networks. We contend, however, that the aim of such measures – at least in rights-respecting societies – should be to protect the rights of people from 'adverse consequences' caused by 'intentional and unwarranted actions'. Put otherwise, we are suggesting that human beings and the rights they possess should be the *assets* or *acquired values* that cybersecurity seeks to protect. This is consistent with the emerging notion of 'human-centric cybersecurity',[41] which has been described as the 'principle that all cybersecurity laws, policies, and practices should respect international human rights and humanitarian laws'.[42]

In view of this, we further contend that the trade-offs that every security measure necessarily entails should also be recast in terms of human rights. This allows for the benefits and harms of particular cybersecurity measures on various rights held by different rights-holders to be assessed using legal tools (most notably the doctrines of legality, necessity, and proportionality) that have been developed in the last 75 years to evaluate and manage such balances.

A. (Cyber-)Security and Human Rights Trade-Offs

Security always involves costs and trade-offs.[43] Even something as simple as locking one's door (a security measure against burglars) involves costs (eg, the time it takes to lock your door) and trade-offs (eg, the risk of being locked out).[44] Consequently, it seems reasonable that there might be a trade-off between 'security' and privacy,

---

[41] MD Cavelty, 'Breaking the Cyber-Security Dilemma: Aligning Security Needs and Removing Vulnerabilities' (2014) 20 *Science and Engineering Ethics* 701, 703; RJ Deibert, 'Toward a Human-Centric Approach to Cybersecurity' (2018) 32 *Ethics & International Affairs* 411, 412–13.
[42] Deibert, 'Toward a Human-Centric Approach' 412–13.
[43] See Baldwin, 'The Concept of Security' 18; see also Schneier, *Beyond Fear*.
[44] Schneier, *Beyond Fear* 7.

both online and offline, as is widely stated by pundits, scholars, and policymakers alike.⁴⁵

The debate on encryption policy is an example par excellence of this purported trade-off. Certain prominent voices – including the states comprising the 'Five Eyes' intelligence sharing arrangement⁴⁶ – have called for the installation of 'backdoor' access points into various kinds of encrypted digital systems as a means of enhancing 'security'.⁴⁷ The proposals cover everything from operating systems, such as Apple's iOS,⁴⁸ to particular pieces of communications software, such as Facebook's WhatsApp Messenger.⁴⁹

The purpose of doing so is to address what is often described as the 'Going Dark' problem,⁵⁰ wherein law enforcement and intelligence agencies claim that they are unable to prevent, detect, and prosecute criminal and terrorist activities due to their use of encrypted systems.⁵¹ In so suggesting, the Five Eyes governments claim that they are seeking to strike a more reasonable balance between 'security' and 'privacy',⁵² after the pendulum swung too far in the direction of privacy following the Snowden revelations.⁵³

When those on the 'pro-backdoor' side of the 'Going Dark' debate talk about 'security', they appear to be referring to traditional notions of 'national security' – as in security against crime and terrorism. Since the protection of life, liberty, and property against criminal and terrorist threats is among the highest duties of any government, 'pro-backdoor' partisans are therefore claiming that it is worth trading off some 'privacy' for more 'security' against these admittedly serious threats.

---

⁴⁵ cf D Solove, *Nothing to Hide: The False Trade-Off Between Privacy and Security* (New Haven, Yale University Press, 2011) (exposing and debunking common myths that there is a trade-off between privacy and security).

⁴⁶ The 'Five Eyes' are Australia, Canada, New Zealand, the UK, and the US.

⁴⁷ See, eg, D Sanger and S Frenkel, '"Five Eyes" Nations Quietly Demand Government Access to Encrypted Data' *The New York Times* (4 September 2018); Five Country Ministerial, Quintet Meeting of Attorneys-General, 'Statement of Principles on Access to Evidence and Encryption' (30 August 2018) available at www.ag.gov.au/About/CommitteesandCouncils/Documents/joint-statement-principles-access-evidence.pdf; Remarks of Attorney General William P Barr to the International Conference on Cyber Security (23 July 2019) available at www.justice.gov/opa/speech/attorney-general-william-p-barr-delivers-keynote-address-international-conference-cyber.

⁴⁸ See, eg, B Barrett, 'The FBI Backs Down Against Apple – Again' (*Wired*, 10 May 2020) available at www.wired.com/story/fbi-backs-down-apple-encryption-pensacola-iphones.

⁴⁹ See, eg, 'India Threatens to Tear Apart Any Semblance of Digital Privacy' *Washington Post* (13 January 2020).

⁵⁰ J Zittrain et al, 'Don't Panic: Making Progress on the "Going Dark" Debate' (Berkman Center for Internet and Society, 2016) available at https://cyber.harvard.edu/pubrelease/dont-panic/Dont_Panic_Making_Progress_on_Going_Dark_Debate.pdf.

⁵¹ ibid.

⁵² T Cushing, 'After FBI Successfully Breaks Into iPhones, Bill Barr Says It's Time for Legislated Encryption Backdoors' (*Techdirt*, 21 May 2020) available at www.techdirt.com/articles/20200519/12513944529/after-fbi-successfully-breaks-into-iphones-bill-barr-says-time-legislated-encryption-backdoors.shtml; JC Wong, 'US, UK and Australia Urge Facebook to Create Backdoor Access to Encrypted Messages' *The Guardian* (4 October 2019).

⁵³ A Blake, 'FBI Revamping Plan For Tackling "Going Dark" Encryption Problem' *The Washington Times* (28 Match 2018).

And given that 'privacy' is a human right, a trade-off between security in the digital realm and human rights appears to come into view.

Other voices in the 'Going Dark' debate, however, dispute the notion of there being a trade-off between 'privacy' and 'security'.[54] On this view, the real trade-off is between 'security' and 'security' – ie, security against different kinds of threats. For example, Schneier has argued that while mandating 'backdoors' might make it easier for governments to intercept and examine the encrypted communications of terrorists and criminals, such a policy measure would make every electronic device containing these 'backdoor' access points more vulnerable to a wide range of attacks.[55] Given that heads of state,[56] airline pilots,[57] corporate titans,[58] and mass shooting suspects[59] may all use the same electronic devices running the same operating systems, mandating the inclusion of a backdoor in every device may create weaknesses that any number of adversaries – from hostile foreign governments to domestic and international criminal syndicates – can use to perpetrate any number of attacks.

While reasonable people can disagree as to whether the benefits associated with backdoors (in investigating crime and terrorism) are worth their costs (reduced security against all kinds of electronic attacks),[60] reconceptualising the trade-offs

---

[54] See, eg, J Ribeiro, 'Tim Cook: There's No Trade-Off Between Security and Privacy' (*PCWorld*, 21 December 2015) available at www.pcworld.com/article/3017517/security/tim-cook-says-there-isnt-a-trade-off-between-security-and-privacy.html (quoting Apple CEO Tim Cook); see also, eg, H Greenfield, 'Governments Should Avoid Mandates to Weaken Digital Security' (*Computer & Communications Industry Association*, 17 February 2016) available at www.ccianet.org/2016/02/governments-should-avoid-mandates-to-weaken-digital-security (quoting CEO of CCIA, Ed Black).

[55] A Stepanovich and M Karanicolas, 'Why an Encryption Backdoor for Just the "Good Guys" Won't Work' (*Just Security*, 2 March 2018) available at www.justsecurity.org/53316/criminalize-security-criminals-secure; 'Encryption Backdoors are a Dangerous Idea' (*New America*, 27 November 2018) available at www.newamerica.org/oti/blog/encryption-backdoors-are-dangerous-idea.

[56] M Rosenberg and M Haberman, 'When Trump Phones Friends, the Chinese and the Russians Listen and Learn' *The New York Times* (24 October 2018).

[57] The US Federal Aviation Administration has authorised the use of Apple iPads as Electronic Flight Bags. See Federal Aviation Administration, 'The Apple iPad and Other Suitable Tablet Computing Devices as Electronic Flight Bags (EFB)' InFO 11011 (13 May 2011) available at www.faa.gov/other_visit/aviation_industry/airline_operators/airline_safety/info/all_infos/media/2011/InFO11011.pdf.

[58] K Zetter and J Cox, 'Here is the Technical Report Suggesting Saudi Arabia's Prince Hacked Jeff Bezos' Phone' (*Vice*, 22 January 2020) available at www.vice.com/en_us/article/v74v34/saudi-arabia-hacked-jeff-bezos-phone-technical-report.

[59] Eg, the gunman in a 2015 mass shooting in California used an encrypted iPhone, sparking a major legal battle between Apple and the US Government over unlocking it. See, eg, E Lichtblau and K Benner, 'Apple Fights Order to Unlock San Bernardino Gunman's iPhone' *The New York Times* (17 February 2016).

[60] We hasten to note, however, that most security experts suggest that the magnitude of the threat to which we would be exposed by weakening encryption is so great as to outweigh any security benefits we would gain from this measure. See United Nations Special Rapporteur on the promotion and protection of the right to freedom of opinion and expression, 'Encryption and Anonymity follow-up report' (June 2018), para 13, available at www.ohchr.org/Documents/Issues/Opinion/EncryptionAnonymityFollowUpReport.pdf. See also National Academies of Sciences, Engineering, and Medicine, *Decrypting the Encryption Debate: A Framework for Decision Makers* (Washington DC, The National Academies Press, 2018) ch 4.

involved so as to be able to make a like-vs-like comparison allows for these benefits and costs to be assessed against a common denominator.

Consistent with this approach, we believe that the security-vs-security trade-off that Schneier has identified in the 'Going Dark' debate can also be conceptualised as a balancing exercise between different human rights. Consider that the International Covenant on Civil and Political Rights (ICCPR) guarantees the right of every individual to life (Article 6), and to liberty and security of the person (Article 9). The UN Human Rights Committee has explained that 'security of the person' refers to 'freedom from injury to the body and the mind, or bodily and mental integrity'.[61] The General Comment goes on to explain the state duty under Article 9 'to take appropriate measures … to protect individuals from foreseeable threats to life or bodily integrity',[62] including from 'individual criminals or irregular groups, including armed or terrorist groups, operating within their territory'.[63] Correspondingly, the argument being made by the 'pro-backdoor' camp in the Going Dark debate could be recast in terms of fulfilling the state's duty under Articles 6 and 9 to protect the life, survival, liberty, and security of every person against certain criminal and terrorist threats (ie, those that can be mitigated with access to the bad actors' encrypted communications).

At the same time, the argument that weakening encryption opens the door to new kinds of threats can also be recast in terms of human rights – specifically, in terms of Articles 6 and 9 of the ICCPR. If mandating backdoors makes it easier for any number of adversaries to compromise electronic systems that are important to our very survival, we then have a 'foreseeable threat[] to life [and] bodily integrity' stemming from a policy measure that is supposed to enhance the protection of these very rights. Hence, we have a situation where the measure in question has contradictory effects on both Articles 6 and 9 of the ICCPR: backdoors help to secure the enjoyment of these rights against certain threats, while making them more vulnerable to others. So as in the security-vs-security conceptualisation above, we now have a like-to-like, rights-vs-rights trade-off that clarifies what is at stake in devising measures to address this public policy issue.

Yet there are still more rights implicated by the notion of mandating encryption backdoors than those guaranteed by ICCPR Articles 6 and 9. The most obvious is, of course, the right to privacy, which is guaranteed by ICCPR Article 17 and features prominently in the conventional 'security vs privacy' dichotomy described above.[64] It is widely recognised that encryption helps to protect the right to privacy by making it more difficult for third parties to access individuals' data both in

---

[61] UN Human Rights Committee, General Comment No 35, 'Article 9 (Liberty and security of person)' (16 December 2014) UN Doc CCPR/C/GC/35, 3.
[62] ibid 9.
[63] ibid 7.
[64] See, eg, S Schulhofer, 'An International Right to Privacy? Be Careful What You Wish for' (2015) 14 *International Journal of Constitutional Law* 238, 253.

transit and at rest.⁶⁵ Yet there is also a growing recognition that strong encryption is essential to enjoyment of the rights to free expression and opinion, enshrined in ICCPR Article 19, given that individuals may be 'chilled' from stating their true thoughts and opinions on the dominant electronic media of our era – even in the relative privacy of their own hard drives or cloud storage accounts – without the strong additional privacy guarantees that encryption provides.⁶⁶ Moreover, in increasingly authoritarian countries, the ability of actors to safely organise and fight for democratic space may also depend on encryption. The battles to maintain this democratic space in turn influence access to an impartial judicial system (ICCPR Article 14) and the right to peacefully assemble (ICCPR Article 21).

Correspondingly, what is at stake in the 'Going Dark' debate is more than just a trade-off between 'security' and 'privacy', or between 'security' and 'security'. There is also a trade-off between the protection of several different human rights and the rights of different rights-holders. Weakening encryption and building backdoors might help protect the rights guaranteed under ICCPR Articles 6 and 9 for some people at some times against certain kinds of threats (such as by facilitating the detection of a terrorist plot), but it comes at a price for the enjoyment of these exact same rights in other circumstances (such as by creating vulnerabilities in critical electronic systems that can be exploited by wrongdoers). Furthermore, such measures also adversely impact the enjoyment of the rights to free expression and privacy in our digital age. (In the next section, we demonstrate how this recasting exercise permits these differential impacts of a single measure on different rights to be assessed using the tests of legality, necessity, and proportionality drawn from human rights law.)

A similar analysis can be applied to the efforts of Facebook and other companies to combat actors that are spreading disinformation on their platforms, which they characterise as a matter of cybersecurity.⁶⁷ For example, the company prohibits 'offers to buy or sell votes as well as misrepresentations about the dates, locations, times and qualifications for casting a ballot'.⁶⁸ And in response to Covid-19, Facebook is removing 'misinformation that could lead to imminent physical harm', including claims such as 'drinking bleach cures the virus and theories like physical distancing is ineffective in preventing the disease from spreading'.⁶⁹

The first of these measures can be characterised as protecting the right 'to vote and to be elected at genuine periodic elections […] by universal and equal

---

⁶⁵ See, eg, UN Human Rights Council, 'Report of the Special Rapporteur on the Promotion and Protection of the Right to Freedom of Opinion and Expression, David Kaye' (22 May 2015) UN Doc A/HRC/29/32, 3.
⁶⁶ ibid 8.
⁶⁷ See text accompanying nn 19–25.
⁶⁸ J Leinwand, 'Expanding Our Policies on Voter Suppression' (*Facebook Newsroom*, 15 October 2018) available at https://newsroom.fb.com/news/2018/10/voter-suppression-policies.
⁶⁹ G Rosen, 'An Update on Our Work to Keep People Informed and Limit Misinformation about COVID-19' (*Facebook*, 16 April 2020) available at https://about.fb.com/news/2020/04/covid-19-misinfo-update.

suffrage', as guaranteed by Article 25(b) of the ICCPR.[70] The second, in turn, can be conceptualised as protecting the rights to life and health, as protected by Article 6 of the ICCPR and Article 12 of the International Covenant on Economic, Social, and Cultural Rights, respectively. Both measures, however, involve at least some interference with the freedom of opinion and expression, as guaranteed by Article 19 of the ICCPR. Correspondingly, as in the 'Going Dark' example, we have two additional measures relating to cybersecurity (as that term is viewed by one of the world's leading internet companies) that can also be characterised as measures to protect certain human rights (democratic rights, life, and health) with some interference upon another (free expression).

B. Implications

Having shown in the previous section that many security vs human rights trade-offs can be recast as trade-offs between securing different human rights for different rights-holders, this section explains why doing so is useful. Our contention is that when the trade-offs implicated by security measures and policies are viewed in terms of the varied impacts on the rights of different rights-holders, we can use the mechanisms that human rights law provides – notably the tests of legality, necessity, and proportionality – to weigh and assess these trade-offs. This process can help us decide in a clear-eyed manner whether the costs associated with a particular policy proposal in terms of certain human rights are worth the benefit in terms of protecting other rights.

To begin, it is important to note that many international and domestic human rights instruments distinguish between rights that are inviolate, and those which may be subject to limitation. As a general matter, Article 4 of the ICCPR recognises that states may take measures 'derogating from their obligations under the present Convention' in times of 'public emergency which threatens the life of the nation', although this provision forbids any derogation from numerous rights guaranteed by the Convention ('non-derogable rights') – including the right to life under Article 6.[71] More specifically, Article 17 of the ICCPR guarantees the right not to have one's privacy, family, home or correspondence 'subjected to arbitrary

---

[70] It is noteworthy that General Comment No 25 (regarding ICCPR Art 25) advises that 'abusive interference with registration or voting as well as intimidation or coercion of voter should be prohibited by penal laws' and that '[v]oters should be able to form opinions independently of […] inducement or manipulative interference of any kind'. UN Human Rights Committee, 'General Comment adopted by the Human Rights Committee under Article 40, paragraph 4, of the International Covenant on Civil and Political Rights: General Comment No 25' (27 August 1996) UN Doc CCPR/C/21/Rev.1/Add.7, 11, 19.

[71] The Siracusa Principles provide authoritative interpretive guidance on derogations during emergencies. UN Commission on Human Rights, 'The Siracusa Principles on the Limitation and Derogation Provisions in the International Covenant on Civil and Political Rights' (28 September 2014) UN Doc E/CN.4/1985/4.

or unlawful interference', while the freedoms of opinion and expression guaranteed by Article 19 of the ICCPR are subject to 'restrictions [...] provided by law' that are 'necessary' for the protection of the 'rights or reputations of others' or for the protection of national security, public order, or public health or morals.

Many modern domestic constitutions contain structurally similar limitations provisions. Some, like Germany's Basic Law and India's Constitution, detail how each of the rights that they enumerate may be specifically limited.[72] Others, like the Canadian Charter of Rights and Freedoms and the South African Bill of Rights, set forth general limitation clauses while specifying certain rights as non-derogable.[73] Especially since the end of the Second World War, international and domestic courts have largely relied upon proportionality and related doctrines to determine when and how rights may be limited to achieve important public policy objectives.[74] A limitation upon the rights guaranteed by international human rights treaties or domestic bills of rights is permissible only if it satisfies the principle of legality (ie, it is prescribed in a law of general application that is clear and ascertainable),[75] and then only if the limitation:

> (i) [...] is designated for a proper purpose; (ii) the measures undertaken to effectuate such a limitation are rationally connected to the fulfilment of that purpose; (iii) the measures undertaken are necessary in that there are no alternative measures that may similarly achieve that same purpose with a lesser degree of limitation; and finally (iv) there needs to be a proper relation ('proportionality *stricto sensu*' or 'balancing') between the importance of achieving the proper purpose and the social importance of preventing the limitation on the constitutional right.[76]

The doctrine of proportionality and other specific tests that have been developed to evaluate the appropriateness of limitations on specific rights (such as the three-part test for ICCPR Article 19[77]) have important applications for cybersecurity

---

[72] See, eg, Art 11 of Germany's Basic Law (declaring the freedom of movement of German citizens and subjecting them to particular limitations) (Basic Law for the Federal Republic of Germany 1949, Art 11); Arts 19(1)(d) and (e) of the Indian Constitution (guaranteeing the freedom of movement of Indian citizens yet subjecting them to specific limitations specified in Art 19(5) of the same) (The Constitution of India 1950, Arts 19(1)(d), (19(1)(e), and 19(5)).

[73] Specifically, s 1 of the Canadian Charter of Rights and Freedoms subjects all of the rights it guarantees to 'reasonable limits prescribed by law as can be demonstrably justified in a free and democratic society', while s 32, which permits governments to enact legislation 'notwithstanding' the Charter's rights guarantees, exempts certain enumerated rights from this provision (Canadian Charter of Rights and Freedoms, ss 1 and 32, Pt 1 of the Constitution Act 1982, being Sch B to the Canada Act 1982 (UK), c 11). Similarly, s 36 of the South African Constitution sets forth a general limitation clause, while s 37, which permits the derogation of certain rights during states of emergency, declares other rights to be non-derogable in all circumstances (The Constitution of the Republic of South Africa 1996, ss 36–37).

[74] See generally A Barak, *Proportionality: Constitutional Rights and Their Limitations* (Cambridge, Cambridge University Press, 2012) (chronicling the evolution of proportionality and related doctrines in numerous countries around the world).

[75] ibid 107–8.

[76] ibid 3.

[77] The operation of the test is well described in A Callamard, 'Freedom of Expression and National Security: Balancing for Protection' (*Columbia Global Freedom of Expression*, December

policy-making. If one accepts our parsimonious definition of cybersecurity as the 'prevention of adverse consequences caused by the intentional and unwarranted actions of others through the use of electronic systems', reconceptualising the trade-offs that are inherent in most cybersecurity measures in terms of human rights allows for the use of such tests to assess whether the benefits of a policy are worth their human rights costs.

Returning to the encryption policy debate, reconceptualising the argument for 'backdoors' in terms of advancing the rights to life and security of the person allows us to use appropriate legal tests to see if the costs (in terms of the rights to privacy and free expression) are worth the benefits. In circumstances where the legality principle is met, a 'backdoor' mandate could be a measure undertaken for the proper purpose of protecting the rights to life and proper security, and which bears a rational connection to this purpose. Likewise, whether such measures are necessary to achieve the proper purpose to which they are directed (in the sense of whether they are the least restrictive means of doing so) can also be assessed, as can whether there is an appropriate balance between the proper purpose being achieved and the limitations that are being imposed on individual rights.

Our larger point, however, is that if we conceptualise the aim of cybersecurity measures (and indeed of all security measures) as striving to secure the rights that belong to the people, we can more fully understand the varied implications of those measures on rights, and make better public policy decisions using an analytically consistent framework.

Moreover, such a framework helps policymakers to more easily see how their policies might impact disparate rights holders differently. We noted in the 'Going Dark' example how some cybersecurity measures might enhance the enjoyment of some rights in some circumstances, while interfering with them in others. The same is true of other cybersecurity measures, such as the real-name policies that many online platforms enforce upon their users.[78] Such policies might protect some individuals from anonymous online harassment, yet they might also expose vulnerable populations (including journalists and ethnic and sexual minorities) to online harassment or physical violence.[79] Likewise, weakening encryption by creating backdoors may disproportionately impact minority communities who are already subject to over-policing,[80] but also others who are likely to be targeted by government officials for unlawful or excessive surveillance, such as journalists,

---

2015) available at https://globalfreedomofexpression.columbia.edu/wp-content/uploads/2016/01/A-Callamard-National-Security-and-FoE-Training.pdf.

[78] 'What Names Are Allowed On Facebook?' (*Facebook*) available at www.facebook.com/help/112146705538576.

[79] UNHRC, 'Report of the Special Rapporteur on the Promotion and Protection of the Right to Freedom of Opinion and Expression' (6 April 2018) UN Doc A/HRC/38/35, 30.

[80] S Renderos and M Tseng Putterman, 'To the Next POTUS: For Communities of Color, Encryption is a Civil Right' (*TechCrunch*, 6 May 2016) available at https://techcrunch.com/2016/05/06/to-the-next-potus-for-communities-of-color-encryption-is-a-civil-right.

activists, and dissidents.[81] To cite an important historical example that encapsulates these risks, Martin Luther King, Jr was labelled a national security threat by the US Federal Bureau of Investigation two days after delivering his famous 'I Have a Dream' speech, which led to the National Security Agency unlawfully tapping his phones for the rest of his life.[82]

III. Conclusion

In a world where everything is fast becoming an internet-connecting thing, cybersecurity policies will pervade many more aspects of our lives. Once cybersecurity is defined in a neutral manner (rather than an empty vessel to be filled with ambitious agendas), it becomes clear that cybersecurity issues touch most every human being, as our society becomes increasingly reliant on electronic systems to provide us with both the essentials and the good things in life.

This fact is at the core of our attempt in this chapter to probe the relationship between cybersecurity and human rights. We show that many cybersecurity measures in the world today already have as their aim, mostly implicitly but sometimes explicitly, the protection of human rights and the people who enjoy them. From here, it does not take much to recast the aims of these measures in terms of human rights, and to measure their costs and benefits in human rights terms as well.

Given that human rights are to be found on every side of the cybersecurity policy equation, we believe that the well-established framework of human rights law best provides a consistent framework for analysing and making decisions about the multi-faceted implications of various cybersecurity measures. To be sure, cybersecurity measures entail other costs that are beyond the scope of this chapter, such as financial costs, where a human rights framework might have less to contribute. Yet given the fundamental importance of human rights and their status as our highest form of law, defining the costs and benefits of cybersecurity measures in terms of human rights ensures that such policies are truly advancing human well-being.

---

[81] Amnesty International, 'Encryption: A Matter of Human Rights' (March 2016) available at www.amnestyusa.org/reports/encryption-a-matter-of-human-rights.

[82] See NSA Archive, DocID: 523696 Ref ID: A523696, https://nsarchive2.gwu.edu//NSAEBB/NSAEBB441/docs/minaret%20after.pdf; AM Bedoya, 'The Color of Surveillance' (*Slate*, 18 January 2016) available at https://slate.com/technology/2016/01/what-the-fbis-surveillance-of-martin-luther-king-says-about-modern-spying.html; M Cyril, 'Black Americans and Encryption: The Stakes are Higher Than Apple v FBI' *The Guardian* (21 March 2016).

3

Perils of Data-Intensive Systems in the Philippines and Asia

JAMAEL JACOB

For the better part of the past couple of decades, information has earned itself the title of the most valuable resource of this era. Its ubiquity and the constant build-up of its use cases have made believers out of businesses and policymakers alike. The result: anywhere one turns to look, there is a programme, a system, or framework that lends itself to the idea that *the* way forward, *the* correct path towards the future inevitably goes through data.

Validating the mystique is the unabated growth of technology companies in size, wealth, and influence. For many, their entire business model revolves around the trove of information they gather from different sources, particularly their customers, clients, or users. They funnel the data into massive processing machineries that maximise not just the serviceability of data, but also their profit potential. These systems are sometimes referred to as data-intensive systems (DIS). The revenues they bring in are of such unprecedented scale, they already rival the finances of nation-states.[1] As a result, certain businesses have been able to expand into other industries, often at the expense of their brick-and-mortar contemporaries. Invariably, governments have not been left out, albeit it took most of them a while to catch up. Many are now on a spending spree, investing heavily on technologies and their own DIS. Their efforts usually lead to partnerships with private actors and are justified by boilerplate state policies like effective governance, better delivery of government services, national security, and general welfare. The trend also rings true in Asia. A remarkable distinction for a region which, from a purely economic standpoint, has already been basking under a similar stature for quite some time. Today, there is an abundance of local businesses and governments firmly latched on to the data bandwagon. With the territory home to roughly

---

[1] See F Benchón and R Moynihan, '25 Giant Companies that Are Bigger than Entire Countries' (*Business Insider*, 25 July 2018). See also J Myers, 'How Do the World's Biggest Companies Compare to the Biggest Economies?' (*World Economic Forum*, 19 October 2016).

60 per cent of the world's population,² they now appreciate sitting on a virtual goldmine that could ostensibly catapult them over their western counterparts.

All that potential, though, has a steep price. Questions ranging from the actual effectiveness of DIS to the harm and negative consequences they inflict on individual freedoms have been brought to the fore. Regulatory capture, outdated policies, and incompetent regulatory authorities have made them more difficult to address. Nonetheless, as the dangers posed by these systems increase in scope, the need to document and discuss them has never been more critical than now. For all stakeholders – state actors, above all else – there must be an honest resolve to take immediate and decisive action. True progress promised by a digital future ought not be at the expense of fundamental liberties.

This chapter aims to contribute to such a discussion by drawing attention to the Philippines, a relatively young democracy nestled in Southeast Asia. Parts I and II highlight the ongoing global exodus towards a more digital and interconnected environment and the central role of information and DIS in this transformation. Part II in particular steers the discussion to the Asian continent. In both segments, common examples of data-intensive systems will also be taken up. Part III is an abridged impact analysis of DIS by presenting both their positive uses and drawbacks. The Philippine context is finally featured in Part IV, focusing mainly on a number of government-initiated DIS. Part V concludes by offering strategy and policy recommendations designed to keep the proliferation and use of DIS in check, particularly in countries handicapped by defective to non-existent controls, including weak regulators and democratic institutions.

I. A Digital and Data-Driven World

The world is becoming more digital by the minute. In 2017, the International Telecommunications Union (ITU) estimated that 46 per cent of households already owned a computer.³ In 2020, internet connectivity is already pegged at 59 per cent of the global population.⁴ And while people are spending a bit less time online every day, the annual total is still more than 100 days of connected time per year, per internet user.⁵ Meanwhile, mobile phone users are up to 5.19 billion, which is about 67 per cent of the total population.⁶ In social media, active users now represent almost half of the population, spending nearly two and a half hours per day on the medium.⁷ Ecommerce is also surging, with three-quarters

---

[2] World Population Review, 'Continent and Region Populations 2020' available at https://worldpopulationreview.com/continents.
[3] W Chua, 'ITU's IDI Ranks Philippines at 15th Place' *Manila Bulletin* (16 November 2017).
[4] S Kemp, 'Digital 2020: Global Digital Review' (*Datareportal*, 30 January 2020).
[5] ibid.
[6] ibid.
[7] ibid.

of the world's digital citizens now purchasing online every month.[8] As Internet of Things (IoT) technologies transition from a niche market to an everyday norm, these figures are expected to climb further at full tilt.[9]

The fuel that keeps this vehicle in transit is data. In today's connected world, it has become both pervasive and ubiquitous. Some are knowingly shared, while most are generated behind the opaque algorithms of tech companies or via state-sanctioned data collection schemes. Outside of civil society, this status quo has encountered little to no resistance – accepted as a necessary compromise in exchange for convenience and services, including those extended by government. Whichever is the case, all available evidence affirms the indispensable role of data. In 2019, it is said that any one of the following occurred within a 60-second timeframe: 18.1 million texts were relayed; 188 million emails were sent out; 390,030 apps were downloaded via Apple's App Store and Google Play; and 3.8 million search queries were made on Google.[10] Wearable devices were also generating 28 petabytes of data within the same period.[11] These numbers, incredible as they are, become even harder to grasp once it becomes clear that they do not yet take into account government data-processing activities. Still, they suffice to explain the increasing number of tech companies that find themselves among the world's top businesses.[12] Some in policy-making have suggested that a so-called 'data dividend plan' is necessary, to require entities such as Facebook and Google to pay individual users a fraction of the revenue derived by these companies from their personal data.[13] The basic premise is that people should be compensated, and thus share in the windfall attributable to the data they themselves have created.

The second critical component is the engine that transforms information from mere potential into a serviceable and profitable format. It consists of the systems and technologies operating around the collection and subsequent processing of data on large scales. Among civil society organisations, they are sometimes referred to as data-intensive systems.[14] The breadth of technologies in the fintech sector are cited as prime examples.[15] However, state-sponsored DIS are just as prevalent at this point – if not more. National identity systems, SIM card registers, and health information exchanges represent the older and more familiar, while big data centres and smart city initiatives are the new arrivals. Unlike their peers,

---

[8] ibid.
[9] GD Maayan, 'The IoT Rundown For 2020: Stats, Risks, and Solutions' (*Security Today*, 13 January 2020).
[10] J Desjardins, 'What Happens in an Internet Minute in 2019' (*Visual Capitalist*, 13 March 2019).
[11] J Desjardins, 'How Much Data Is Generated Each Day?' (*World Economic Forum*, 17 April 2019).
[12] A Murphy et al, 'Global 2000: The World's Largest Public Companies' *Forbes* (13 May 2020).
[13] A García Martínez, 'No, Data is Not the New Oil' *Wired* (26 February 2019).
[14] Privacy International, 'The Keys to Data Protection' (August 2018) available at https://privacyinternational.org/sites/default/files/2018-09/Data%20Protection%20COMPLETE.pdf.
[15] Privacy International, 'Fintech: Privacy and Identity in the New Data-Intensive Financial Sector' (November 2017) available at https://privacyinternational.org/sites/default/files/2017-12/Fintech%20report.pdf.

the latter two are associated mainly with the private sector and public-private collaborations, respectively. Through the years, these systems have increased in numbers owing to rapid advancements in data processing and internet connectivity.

Consider national ID programmes, which are in essence centralised mechanisms that allow individuals to identify themselves to their communities and governments. In 2018, around 174 countries were already using some form of a national ID card.[16] One of the more well-known programmes involved Estonia's *isikukood*, or Personal Identification Code.[17] Originally restricted to Estonian nationals, it was eventually extended to resident non-citizens.[18] Today, Estonia's eID card is regarded as one of the most successful deployments of smart, card-based national ID card systems in the world in terms of dissemination and active use.[19] The evolution of Estonia's ID system is no isolated case. In 2019, it was announced that France, which already has an ID system, would be the first European country to use facial recognition technology in identity verification via the use of a mobile app.[20]

Another type of DIS that operates around individual identity but which is firmly linked to mobile phone use is a SIM card registration programme. It is among those assimilated by the greatest number of nations and works by making it mandatory for a person to sign up and provide personal details when purchasing or activating a pre-paid SIM card. As of January 2020, 155 countries already had mandatory SIM card registration laws in place.[21] Some are doubling down by incorporating biometric information into the registration process.

There are also DIS that are inherently complex in terms of structure. They offer functions more elaborate than something as one-dimensional as identity verification. Health information exchanges (HIEs) are one such type. Their objective is to leverage improved information flow in support of better health service delivery and health system management. Not only do they enhance clinical care, they also improve government response to public health crises. Most countries have already committed to adopting HIEs, differing only in the level of adoption, scope, and allocated resources.[22] Developed countries were early adopters. Finland, for instance, has regional health information systems that have been in use for a dozen years already.[23]

---

[16] The World Bank, '2018 Global ID4D Dataset' (April 2018) available at https://datacatalog.worldbank.org/dataset/identification-development-global-dataset.

[17] T Kotka, CI Vargas Alvarez del Castillo and K Korjus, 'Estonian e-Residency: Redefining the Nation-State in the Digital Era' (2015) 9 *Cyber Studies Programme* 3.

[18] ibid.

[19] ibid.

[20] H Samuel, 'France to Become First EU Country to Use Nationwide Facial Recognition ID App' *The Telegraph* (3 October 2019).

[21] Privacy International, 'SIM Card Registration' available at https://privacyinternational.org/learn/sim-card-registration.

[22] L Wu, 'Recommendations for a Global Framework to Support Health Information Exchange in Low- and Middle-Income Countries' (Regenstrief Institute, 14 November 2016).

[23] H Hyppönen et al, 'Health Information Exchange in Finland: Usage of Different Access Types and Predictors of Paper Use' (2019) 122 *International Journal of Medical Informatics* 1.

Most private sector examples are self-evident since they revolve around the business model of the companies behind them. In the fintech sector, for instance, DIS are primarily designed to facilitate credit scoring.[24] For those who depict their products and services as 'free', DIS are all about converting user data into the profiles or data sets so coveted by businesses, especially those in advertising. This practice of harvesting complex data about potential customers in order to offer them tailored goods has also been referred to as 'Surveillance Capitalism'.[25] Occasionally, a new DIS puts the concept into action in its own unique way. A fairly recent example is the controversial facial recognition software of the company Clearview AI. While facial recognition technology itself is no longer novel, the powerful image database that acts as base for the company's programme sets the latter apart from other similar tools. It boasts of over three billion photos that have been scraped from all over the web.[26]

Occasionally, collaborative efforts between governments and private companies also result in DIS. Smart city initiatives are a case in point. A smart city has been described as 'an urban setting that applies technology to enhance the benefits and diminish the shortcomings of urbanisation'.[27] Putting this into operation can cover a range of activities, from street-level gunshot detectors to so-called intelligent power grids, and smart traffic lights schemes.[28] While innovative solutions are introduced mainly by tech companies, government involvement is integral to their success because data is collected primarily via public spaces, thereby requiring authorisation and effective regulations. In 2017, more than 250 smart city projects already existed across 178 countries.[29] Europe was leading the way with 12 of the top 25, as ranked by the IESE Cities in Motion Index.[30]

II. Shifting to the East

While the digital transformation is exhibiting no signs of let-up, its focus of activity has shifted from Silicon Valley to the eastern end of the globe. In 2014, Asia was already home to more technology firms than the US.[31] Those based in the

---

[24] Privacy International, 'Fintech: Privacy and Identity'.
[25] S Zuboff, 'Big Other: Surveillance Capitalism and the Prospects of an Information Civilization' (2015) 30 *Journal of Information Technology* 25.
[26] K Hill, 'The Secretive Company That Might End Privacy as We Know It' *The New York Times* (18 January 2020).
[27] WY Yip, 'Singapore Is World's Smartest City: IMD Smart City Index' *The Straits Times* (3 October 2019).
[28] J Qi, 'Urban Intelligence: Smart Cities and the Future of Inclusive Growth' *Harvard International Review* (20 September 2019).
[29] Guidehouse Insights, 'More than 250 Smart City Projects Exist in 178 Cities Worldwide' (*Guidehouse Insights*, 16 March 2017).
[30] P Berrone et al, 'New York, London and Paris Firmly Established as the Smartest Cities' (*IESE Insight*, 2018).
[31] L Chen '2014 Fab 50: Asia's Tech Takes Over the World' *Forbes* (27 August 2014).

region are not just more willing to exploit the latest technological advances, but are actually leading in nearly every aspect of digitalisation.[32] Available statistics suggest this is no mere coincidence. Internet connectivity was already at 55.1 per cent as of May 2020, enough to claim 50.9 per cent of the global internet population.[33] Six of the top 10 countries in the world in terms of hours spent online hail from the continent.[34] The Asia-Pacific region now also boasts of 4.43 billion mobile phone connections and 2.14 billion active social media users.[35] With Facebook, in particular, Asia accounts for half of its total users.[36] Meanwhile, ecommerce revenue is expected to reach US$1.623,264 million in 2021, with a 7 per cent annual growth rate.[37] Ecommerce adoption rates are highest in Indonesia (88 per cent) and Thailand (82 per cent).[38] They are joined by four other Asian countries in the world's top 10.[39] East and Southeast Asia also make for an interesting footnote. The two already account for one-third of the total internet population.[40] In 2019 alone, they were responsible for 50 million new users.[41] Taken together, these figures offer a vast terrain ideal for DIS implementation.

National ID systems are now commonplace, with none perhaps more famous than India's *Aadhaar*. Administered by the Unique Identification Authority of India (UIDAI), the programme is regarded as the largest in the world, with around 1.3 billion registered individuals since its launch in 2010.[42] To facilitate identity verification, ID holders can use their mobile device, along with a Personal Identification Number (PIN), or a biometric via a biometric reader or kiosk. Today, people use the ID for a whole range of purposes, including healthcare transactions and marriage registration. When the enrolment began, there was no specific law governing the programme outside of the Notification[43] that paved the way for the creation of the UIDAI as an attachment to the country's Planning Commission. That issuance only provided for the initial staff composition of the agency and its general functions. It was only in 2016 that the government proposed and passed the *Aadhaar* Act (Target Delivery of Financial and Other Subsidies, Benefits, and Services)[44] to serve as the system's enabling law. In 2019, amendments[45]

---

[32] T Saadi Sedik, 'Asia's Digital Revolution' (2018) 55 *Finance & Development* 31.
[33] Internet World Stats, 'Internet Usage in Asia' (*Internet World Stats*, 2020).
[34] Kemp, 'Digital 2020: Global'.
[35] ibid.
[36] Internet World Stats, 'Internet Usage in Asia'.
[37] Statista, 'eCommerce: Asia' available at www.statista.com/outlook/243/101/ecommerce/asia.
[38] Kemp, 'Digital 2020: Global'.
[39] ibid.
[40] ibid.
[41] ibid.
[42] P Blumenthal and G Sathe, 'India's Biometric Database Is Creating a Perfect Surveillance State – And U.S. Tech Companies Are on Board' *Huffington Post* (25 August 2018).
[43] Planning Commission, Notification No A.03011/02/2009-Adm dt (28 January 2009).
[44] The Aadhaar Act (Targeted Delivery of Financial and Other Subsidies, Benefits and Services) *The Gazette of India*, 26 March 2016/Chaitra 6, 1938 (Saka).
[45] See The Aadhaar and Other Laws (Amendment) Act, *The Gazette of India*, 24 July 2019/Shravana 2, 1941 (Saka).

to the statute and a few others were introduced to address privacy and security concerns. Another sizeable ID system is Indonesia's *Electronic Kartu Tanda Penduduk* which was launched in 2011. Under the programme, registered residents are given an electronic ID card with a unique number and encrypted fingerprint, photo, and demographic data. Enrolment takes place at registration centres, where an individual's fingerprints, iris, and face are captured as images through biometric equipment and personal details are placed on record.[46] It is currently being used to obtain other government IDs such as passports, driving licences, and state health insurance cards.[47] After *Aadhaar* the next most widely known DIS in Asia is China's Social Credit System. It is essentially a massive ranking system that requires behavioural surveillance of the entire population in order to create a ranking mechanism based on each individual's 'social credit'.[48] The programme is made up of three interconnected components – a master database, a blacklisting system, and a punishment and rewards mechanism – and is meant to 'engineer better individual and business behaviour by awarding the trustworthy and punishing the disobedient'.[49] When it was announced in 2014, the government made sure to emphasise that the system is 'an important component part of the Socialist market economy system and the social governance system'.[50] Similar to a private credit score, a person's 'social score' could also move up or down, except that the catalyst is their behaviour. This 'carrot and stick' approach already has human rights advocates on alert, but what really transforms the programme into a sinister tool is its opaque methodology. Thus far, the types of infractions associated with the system indicate that it casts a very wide net: poor driving, violating no-smoking policies, loitering, late payment of utility bills, and spreading 'fake news'.[51] This list is rivalled in variety by the kinds of penalties that have so far been meted out (eg, travel restrictions, denial of entry into the top schools, public shaming, etc).[52] Other DIS that have been embraced in Asia include HIEs. Among the countries that have one in place are Singapore, India, China, and Malaysia. Despite the systems' popularity, though, implementation has been inconsistent at best and riddled with challenges.

---

[46] E Messmer, 'Indonesia Advances World's Most Ambitious Biometric-Based National Identity Card Project' *Networked World* (20 September 2012).
[47] The Institute for Policy Research and Advocacy, 'State of Privacy Indonesia' (*Privacy International*, 26 January 2019) available at https://privacyinternational.org/state-privacy/1003/state-privacy-indonesia#identification.
[48] A Ma, 'China Has Started Ranking Citizens with a Creepy 'Social Credit' System – Here's What You Can Do Wrong, and the Embarrassing, Demeaning Ways They Can Punish You' *Business Insider* (30 October 2018).
[49] C Zhou and B Xiao, 'China's Social Credit System Is Pegged to Be Fully Operational by 2020 – But What Will It Look Like?' *ABC News* (2 January 2020).
[50] State Council, 'Planning Outline for the Construction of a Social Credit System (2014–2020)' (14 June 2014) GF No (2014)21.
[51] Ma, 'China Has Started Ranking Citizens'. See also 'China's "Social Credit" Scheme Involves Cajolery and Sanctions' (*The Economist*, 28 March 2019).
[52] ibid.

In Malaysia, for instance, nine years after its HIE (MyHiX) was launched, it had only been implemented successfully in eight healthcare institutions.[53] Meanwhile, as recently as 2017, only three per cent of private healthcare providers had been integrated into Singapore's then six-year-old National Electronic Health Record (NEHR).[54] In stark contrast, the adoption of SIM card registration has more or less been unanimous, with only the Philippines as the last major holdout.[55] The difference lies in the nature of implementation. In some countries like China and Pakistan, they require biometric data collection during registration.[56] Others are already looking at innovations, with countries such as Laos developing apps to speed up the registration process. In 2019, only 72 per cent of the total number of active SIM cards in the country were registered.[57] Smart city initiatives are also growing in number, more so these recent years. China has become a global leader with a record number of 800 pilot programmes underway or in planning, accounting for more than half of the world's total.[58] In 2015, the Indian Government also committed to invest in 100 smart cities over the next five years to address the country's rapidly growing population juxtaposed against its urban centres which are plagued with poor infrastructure and inadequate services.[59] In terms of milestones, South Korea stakes its claim as the first to adopt the 'ubiquitous city' (u-city) concept when it began building New Songdo City in 2005.[60] In a u-city, all major information systems share data, with computers built into people's houses, the streets and office buildings. Meanwhile, according to the IMD Smart City Index, Singapore is the world's smartest city, besting 102 others, including Taipei which is the only other Asian city to make it into the top 10.[61] Rounding off the DIS list are big data centres which, thus far, are attributed mostly to the private sector. They are essentially centralised locations that house servers and networking equipment used to retain and process large swathes of data. There are indications though that states are finally warming up to the idea. In 2019, the Indonesian Government established via a Presidential issuance[62] *Satu Data Indonesia*, an integrated data-management system that allows for the collection of 'accurate, up-to-date,

---

[53] NI Ismail and NH Abdullah, 'Malaysia Health Information Exchange: A Systematic Review' (2017) 13 *Business and Economic Horizons* 706.

[54] C Luo Er, 'National Electronic Patient Database Soon to Be Mandatory for Healthcare Providers' *Channel News Asia* (8 November 2017).

[55] GSMA Association, 'Access to Mobile Services and Proof of Identity 2020: The Undisputed Linkages' (March 2020) 7.

[56] GSMA Association, 'Access to Mobile Services and Proof of Identity 2020'.

[57] E Phouthonesy, 'Telecom Regulator Proposes Online Sim Card Registration' *Vientiane Times* (16 May 2019).

[58] K Atha et al, 'China's Smart Cities Development' (Research Report Prepared on Behalf of the US–China Economic and Security Review Commission, January 2020).

[59] V Khare, 'India Election 2019: Have 100 "Smart Cities" Been Built?' (*BBC News*, 25 March 2019).

[60] P Licalzi O'Connell, 'Korea's High-Tech Utopia, Where Everything Is Observed' *The New York Times* (5 October 2005).

[61] Yip, 'Singapore Is World's Smartest City'.

[62] Presidential Regulation Number 39 of 2019 (12 June 2019).

integrated, accountable, easily accessible, and shared' data for the specific purpose of improving government data governance.[63] It remains to be seen how much of an influence the move will be on neighbouring countries, or even the region.

III. Impact of Data-Intensive Systems

Proponents of data-intensive systems rely on a menu of justifications attesting to the benefits they supposedly account for. A constant on this list is that a DIS enables its owner to make evidence-based decisions consistently and more effectively. For governments, this means being in a position to develop new insights from which they can devise policies and programmes that are more responsive to people's needs. In smart city projects, for instance, data allow the government to match more accurately the availability and supply of public services with real-time needs and to surface emerging problems before they become unmanageable.[64] The same argument has been made in favour of government-initiated data centres whose ability to generate statistical geospatial data is proclaimed as key to policy-making and development programmes.[65] Another common pretext is better public access to government services and facilities. The national ID program of Estonia allows access to all government e-services.[66] It earned the country the distinction of being the first to offer 'i-voting' in a general election.[67] Proponents of SIM card registers offer the same argument. In Egypt, one study showed increased citizen engagement during the elections after a prototype mobile voting system anchored on the SIM card programme was introduced.[68] Smart cities, on the other hand, are able to use data to prioritise the most vulnerable populations. In São Paulo, a comprehensive geographic database of socioeconomic and physical indicators allowed the city to prioritise housing and upgrading investments in marginalised communities.[69] There is also the familiar claim that data-intensive systems are important (indispensable even) tools for crime prevention.[70] This is often the primary reason cited to boost support for SIM card registration schemes.[71] Nigeria's system was

---

[63] B Nugroho, 'President Jokowi Signs Presidential Regulation No. 39/2019 Concerning Indonesia One Data' *RRI Radio* (27 June 2019).
[64] The World Bank, 'Smart Cities' in *World Development Report 2016: Digital Dividends* (Washington DC, The World Bank, 2016) 240.
[65] Y Nugroho, 'We Urgently Need One Data, Open Govt' *Jakarta Post* (7 December 2017).
[66] Kotka, Vargas Alvarez del Castillo and Korjus, 'Estonian e-Residency'.
[67] ibid.
[68] GSMA Association, 'The Mandatory Registration of SIM Card Users: A White Paper' (2013).
[69] The World Bank, 'Smart Cities'.
[70] See D Lyon, 'National ID Cards: Crime-Control, Citizenship and Social Sorting' (2007) 1 *Policing* 111. See also Privacy International, '101: SIM Card Registration' (9 January 2019) available at https://privacyinternational.org/explainer/2654/101-sim-card-registration.
[71] See N Hasan et al, 'Mobile Phone SIM Card: A Security Concern in the Perspective of Bangladesh' (16th International Conference on Computer and Information Technology, Khulna, March 2014). See

established on the premise that unregulated mobile phone use facilitated felonies like robbery, kidnapping, and internet banking fraud.[72] In Ecuador, the SIM register was enforced to address the proliferation of handset theft.[73] The same premise has also been invoked in the promotion of smart cities. News of police departments implementing city-wide 'predictive-policing' systems[74] in order to prevent crimes even before they occur are highlighted for optimal effect. Other potential benefits for states are highlighted by the experience of countries like Estonia whose ID system also secured cost-free positive media attention which, in turn, was seen as providing a significant boost to foreign trade investment, tourism, export business, and even national security.[75] For the private sector, the principal function of most DIS is to work towards the maximisation of profits, with more efficient and cost-effective processing activities as common prerequisites. Nonetheless, it is important to point out that businesses stand to benefit from government DIS as well. Once again, Estonia's eID presents a good case study. Its digital signature feature makes it easier to execute legally binding contracts and encrypt sensitive documents. It can also be used to establish an Estonian company, access Estonian e-banking, and make digital payments to service providers.[76] Meanwhile, telecommunications firms are often advised that SIM registration programmes will improve their service delivery capacity. In Nigeria and Kenya, targeted marketing activities informed by SIM user data reportedly led to an increase in the take-up of offers among customers.[77]

Despite all the plaudits and praise heaped on DIS, the list of attendant risks they are associated with is daunting. The danger they pose is particularly high when social data (or big social data) is involved.[78] 'Social data' pertain to large amounts of information relating to people, often describing their behaviour and technology-mediated social interactions online.[79] Indeed, the potential abuse and misuse of DIS is fast becoming a major concern. In 2019, 64 per cent of internet users claimed to be worried about how companies use their data.[80] There is plenty

---

also K Kitiyadisai, 'Privacy Rights and Protection: Foreign Values in Modern Thai Context' (2005) 7 *Ethics and Information Technology* 17.

[72] M2SYS Technology, 'Fingerprint Biometric Based SIM Card Registration System Deployed in Nigeria' available at www.m2sys.com/blog/wp-content/uploads/2015/07/Case-Study-SIM-Card-Registration-System-Deployed-in-Nigeria-BioPlugin.pdf.

[73] GSMA Association, 'Mandatory Registration of Prepaid SIM Cards: Addressing Challenges Through Best Practice' (2016).

[74] M Meuse, 'Vancouver Police Now Using Machine Learning to Prevent Property Crime' (*CBC News*, 23 July 2017).

[75] Kotka, Vargas Alvarez del Castillo and Korjus, 'Estonian e-Residency'.

[76] ibid.

[77] GSMA Association, 'The Mandatory Registration of SIM Card Users'. See also KP Donovan and AK Martin, 'The Rise of African SIM Registration: Mobility, Identity, Surveillance and Resistance' Information Systems and Innovation Group Working Paper Series, no 186, London School of Economics and Political Science (7 November 2012).

[78] A Weigand, *Data for the People: How to Make Our Post-Privacy Economy Work for You* (New York, Basic Books, 2017) 2.

[79] E Olshannikova et al, 'Conceptualizing Big Social Data' (2017) 4 *Journal of Big Data*.

[80] Kemp, 'Digital 2020: Global'.

of evidence to validate this number, too. Take the case of ID systems which have a history of fostering new forms of discrimination and harassment.[81] In Kenya, there have been reports of ethnic, racial, and cultural minorities being confronted with obstacles and additional scrutiny when they apply for a biometric ID, leading some civil society groups to accuse the government of 'digitising discrimination'.[82] The Chinese Government, on the other hand, has been accused of using a smart city surveillance platform to monitor and control millions of people from Muslim ethnic groups.[83] Across the aisle, private sector entities have also been involved in related controversies. The companies behind ride-hailing apps Uber and Lyft have both been accused of using collected data to track journalists, ex-lovers of employees, and even regular users.[84] A contributing factor is the absence of data protection regulation that could rein in most types of misconduct. For instance, only 59 per cent of countries mandating SIM card registration have a privacy or data protection framework in place.[85] Neither does India, which has its controversial ID system, nor Indonesia, despite the latter's recent focus on big data centres.

Surveillance is another major concern. Powerful data-intensive technologies combine to create an intrusive digital environment where both governments and businesses are able to conduct surveillance activities like never before.[86] ID systems are a good example. National ID cards are especially notorious for being treated by governments as 'internal passports' that allow the tracking of people's movements.[87] Mandatory SIM card registration systems have the same potential. They pose a threat to a wide spectrum of individuals, including journalists, whistle-blowers, witnesses, marginalised groups, and even victims of discrimination and oppression. In Zimbabwe, the SIM card registration law rendered obsolete anonymity of communications by enabling location-tracking and simplifying communications surveillance and interception.[88] A security lapse in China also offered a glimpse on the extent of the country's smart city surveillance system. Researchers discovered that the exposed data were more than

---

[81] See C Leigh Anderson et al, 'Review of National Identity Programs' (International Telecommunication Union, 2016) 34; See also D Lyon, 'Identity Cards: Social Sorting by Database' (Oxford Internet Institute, November 2004) Internet Issue Brief No 3.

[82] AL Dahir, 'Kenya's New Digital IDs May Exclude Millions of Minorities' *The New York Times* (28 January 2020).

[83] C Buckley and P Mozur, 'How China Uses High-Tech Surveillance to Subdue Minorities' *The New York Times* (22 May 2019).

[84] See A Hern, 'Uber Investigates Top Executive After Journalist's Privacy Was Breached' *The Guardian* (19 November 2014); J Constine, 'Former Employees Say Lyft Staffers Spied on Passengers' *TechCrunch* (26 January 2018).

[85] GSMA Association, 'Access to Mobile Services and Proof of Identity 2020', 17.

[86] UN Human Rights Council, 'The Right to Privacy in the Digital Age: Report of the United Nations High Commissioner for Human Rights' (3 August 2018) UN Doc A/HRC/39/29.

[87] American Civil Liberties Union, '5 Problems with National ID Cards' available at www.aclu.org/other/5-problems-national-id-cards.

[88] Privacy International, 'The State of Privacy 2014' (24 February 2014) available at https://privacyinternational.org/blog/1509/state-privacy-2014.

enough to build 'a picture of a person's day-to-day life'.[89] Also causing problems is the consequent expansion of the intended uses of a particular DIS.[90] ID systems are classic examples, given the way they draw in government agencies that end up seeking linkages, followed by private sector entities. Designed primarily to facilitate identity verification, national IDs later become mandatory requirements even for services or transactions that are not contingent on people's identities. This illustrates how rudimental it is to turn an ID programme into an effective surveillance mechanism. When the Indian Government sought to expand the use cases for the *Aadhaar*, a legal challenge was brought before the Supreme Court which thereafter ruled that state directives mandating the linking of *Aaadhar* numbers to bank account numbers and mobile numbers were not valid for failing the proportionality test and for having no legal basis, respectively.[91] The Court held that deactivating bank accounts not linked to the *Aadhaar* numbers of their owners amounts to the unlawful deprivation of private property, while mandating the linking of mobile numbers with *Aadhaar* numbers is not authorised by any existing law. Meanwhile, securing data-intensive systems projects a world of problems all of its own considering the enormity of the challenge it sets forth. The size of its data inventory makes a DIS an ideal target for bad actors, while its complex nature allows for a lot of possible mishaps. HIEs in particular are far more at risk because of the sensitive nature of the data they handle. The actions of one rogue employee can lead to a data breach involving thousands of patient records accessible through the network.[92]

A number of security incidents have also involved voters' databases. The personal information of over two million Indonesian voters was leaked online in the midst of the Covid-19 pandemic.[93] Earlier in 2020, a software flaw supposedly exposed the entire voters' registry of Israel.[94] On occasion, the problem is one of implementation. Their very nature makes DIS a challenge to implement. SIM card registration, for instance, can be very demanding with its information infrastructure requirements. In Nigeria, the regulator and telecom operators reportedly spent around US$128 million within a six-year period but still encountered plenty

---

[89] Z Whittaker, 'Security Lapse Exposed a Chinese Smart City Surveillance System' *TechCrunch* (4 May 2019).

[90] See S Straub, 'The Limits of Control – (Governmental) Identity Management from a Privacy Perspective' in J Camenisch, S Fischer-Hübner and K Rannenberg (eds), *Privacy and Identity Management for Life* (Berlin, Springer, 2011).

[91] *KS Puttaswamy v Union of India*, Writ Petition (Civil) No 494 of 2012 (Sup Ct India, 24 August 2017).

[92] See L Zhang, M-S Pang and S Wattal, 'Does Sharing Make My Data More Insecure? An Empirical Study on Health Information Exchange and Data Breaches' (Workshop on the Economics of Information Security, Boston, 3–4 June 2019).

[93] The Straits Times, 'Indonesia Investigates Data Breach on Over Two Million Voters' *The Straits Times* (23 May 2020).

[94] D Victor, S Frenkel and I Kershner, 'Personal Data of All 6.5 Million Israeli Voters Is Exposed' *The New York Times* (10 February 2020).

of problems during implementation.[95] One should expect nothing less from smart cities projects which are bigger and more complex. To be sure, reality has not always mirrored the lofty projections for these big-ticket ventures. In South Korea, more than a decade from its inception, Songdo is still nowhere near its advertised form, with a population less than a quarter of the target and with few people and businesses interested in making the city their home.[96] On occasion, this has led to DIS failing to deliver on their promises. Take for example ID systems which are often promoted by alluding to their ability to prevent terrorism. A study by Privacy International has already shown that there is no sound evidence to support such a claim.[97] Most terrorist attacks are committed by individuals who actually have legitimate ID cards. Meantime, with SIM card registration, the notion that it is a boon for law enforcement has also been debunked across jurisdictions.

In Pakistan, one account narrates how a DIS led law enforcement to apprehend innocent civilians.[98] Worse, SIM card registries can even cause surges in certain types of crimes and encourage black markets to flourish.[99] Accounts like these have dissuaded some countries from adopting a similar system and convinced others to abandon their existing ones. Mexico repealed its SIM registration law just three years after implementation.[100] There have also been scenarios where a DIS created problems worse than the one it was meant to address. For example, vulnerable persons and marginalised groups could end up getting disincentivised or discriminated against if SIM card registration is poorly executed. An ID system, on the other hand, has led to people starving to death[101] or dying of illness[102] after they were refused assistance for failing to produce an ID. What makes it all the more tragic is that when DIS falls short of expectations, calls for their further expansion tend to surface instead of viable solutions. When such demands are accommodated, they could translate to the amplification of the lingering issues. In France, a 2016 proposal sought to develop a 'mega-database' consisting of personal information already featured in two existing databases (ie, passport and national ID). The single database setup was denounced for being susceptible to abuse and highly vulnerable to hacks and data breaches.[103] The country's Justice Minister,

---

[95] E Okonji, 'Nigeria: MTN Apologises to Customers Over SIM Validation' (*allAfrica*, 7 September 2015) available at http://allafrica.com/stories/201509072401.html.
[96] C White, 'South Korea's "Smart City" Songdo: Not Quite Smart Enough?' *South China Morning Post* (25 March 2018).
[97] M Tempest, 'ID Cards "Will Not Stop Terrorism"' *The Guardian* (27 April 2004).
[98] S Varandani, 'Peshawar School Attack: 4 Suspects Arrested in Bahawalpur, Pakistani Taliban Used Woman's SIM Card' *International Business Times* (19 December 2014). See also A Shahzad, 'Pakistan Tightens Cellphone Control After Taliban Massacre' *The Hindu* (26 February 2015).
[99] GSMA Association, 'Mandatory Registration of Prepaid SIM Cards'.
[100] ibid.
[101] R Ratcliffe, 'How a Glitch in India's Biometric Welfare System Can Be Lethal' *The Guardian* (16 October 2019).
[102] Asian News International, 'No Aadhaar Card: Hospital Allegedly Denies Treatment; Woman Dies in Sonipat' *Business Standard* (30 December 2017).
[103] P Kirby, 'French Privacy Row Over Mass ID Database' (*BBC News*, 8 November 2016).

who was the system's initial proponent, even became its foremost critic after noting the significant departure of the project from the original concept which envisioned a more secure multi-dimensional and multi-local database.[104]

IV. The Philippines: A Case Study

The Philippines, a developing country of more than 109 million people, makes for an interesting test case when evaluating the potential impact of data-intensive systems. Having survived a long colonial past and authoritarian rule, it is regarded as a functioning democracy despite chronic political unrest and economic challenges. Poverty is prevalent, with the political landscape dominated by political dynasties and landed elites. This has in part helped nurture two protracted internal armed conflicts involving communist rebels and Muslim separatists. In terms of ICT development, the country formally linked to the internet in 1994. The medium remains largely unregulated today due to limited state capacity, making it susceptible to regulatory capture by the dominant market players who also own most of the internet infrastructure.[105] Despite having one of the slowest (yet most expensive) connections in the world,[106] the popularity of the internet seems unaffected. Sixty-seven per cent of the population are considered active internet users[107] who spend an average of nine hours and 45 minutes online everyday – the highest in the world.[108] Remarkable numbers, considering that in 2017 the ITU estimated that only around 39 per cent of Filipino households owned a computer, well below the global average.[109] With 73 million active social media users, Filipinos also top the list for most time spent on these platforms, averaging three hours and 53 minutes a day.[110] The ecommerce adoption rate is 76 per cent which is already among the highest in the world.[111]

On paper, the country appears primed for the type and rate of technological assimilation it is going through. It is a signatory to the Universal Declaration of Human Rights and has ratified eight core international human rights instruments. Its Constitution includes a Bill of Rights, emphasises social justice and human rights, and mandates the creation of an independent Commission on Human

---

[104] R Albano, 'France's "Mega-Database" Halted for Data Breach Fears' *The Gospel Herald* (19 November 2016).

[105] MG Mirandilla-Santos, 'Philippine Broadband: A Policy Brief', USAID Policy Brief No 4. The Arangkada Project (February 2016) available at www.investphilippines.info/arangkada/wp-content/uploads/2016/02/BROADBAND-POLICY-BRIEF-as-printed.pdf.

[106] YV Gonzales, 'PH Internet 2nd Lowest in Asia, One of the Most Expensive' (*Inquirer.net*, 19 May 2015).

[107] S Kemp, 'Digital 2020: The Philippines' (*Datareportal*, 18 February 2020).

[108] Kemp, 'Digital 2020: Global'.

[109] Chua, 'ITU's IDI Ranks Philippines at 15th Place'.

[110] Kemp, 'Digital 2020: Global'.

[111] ibid.

Rights which is complemented by human rights offices in the critical sectors of law enforcement and the armed forces. There are also statutes that deal primarily with the internet and technology, such as the E-Commerce Act 2000, the Anti-Child Pornography Act 2009, the Anti-Photo and Video Voyeurism Act 2012, the Data Privacy Act 2012, the Cybercrime Prevention Act 2012 and the Telecommuting Act (2019). ICT regulations are now being issued on account of the Department of Information and Communications Technology (DICT) and its two attached agencies – the National Telecommunications Commission and the National Privacy Commission (NPC). In the field of data protection, the country has already been accredited as Observer to the Consultative Committee of Convention 108+[112] and, in 2020, its application to participate in the Asia-Pacific Economic Forum Cross-Border Privacy Rules System was approved.[113] Unfortunately, these legal and institutional safeguards have all been exposed as exceptionally weak by the rise to power of populist President, Rodrigo Duterte, who openly conveys his aversion towards human rights and their advocates.[114] The impact of his posturing is pronounced, judging by the dismal state of the local human rights landscape.[115] According to the UN High Commissioner for Human Rights, Duterte's fixation on national security threats (both real and perceived) have resulted in grave rights violations.[116] Freedom House gives the country a score of 59/100 in its 2020 report on political rights and civil liberties, noting the inconsistent application of the rule of law which tends to favour those who wield significant political and economic capital.[117] The non-profit organisation has also highlighted the prevailing culture of impunity that has resulted in crimes targeting activists and journalists and the thousands of extrajudicial killings associated with a controversial drug war.[118] These conditions that currently frustrate people's civil liberties have also become the catalysts that have allowed data-intensive systems to gain ground and thrive.

As is the case in many countries, the Philippines has long had centralised, state-owned databases. Most have to do with ID systems maintained by different government agencies pursuing their respective mandates. The Commission on Elections (Comelec), for instance, has several relating to the conduct of national and local elections. The Department of Foreign Affairs (DFA) maintains one to facilitate passport issuance. The same is true for those institutions in charge of drivers' licences, universal health insurance, taxation, and a number of other

---

[112] G Greenleaf, 'How Far Can Convention 108+ "Globalise"?: Prospects for Asian Accessions' (*Social Science Research Network*, 3 February 2020).

[113] Cross-Border Privacy Rules System Joint Oversight Panel, 'Findings Report' (9 March 2020).

[114] M Ramos, 'Duterte Threatens to Kill Rights Activists If Drug Problem Worsens' (*Inquirer.net*, 29 November 2016).

[115] UN Human Rights Council, 'Situation of Human Rights in the Philippines: Report of the United Nations High Commissioner for Human Rights' (29 June 2020) UN Doc A/HRC/44/22.

[116] ibid.

[117] Freedom House, 'Freedom in the World 2020' (Freedom House, 2020) available at https://freedomhouse.org/country/philippines/freedom-world/2020.

[118] ibid.

government services and benefits. It is the digitalisation of these systems that is a more recent development. Take the case of Comelec which only began building a central computer database of registered voters in 2003 in the run-up to the country's first automated elections in 2010. The DFA's passport modernisation programme, on the other hand, was launched sometime in 2006[119] and culminated in the issuance of ePassports beginning in 2009. It was after these changes that interest in DIS quickly intensified, coinciding with the enactment of most ICT-related laws. The fascination persists today with a number of DIS already at different stages of implementation.

At the top of the list is the Philippine Health Information Exchange (PHIE)[120] which seeks to enable patient information sharing between healthcare providers. The programme believes that comprehensive and secure access to health information improves decision-making in patient care.[121] It recognises the need for a central system for identifying patients, particularly those with highly communicable diseases and special health conditions, using a secure platform that allows electronic access and exchange of health data.[122] The system helps avoid repetitive data collection, improves data quality, monitors the efficiency of data flow, and reduces operational costs.[123] Apprehension expressed towards the system include data privacy concerns.[124] Since it will require one lead implementer (ie, Philippine Health Insurance Corporation or PHIC) to process its members' health information outside its primary mandate, it runs the risk of violating the data protection law. It is possible that the 2019 universal health care statute[125] addresses this issue but this view is untested and may be disputed before a court. The new law does not explicitly mention the use of member information and even underlines the importance of patient privacy and confidentiality. Questions have also been raised about the government's capacity to host, secure, and sustain the system. Security is another major sticking point, in view of the state's lacklustre history with securing its major databases.[126]

---

[119] GMANews.TV, 'DFA Eyes Taking Over Passport Modernization Program' (*GMA News Online*, 8 June 2006).

[120] S&T Media Service, 'MOA Signing for DOST's Phil. Health Info Exchange' *Department of Science and Technology* (19 March 2015) available at www.dost.gov.ph/knowledge-resources/news/44-2015-news/668-moa-signing-for-dost-s-phil-health-info-exchange.

[121] See Philippine Health Insurance Corporation, 'National eHealth Program Briefer' (2015).

[122] See DOH-DOST-PhilHealth Joint Adm O No 2016-001 (2016).

[123] See Department of Health and Department of Science and Technology, 'Philippines eHealth Strategic Framework and Plan 2013–2017' (11 September 2013).

[124] The Manila Times, 'Government Launches eHealth System' *The Manila Times* (7 February 2014). See also B Cahiles-Magkilat, 'Private Hospitals Vow to Comply with Data Privacy Rules' *Manila Bulletin* (23 September 2017).

[125] Rep Act No 11223 (2019), s 36.

[126] See A Hern, 'Philippine Electoral Records Breached in "Largest Ever" Government Hack' *The Guardian* (11 April 2016). See also LB Salaverria, 'Stradcom Earned P2B Using LTO Data-COA' (*Inquirer.net*, 7 October 2011). See also M Bueza, 'Ex-DFA Contractor "Took Off" with Passport Data, Says Locsin' (*Rappler*, 12 January 2019).

The country now also has its national ID programme: the Philippine Identification System (PhilSys). Established by law in 2018, it is to be the central identification platform for all Filipinos and resident foreigners. It has three key components: (a) PhilSys Number (PSN); (b) PhilID; and (c) PhilSys Registry.[127] The PSN is assigned upon birth or registration,[128] while the PhilID is a non-transferable physical card featuring essential information about the registrant.[129] The PhilSys Registry is the database and contains all registered information, including the ID's record history.[130] Managing it is the Philippine Statistics Authority (PSA).[131] Proponents expect the system to address the needs of Filipinos without access to proper birth certificates.[132] It supposedly eliminates the government's multiple ID system[133] and reduces associated costs by as much as 80 per cent.[134] They predict it will be this social and economic platform that enables seamless service delivery, enhanced governance, corruption reduction, financial inclusion, and even the ease of doing business. Duterte himself extols the role of the programme in the drive against poverty, corruption, crime, including terrorism and violent extremism.[135] His message is echoed by allies who frequently highlight its financial inclusion potential[136] and its place in the national security apparatus.[137] The military believes PhilSys will promote peace and security while those in law enforcement see potential uses in their operations.[138]

PhilSys is also expected to benefit transactions in the private sector. The risks and transaction costs for fintech companies will be greatly reduced while the use of electronic payments could increase by more than 50 per cent.[139] Despite this optimism, an assortment of issues has haunted PhilSys ever since its enabling law was passed. First, there is the inexperience and lack of technical competence of the PSA as an ID system implementor. Its designation alone was already a surprise since ID development has never been a statistical function.[140] This prompted the agency to make it clear from the start that it would need third-party service providers to

---

[127] Rep Act No 11055 (2018), s 7.
[128] ibid, s 7(a).
[129] ibid, s 7(c).
[130] ibid, s 7(b).
[131] ibid, s 15.
[132] J Villanueva, 'PSA to Roll Out 7-M Nat'l IDs in 2019' *Philippine News Agency* (14 November 2018).
[133] C Ordinario, 'Mobile App Payment May Soon Be the Norm in Paying PUV Fares' *Business Mirror* (9 October 2019).
[134] DL Lucas, 'It's Final: BSP to Print Nat'l IDs' (*Inquirer.net*, 8 October 2019).
[135] AL Colina IV, '"Nothing to Worry About Phil ID System" – Duterte' *MindaNews* (7 August 2018).
[136] D Rekhi, 'Philippines to Launch "Aadhaar"' *The New Indian Express* (29 June 2018).
[137] DJ Esguerra, 'National ID System Can Help Deter Criminality, Terrorism – Lacson' (*Inquirer.net*, 6 August 2018).
[138] R Acosta, 'Separating the Good from the Bad Through a National ID System' *Business Mirror* (12 August 2018).
[139] Ordinario, 'Mobile App Payment'.
[140] C Ordinario, 'Technology Aids Government Collection of "New Oil"' *Business Mirror* (10 October 2019).

execute this additional mandate.[141] The PSA took some time combing through its options[142] before finally coming to an agreement with the central monetary authority.[143] By then, its search for an able collaborator had already caused significant delay in the project rollout.[144] Budget woes may have also contributed to the problem.[145] Once the system is in place, it is likely that complications are only going to increase, with its ability to deliver on its promises – including its adherence to data protection and information security standards – coming into play. That it would not be used for unsanctioned state surveillance is foremost among people's concerns. Many sectors underscore its ability to monitor all ID-related transactions and how this could allow the government to establish a comprehensive profile of each registered individual.[146] That, in turn, could be used to facilitate harassment of political opponents.[147] The large number of former military officers now occupying executive positions in the government and the alarming trend of 'discreet but systematic passage of repressive laws' have only reinforced people's fears.[148] Compounding the situation are concerns about the security of the system. One weak point is the absence of a government-owned broadband network which means remote system access goes through commercial telecommunication facilities that are designed for public use. Coupled with the poor network security capacity of government agencies, parties are wary of the possible disaster scenarios.[149] Beyond privacy and security, the ability of PhilSys to actually live up to its potential is also suspect. For instance, the claim that it will consolidate all current government IDs[150] appear to be false, since the PhilID is unable to verify anything outside of a person's identity. It was never designed to be a proxy for something like a passport or a voter's ID. The same may be said of the other sweeping claims made by its proponents such as the assertion that it will significantly improve public access to government services. That statement glosses over other major causes of delay in government transactions like widespread corruption and bureaucratic red tape. When confronted with the system's limitations, advocates

---

[141] G Kabiling, 'P30 Billion Needed to Fully Implement PH ID System' *Tempo* (8 August 2018).
[142] Villanueva, 'PSA to Roll Out 7-M Nat'l IDs in 2019'.
[143] Lucas, 'It's Final: BSP to Print Nat'l IDs'.
[144] L Gatpolintan, 'Nat'l ID to Be Rolled Out in March: PSA' *Philippine News Agency* (5 October 2018). See also NA Mercado, 'National ID System Target: 105M Filipinos Covered by 2022' (*Inquirer.net*, 1 July 2019); FM Macapagat, 'Info Campaign Crucial to Phil ID Mass Registration on July 2020' *Philippine Information Agency* (21 September 2019); Villanueva, 'PSA to Roll Out 7-M Nat'l IDs in 2019'.
[145] See CA Aguinaldo, 'PSA Seeks Restoration of Original Budget for National ID Registration' *BusinessWorld* (2 October 2018). See also K Aguilar, 'Recto Fears Lack of Budget May Derail National ID System Rollout' (*Inquirer.net*, 19 November 2019).
[146] JM Aurelio, 'Duterte: Data Privacy Secure with National ID' (*Inquirer.net*, 7 August 2018).
[147] S Alegado and C Yap, 'Philippines Does an India, Gets Aadhaar-Like ID System' *Hindustan Times* (29 August 2018).
[148] Aurelio, 'Duterte: Data Privacy Secure'.
[149] AS Vitangcol, 'Risk of Exposing Our Private Data to the Public' *The Manila Times* (19 August 2016).
[150] GK Cabico, 'What You Need to Know About the Proposed National ID' *Philstar* (29 May 2018). See also Esguerra, 'National ID System Can Help Deter Criminality'.

simply call for more features to be integrated into the PhilSys,[151] which, as noted earlier, highlights another key DIS issue. This early, even before mass registration for the system has begun, one legislator has already declared his intention to lobby for amendments to the PhilSys law that will enable expanded data collection.[152] Notwithstanding all these warnings, proponents still managed to find surprising allies, not least of whom is the country's data protection authority. Describing it as 'privacy-designed', the Privacy Commissioner has consistently toed the government line when asked to comment on PhilSys,[153] going so far as to guarantee that appropriate measures are in place to protect the system.[154] As for the President, he has casually dismissed criticism of the system, noting that those harbouring fears are likely involved in something illegal.[155] He assured the public that all privacy and security concerns would be addressed and pointed to the close coordination between PSA, the DICT, and NPC as proof.[156]

There have also been many attempts to establish a SIM card registration system. In the current Congress alone, a combined total of 16 Bills are being considered, most of which share similar features. Proposals are often justified by the need to promote accountability in SIM use and to equip law enforcement with tools necessary for resolving mobile phone-related crimes. Under the regime being taken up, a public telecommunications entity (PTE) or vendor may refuse to sell and issue a SIM card to someone who is against registration, including foreign nationals.[157] Registrations forms are to be kept by the PTEs who are the ones required to maintain a SIM Card Register.[158] While the proposal makes all information on a SIM card record 'absolutely confidential', this protection may be set aside if the PTE receives either a subpoena, court order, or even a mere written request by a law enforcement agency on the ground that a particular number is being used in the commission of or as a means to commit a crime.[159] Motivations behind SIM registration proposals are usually high in the wake of high-profile incidents where mobile phone use is prominent in the public narrative; often, it is incidents involving bombing attacks where the explosion is believed that have been triggered by phone.[160] Over the years, critics have consistently based their opposition

---

[151] NA Mercado, 'Solon Wants National ID Mass Registration to Begin Before June 30' (*Inquirer.net*, 23 April 2020).
[152] ibid.
[153] AJ Pateña, 'Commission Backs Creation of Privacy-Designed Nat'l ID System' *Philippine News Agency* (28 May 2018).
[154] ibid.
[155] J Torres Jr, 'Bishops Back Philippines' National ID System' *Union of Catholic Asian News* (7 August 2018).
[156] ibid. See also L Alimondo, 'Benguet Eyed as National ID Pilot Testing Area' (*Sunstar Baguio*, 10 October 2019). See also Colina IV, '"Nothing to Worry About Phil ID System" – Duterte'.
[157] Comm On Information and Communications Technology, H Rpt 131, 18th Cong, 1st Sess (2019).
[158] ibid, ss 6, 10.
[159] ibid, s 9.
[160] LA So, 'Davao Blast: IED Detonated Via Cellphone' *Philstar* (4 September 2016).

on grounds that include the following: (a) it calls for real-time collection of data;[161] (b) it entails additional costs that will be passed on to users;[162] (c) it is an added administrative burden on the regulator;[163] (d) lack of a reliable government ID system;[164] (e) unproven effectiveness, and susceptibility to circumvention;[165] and (f) disenfranchisement of certain sectors.[166] Thus far, they have been enough to keep this proposition at bay.

Another DIS project enjoying exposure of late calls for the establishment of the National Big Data Center, whose purpose is to process big data that will allow policies and programmes to address more effectively the country's current and emerging development issues.[167] In recognition of the attendant privacy issues, part of the centre's function is to ensure the confidentiality of any personal information it collects.[168] The projected sources of data include mobile (phone) companies and 'internet companies' (eg, social media platforms, search engines, etc).[169] The proposed law lists a number of acts it will consider as violations and classifies them as crimes.[170] Ambiguity is a major drawback of the Bill, particularly as regards the type of data the centre will process. The proposal states that any personal data will be anonymised prior to processing, and yet data privacy and the country's data protection law is referred to numerous times, suggesting otherwise. Data ownership is also a point at issue. Data that 'comes to the possession and knowledge' of the centre are supposed to become the property of public dominion.[171] This notwithstanding, the Bill states that data partners may define the ownership of data when engaging with the centre.[172]

Other DIS examples, such as smart city projects, usually take the form of public-private partnerships between local government units and technology companies. In 2017, the country's financial hub, Makati City, collaborated with a telecommunications firm to develop a city card that functions both as a government ID and an Automated Teller Machine (ATM) card.[173] It gives residents access to city government services and benefits, such as cash allowances, stipends, and even salaries. The capital city, Manila, is also looking to establish its own resident ID system, along with innovations in its traffic, solid waste, and flood management programmes, except that the expected tie-up may be with the governments of Singapore and the US.[174] In recent years, there are signs that the national

---

[161] M Cruz, 'Solon: Great Risk in SIM Registration' (*Manilastandard.net*, 18 September 2016).
[162] ibid.
[163] ibid.
[164] LP Gomez, 'SIM Registration Opposed' *Manila Standard* (23 October 2013).
[165] ibid.
[166] ibid.
[167] H No 362, 18th Cong, 1st Sess (2019).
[168] ibid, s 13.
[169] ibid, s 11.
[170] ibid, ss 14–16.
[171] ibid, s 18.
[172] H No 362.
[173] EV Abadilla, 'Makati First to Launch Smart Card for Residents' *Manila Bulletin* (30 March 2017).
[174] K Doming, 'Manila Bags US, Singapore Support to Turn Capital Into 'Smart City' (*ABS-CBN News*, 8 August 2019).

government is keen on assuming a more prominent role. Cases like the closed-circuit television network that will be installed in the National Capital Region and Duterte's hometown, Davao City, offer a concrete demonstration. Known as the 'Safe Philippines Project', it is a joint undertaking between the Department of the Interior and Local Government and China International Telecommunications and Construction Corporation – a state-owned entity.[175] Its proponents claim that it shall induce a 15 per cent reduction in the crime rate while significantly improving police response time.[176] Critics, on the other hand, have expressed alarm over the participation of China, given the ongoing territorial dispute between the two nations over portions of the South China Sea. Meanwhile, there is scant evidence to date of local companies managing to establish their own data-intensive systems. This is not to say though that they do not exist. Amid this ongoing Covid-19 pandemic, the proliferation of contact tracing applications[177] developed by the private sector indicates a budding potential. Also of note is that notwithstanding existing limitations, some actors have not shied away from taking advantage of the capabilities of dominant platforms like Facebook. In 2019, when the social media giant removed at least 200 pages, groups, and accounts for engaging in coordinated inauthentic behaviour, it was able to link them to a network organised by the President's electoral campaign social media manager.[178] It proved that DIS can work not only for the benefit of their owners, but even third parties familiar with the way they operate.

All told, the DIS landscape in the Philippines bears a striking resemblance to those found in other jurisdictions. For the most part, the measures being introduced are similar and so are the issues they have brought with them. This bodes well for efforts aimed at generating controls and solutions, which could concentrate on the most persistent problems with a genuine hope that comparable degrees of effectiveness will also be realised.

V. Conclusion

It is said that one major challenge that twenty-first century information societies face today is reconciling the benefits of new technologies with the protection of fundamental human rights.[179] While these technologies could potentially help states to fulfil their human rights obligations, they are equally capable of

---

[175] P Romero, 'DILG, Chinese Firm to Install P20 Billion CCTV Network' *Philstar* (13 December 2018).

[176] C Elemia, 'Senators Sound Alarm Over China-Funded DILG Surveillance Project' (*Rappler*, 14 December 2018).

[177] See G Gonzales, 'LIST: Coronavirus Contact Tracing Apps in the Philippines' (*Rappler*, 14 April 2020).

[178] UNHRC, 'Situation of Human Rights in the Philippines'.

[179] UN General Assembly, 'Report of the Special Rapporteur on the Right to Privacy' (19 October 2017) UN Doc A/72/43103.

undermining some of these very same rights. This dilemma persists in lockstep with the evolution and growth of data processing. In terms of volume alone, one estimate declares that the amount of information created two decades ago is now produced in less than an hour.[180]

Naturally, this means data-intensive systems will also continue to grow bigger, become more powerful, and more influential. Data will continue to remain a key economic asset, similar to labour and capital. A more level playing field is likely to manifest as the flow and exchange of ideas cease to follow a West-to-the-rest trajectory. Rapid technological developments and urbanisation guarantee this by allowing Asia and other developing nations to leapfrog over their peers. The populace will also continue to grapple between their basic rights and the promises offered by a digital world. Current sentiments suggest the privacy paradox is very much alive. While more people are now concerned about their privacy, they are also more likely to welcome new technologies, even those designed to share more of their intimate data.[181] All this bears down on states which are duty-bound to maintain order through appropriate, effective, and timely interventions. They must rise to the challenge of addressing the negative impact of DIS and treat it as the urgent concern it represents. This is crucial particularly for those who still find themselves trailing in the wake of technological advancements. They must make sure to cover a number of points when formulating an effective response.

First, it has become clear that the operation of data-intensive systems must always take place in accordance with a suitable legal framework. To the extent possible, those systems operated by governments must have a legal basis against which their functions shall be regularly measured and, in case of divergence, recalibrated. The purpose for each system must be limited and clearly delineated to afford safeguards against abuses and function creep. The enabling law ought to ensure there is transparency in the system's operation, allowing for public scrutiny especially where automated decision-making processes are involved. Together with their private sector peers, state-sanctioned DIS must also adhere to strong data protection legislation. In the current information age, these policies are even more essential given the volumes of personal data being collected and stored by intermediaries and the disturbing trend of states pressuring these private actors to give access to their data inventory.[182] Thankfully, the legacy principles of the Organisation for Economic Cooperation and Development's Guidelines on the Protection of Privacy and Transborder Flows of Personal Data, the 1981 Council of Europe's Data Protection Convention,[183] and the 1990 United Nations Guidelines

---

[180] Weigand, *Data for the People* 3.
[181] Kemp, 'Digital 2020: Global'.
[182] UNHRC, 'Report of the Special Rapporteur on the Promotion and Protection of the Right to Freedom of Opinion and Expression' (16 May 2011) UN Doc A/HRC/17/27.
[183] Council of Europe, 'Convention for the Protection of Individuals with Regard to the Automatic Processing of Individual Data' (28 January 1981) ETS 108.

for the regulation of computerised personal data files[184] live on through most data protection laws today and offer a solid policy framework. Data subject rights are another critical component for data protection policies. To the extent possible, they should allow individuals to choose whether they wish to participate in a DIS. Access to their data, the right to object, to redress and indemnity must be ensured. There should also be minimum security requirements, including mandatory breach reporting protocols. This is crucial especially for systems that handle sensitive and other confidential information. Given the uneven emphasis placed in recent years on public order and national security at the expense of human rights, governments should aim to match the risks posed by their data processing activities with the necessary and appropriate protections. The preservation of democracies requires checks and balances that ensure government initiatives are undertaken to protect a free society. Other policies worth considering include the adoption of data localisation or data sovereignty, and active support for the creation and use of privacy-enhancing technologies. Indonesia, Vietnam, and China have all started tightening data retention and data security requirements for the purpose of data protection. This aligns with the trend of government agencies and other data collectors and data processors preferring domestic data centres out of security concerns. Finally, effective oversight by an independent and competent data protection authority should be of utmost priority. Regulatory powers should be commensurate with the new challenges posed by DIS and advances in data processing. The experience of countries like the Philippines has shown that even with legal, constitutional, and institutional safeguards in place, enforcement can be futile if the regulator or implementing agency is ill-equipped to enforce its mandate, ambivalent in its position on issues, or worse, becomes an enabler of the practices it is charged with reining in.

Civil society will continue to play a pivotal role by supplying stakeholder insight and assistance and by keeping state actors in line. In weak democracies, where controls and institutions are either compromised or non-existent, its work is indispensable. At the rate technological developments occur today, harnessing data is bound to become easier and more potent. DIS in greater numbers should be anticipated, together with their concomitant legal and logistical challenges. It will be one balancing act after another, participated in and decided by what will hopefully be a representative set of stakeholders. For states, the duty to effect policies such as facilitating commerce and better information flows should always be offset by a concurrent obligation to uphold individual rights. Where there is conflict, paramount effort must be exerted to reconcile opposing interests. Only when compromise is impossible, after a thorough and careful assessment, should they make the difficult but necessary decision to pursue that end they believe society considers more valuable.

---

[184] See UN Commission on Human Rights, 'Human Rights and Scientific and Technological Developments' (20 February 1990) UN Doc E/CN.4/1990/72.

4
Freedom of Peaceful Assembly and Association in an Age of Online Networks and Mobile Sensing

JONATHAN ANDREW

I. Introduction

Relationships are a key element of our personal identities and integral to each individual's enjoyment of human dignity. The digital technologies that increasingly facilitate these relationships – whether in the context of our personal, political or professional lives – have already altered how we frame seemingly straightforward notions such as friendship or community. Social networking online reflects a wider sociocultural transformation whereby tight-knit, face-to-face communities are shifting towards 'networked individualism', a system of social interaction in which the individual is at the centre of personal relationships unencumbered by physical limitations.[1] Our networks of association online can expose us to information from more widely disparate sources and involve us in concerns far beyond our own immediate private or intimate sphere.[2]

Meanwhile, our lives are increasingly subject to the influence of technologies that can track, trace, and determine activities and interactions in ever greater detail. The localisation of the individual and proximity of others are becoming more valuable in delivering a range of services.[3] Increasingly sensitive sensing technologies,

---

[1] See AM Manago and L Vaughn, 'Social Media, Friendship, and Happiness in the Millennial Generation' in M Demir (ed), *Friendship and Happiness: Across the Life-Span and Cultures* (Dordrecht, Springer, 2015). See also S Joseph, 'Social Media, Human Rights and Political Change' (2012) 35 *Boston College International and Comparative Law Review* 145, 148; K Wilcox and AT Stephen, 'Are Close Friends the Enemy? Online Social Networks, Self-Esteem, and Self-Control' (2013) 40 *Journal of Consumer Research* 90.

[2] See E Gordon and A de Souza e Silva, *Net Locality: Why Location Matters in a Networked World* (Chichester, Wiley Blackwell, 2011).

[3] See G Danezis, S Lewis and R Anderson, 'How Much is Location Privacy Worth?' (Workshop of the Economics of Information Security, Harvard University, June 2005) 2; SE Henderson, 'Carpenter v. United States and the Fourth Amendment: The Best Way Forward' (2017) 26 *William & Mary Bill*

including GPS, Bluetooth and ECG monitoring, embedded into personal devices such as mobile phones, smartwatches and other wearables, allow applications to detect our location and proximity to others in real time.[4] In addition, the diffusion of Web 2.0 functionality in the first decade of the twenty-first century has prompted a huge expansion in the social component of activities online.[5] More recently, rapidly falling data storage costs associated with cloud computing have provided further opportunities for developing these social spaces.[6] Moreover, the availability of cellular data derived from the use of mobile devices has enabled the detailed mass monitoring of geographic positions and social interactions of individuals and groups on a scale previously considered unfeasible.[7] Some early research on this type of monitoring suggested that it would enable us to look past cultural and psychological biases to see ourselves in a new, more objective light.[8] However, risks associated with exploiting nuanced measurements of behaviour, associations and activities through increasingly complex data-mining techniques were also noted early on.[9] Details pertaining to interactions with others can furnish information about individuals' political beliefs, religious faith and sexual identity.

This chapter considers the implications of these changes for freedom of peaceful assembly and association. It begins with a brief survey of European and US jurisprudence pertaining to interferences in these rights by digital means. It then explores how association and assembly have evolved under the influence of digital messaging and various types of social media. It goes on to examine how these tools, together with location monitoring and augmented and pervasive sensing in our surroundings, may be exploited by law enforcement and other public agencies to engage in a level of surveillance that threatens fundamental rights.

---

of Rights Journal 495; K Martin and H Nissenbaum, 'What Is It About Location?' (2020) 35 *Berkeley Technology Law Journal* 101.

[4] See P Klasnja et al, 'Exploring Privacy Concerns About Personal Sensing' in H Tokuda et al (eds) *Pervasive Computing* (Berlin, Springer, 2009); T Althoff et al, 'Large-Scale Physical Activity Data Reveal Worldwide Activity Inequality' (2017) 547 *Nature* 336.

[5] See JA Obar and S Wildman, 'Social Media Definition and the Governance Challenge: An Introduction to the Special Issue' (2015) 39 *Telecommunications Policy* 745, 745.

[6] See K Chard et al, 'Social Cloud Computing: A Vision for Socially Motivated Resource Sharing' (2012) 5 *IEEE Transactions on Services Computing* 551; GA Dagnaw and SE Tsige, 'Challenges and Opportunities of Cloud Computing in Social Network; Survey' (2019) 7 *Internet of Things and Cloud Computing* 73, 73.

[7] See J-P Onnela et al, 'Geographic Constraints on Social Network Groups' (2011) 6(4) *PLoS ONE*.

[8] See, eg, A Pentland, *Honest Signals: How They Shape our World* (Cambridge, MA, MIT Press, 2010) 84; W Dong, B Lepri and A Pentland, 'Modeling the Co-Evolution of Behaviors and Social Relationships Using Mobile Phone Data' in *Proceedings of the 10th International Conference on Mobile and Ubiquitous Multimedia* (New York, Association for Computing Machinery, 2011) 134; R Ferguson and S Buckingham Shum, 'Social Learning Analytics: Five Approaches' in *Proceedings of the 2nd International Conference on Learning Analytics and Knowledge* (New York, Association for Computing Machinery, 2012) 23.

[9] See KJ Strandburg, 'Surveillance of Emergent Associations: Freedom of Association in a Network Society' in A Acquisti et al (eds), *Digital Privacy: Theory, Technologies, and Practices* (Boca Raton, Auerbach Publications, 2008) 435, 438.

II. The Limits of Surveillance in European and US Jurisprudence

While mass surveillance and bulk data retention are not entirely new phenomena, advances in information and communication technologies (ICTs) have continued to supplement governments' ability to develop uses of monitoring that risk interferences in fundamental rights. The case law of the European Court of Human Rights testifies to states' propensity for creating increasingly pervasive, large-scale monitoring programmes of populations in Europe for use by the intelligence services, law enforcement and other public authorities.[10] More recently, the Court has highlighted the importance of examining compliance with the privacy principles of Article 8 of the European Convention on Human Rights when the powers vested in the state are obscure, thereby 'creating a risk of arbitrariness especially where the technology available is continually becoming more sophisticated'.[11] As digital technologies augment the capacity to collate a greater volume of more detailed information pertaining to individual citizens with far more efficiency, in many instances the personal data collected may concern completely innocuous activities and be unrelated to any, even minor, unlawful activity – let alone more serious crime that might possibly cross the threshold by which a proportionality test could reasonably be applied. Recognition of citizens' right to privacy implies that the state generally refrain from the indiscriminate monitoring of populations. Thus, the law must adequately define the basis on which targets are identified for monitoring by a public authority authorised to do so, though authorities need not notify those persons subject to surveillance measures, as elucidated in judgments from Strasbourg dating back as far as 1978. *Klass and Others v Germany* was notable for the fact that the Court found that democratic societies are threatened by such sophisticated forms of terrorism and espionage that, in order to counter them, states must be able to undertake 'secret surveillance of subversive elements operating within its jurisdiction'.[12] The Court therefore accepted the necessity of legislation allowing for the surveillance of telecommunications under exceptional conditions in a democratic society in the interests of national security or for the prevention of disorder or crime.

In *Klass and Others* the applicants also alleged a breach of Article 13 of the European Convention on Human Rights, the right to an effective remedy for individuals whose rights are violated. In the context of covert surveillance measures, it may be difficult to ascertain whether a violation has in fact occurred. As the Court

---

[10] For precedent established in respect of earlier forms of mass surveillance, see, eg, *Rotaru v Romania* [GC], no 28341/95 (4 May 2000); *Weber and Saravia v Germany*, no 54934/00 (29 June 2006); *Liberty and Others v UK*, no 58243/00 (1 July 2008).

[11] *Catt v UK*, no 43514/15 (24 January 2019) 114. See also *Roman Zakharov v Russia* [GC], no 47143/06 (4 December 2015) 229; *Szabó & Vissy v Hungary*, no 37138/14 (12 January 2016) 68.

[12] *Klass and Others v Germany*, no 5029/71 (6 September 1978).

noted, 'it is the secrecy of the measures which renders it difficult, if not impossible, for the person concerned to seek any remedy of his own accord, particularly while surveillance is in progress'.[13] Taking this into consideration, it took a pragmatic approach to interpreting Article 13:

> Article 13 ... requires that where an individual considers himself to have been prejudiced by a measure allegedly in breach of the Convention, he should have a remedy before a national authority in order both to have his claim decided and, if appropriate, to obtain redress.[14]

Although the Court ultimately rejected the applicants' complaint, it clearly articulated its underlying aversion towards monitoring, while accepting its inevitability:

> Secret surveillance and its implications are facts that the Court, *albeit to its regret*, has held to be necessary, in modern-day conditions in a democratic society, in the interests of national security and for the prevention of disorder or crime. (Emphasis added)[15]

A further important consideration is the effect that the rapid augmentation of data storage has had on the potential invasiveness of detection and screening activities. The deliberations in *S and Marper v UK* emphasised data retention as a particular concern. In this case, the Court reaffirmed the notion that the fight against crime should indeed make use of modern techniques as they become available:

> The Court finds it to be beyond dispute that the fight against crime, and in particular against organised crime and terrorism, which is one of the challenges faced by today's European societies, depends to a great extent on the use of modern scientific techniques of investigation and identification.[16]

But the techniques used must not violate fundamental rights. Behavioural details that relate to personal interests, activities and relationships can be inferred through increasingly complex processing of personal data, as the European Court of Justice's final judgment in *Digital Rights Ireland and Seitlinger and Others* made clear:

> [the data which providers of publicly available electronic communications services or of public communications networks must retain,] taken as a whole, may allow very precise conclusions to be drawn concerning the private lives of the persons whose data has been retained, such as the habits of everyday life, permanent or temporary places of residence, daily or other movements, the activities carried out, the social relationships of those persons and the social environments frequented by them.[17]

---

[13] ibid 68.
[14] ibid 64.
[15] ibid 68.
[16] *S and Marper v UK* [GC], nos 30562/04 and 30566/04 (4 December 2008) 105.
[17] Judgment in Joined Cases C-293/12 and C-594/12, *Digital Rights Ireland and Seitlinger and Others* (8 April 2014) 27.

The judgment in this case was significant for its deliberation of the possible harm caused by surveillance in light of the rights to privacy, data protection and freedom of expression (Articles 7, 8 and 11 of the Charter of Fundamental Rights of the European Union). It also underscored the finding from the earlier *Rundfunk* case[18] that an interference with the right to privacy can be established irrespective of whether the information concerned is sensitive, or whether the individuals concerned have been caused any inconvenience.[19] This affirmation is particularly pertinent to the measurement of previously indiscernible aspects of our lives, which determine whether our conduct conforms to standards or norms of personal behaviour that may be unclear to the individual concerned.

Across the Atlantic, the courts have also deliberated how information technologies challenge normative precepts around the social construction of spaces, as well as the role surveillance may play in inhibiting our capacity to interact with one another and form relations. In *United States v Jones*, Justice Sotomayor recognised the privacy interests relative to a person's specific location: 'GPS monitoring generates a precise, comprehensive record of a person's public movements that reflects a wealth of detail about her familial, political, professional, religious, and sexual associations.'[20] In determining the limits to which constitutional protections extend, the Supreme Court considered inter alia the scope of a person's subjective expectation of privacy and the relevance of whether they had taken actions to shield their activity from the public. This consideration reaches to the heart of a concern that is becoming more critical – namely how to delineate the responsibilities of different parties when the capabilities for ubiquitous monitoring are rapidly evolving. The case proved insightful for its review of the extent to which citizens should proactively engage in efforts to protect their own fundamental rights, considering the relatively limited measures at their disposal compared with government authorities. The Court's deliberations confirmed the belief that Jones (and others) need not be burdened from having to defend their privacy, but that the onus was on the government to refrain from interfering in the first place. This was especially important as individuals generally have little recourse to measures that can protect them from such breaches (even if they have the knowledge and funds to do so).

In the recent case *Carpenter v United States*, the Supreme Court deliberated how far the Fourth Amendment, which prohibits unreasonable searches and seizures, should extend to safeguarding a person's electronic devices. It ruled that this constitutional protection afforded individual freedom from unreasonable intrusions by the government into personal communication devices, including smartphones, which might be co-opted as de facto monitoring tools, as opposed to covert surveillance instruments such as those used by law enforcement in the

---

[18] Judgment in Joined Cases C-465/00, C-138/01 and C-139/01, *Österreichischer Rundfunk and Others* (20 May 2003) 75.

[19] *Digital Rights Ireland and Seitlinger and Others* 33.

[20] Justice Sotomayor, Concurrence in the judgment *United States v Jones*, 132 S.Ct.945 (2012) 3.

earlier *Jones* case. The Court asserted that historical cellular site records of a mobile device provide the government with 'near perfect surveillance and allow it to travel back in time to retrace a person's whereabouts'.[21] The ability to monitor an individual's movement in this way present distinct concerns for the enjoyment of freedom of peaceful assembly and association where multiple records of mobility are cross-referenced to determine patterns of interaction between people.

These cases highlight the challenge of applying a framework of constitutional provisions in a way that accommodates the changes brought by digital transformation, while running the risk of being overtaken by further technological developments. Nonetheless, we must not lose sight of the fact that technological innovations can continue to play an essential, positive role in the environment that we develop as a society.[22] As such, it is crucial that a coherent shared framework of complementary legal and technical parameters that safeguards citizens, while facilitating the beneficial innovations of advances in digital technologies, be created.

III. From Labour Relations and Political Representation to Interactive Gaming: The Evolution of Assembly and Association

The premise established in the Universal Declaration of Human Rights – that 'Everyone has the right to freedom of peaceful assembly and association' (Article 20(1)) – is elaborated in the International Covenant on Economic, Social and Cultural Rights (Article 8) and the International Covenant on Civil and Political Rights (Articles 21 and 22), which underscore its importance to labour relations and political representation.[23] Notwithstanding the connection with trade unions, freedom of association in particular is interpreted broadly to apply

---

[21] Justice Roberts, Opinion in the judgment *Carpenter v United States*, 585 U.S. (2018).

[22] See L Lessig, *Code: Version 2.0* (New York, Basic Books, 2006). See also JR Reidenberg, 'Lex Informatica: The Formulation of Information Policy Rules Through Technology' (1997) 76 *Texas Law Review* 553; RE Leenes and B-J Koops, '"Code" and Privacy – Or How Technology is Slowly Eroding Privacy' in EJ Dommering and LF Asscher (eds), *Essays on the Normative Role of Information Technology* (The Hague, TMC Asser Press, 2006).

[23] The main regional standards across Africa, the Americas and Europe each incorporate the human right to freedom of peaceful assembly and association: see the African Charter on Human and Peoples' Rights, Arts 10 and 11; American Declaration of the Rights and Duties of Man, Arts 21 and 22; American Convention on Human Rights, Arts 15 and 16; European Convention on Human Rights, Art 11; and Charter of Fundamental Rights of the European Union, Art 12. See also the ASEAN Human Rights Declaration, which includes the right to freedom of peaceful assembly (Art 24) and the freedom to form and join trade unions (Art 27(2)). The right to form and participate in trade unions is also explicitly guaranteed in the ILO Convention of 1948 concerning Freedom of Association and Protection of the Right to Organize (ILO Convention No 87) and the ILO Convention of 1949 concerning the Application of the Principles of the Right to Organize and Collective Bargaining (ILO Convention No 98).

to a huge range of groups, movements and organisations, whose activities are now frequently mediated by online tools.[24]

The capability of online networks and platforms to transcend barriers and facilitate the organisation of groups has had a profound influence on assembly and association. The immediacy and asynchronous nature of online communications make them particularly effective for connecting the once disassociated,[25] allowing parties to organise and recruit others in a process that may obviate the need for either hierarchy or the refinement of a strategy,[26] as well as to raise funds.[27] A further benefit of online tools is their capacity to enable and embolden vulnerable or marginalised groups, encouraging greater dialogue with those with disabilities or impairments that might inhibit their capacity to meet offline and minimising exposure to harassment for individuals who are subject to intimidation or discrimination. Individuals with marginalised identities may use anonymity and the intrinsic spatial separation afforded by online discourse as protective tools that aid their participation in online interaction.[28] Participation in online associations is more highly valued by people with marginalised, concealed or stigmatised identities: those who may not feel able to disclose their sexual orientation publicly, for example, or those with extreme political beliefs.[29]

The digital space is of fundamental importance where the right for citizens to participate in the conduct of public affairs intersects with the exercise of the right to freedom of peaceful assembly and association.[30] Just over a decade ago,

---

[24] See, eg, UNHRC Res 24/5 (2013); UNHRC, 'Report of the Special Rapporteur on the Rights to Freedom of Peaceful Assembly and of Association, Maina Kai' (2013) UN Doc A/HRC/23/39; European Commission for Democracy through Law (Venice Commission) and OSCE Office for Democratic Institutions and Human Rights, 'Joint Guidelines on Freedom of Association' (2014) 10–16; European Court of Human Rights Press Unit, 'Factsheet – Political Parties and Associations' (2016); International Labour Office, *Freedom of Association. Compilation of Decisions of the Committee on Freedom of Association* (Geneva, ILO, 2018); UNHRC, 'Report on the Rights to Freedom of Peaceful Assembly and of Association' (2019) UN Doc A/HRC/41/41.

[25] See DB Boyd and NB Ellison, 'Social Network Sites: Definition, History, and Scholarship' (2007) 13 *Journal of Computer-Mediated Communication* 210.

[26] See, eg, Strandburg, 'Surveillance of Emergent Associations' 437; D Runtzen and J Zenn, 'Association and Assembly in the Digital Age' (2011) 13(4) *The International Journal of Not-for-Profit Law* 53.

[27] See, eg, N Shapovalova, 'Assessing Ukrainian Grassroots Activism Five Years After Euromaidan' (*Carnegie Europe*, 6 February 2019) available at https://carnegieeurope.eu/2019/02/06/assessing-ukrainian-grassroots-activism-five-years-after-euromaidan-pub-78248.

[28] See, eg, H Noman, 'Arab Religious Skeptics Online: Anonymity, Autonomy, and Discourse in a Hostile Environment' (2015) Berkman Center Research Publication No 2015-2; S Steinberg, 'Sharenting: Children's Privacy in the Age of Social Media' (2017) 66 *Emory Law Journal* 839.

[29] See, eg, K McKenna and J Bargh, 'Coming Out in the Age of the Internet: Identity "Demarginalization" through Virtual Group Participation' (1998) 75 *Journal of Personality and Social Psychology* 681; S Watt, M Lea and R Spears, 'How Social Is Internet Communication? A Reappraisal of Bandwidth and Anonymity effects' in S Woolgar (ed) *Virtual Society? Technology, Cyberbole, Reality* (Oxford, Oxford University Press, 2002).

[30] See E Gordon, J Baldwin-Philippi and M Balestra, 'Why We Engage: How Theories of Human Behavior Contribute to Our Understanding of Civic Engagement in a Digital Era' (2013) Berkman Center Research Publication No 21. See also N Jung, Y Kim and H de Zuniga, 'The Mediating Role of Knowledge and Efficacy in the Effects of Communication on Political Participation' (2011) 14 *Mass Communication and Society* 407.

the Arab Spring prominently revealed how the online sphere could contribute to political engagement: in 2010, just four years after its launch, Twitter was used to organise protests in public spaces and massive pro-democracy uprisings throughout North Africa and the Middle East.[31] Social media networks and messaging platforms now play an even more decisive role in influencing civic engagement. In many communities, they have become essential conduits for dialogue leading to the formation and development of associations and for civic discourse including calls to participate in peaceful assemblies. In Sudan, for example, private Facebook groups have become a favoured means for women to expose abuses allegedly committed by members of the security forces against assemblies and during protests in the country.[32] Social media platforms thrive on both sharing causes and establishing causes to rally around.[33] Sites such as Change.org or Facebook's integrated 'Community Actions' petition feature seek to facilitate civic participation by allowing users to start petitions and develop interactions with decision-makers to achieve change in the public sphere.[34]

The critical role that the internet and, in particular, social media and digital messaging now play in enabling civic discourse is also a challenge for civil society. Their pervasiveness and impact are such that failure to participate risks 'digital exclusion'. Further complicating this issue is the opacity of many of the digital communication channels upon which civil society organisations and activists have become reliant. When the audience of a message or communication is determined by algorithm-based decisions, actors in the civil space may be impeded in their ability to effectively engage and impart information. Similarly, when social media platforms such as LinkedIn and Facebook use proprietary algorithms and artificial intelligence to suggest who users might connect and interact with, it is difficult to determine the degree to which users *voluntarily* associate with others. There are inherent risks in building profiles based on subjective interpretations of associations between different parties. Oversimplified models that infer relationships between members of an association may not in fact credibly reflect the nature of those ties.[35] They may also replicate or engender new biases or discriminatory effects in engineering social interactions between individuals and groups.

---

[31] See PN Howard et al, 'Opening Closed Regimes: What Was the Role of Social Media During the Arab Spring?' (Project on Information Technology and Political Islam, 2011) 23; MM Charrad and NE Reith, 'Local Solidarities: How the Arab Spring Protests Started' (2019) 34(S1) *Sociological Forum* 1174; N Waechter, 'The Participative Role of Social Media for the Disadvantaged Young Generation in the Arab Spring' (2019) 44 *Österreichische Zeitschrift für Soziologie* 217.

[32] See T Griffin, 'These Women Joined Facebook to Follow their Crushes. Now They're Using their Skills to Expose Abusive Police' (*Buzzfeed*, 16 February 2019). See also M Alamin, 'Facebook Is No Substitute for an Election, Sudan's Embattled Leader Says' (*Bloomberg*, 31 January 2019).

[33] R Thompson, 'Radicalization and the Use of Social Media' (2011) 4(4) *Journal of Strategic Security* 176.

[34] J Constine, 'Facebook Launches Petition Feature, Its Next Battlefield' (*TechCrunch*, 1 February 2019).

[35] See, eg, AL Barabási, *Linked: The New Science of Networks* (Cambridge MA, Perseus, 2002); PJ Carrington, J Scott and S Wasserman, *Models and Methods in Social Network Analysis* (New York, Cambridge University Press, 2005).

On the other hand, the notion that the news and feed update algorithms deployed by social media exploit our tendency to reinforce strongly held convictions through the power of confirmation bias is contested.[36] 'Filter bubbles' have always existed. Their appearance in social media networks is simply due to information and users' beliefs and judgments now being channelled through this conduit. Closed discussion groups may shield members from exposure to a plurality of opinions and from fact-checking,[37] but the inclination to isolate ourselves from views that rebut our own certainly preceded the rise of internet chat fora.

Other types of social media that have a large associative and interactive component include content communities such as YouTube, virtual worlds such as Animal Crossing,[38] collaboration projects such as Wikipedia, Quora or GitHub,[39] and gaming. By 2020, the most popular online games, including Fortnite and Minecraft, had a combined following in the hundreds of millions globally.[40] Initially designed solely around gameplay, gaming platforms are now hubs for broader social interconnections and the formation of groups and communities with shared interests.[41]

The users of social media and other online platforms who create content through their interactions and are primarily responsible for its (re)distribution have a duty to treat others with dignity and respect, as important as the obligations and responsibilities prescribed for public authorities and businesses. Principled behaviour on the part of individuals in the associative context affords scope for relationships to form and promotes the various facets of engagement. The freely chosen actions of the individual should not be disregarded in the discussion of rights and responsibilities.

---

[36] See, eg, A Alsaad, A Taamneh and MN Al-Jedaiah, 'Does Social Media Increase Racist Behavior? An Examination of Confirmation Bias Theory' (2018) 55 *Technology in Society* 41.

[37] See DK Citron, 'Cyber Mobs, Disinformation, and Death Videos: The Internet as It Is (and as It Should Be)' (2020) 118 *Michigan Law Review* 1073, 1078. For changes made by Facebook following criticism of its 'Secret Groups' platform feature, see G Gebhart, 'Understanding Public, Closed, and Secret Facebook Groups' (*Electronic Frontier Foundation*, 13 June 2017) available at www.eff.org/deeplinks/2017/06/understanding-public-closed-and-secret-facebook-groups.

[38] See, eg, L Zhu, 'The Psychology Behind Video Games During COVID-19 Pandemic: A Case Study of *Animal Crossing: New Horizons*' (2020) *Human Behaviour and Emerging Technologies*.

[39] See, eg, G Murić et al, 'Collaboration Drives Individual Productivity' (2019) 3 *Proceedings of the ACM on Human–Computer Interaction*; X Cheng et al, 'Open Collaboration Between Universities and Enterprises: A Case Study on GitHub' (2020) 30 *Internet Research* 1251; A Chhabra and SRS Iyengar, 'Who Writes Wikipedia? An Investigation from the Perspective of Ortega and Newton Hypotheses' in *Proceedings of the 16th International Symposium on Open Collaboration* (New York, Association for Computing Machinery, 2020). See also J Mistry, 'Analysing Government Use of GitHub for Collaboration: An Empirical Approach to Measuring Open Government and Open Collaboration' (Masters Thesis, University of Waterloo, 2020).

[40] C Gough, 'Fortnite – Statistics & Facts' (*Statista*, 5 March 2020) available at www.statista.com/topics/5847/fortnite; C Gough, 'Number of active players of Minecraft worldwide as of May 2020' (*Statista*, 26 August 2020) available at www.statista.com/statistics/680139/minecraft-active-players-worldwide.

[41] See T Malaby, 'Coding Control: Governance and Contingency in the Production of Online Worlds' (2006) Special Issue Number 7, *First Monday*; S Humphreys, 'Predicting, Securing and Shaping the Future: Mechanisms of Governance in Online Social Environments' (2013) 9 *International Journal of Media & Cultural Politics* 247.

The capabilities of certain fora in the digital domain to develop debate and mobilise associations into action are not always used by individuals and groups in a manner that safeguards the rights of others. Online chat fora such as 4chan and 8chan have been used by extremists to circulate calls to arms and violence towards certain ethnic groups.[42] Threatening and offensive material continues to circulate on Reddit despite concerns regarding racist content and intimidation on the online platform being raised as early as 2015.[43] Concerns have also arisen with regard to harassment and intimidation in the gaming environment.[44] Tech companies streaming video games, including Twitch, Microsoft and YouTube, have recently launched investigations into allegations of inappropriate behaviour including physical threats, stalking, and sustained harassment.[45] With online interactive gaming constituting an environment ripe for surveillance,[46] various intelligence services and law enforcement agencies have, via the analysis of metadata processed through packet-sniffing software, determined that certain online players use the platforms for illicit activities linked to organised crime including people trafficking, the sale of materials connected to nuclear proliferation, arms dealing and terrorism.[47] Other online services are equally used for unlawful activities.[48]

Social media also allows for the collection and processing of location data,[49] though lack of transparency and accessibility around data quality and consent continue to compromise potentially beneficial location-based functionality. Several of the earliest interactive platforms that exploited location data, such as Foursquare[50] and the now defunct location-based messaging app

---

[42] See K Abraham and R Marlin-Bennett, 'Cyberplace: Conceptualizing Power and Politics in Extended Reality' (American Political Science Association Annual Meeting, Chicago, 29 August–1 September 2013).

[43] See K Hankes, 'Black Hole' [2015] *Intelligence Report*.

[44] See, eg, B Stephen, 'Twitch Overhauls its Rules Around Harassment and Hateful Conduct' (*The Verge*, 9 December 2020).

[45] See, eg, D Smith, 'Most People Who Play Video Games Online Experience "Severe" Harassment, New Study Finds' (*Business Insider*, 25 July 2019).

[46] See JR Whitson and B Simon, 'Game Studies Meets Surveillance Studies at the Edge of Digital Culture: An Introduction to a Special Issue on Surveillance, Games and Play' (2014) 12 *Surveillance & Society* 309, 311; R Shimonski, J Zenir and A Bishop, 'Web Camera and Video Tracking' in R Shimonski, J Zenir and A Bishop (eds), *Cyber Reconnaissance, Surveillance and Defense* (Waltham, MA, Syngress, 2015); B Gellman, 'Inside the NSA's Secret Tool for Mapping Your Social Network' (*Wired*, 24 May 2020).

[47] See J Elliott, 'World of Spycraft: NSA and CIA Spied in Online Games' (*ProPublica*, 9 December 2013).

[48] See, eg, Europol, *Internet Organised Crime Threat Assessment 2018* available at www.europol.europa.eu/internet-organised-crime-threat-assessment-2018; S Andrews, B Brewster and T Day, 'Organised Crime and Social Media: A System for Detecting, Corroborating and Visualising Weak Signals of Organised Crime Online' (2018) 7 *Security Informatics* 3.

[49] See S Das, J Dev and JL Camp, 'Privacy Preserving Policy Framework: User-Aware and User-Driven' (*Social Science Research Network*, 31 August 2019).

[50] Foursquare differentiated itself from its competitors largely on the basis of its location feature to encourage 'check-ins' and self-identify and share patterns of movement. See, eg, J Cranshaw et al, 'The Livehoods Project: Utilizing Social Media to Understand the Dynamics of a City' (International AAAI Conference on Weblogs and Social Media, Trinity College Dublin, *Social Science Research Network*, June 2012) 58.

Yik Yak,[51] openly called attention to this feature, publicising the value of dialogue with others in the vicinity. Facebook or Twitter also collect vast amounts of location data and profile their users' patterns of mobility but are noticeably warier of advertising their interest in knowing their whereabouts.[52] More recently, some Covid-19 contact tracing apps, whose primary function is to discern patterns of association based on location data from the overt (opt-in) surveillance of mobile devices, have raised concerns, with some apps having access to 'social graphs', information about whom, where and when people have physically met, and thus their mobility record.[53]

IV. Ubiquitous Sensing Networks: A Paradigm Shift for Monitoring Capabilities

ICTs, including mobile sensing, are exerting a growing and pervasive influence in urban centres in particular.[54] Strategy studies have highlighted that policy interventions and management decisions relating to the operation of vital infrastructure will in part be shaped by mapping individuals' patterns of mobility and interactions.[55] Public authorities, national governments and regional entities such as the European Union have allocated resources to studying the possible uses of technologies enhanced by the processing of data from communication networks.[56] They include the monitoring of urban dynamics, public transportation networks and more nuanced personal and contextual services.[57] Much of the promise of

---

[51] At the height of its popularity, in 2015, Yik Yak raised the ire of parents and educators in fomenting disruption and facilitating the harassment of students through anonymous messaging to peers in the locality. See V Safronova, 'The Rise and Fall of Yik Yak, the Anonymous Messaging App' *The New York Times* (27 May 2017). See also NC Russell at al, 'APIs and Your Privacy' (*Social Science Research Network*, 2019).

[52] See L Humski, D Pintar and M Vranić, 'Analysis of Facebook Interaction as Basis for Synthetic Expanded Social Graph Generation' (2019) 7 *IEEE Access* 6622. See also the early identification of location as a means to draw inferences in social relations between users in N Akhtar, H Javed and G Sengar, 'Analysis of Facebook Social Network' (5th International Conference and Computational Intelligence and Communication Networks, Mathura, 2013) 451.

[53] See LR Bradford, M Aboy and K Liddell, 'COVID-19 Contact Tracing Apps: A Stress Test for Privacy, the GDPR, and Data Protection Regimes' (2020) 7 *Journal of Law and the Biosciences*; 'Report: Reassessing COVID-19 Contact Tracing Apps, Security and Privacy Risks Persist' (*Guardsquare*, 10 December 2020).

[54] See, eg, R Kitchin, 'The Real-Time City? Big Data and Smart Urbanism' (2014) 79 *GeoJournal* 1; Z Allam and ZA Dhunny, 'On Big Data, Artificial Intelligence and Smart Cities' (2019) 89 *Cities* 80.

[55] See, eg, ID Constantiou and J Kallinikos, 'New Games, New Rules: Big Data and the Changing Context of Strategy' (2015) 30 *Journal of Information Technology* 44.

[56] See, eg, K Kourtit, P Nijkamp and D Arribas-Bel, 'Smart Cities Perspective – A Comparative European Study by Means of Self-Organizing Maps' (2012) 25 *Innovation* 229; M Batty et al, 'Smart Cities of the Future' (2012) 214 *European Physical Journal Special Topics* 481; A Townsend, *Smart Cities: Big Data, Civic Hackers, and the Quest for a New Utopia* (New York, Norton, 2013).

[57] See M Gonzalez, C Hidalgo and A-L Barabási, 'Understanding Individual Human Mobility Patterns' (2008) 453 *Nature* 779. See also X Cheng et al, 'Exploiting Mobile Big Data: Sources, Features, and Applications' (2017) 31 *IEEE Network* 72.

'smart cities' delivering more secure, liveable and functional environments is based on real-time awareness of population dynamics.[58]

There are concerns, however, that these developments will be based on skewed data. Indeed, the lives of individuals who, due to 'poverty, geography, or lifestyle', live on the margins of society are 'less "datafied" than the general population's'.[59] 'Because not all data is created or even collected equally, there are "signal problems" in big-data sets – dark zones or shadows where some citizens and communities are overlooked or underrepresented.'[60] Data-generating activities should be understood in the context of social mobility: different groups within communities have differentiated access to and relatively less fluency in the new technologies.[61]

The monitoring of open-source data from social media and other ICTs may also fall within the law enforcement remit of detecting crime.[62] Social media platforms constitute an extremely attractive source of such 'open-source intelligence' because of the level of trust placed in them by users.[63] The monitoring of the use of location-aware networks that allow for the development of associations all but invisible to the offline world is simply an extension of open-source intelligence surveillance activity.[64]

Technological and methodological developments have brought about a paradigm shift in the way in which citizens' activities can be monitored and interpreted. Advances in computing make it possible to analyse larger and larger data sets and to uncover 'suspicious' patterns of association. Social network analysis can provide a powerful set of tools for describing and modelling the relational context and dimensions of a behaviour.[65] Earlier forms of relational surveillance – which aspires to explain the nature of interactions and their purpose – already harbour inherent risks to associational activity and free expression. Protests and other public assemblies have prompted debate as to whether use by public authorities of social network analysis bodes well for civil society.[66]

---

[58] See T Althoff et al, 'Large-Scale Physical Activity Data Reveal Worldwide Activity Inequality' (2017) 547 *Nature* 336.

[59] J Lerman, 'Big Data and its Exclusions' (2013) 66 *Stanford Law Review Online* 55.

[60] See K Crawford, 'Think Again: Big Data' (*Foreign Policy*, 9 May 2013).

[61] S Barocas and AD Selbst, 'Big Data's Disparate Impact' (2016) 104 *California Law Review* 671, 685.

[62] See Appendix to the Recommendation Rec(2001)10 of the Committee of Ministers to Member States on the European Code of Police Ethics, adopted by the Committee of Ministers on 19 September 2001.

[63] See L Vomfell, WK Härdle and S Lessmann, 'Improving Crime Count Forecasts Using Twitter and Taxi Data' (2018) 113 *Decision Support Systems* 73.

[64] See HJ Williams and I Blum, *Defining Second Generation Open Source Intelligence (OSINT) for the Defense Enterprise* (Santa Monica, Rand Corporation, 2018); BH Miller 'Open Source Intelligence (OSINT): An Oxymoron?' (2018) 31 *International Journal of Intelligence and CounterIntelligence* 702; JRG Evangelista et al, 'Systematic Literature Review to Investigate the Application of Open Source Intelligence (OSINT) with Artificial Intelligence' [2020] *Journal of Applied Security Research*.

[65] Strandburg, 'Surveillance of Emergent Associations' 437.

[66] For the role of social network analysis in tracking disturbances in public protest during the 2011 London riots, see HMIC, 'The Rules of Engagement: A Review of the August 2011 Disorders' (2011), available at www.justiceinspectorates.gov.uk/hmicfrs/media/a-review-of-the-august-2011-disorders-20111220.pdf. See also S Owen, 'Monitoring Social Media and Protest

Advances in computing may also allow for more nuanced forecasting of crime, based on extrapolating trends and patterns from assembled data.[67] However, this approach is predicated on qualifying behavioural attributes and construing potentialities based on ostensibly rational criteria.[68] It presumes that there is a correlation between the behaviour of individuals – a homogeneity of 'types' – and that the data is reliable.[69] There are dangers in tacitly accepting that our movements and associations be recorded and correlated for the purpose of forecasting illicit pursuits.[70] Exceptional care is needed when attempting to determine whether an association or an interaction at the early stage heralds a tendency or inclination towards an engagement in unlawful activity. Predictive profiling of this nature risks repressing emergent associations before members even recognise or comprehend their own affiliation. Where profiling of associations between parties is based on, for example, gender, religion, political or other opinions, it may jeopardise equality.[71] The tendency to use empirical data analysis to supposedly eliminate non-commensurability and ambiguity also reduces intricate facets of life to simple categorisations and risks grave miscalculations.[72] Moreover, attempting to make individual behaviours and preferences fit pre-existing frameworks may lead to social conformity, marginalising those who deviate from the norm.[73] Social norms that would have once been considered inhibiting may well eventually be fully internalised and pursued unconsciously, influenced by shifts emanating from technological change.

Even citizens who are aware of a surveillance capability of a technology that has been implemented are unlikely to be able to discern how exactly their own behaviour is being observed.[74] This can give rise to subtle changes in individuals'

Movements: Ensuring Political Order Through Surveillance and Surveillance Discourse' (2017) 23 *Social Identities* 688; R Levinson-Waldman, 'Government Access to and Manipulation of Social Media: Legal and Policy Challenges' (2018) 61 *Howard Law Journal* 523.

[67] See C McCue, *Data Mining and Predictive Analysis: Intelligence Gathering and Crime Analysis* (Oxford, Elsevier, 2007); T Scassa, 'Law Enforcement in the Age of Big Data and Surveillance Intermediaries: Transparency Challenges' (2017) 14 *SCRIPTed* 239.

[68] See E Murphy, 'The New Forensics: Criminal Justice, False Certainty, and the Second Generation of Scientific Evidence' (2007) 95 *California Law Review* 721. See also President's Council of Advisors on Science and Technology (PCAST), *Forensic Science in Criminal Courts: Ensuring Scientific Validity of Feature-Comparison Methods* (September 2016) available at https://obamawhitehouse.archives.gov/sites/default/files/microsites/ostp/PCAST/pcast_forensic_science_report_final.pdf.

[69] See, eg, N Bouhana, SD Johnson and M Porter, 'Consistency and Specificity in Burglars Who Commit Prolific Residential Burglary: Testing the Core Assumptions Underpinning Behavioural Crime Linkage' (2016) 21 *Legal and Criminological Psychology* 77; J Roach and K Pease, 'Police Overestimation of Criminal Career Homogeneity' (2014) 11 *Journal of Investigative Psychology and Offender Profiling* 164.

[70] See C Castelluccia, 'Behavioural Tracking on the Internet: A Technical Perspective' in S Gutwirth et al (eds), *European Data Protection: In Good Health?* (Dordrecht, Springer, 2012) 22.

[71] See UN International Covenant on Civil and Political Rights, Arts 2(1) and 26.

[72] See DJ Solove, 'Privacy and Power: Computer Databases and Metaphors for Information Privacy' (2001) 53 *Stanford Law Review* 1393, 1425.

[73] See BE Harcourt, 'Against Prediction: Sentencing, Policing, and Punishing in an Actuarial Age', Chicago Public Law and Legal Theory Working Paper No 94 (2005), 36.

[74] See S Lockwood, 'Who Knows Where You've Been? Privacy Concerns Regarding the Use of Cellular Phones as Personal Locators' (2004) 18 *Harvard Journal of Law and Technology* 307, 313–14.

mental states (to their sense of seclusion, for example), a feeling of agitation, or anxiety as to whether interactions with others might be misinterpreted.[75] A further consideration in respect of the harm of seemingly intangible interferences to the enjoyment of the right to association is the significance of heuristics. In this regard, the public's demand for the protection of the law is far greater where citizens can perceive the harm in question. If the harm is otherwise complex to understand and appreciate, then it is very likely that the pressure for greater oversight and regulation will be diminished.

V. Conclusion

The digital age has opened new space for the enjoyment of the rights to freedom of peaceful assembly and association and may yet furnish beneficial insights on the dynamics of individuals, groups and communities. However, it also enables governments, public authorities and other agencies to monitor citizens' interactions and relationships in increasingly fine detail. The jurisprudence may provide some guidance as to what constitutes a reasonable level of surveillance, but it necessarily lags behind the latest technological developments. Increasingly complex processing of open-source data, including location data, risks interfering with freedom of assembly and association, particularly when predictive profiling may stamp out interactions almost before they have begun.

The reordering of our social relationships constitutes an ongoing, major shift in human activity. Despite increasing recognition of the impact of what has been, in effect, a largely experimental approach to the widescale social engineering of society, the process remains an iterative one guided by short-term interests. It is crucial that digital tools be developed that maximise the welfare of communities and the protection of their fundamental rights, for the benefit of all.

---

[75] See DJ Solove, 'Reconstructing Electronic Surveillance Law' (2004) 72 *George Washington Law Review* 1701, 1708.

5

Algorithms of Occupation: Use of Artificial Intelligence in Israel and Palestine

MARWA FATAFTA

I. Introduction

In October 2017, the Israeli police arrested a Palestinian construction worker after he posted on Facebook a picture of himself leaning against a bulldozer with a cup of coffee and a cigarette in his hands.[1] After a few hours of interrogation, the Israeli police realised that they had arrested him based on an error in Facebook's transliteration and translation of his post. The platform automatically translated what he wrote in Arabic, 'ysabihum', which means good morning, to 'attack them' in Hebrew and 'hurt them' in English. Upon making international news, Facebook quickly apologised for the mistake and admitted that 'mistakes like these might happen from time to time'.[2] Facebook uses its automatic translation service to translate around 6 billion posts a day using Artificial Intelligence (AI).[3]

The incident is far more indicative and alarming than just an embarrassing system glitch. The case of the Palestinian construction worker, who deleted his post right after his release, is an example of the potential harm of AI systems to human rights, particularly when they are deployed in a context of military occupation. On the one hand, the Israeli authorities have been using an AI-powered predictive policing system, which combs through Palestinian social media data to flag individuals who could be likely attackers. Since October 2015, hundreds of

---

[1] Y Berger, 'Israel Arrests Palestinian Because Facebook Translated "Good Morning" to "Attack Them"' *Haaretz* (22 October 2017).

[2] S Fussell, 'Palestinian Man Arrested After Facebook Auto-Translates "Good Morning" as "Attack Them"' (*Gizmodo*, 23 October 2017) available at https://gizmodo.com/palestinian-man-arrested-after-facebook-auto-translates-1819782902.

[3] P Guzman and D Husa, 'Expanding Automatic Machine Translation to More Languages' (*Facebook Engineering*, 11 September 2018) available at https://engineering.fb.com/ml-applications/expanding-automatic-machine-translation-to-more-languages.

Palestinians have been arrested by the Israeli authorities – with the help of these technologies – in relation to their social media activity, including 19 children in 2016 alone.[4] In 2017, an estimated 300 Palestinians were arrested on charges of incitement to violence online,[5] and in 2018, the Israeli authorities arrested 350 Palestinians on the same charge.[6] On the other hand, the lack of transparency and accountability about how exactly AI works makes it difficult for harmed individuals to seek clarity, let alone redress, when such systems err. Facebook's translation mistake raises questions beyond the language processing abilities of its proprietary system. Bulldozers have been used by Palestinians in ramming attacks in the past, particularly in Jerusalem near the Israeli settlement where the Palestinian man worked. This leads to the question: what correlations were made between the photo content, the location of the man at the time, his nationality, gender and age?

AI has increasingly become a part of our everyday experience. It curates content on social media feeds, sorts results on search engines, recommends what to see next on YouTube, estimates how much an Uber ride would cost, diagnoses illness in health apps, and runs self-driving cars. Yet despite its promising potential, AI draws a lot of criticism, especially when used in justice and law enforcement, for its harmful effects on human rights enshrined in the Universal Declaration of Human Rights (UDHR), the International Covenant on Civil and Political Rights (ICCPR) and the International Covenant on Economic, Social and Cultural Rights (ICESCR). Predictive policing systems analyse data in order to make statistical predictions about when and where a crime may occur (hotspot analysis) or who could be a likely perpetrator or victim of a crime.[7] Many law enforcement and security agencies around the world aspire to deploy AI-powered predictive tools. The Chinese Government has been reported to use a predictive policing system, analysing big data, to detain and interrogate people in the western minority region of Xinjiang.[8]

---

[4] Defense for Children International Palestine, 'Facebook Posts Land Palestinian Teens in Administrative Detention' (17 October 2016) available at www.dci-palestine.org/facebook_posts_land_palestinian_teens_in_administrative_detention.

[5] Palestinian human rights organisation Addameer notes that the number of Palestinians arrested include those who were arrested for other reasons but later charged with incitement online for their social media activity: Addameer, 'Arrests on Charges of "Incitement" on Social Media Platforms and Israeli Government Policy: A Facebook Case Study' (7 January 2019) n 1 available at www.addameer.org/publications/arrests-charges-%E2%80%9Cincitement%E2%80%9D-social-media-platforms-and-israeli-government-policy.

[6] 7amleh – The Arab Center for the Advancement of Social Media, 'Silenced Networks: The Chilling Effect among Palestinian Youth in Social Media' (October 2019) available at https://7amleh.org/wp-content/uploads/2019/10/7amleh_Net_0919_ENGLISH1.pdf.

[7] WL Perry et al, 'Predictive Policing: The Role of Crime Forecasting in Law Enforcement Operations' (*RAND Corporation*, 2013) available at www.rand.org/content/dam/rand/pubs/research_reports/RR200/RR233/RAND_RR233.pdf.

[8] Human Rights Watch, 'China: Big Data Fuels Crackdown in Minority Region' (26 February 2018) available at www.hrw.org/news/2018/02/26/china-big-data-fuels-crackdown-minority-region.

The Danish Security and Intelligence Service purchased a policing system from Palantir Technologies, a controversial American private firm specialised in big data analysis, in the aftermath of the terrorist shootings that took place in Copenhagen in 2015.[9] The Netherlands has developed its own Crime Anticipation System (CAS), which analyses data to detect crime patterns and deploy police accordingly.[10] Similarly, Indian media reported in 2017 that the police aimed to deploy a predictive policing system throughout India to detect crime patterns and hotspots.[11] One Indian official cited the experience of the US in deploying such tools as showing 'great results'. Contrary to the claims of the Indian official, such systems, particularly those used in criminal justice in the US, have become notorious for all the wrong reasons. Research has found that predictive policing in the US has not only failed at reducing crime rates but has rather resulted in exacerbating corrupt, unconstitutional and racially biased practices.[12]

AI technologies are not created in a vacuum. They are designed and used to make decisions or solve problems in certain social, economic and political contexts in which bias, discrimination or human rights violations already exist. Predictive policing tools rely on historical police data, which means that communities or areas which already have high crime rates or are heavily policed are most likely to be flagged by these systems. What makes the use of these technologies even more problematic is the lack of transparency, and therefore accountability, of these predictive policing models. Algorithms used in these models are opaque and their decisions are difficult to interpret even by experts. When decisions take place in a context where security forces are not regulated or are under-investigated, it opens the door to bias and abuse justified by automated decision-making. What happens when AI is deployed in more volatile contexts of conflict where discrimination and human rights violations are structural and systematic? This chapter builds on the investigations of the harmful effects of AI by looking into the human rights implications of Israel's use of a predictive policing system in the Occupied Palestinian territories. The use of predictive policing by the Israeli authorities has led to the invasive monitoring and surveillance of activity on the Palestinian internet, the arrest of hundreds of Palestinians without due process or access to fair trial, as well as a chilling effect and self-censorship on social media in fear of arrest or prosecution.

---

[9] European Digital Rights (EDRi), 'New Legal Framework for Predictive Policing in Denmark' (22 February 2017) available at https://edri.org/new-legal-framework-for-predictive-policing-in-denmark.

[10] J Pieters, 'Dutch Police Use Big Data to Predict Crime, Manage Resources' *NL Times* (15 May 2017) available at https://nltimes.nl/2017/05/15/dutch-police-use-big-data-predict-crime-manage-resources.

[11] V Sharma, 'Indian Police to Be Armed with Big Data Software to Predict Crime' *The New Indian Express* (23 September 2017) available at www.newindianexpress.com/nation/2017/sep/23/indian-police-to-be-armed-with-big-data-software-to-predict-crime-1661708.html.

[12] J Asher and R Arthur, 'Inside the Algorithm that Tries to Predict Gun Violence in Chicago' *The New York Times* (13 June 2017).

II. Artificial Intelligence and Human Rights

What is Artificial Intelligence? There is no widely agreed definition of what AI actually is. It is an umbrella term that describes 'a variety of computational techniques and associated processes dedicated to improving the ability of machines to do things requiring intelligence'.[13] One of the leading scholars on AI, John McCarthy, who coined the term in 1955, defines AI as 'the science of making machines do things that would require intelligence if done by men'.[14]

A study by the Berkman Klein Center for Internet & Society at Harvard University classifies AI systems currently in use into two main categories: systems that can learn by themselves and systems that cannot. The first group of AI technologies use accumulative data to improve their performance and automatic decision-making over time. These include machine learning, deep learning, facial recognition, and natural language processing. The second group of technologies, called knowledge-based systems or closed-rule algorithms, can only perform specific tasks in specific domains based on predefined rules. Unlike the first group, they do not have the capacity to learn on their own and improve.

AI technologies are rapidly evolving, which makes it difficult to identify what is AI and what is not: a phenomenon termed the 'AI effect'. This is when 'formerly cutting-edge innovations become mundane and routine, losing the privilege of being categorized as AI, while new technologies with more impressive capabilities are labeled as AI instead'.[15] Contrary to how AI is sometimes perceived – especially in the media and pop culture – as futuristic robots that possess human-like cognitive capacities and intelligence, the current forms of AI fall within the realm of so-called Narrow AI. This is the application of a single task in a specific domain.[16] Artificial General Intelligence (AGI), where machines resemble humans in their intelligence or even outsmart them, is an evolving area of research that remains far from being realised.

AI and automated decision-making algorithms are often perceived and promoted by private companies and other parties who design or adopt them as neutral technologies that make decisions based on data processing and analysis, rather than subjective human judgement. This perception of neutrality, where technology is seen as merely a 'tool' is a common fallacy.[17] Algorithms, the building

---

[13] F Raso et al, 'Artificial Intelligence & Human Rights: Opportunities & Risks' (Berkman Klein Center for Internet & Society, 2018) available at https://cyber.harvard.edu/publication/2018/artificial-intelligence-human-rights.

[14] Access Now, 'Human Rights in the Age of Artificial Intelligence' (2018) available at www.accessnow.org/cms/assets/uploads/2018/11/AI-and-Human-Rights.pdf.

[15] Raso et al, 'Artificial Intelligence & Human Rights'.

[16] B Goertzel, 'Artificial General Intelligence: Concept, State of the Art, and Future Prospects' (2014) 5 *Journal of Artificial General Intelligence* 1.

[17] Z Tufekci, *Twitter and Tear Gas: The Power and Fragility of Networked Protest* (New Haven, Yale University Press, 2017).

blocks of AI, are associated with being mathematical, logical and hence objective and impartial. Such claims to neutrality are dangerous since they deem the automated decisions of algorithms and AI unquestionable: 'conclusions described as having been generated by an algorithm wear a powerful legitimacy, much the way statistical data bolster scientific claims'.[18] To demonstrate this point, a study on an algorithmic risk-assessment software called COMPAS, used by US courts to determine the likelihood of reoffending, found that the accuracy rate of the software was the same as the accuracy rate of predictions made by 400 random volunteers recruited on the internet.[19] One of the researchers of this study, Hany Farid, explains:

> Imagine you're a judge and your court has purchased this software; the people behind it say they have big data and algorithms, and their software says the defendant is high-risk. Now imagine I said: Hey, I asked 20 random people online if this person will recidivate and they said yes. How would you weigh those two pieces of data? I bet you'd weigh them differently.[20]

Furthermore, the association of algorithms with neutrality and legitimacy can create a distance between the decisions made by the system and the institutional or corporate owner of such a system, creating 'an entity that is somehow separate, like the assembly line inside the factory, that can be praised as efficient or blamed for mistakes'.[21] Going back to the case of the Palestinian construction worker, his arbitrary detention and interrogation were pinned on the error of a system that occasionally makes mistakes but learns to do better. Such a claim to neutrality completely ignores the fact that technologies are not created or deployed in a social vacuum. They are designed by humans or social institutions to provide solutions for social problems or to achieve desired outcomes, which makes them a social construct.[22]

The existing literature points out that AI technologies can be inherently biased, and therefore make biased decisions, recycle or exacerbate racial, ethnic and gender bias and discrimination. Dispelling the myth of neutrality around algorithmic decision-making as well as AI systems is critical to understanding how such systems can facilitate and exacerbate further biases, discrimination and violations of human rights. For example, an AI-powered image-recognition software was found to produce sexist results as it associated images of cooking and

---

[18] B Peters, *Digital Keywords: A Vocabulary of Information Society and Culture* (Princeton, NJ, Princeton University Press, 2016).

[19] J Dressel and F Hany, 'The Accuracy, Fairness, and Limits of Predicting Recidivism' (2018) 4 *Science Advances*.

[20] E Yong, 'A Popular Algorithm Is No Better at Predicting Crimes Than Random People' (*The Atlantic*, 17 January 2018) available at www.theatlantic.com/technology/archive/2018/01/equivant-compas-algorithm/550646.

[21] Peters, *Digital Keywords*.

[22] Tufekci, *Twitter and Tear Gas*.

cleaning with women while images of sports were associated with men.[23] Google also came under fire after its AI-powered photos app classified an image of two black people as gorillas.[24] The bias delivered by AI systems is a result of two factors: first, the design of the system itself, and second, the quality of data used to train and operate the system. To start with, the design process involves the designers making social and political judgments. In designing an algorithmic model, human developers make decisions in defining the problem to be solved, the way it is operationalised, what the desired outcome should be, and which variables should accordingly be prioritised and optimised. When complex social situations and activities are translated into computational terms, there is human judgement involved in how values are assigned to data. For example, what criteria does Facebook's algorithmic model use to decide what is 'relevant' content to show on someone's newsfeed? Even when developers intentionally exclude values or parameters that could lead to bias, such as ethnicity, data proxies related to race, such as income, education or residence area, could still lead to biased results.[25]

The second factor that contributes to bias is the quality of data used to train and run these systems. The feedback loop in these systems will only reproduce whatever it is fed. This is particularly precarious when an AI system is fed 'dirty data', a term used to describe 'missing data, wrong data, and non-standard representations of the same data'.[26] Predictive policing systems, for example, are notorious for reproducing existing bias and discrimination especially against minorities and over-policed communities. A recent study by New York University that looked into the use of dirty data for predictive policing in 13 US jurisdictions found that some police departments used intentionally manipulated and falsified data, facilitated by corrupt, unlawful and racially discriminatory police practices in order to fulfil certain statistical quotas such as reducing crime rates for public relations and receiving more funding. The historical data used is 'a reflection of the department's practices and priorities rather than actual rates of crimes'.[27] There is also the issue of how data is collected; when there is no standardised collection process, it is left to the subjective discretion of the police officer to decide when and which crimes are recorded. Not all crimes are treated and recorded equally. For example, white-collar crimes as opposed to street crimes are under-investigated and overlooked in

---

[23] N Alang, 'Turns Out Algorithms Are Racist' (*The New Republic*, 31 August 2017) available at https://newrepublic.com/article/144644/turns-algorithms-racist.
[24] P Pachal, 'Google Photos Identified Two Black People As "Gorillas"' (*Mashable*, 2015) available at https://mashable.com/2015/07/01/google-photos-black-people-gorillas.
[25] Access Now, 'Human Rights in the Age of Artificial Intelligence'.
[26] W Kim et al, 'A Taxonomy of Dirty Data' (2003) 7 *Data Mining and Knowledge Discovery* 81.
[27] R Richardson, JM Schultz and K Crawford, 'Dirty Data, Bad Predictions: How Civil Rights Violations Impact Police Data, Predictive Policing Systems, and Justice' (2019) 94 *New York University Law Review Online* 15.

police data sets.[28] Furthermore, communities who have a history of being particularly targeted by the police are less likely to report crimes.[29]

The former United Nations Special Rapporteur for the promotion and protection of the right to freedom of opinion and expression, David Kaye, highlighted, in a report on the implications of AI technologies for human rights, the detrimental effects of such technologies on freedom of expression and opinion, and consequently on human autonomy, dignity, and self-determination. AI that is used to promote, demote and present content on social media platforms and search engines is very opaque and influences which information is displayed for users to see and consume. This non-transparent personalisation of content feeds to individual users reinforces existing world views and beliefs and prevents users from enjoying their right to develop personal opinions based on various information and opinions.[30]

AI technologies also threaten the right to privacy, a right that is fundamental to human dignity, as they prey on multitude upon multitude of personal data and may be able to infer further personal information from data sets such as age and sexual orientation even when the collected data is anonymised. In 2016, two German researchers were able to re-identify people from the anonymised browsing history datasets of more than 3 million German citizens.[31] Researchers from Imperial College London and Belgium's Université Catholique de Louvain have also recently shown that 99.98 per cent of Americans would be correctly re-identified in any anonymised dataset using 15 demographic attributes such as gender, class, race, occupation and marital status.[32]

III. Predictive Policing in Israel and Palestine

In late 2015, a wave of anger and violence broke out in Israel and the Occupied Palestinian territories amid the lack of a political horizon, the expansion of illegal Israeli settlements in the West Bank and East Jerusalem, and the systematic suppression and violation of Palestinians' fundamental rights. Tens of thousands of young Palestinians marched on the streets demanding an end to the decades-long Israeli military occupation of the West Bank, East Jerusalem and Gaza. The Israeli Defence Forces (IDF) responded to the demonstrations with lethal force. Israeli settlers also escalated their attacks on Palestinians and their property, in what is

---

[28] ibid.
[29] ibid.
[30] United Nations General Assembly, 'Report of the Special Rapporteur on the Promotion and Protection of the Right to Freedom of Opinion and Expression' (29 August 2018) UN Doc A/73/348.
[31] A Hern, '"Anonymous" Browsing Data Can Be Easily Exposed, Researchers Reveal' *The Guardian* (1 August 2017).
[32] L Rocher, JM Hendrickx and Y-A de Montjoye, 'Estimating the Success of Re-Identifications in Incomplete Datasets Using Generative Models' (2019) 10 *Nature Communications*.

known as 'price tag' attacks.[33] What marked this uprising, the so-called *Habba* or the Intifada of Individuals, was the surge of unprecedented 'lone-wolf' attacks by Palestinians teenagers who carried out attacks on Israelis on the streets, especially Israeli security forces, with a kitchen knife or any other sharp household object. Historically, armed resistance against the Israeli occupation was exclusive to the military wings of Palestinian political factions such as Fatah and Hamas. This time around, however, the attacks were not planned or coordinated by any Palestinian leadership or political faction, but were, rather, leaderless and sporadic.

Social media was at the forefront of this wave. Young Palestinian activists, living in geographically fragmented areas, used social media, particularly Facebook, to connect, organise peaceful protests, mobilise Palestinians at grassroots level and overcome the geographical fragmentation. Israeli politicians and media commentators, on the other hand, blamed social media for inciting young Palestinians to violence, a claim which disregards the consistent warnings for two years prior from Israeli defence officials and the Israeli intelligence that the situation on the ground was likely to explode in the absence of any political horizon for Palestinians.[34] In 2016, the Israeli Public Security Minister, Gilad Erdan, speaking on television, blamed Facebook and said that:

> some of the victims' blood is on Zuckerberg's hands. Facebook has turned into a monster. The younger generation in the Palestinian Authority runs its entire discourse of incitement and lies and finally goes out to commit murderous acts on Facebook's platform.[35]

As a result, the Israeli authorities started to exert pressure on social media companies to remove what they deemed to be inciting content published by Palestinian users on these platforms. A new 'Cyber Unit' was created under the General Attorney's office to collaborate with social media platforms in order to remove online content, and to restrict or block access to certain websites. The Israeli Government held a number of meetings with Facebook, YouTube and Google in order to discuss how inflammatory online material could be monitored and removed. The Israeli Minister for Justice, Ayelet Shaked, announced in September 2016 that Facebook had cooperated on 95 per cent of the government's requests to remove content it found 'inciteful'.[36] According to the Palestinian human rights organisation, Adalah, these requests put forward by the Israeli Government to remove users' online content, as well as the operation of the cyber unit, are considered illegal

---

[33] United Nations Office for the Coordination of Humanitarian Affairs, '2015: Interactive, Community-Level Infographics on Humanitarian Vulnerability – Settler Violence' available at www.ochaopt.org/page/2015-interactive-community-level-infographics-humanitarian-vulnerability-settler-violence.
[34] A Issacharoff, 'When All Else Fails, Blame Facebook' *The Times of Israel* (10 July 2016) available at https://blogs.timesofisrael.com/when-all-else-fails-blame-facebook.
[35] J Lis, 'Israeli Minister Slams Facebook: "Terror Victims' Blood Is on Zuckerberg's Hands"' *Haaretz* (3 July 2016).
[36] S Pulwer and E Vidal, 'Facebook Complying with 95% of Israeli Requests to Remove Inciting Content, Minister Says' *Haaretz* (12 September 2016).

and constitute a grave form of censorship as freedom of expression is criminalised based on an administrative decision rather than a court order.[37]

In addition to removing online content, Israeli military intelligence developed a predictive policing system that monitors and mines social media content and flags Palestinians considered likely to commit an attack in the near future. In July 2016, the IDF revealed in a number of press briefings how the system generally works. According to the Israeli newspaper *Haaretz*, the system collects and analyses data from social media and flags individuals who match a potential terrorist profile, then tracks their social media posts as well as the accounts of their friends and relatives. These terrorist profiles were built by Israeli intelligence officers based on a number of data points such as age, area of residence and other factors such as state of mental health. In one of those briefings, an Israeli intelligence officer said that psychologists were present during the interrogations of some of the attackers in order to observe and understand their motivation and general characteristics, information that could then be used to construct an archetype of Palestinian lone-wolf attackers. The system also looks for certain word cues such as the word 'Shaheed', which means martyr in Arabic, or 'Zionist', 'Gaza', or 'Al-Aqsa'. These words change and the algorithm is adjusted based on the current political trends and developments on the ground.[38] With this system, the Israeli authorities arrested and interrogated between 300 and 400 Palestinians for posts and comments they wrote or photos they shared on social media in the period from October 2015 to the end of 2018.

Similar to other predictive policing and surveillance technologies, these systems are opaque and their inner workings are considered confidential. The patterns of the arrests and charges, however, disclose the logic behind the operationalisation of such technology, that is, the immediate detention of any Palestinians, particularly young ones, where there might be a slight suspicion for crimes they have not committed yet on the assumption that they might commit one in the near future. 'Unlike terrorists who belong to Hamas or the Islamic Jihad, if you get to their house a week before the attack the kid doesn't know that he is a terrorist yet', explained one Israeli officer in July 2016 at an IDF briefing on this system.

In the absence of any form of legal protection for Palestinians, or in the presence of legal frameworks that deprive them of their rights, the use of predictive policing has facilitated and proliferated arrests and human rights abuses, particularly the right to privacy and right to freedom of expression and opinion. Palestinians who are residents or citizens of Israel or have a West Bank or Gaza ID are subject to different legal jurisdictions and are therefore granted or deprived of different legal rights. Palestinians who are citizens of Israel and are residents of Jerusalem are subject to Israeli civilian law, while Palestinians living in the West Bank and Gaza are subject

---

[37] Adalah – The Legal Center for Arab Minority Rights in Israel, 'Israel's "Cyber Unit" Operating Illegally to Censor Social Media Content' (14 September 2017) available at www.adalah.org/en/content/view/9228.

[38] R Eglash and L Morris, 'Israel Says Monitoring Social Media Has Cut Lone-Wolf Attacks. Palestinians Are Crying Foul' *Washington Post* (9 July 2018).

to Israeli military orders and military courts, which criminalise any form of political or cultural expression and activity that is deemed to 'threaten Israeli security or to adversely affect the maintenance of order and control of the territories'.[39] It is worth mentioning that military rule does not apply to Israeli settlers who live in the West Bank. These people are subject to Israeli civil and criminal law, rather than military law. Therefore, what happens to Palestinians after they are detained depends on what ID they carry and under which legal framework they are prosecuted. For example, in the West Bank and Gaza, the Israeli military court could prosecute any Palestinian on charges of incitement to violence

> who attempts, orally or otherwise, to influence public opinion in the Area in a manner which may harm public peace or public order, or … carries out an action expressing identification with a hostile organisation, with its actions or its objectives or sympathy for them, by flying a flag, displaying a symbol or slogan or playing an anthem or voicing a slogan, or any similar explicit action clearly expressing such identification or sympathy.[40]

The Israeli military courts have applied a broad legal definition of incitement with a great degree of flexibility. For instance, the court treats each social media post as a separate offence. The court can also take into consideration the number of friends the suspect has, and the number of likes, shares and comments on each post, to determine the severity of the sentence. Furthermore, the evidence is often not disclosed for 'security reasons'. Under military rule, Israel extensively and routinely uses administrative detention to detain Palestinians for an indefinite period of time on the basis of secret evidence, which cannot be accessed by the detainee or his/her lawyer, and without charge or trial.[41] Since the beginning of the Israeli occupation in 1967, thousands of Palestinians have been held in administrative detention from six months up to several years.[42]

Palestinians who are citizens of Israel, on the other hand, are subject to Israeli civil and criminal law. The legal definition of incitement there is equally broad and allows the Israeli court to tailor evidence as it sees fit. According to Article 144.D2 on Incitement to Violence or Terror of the Israeli Penal Code of 1977:

> If a person publishes a call to commit an act of violence or terror or praise, words of approval, encouragement, support or identification with an act of violence or terror (in this section: inciting publication) and if – because of the inciting publication's contents and the circumstances under which it was made public there is a real possibility that it will result in acts of violence or terror, then he is liable to five years imprisonment.

---

[39] Addameer, 'The Israeli Military Courts' (July 2017) available at www.addameer.org/israeli_military_judicial_system/military_courts.

[40] Articles 251 and 199 of chapter G of the order regarding Security Provisions (consolidated version) No 1651 of 2009, cited in Addameer, 'Arrests on Charges of "Incitement" on Social Media Platforms'.

[41] B'tselem, The Israeli Information Center for Human Rights in the Occupied Territories, 'Administrative Detention' (11 November 2017) available at www.btselem.org/administrative_detention.

[42] B'tselem, 'Statistics on Administrative Detention' (22 November 2020) available at www.btselem.org/administrative_detention/statistics.

Under these legal definitions, whether in Israel or the occupied territories, what Palestinians consider as an expression of their collective identity as an occupied people, of their resistance and criticism of the Israeli occupation and its oppressive policies, and as an exercise of their rights to freedom and self-determination, Israel regards as incitement to violence and terrorism and a threat to its national security. Words such as 'Shaheed' (martyr), 'Intifada' (uprising), 'Sumud' (steadfastness) or 'Muqawamah' (resistance), for instance, are part of the Palestinian national discourse and carry positive social, political and historical weight. However, as Israeli scholar Yonatan Mendel explains in his article on the politics of non-translation, the Israeli Government, media, and scholars have deliberately and systematically emptied these words from their contextual meaning and filled them instead with demonised and negative values tied to glorifying death, violence and terrorism.[43]

The prosecution of Dareen Tatour, a Palestinian poet with Israeli citizenship, is a case in point. She was arrested in October 2015 after she published on her Facebook account a poem whose title translates as 'Resist, My People; Resist Them' with a video of Palestinian protestors throwing stones. Addameer, an organisation that supports Palestinian prisoners and human rights defenders, described how the Israeli interrogators and court misinterpreted Tatour's poem:

> Tatour was shown only the Arabic version of the poem despite the fact that the interrogators solely referenced a Hebrew translation during interrogation. Consequently, Tatour was interrogated on expressions and phrases she herself did not include in the poem. She viewed the Hebrew translation for the first time during the court sessions and stated that most of the expressions translated from Arabic to Hebrew were wrong and inaccurate; for instance, the word 'martyr' was translated to 'terrorist'. The main point of contention during interrogation and court sessions centred on adapting, clarifying, and tailoring the words and expressions in the poem. The poem spoke of the child martyrs Ali Dawabsheh and Mohmammad Abu Khdeir who were described as 'innocent martyrs'. However, they were referred to as 'terrorists' during interrogation and in court.[44]

As a result, Tatour was forcibly transferred to a settlement near Tel Aviv where she was placed under house arrest and banned from accessing the internet and receiving visitors. Eight months later, she was allowed to move back to her family but remained under house arrest. It was not until July 2018 that she was sentenced to five months in jail, but she was released two months later. Following Tatour's appeal, the Nazareth District Court reversed her conviction over the poem in May 2019 though it upheld her charges over two other Facebook posts.[45]

---

[43] Y Mendel, 'The Politics of Non-Translation: On Israeli Translations of Intifada, Shahid, Hudna and Islamic Movements' (2010) I *Cambridge Literary Review* 179.
[44] Addameer, 'Arrests on Charges of "Incitement" on Social Media Platforms'.
[45] 'Free Dareen' (2019) available at https://web.archive.org/web/20200110105834/https://freedareentatour.org/trial.

It is important to note that the monitoring of social media and the prosecutions on charges of incitement to violence only target Palestinians and do not apply to Israelis and what they post online. The Index of Racism and Incitement in Israeli Social Media, a survey published annually by the Palestinian digital rights organisation 7amleh, notes an increase in racist and inciting posts against Palestinians on Israeli social media networks. In 2020, there were 574,000 conversations containing violent speech towards Arabs, a 16 per cent increase on the previous year.[46] Yet there have been no prosecutions or measures taken by the Israeli Government to respond to the increasingly explicit calls for violence against Palestinians on social media.

Palestinians use social media platforms to share and comment on the daily realities and political developments under the Israeli military occupation. They use them to connect, organise, and mobilise non-violent protests and campaigns. As one Palestinian activist puts it: 'It's a way to achieve non-violent resistance.'[47] One of the earliest uses of social media by Palestinian youth to organise political campaigns was the 15 March movement. Inspired by the Arab Spring in 2011, a Facebook page called 'End the Division' called all Palestinians in the occupied territories and Palestinian refugees in Jordan, Syria and Lebanon to join in mass protests on 15 March and to unite and end the political division between the two rival political factions Fatah and Hamas. Similar calls for mass marches were made in 2011 by Palestinian youth on Facebook in commemoration of *Nakba Day*, which marks the displacement and dispossession of the Palestinian people from their land and the creation of the state of Israel. In response to the online call, thousands of Palestinians marched towards historical Palestine from Egypt, Jordan, Lebanon and Syria, making up the largest march by Palestinian refugees into Israel in history.[48] Palestinians continue to use social media for political purposes, with Facebook being the main platform with the highest percentage of Palestinian internet users.

Social media simultaneously provided a new sphere for Israel, a renowned exporter of state-of-the-art cybersecurity and surveillance technologies, to persecute Palestinians over their political views and activities online. The use of data-hungry technologies, such as predictive policing, combined with the absence of any ethical or legal boundaries to how far the intelligence apparatus can go in monitoring, collecting and extracting information about Palestinians, has elevated Israeli surveillance and social media policing to an industrial scale. Even before the use of predictive policing, the level of the state's intrusion into Palestinians'

---

[46] 7amleh, 'Index of Racism and Incitement in Israeli Social Networks for the year 2020' (2021) available at https://7amleh.org/2021/03/08/racism-and-incitement-index-2020-the-increase-in-racism-and-incitement-against-palestinians-and-arabs-during-the-pandemic.

[47] D Duncan, 'E-Palestine: Palestinian Youth Bring Their Politics Online' *Time* (29 October 2008).

[48] M Nabulsi, '"Hungry for Freedom" Palestine Youth Activism in the Era of Social Media' in L Herrera (ed), *Wired Citizenship: Youth Learning and Activism in the Middle East* (New York, Routledge, 2014).

privacy led 43 Israeli intelligence soldiers from the elite cyber military intelligence unit, Unit 8200, to protest in 2014 with an open letter to the Israeli Prime Minister Benjamin Netanyahu against 'the continued control of millions of people and in-depth inspection that's invasive to most areas of life'. The letter exposes how severely abusive it can be when deploying surveillance technologies in the context of military occupation, where the use of these technologies and the collection of data to feed AI systems, such as predictive policing, is not regulated or legally restricted:

> the Palestinian population is subject to military rule, completely exposed to espionage and to being tracked by Israeli intelligence. Contrary to Israeli citizens or citizens of other countries, there's no oversight on methods of intelligence or tracking and the use of intelligence information against the Palestinians, regardless [of whether] they are connected to violence or not.[49]

Contrary to the claim that monitoring Palestinians on social media reduced lone-wolf attacks by 80 per cent between 2015 and 2017,[50] the intelligence officers concluded that 'none of this allows for a normal life, fuelling more violence and putting an end to the conflict further away'.[51]

Such mass surveillance and intrusion into Palestinian private life is enabled by the fact that Israel occupies and controls the entire information and communications technology infrastructure.[52] While Palestinians have the right to build and operate their own independent information and communication system under the Oslo peace agreement signed in 1995, they have never been allowed to do so. Israel has placed severe restrictions on importing, installing and operating the required infrastructure throughout the Occupied Palestinian territories. It also controls the electromagnetic sphere and restricts Palestinian telecom operators' use of frequencies. Israel also restricts the number of permits issued to Palestinian operators to deploy, install and maintain infrastructure and equipment in Area C, which constitutes more than 60 per cent of the West Bank.

The level of mass surveillance and the ensuing rise of arrests of Palestinians over content they post and share on social media platforms have undoubtedly had a chilling effect on freedom of expression. When people feel watched, they tend to change their behaviour online and censor themselves, even in private communications.[53] The Israeli security apparatus has established, through its advanced technological capacities and the extent to which it monitors Palestinian

---

[49] E Levy, 'IDF Intelligence Soldiers Refuse to Serve: We Won't Work Against Innocent Palestinians' (*Ynet news*, 12 September 2014) available at www.ynetnews.com/articles/0,7340,L-4570256,00.html.
[50] Eglash and Morris, 'Israel Says Monitoring Social Media Has Cut Lone-Wolf Attacks'.
[51] E Levy, 'IDF Intelligence Soldiers Refuse to Serve'.
[52] N Arafeh and WF Abdullah, 'ICT: The Shackled Engine of Palestine's Development' (*Al-Shabaka – The Palestinian Policy Network*, 9 November 2015) available at https://al-shabaka.org/briefs/ict-the-shackled-engine-of-palestines-development.
[53] J Shaw, 'The Watchers: Assaults on Privacy in America' (January–February 2017) *Harvard Magazine* 56.

communities, a god-like, all-knowing, omnipresent status.[54] In 2016, for example, Israeli forces arrested a Palestinian man, Hiran Jaradat, in a night raid on his house in the West Bank. The Israeli army had shot and killed his brother, who had Down syndrome, two months earlier. 'When they showed me the picture of my brother Arif, they said to me, "Maybe you want to avenge your brother's death and carry out a terror attack?"' Jaradat went on to say: 'With respect to the use of Facebook, I will go back to posting things there – but I will be more careful about what I post. You can't really know if a certain picture is considered incitement or not.'[55] Jaradat is not alone. Two thirds of Palestinian youth who use the internet are afraid to share their political views online because of government surveillance.[56] Some stopped expressing their political views after someone from their social circle was interrogated or prosecuted. In addition to self-censorship, fear of surveillance has affected the Palestinian digital ecosystem and how young Palestinians decide which social media platform to use for political speech. For example, many refrain from using Facebook for being 'particularly risky' and opt for other platforms instead. One of the young men who participated in 7amleh's study on the chilling effect among Palestinian youth on social media said: 'I participate in Palestinian and international issues, but in my opinion, Instagram is the most secure site to express opinion, because I share directly from the source, and Facebook is more monitored which prevents me from using it.'[57] The study shows that fear extends from immediate repression to future harm and loss of education and employment opportunities. This is particularly significant among Palestinians who are citizens of Israel. As explained by one of the participants:

> a school teacher working in the Ministry of Education was fired because they expressed their opinion on social media. ... I see a major barrier imposed on us by the State [Israel] where I may think a lot before I publish my post, and there is no safety in expressions. ... I can think of 20 times, I know today that I share political things but if I apply for a job at the Ministry and they see the posts, I will not be at that place. ... I make some sacrifices so I can feel free in some places and I can lose many things in return, and I think this is an essential aspect that exists in each person's life.[58]

Since 2015, Palestinians have been campaigning against censorship by social media platforms' content moderation algorithms.[59] Facebook has come under fire on a number of occasions for ceding to Israeli pressure to censor and remove Palestinian content and suspend Palestinian accounts.[60] According to the office of

---

[54] H Tawil-Souri, 'Surveillance Sublime: The Security State in Jerusalem' (2016) 68 *Jerusalem Quarterly* 56.

[55] O Hirschauge and H Shezaf, 'How Israel Jails Palestinians Because They Fit the "Terrorist Profile"' *Haaretz* (31 May 2017).

[56] 7amleh, 'Silenced Networks'.

[57] ibid.

[58] ibid.

[59] B McKernan, 'Facebook "Deliberately Targeting" Palestinian Activists by Shutting their Accounts' *The Independent* (25 October 2016).

[60] M Fatafta and N Nashif, 'Surveillance of Palestinians and the Fight for Digital Rights' (*Al-Shabaka*, 23 October 2017) available at https://al-shabaka.org/briefs/surveillance-palestinians-fight-digital-rights.

the Israeli state attorney, the Israeli Government requests that Facebook remove an annual average of 12,000 posts, with an 85 per cent compliance rate.[61] In September 2016, Facebook shut down the accounts of four editors at the Palestinian Shehab News Agency and three journalists from Al Quds News Network. After online protests using the hashtags #FBCensorsPalestine and #FacebookCensorsPalestine, Facebook apologised for the suspension.[62] In February 2018, Palestinians again campaigned (#FBfightsPalestine) against Facebook's targeting Palestinian free speech through removal of content and suspension of Palestinian accounts. A Palestinian group that documents social media's biased content moderation and censorship, called Sada Social, noted in 2019 that Facebook had developed new content moderation algorithms that ban and remove expressions such as Hamas, Hizbollah, Jihad, and Al Qassam. The group noted that years old content with these expressions were being removed from the platforms.[63] Facebook's AI-powered content moderation system has been criticised for being inconsistent, non-transparent and therefore unaccountable, and results in disproportionately censoring already marginalised groups.[64] Despite Facebook and other tech companies' claims that AI can help in the strenuous human effort to moderate content online, AI-automated moderation fails to understand irony, sarcasm, local slang as well as the cultural, political and social nuances and context of published content, which results in discrimination and violations of the users' freedom of expression.

IV. Conclusion

Artificial intelligence has taken the centre stage of how new technologies are seeping into many areas of our everyday life. And even though it remains in its infancy, the potential to cause harm has already manifested in many applications of this technology. From healthcare, online content moderation, facial recognition, to the use of risk-assessment tools and predictive policing systems in law enforcement and criminal justice, the various applications of AI threaten to entrench existing racial and social biases and discrimination as well as to exploit personal data, violate the right to privacy and the right to freedom of expression to unprecedented levels. In criminal justice, predictive policing and risk-assessment tools raise many serious human rights concerns, while more and more governments justify developing and

---

[61] T Nassar, 'How Facebook Protects Israel' (*The Electronic Intifada*, 15 March 2018) available at https://electronicintifada.net/blogs/tamara-nassar/how-facebook-protects-israel.
[62] 'Facebook Apologizes for Suspending Palestinian Journalists' Pages' *The Times of Israel* (26 September 2016).
[63] 'New Facebook Violations Due to Palestinian Terminology' *Sada Social* (19 September 2019) available at http://sada.social/بيانات/انتهاكات-جديدة-لفيسبوك-بسبب-مصطلحات-ف.
[64] JC York and C McSherry, 'Content Moderation Is Broken. Let Us Count the Ways' (*Electronic Frontier Foundation*, 29 April 2019) available at www.eff.org/deeplinks/2019/04/content-moderation-broken-let-us-count-ways.

deploying such tools on the grounds of safeguarding national security and protecting public safety. Despite such claims, as demonstrated in the use of predictive policing by the Israeli authorities to monitor and target Palestinians, AI elevates the suppression of vulnerable and marginalised communities and the violations of their privacy and freedom of expression to a mass automated process that hides behind a veil of efficiency and statistical neutrality.

We cannot detach AI systems from the contexts in which they are deployed. The lack of any legal checks and balances, oversight, and accountability can lead to catastrophic results and aid mass oppression and discrimination. AI-powered technologies, such as facial recognition systems and predictive policing tools, have enabled governments to expand their surveillance to unprecedented levels. As in the case of Israel and Palestine, the harmful impact of AI-powered surveillance on free speech, privacy, and political participation is more acute when a marginalised community is routinely and disproportionately targeted by security forces.

And while the jury is still out on assessing the various impacts of AI as new technologies continue to emerge in different sectors, the use of international human rights law to examine AI systems is crucial to the ongoing debate, and can provide universal standards to a field that lacks clarity in definitions, forms, and standards. Big Tech firms such as Facebook, Amazon, Google, Microsoft, and IBM have partnered to introduce ethical frameworks for the AI industry.[65] Even though ethical guidelines are important, they are not sufficient. Human rights are universal, specific, and have clear mechanisms for accountability as opposed to ethics. In parallel, in 2018, a coalition of human rights organisations put together a declaration on protecting the rights to equality and non-discrimination in machine learning systems, named after the city where it was launched, the Toronto Declaration.[66] Such steps are critical, as AI has

> created new forms of oppression, and in many cases disproportionately affects the most powerless and vulnerable. The concept of human rights addresses power differentials and provides individuals, and the organisations that represent them, with the language and procedures to contest the actions of more powerful actors, such as states and corporations.[67]

Predictive policing in particular must be interrogated further and put under greater scrutiny, especially in relation to how data is collected and used. The automated decision-making of AI-powered systems, even if it were fully accurate, must not

---

[65] A Selyukh, 'Tech Giants Team Up to Tackle the Ethics of Artificial Intelligence' (*NPR*, 28 September 2016) available at www.npr.org/sections/alltechconsidered/2016/09/28/495812849/tech-giants-team-up-to-tackle-the-ethics-of-artificial-intelligence.

[66] 'The Toronto Declaration: Protecting the Rights to Equality and Non-Discrimination in Machine Learning Systems' (May 2018) available at torontodeclaration.org.

[67] C van Veen and C Cath, 'Artificial Intelligence: What's Human Rights Got to Do with It?' (*Data & Society: Points*, 14 May 2018) available at https://points.datasociety.net/artificial-intelligence-whats-human-rights-got-to-do-with-it-4622ec1566d5.

be used as a rubber stamp for unlawful practices which violate people's rights to a fair trial, to liberty and security, and to equality before the courts. Justice systems and law enforcement were built on the legal principle and the fundamental right of presumption of innocence, that individuals are innocent until proven guilty. The introduction of AI-powered predictive and assessment tools is challenging this principle, where the individuals flagged by these systems or scored as high-risk are guilty until proven innocent. The detention and prosecution of individuals based on an assumed future crime, made possible by intelligent computation, is a dangerous precedent despite the claims that such technologies are effective in deterring future violence.

6

The Facebook Oversight Board and the UN Guiding Principles on Business and Human Rights: A Missed Opportunity for Alignment?

STEFANIA DI STEFANO

I. Introduction

People around the world share over 2.5 billion pieces of content on Facebook every day.[1] The platform, with its 2.7 billion monthly active users (as of August 2020), is the biggest social network worldwide.[2] With its stated mission to 'give people the power to build community and bring the world closer together',[3] Facebook constitutes one of the most important means through which individuals exercise their right to freedom of expression. Most importantly, the platform not only represents a significant portion of the digital public sphere's architecture, but it is, through its content moderation policies, also one of the architects of the institutional design of this space.[4]

The internet and social media have, since their advent, been deemed to be facilitators for the promotion of human rights, with the right to freedom of expression being the driving force for the enjoyment of other individual human rights.[5]

---

[1] T Gillespie, *Custodians of the Internet: Platforms, Content Moderation, and the Hidden Decisions That Shape Social Media* (New Haven, Yale University Press, 2018) 114.

[2] 'Number of Monthly Active Facebook Users Worldwide as of 3rd Quarter 2020' (*Statista*, 24 November 2020) available at www.statista.com/statistics/264810/number-of-monthly-active-facebook-users-worldwide.

[3] 'Company Info' (*About Facebook*) available at https://about.fb.com/company-info.

[4] K Klonick, 'The New Governors: The People, Rules, and Processes Governing Online Speech' (2018) 131 *Harvard Law Review* 1598, 1601.

[5] UNHRC, 'Report of the Special Rapporteur on the Promotion and Protection of the Right to Freedom of Opinion and Expression' (2011) UN Doc A/HRC/17/27, 22.

However, the Cambridge Analytica scandal[6] seems to have set in motion a domino effect for technology companies – and for Facebook in particular – casting a shadow on what had been described as 'the liberating power of technology'.[7] The internet is now depicted as 'a place of darkness, danger, propaganda, misogyny, harassment, and incitement, which private actors are doing little to ameliorate'.[8] Social media companies, rather than being enablers of freedom of expression, have been exposed as actively managing and shaping 'the norms and boundaries for how users may form and express opinions, encounter information, debate, disagree, mobilize, and retain a sense of privacy'.[9] Since in the eyes of public opinion they have mutated from promise to peril for freedom of expression, and since calls for regulation, transparency and accountability have become more and more prominent, social media platforms are now under close scrutiny for their policies, product design, and content decisions.

In response to this backlash, on 15 November 2018, Mark Zuckerberg, Founder and CEO of Facebook, revealed the company's intention to create an independent body tasked with reviewing users' appeals on the company's content decisions, and whose deliberations would be transparent and binding on Facebook itself.[10] Since then, Facebook has published a 'Draft Charter'[11] for the 'Oversight Board', organised global consultations,[12] released the 'Charter'[13] and 'Bylaws'[14] that govern this adjudicatory body, and announced its first members.[15] The Oversight Board started accepting cases in October 2020,[16] and publicly announced the first cases

---

[6] C Cadwalladr and E Graham-Harrison, 'Revealed: 50 Million Facebook Profiles Harvested for Cambridge Analytica in Major Data Breach' *The Guardian* (17 March 2018).

[7] EV Morozov, *The Net Delusion: The Dark Side of Internet Freedom* (New York, Public Affairs, 2011) xiii.

[8] D Kaye, 'Foreword' in RF Jørgensen (ed), *Human Rights in the Age of Platforms* (Cambridge, MA, MIT Press, 2019) xii.

[9] RF Jørgensen, 'Introduction' in RF Jørgensen (ed), *Human Rights in the Age of Platforms* (Cambridge, MA, MIT Press, 2019) xvii.

[10] M Zuckerberg, 'A Blueprint for Content Governance and Enforcement' (*Facebook*, 15 November 2018) www.facebook.com/notes/mark-zuckerberg/a-blueprint-for-content-governance-and-enforcement/10156443129621634.

[11] N Clegg, 'Charting a Course for an Oversight Board for Content Decisions' (*Facebook Newsroom*, 28 January 2019) available at https://about.fb.com/news/2019/01/oversight-board.

[12] B Harris, 'Getting Input on an Oversight Board' (*Facebook Newsroom*, 1 April 2019) available at https://about.fb.com/news/2019/04/input-on-an-oversight-board; B Harris, 'Global Feedback and Input on the Facebook Oversight Board for Content Decisions' (*Facebook Newsroom*, 27 June 2019) available at https://about.fb.com/news/2019/06/global-feedback-on-oversight-board.

[13] B Harris, 'Establishing Structure and Governance for an Independent Oversight Board' (*Facebook Newsroom*, 17 September 2019) available at https://newsroom.fb.com/news/2019/09/oversight-board-structure.

[14] B Harris, 'Preparing the Way Forward for Facebook's Oversight Board' (*Facebook Newsroom*, 28 January 2020) available at https://about.fb.com/news/2020/01/facebooks-oversight-board.

[15] N Clegg, 'Welcoming the Oversight Board' (*Facebook Newsroom*, 6 May 2020) available at https://about.fb.com/news/2020/05/welcoming-the-oversight-board.

[16] 'The Oversight Board Is Now Accepting Cases' (October 2020) available at https://oversightboard.com/news/833880990682078-the-oversight-board-is-now-accepting-cases.

on which it was deliberating in December 2020.[17] This initiative has been described as a 'pivotal moment in the history of online speech governance':[18] indeed, the creation of such an adjudicatory body should not only contribute to shaping the contours of online freedom of expression but also address users' grievances.

If the Oversight Board has the potential to increase the legitimacy of the company's content moderation policies and decisions, it could also prove instrumental in Facebook meeting its human rights responsibilities under the United Nations Guiding Principles on Business and Human Rights (Guiding Principles).[19] This chapter assesses whether the Oversight Board, as it has been designed, is aligned with the Guiding Principles, especially with respect to access to remedy for Facebook's users. It is divided into three parts: after presenting content moderation as the central commodity of social media platforms, the first part describes how Facebook governs speech within its platform; the second part explains how the Oversight Board has been designed and how it will adjudicate content disputes; and the third part analyses the Oversight Board through the lens of the Guiding Principles in order to determine the extent to which Facebook, with the creation of this adjudicatory body, meets its human rights responsibilities within this framework.

II. Private Norms Governing the Digital Public Sphere

A. Content Moderation: The 'Essence' of Platforms

> [M]oderation, far from being occasional or ancillary, is in fact an essential, constant, and definitional part of what platforms do. Moderation is the essence of platforms. It is the commodity they offer. It is their central value proposition.[20]

Until recently, social media platforms strove to present themselves as neutral. From their perspective, content moderation was a function to be disavowed. As Facebook's stated mission is 'to give people a voice', the company has often underscored its self-definition as a *technology company* as opposed to a *media company*,[21]

---

[17] 'Announcing the Oversight Board's First Cases and Appointment of Trustees' (December 2020) available at https://oversightboard.com/news/719406882003532-announcing-the-oversight-board-s-first-cases-and-appointment-of-trustees.

[18] E Douek, 'Facebook's "Oversight Board:" Move Fast with Stable Infrastructure and Humility' (2019) 21 *North Carolina Journal of Law and Technology* 1, 4.

[19] UN OHCHR, 'Guiding Principles on Business and Human Rights: Implementing the United Nations "Protect, Respect and Remedy" Framework' (2011) UN Doc HR/PUB/11/04.

[20] T Gillespie, 'Platforms Are Not Intermediaries' (2018) 2 *Georgetown Law Technology Review* 198, 201.

[21] On the strategic relevance of this distinction for platforms as well as its inaccuracy, see PM Napoli and R Caplan, 'When Media Companies Insist They're Not Media Companies and Why It Matters for Communications Policy' (2016) available at https://papers.ssrn.com/abstract=2750148.

and supports its argument by invoking the fact that the platform does not produce any content but merely facilitates the distribution of user-generated content.[22] Indeed, as noted by Gorwa, even the consistent use of the term 'platform' has been deployed in a strategic manner: by presenting themselves as facilitators for distributing user-generated content without creating any of it, social media platforms strengthen their claim that they should not be held liable for it.[23] However, content moderation constitutes, according to Gillespie, the 'essence of platforms'.[24] Gillespie defines platforms as online sites or services that:

a) host, organize, and circulate users' shared content or social interactions for them,
b) without having produced or commissioned (the bulk of) that content,
c) built on an infrastructure, beneath that circulation of information, for processing data for customer service, advertising and profit,
[…]
d) platforms do, and must, *moderate the content and activity of users, using some logistics of detection, review and enforcement.* (emphasis added)[25]

Content moderation processes allow social media platforms to perform two main functions: as *content gatekeepers*, they can determine what categories of content are allowed or prohibited on these spaces; as *content organisers*, they can employ algorithmic personalisation to individualise their users' experiences.[26] Content moderation is the central commodity of social media platforms because, by crafting 'the "right" feed for each user, the "right" social exchanges, and the "right" kind of community', it allows them to 'promote engagement, increase ad revenue, […] facilitate data collection' and ultimately shape user participation into a deliverable experience.[27] This objective is achieved through the combination of three different tools: moderation (through removal, filtering, and suspension), recommendations (through news feeds, trending lists, and personalised suggestions), and curation (through featured content and front-page offerings).[28] As a result, although it may seem that internet users can publish freely and instantly online, the content they share and see is actually actively moderated by the platform on which it appears:[29] far from being an ancillary property of these platforms, content moderation represents their 'essential, constitutional, definitional' characteristic.[30]

---

[22] G Segreti, 'Facebook CEO Says Group Will Not Become a Media Company' (*Reuters*, 30 August 2016).
[23] R Gorwa, 'What Is Platform Governance?' (2019) 22 *Information, Communication & Society* 854, 856.
[24] Gillespie, 'Platforms Are Not Intermediaries' 201.
[25] Gillespie, *Custodians of the Internet* 18–21.
[26] B Sander, 'Freedom of Expression in the Age of Online Platforms: Operationalising a Human Rights-Based Approach to Content Moderation' (2020) 43 *Fordham International Law Journal* 939, 2.
[27] Gillespie, 'Platforms Are Not Intermediaries' 202.
[28] ibid.
[29] Klonick, 'The New Governors' 1601.
[30] Gillespie, *Custodians of the Internet* 21.

Given that social media platforms are a crucial presence within the digital public sphere and that they have developed rules for moderating expression within it, they have now become 'both the architecture for publishing new speech and the architects of the institutional design that governs it':[31] as such, content moderation constitutes a structural pillar of this institutional design. Nonetheless, as underscored by Klonick, 'despite the essential nature of these platforms to modern free speech and democratic culture, very little is known about *how or why* these companies curate user content' (emphasis added).[32] Focusing on why social media companies have decided to integrate values in their platforms and which values have been integrated,[33] she identifies three elements that have influenced content moderation systems: (1) an underlying belief in free speech norms; (2) a sense of corporate responsibility; and (3) the necessity of meeting users' norm expectations.[34] The first element is deeply rooted in the US concept of free speech: by examining the history of Facebook, YouTube and Twitter, Klonick illustrates that a common thread they share is that 'American lawyers trained and acculturated in US free speech norms and First Amendment law oversaw the development of the company content-moderation policy'.[35] The second element embodies the philosophies and values of the companies, usually considered in conjunction with or even aligned with US free speech norms, and then balanced against competing principles of user safety, harm to users, public relations concerns and the revenue implications of certain content for advertisers.[36] The result of such a balancing exercise usually favours free speech, while simultaneously calling for a further development of 'new approaches or rules that would still satisfy concerned users and encourage them to connect and interact on the platform'.[37] Finally, the third element, which can also be considered the primary reason for which companies decide to moderate speech and take down some categories of content, is the threat that such material would pose to potential profits based on advertising revenue: by meeting users' expectations, they ensure that those users spend more time on their platforms,[38] hence capitalising their attention to make profits.[39] A fourth element has been identified by Sander, who argues that regulation, understood as either mandatory regulatory measures or more informal regulatory pressures, also influences content moderation policies.[40] Content moderation policies are thus not developed in a vacuum, but are the result of a combination of different

---

[31] Klonick, 'The New Governors' 1603–04.
[32] ibid 1601.
[33] ibid 1617.
[34] ibid 1618.
[35] ibid 1621.
[36] ibid 1625–26.
[37] ibid 1626.
[38] ibid 1627.
[39] See S Zuboff, *The Age of Surveillance Capitalism: The Fight for a Human Future at the New Frontier of Power* (New York, Public Affairs, 2019).
[40] Sander, 'Freedom of Expression' 950–52.

factors, which in turn shape and define what is permissible or not in these spaces. As highlighted by Sander, this process of content moderation is not static, but is constantly shaped by the interaction of a plurality of actors which include the platforms' policy teams, user communities, governments, advertisers, mass media organisations, civil society groups and academic experts.[41]

B. How Facebook Governs Speech

> Facebook is not a government but it is a platform for voices around the world. We moderate content shared by billions of people and we do so in a way that gives free expression maximum possible range.[42]

The Community Standards are the rules that govern expression within Facebook's platform. Defined as 'a guide for what is and isn't allowed on Facebook',[43] they are rooted in Facebook's commitment to expression but are also based on other, competing values (authenticity, safety, privacy and dignity), against which freedom of expression is balanced when making a decision on content. Intended to be comprehensive, they are divided into six parts (Violence and criminal behaviour, Safety, Objectionable content, Integrity and authenticity, Respecting intellectual property, and Content-related requests and decisions); each of these parts is then further divided into specific categories of prohibited content that elucidate the policy rationale behind the associated rules. When introduced in 2011, the Community Standards regulated ten categories of speech;[44] since then, they have evolved and have been expanded[45] to 26 categories.

The need to create rules for governing speech within the platform emerged concomitantly with the expansion of the platform, which had evolved from a website launched for Harvard University students in 2004 to a platform with a global reach.[46] As described by Klonick, it was only from 2008 that Facebook started to think about and develop content moderation rules and policies: up until that moment, content moderation was essentially based on a one-page document of internal rules applied globally to all Facebook users, and the main tenet

---

[41] ibid 7.
[42] R Allan, 'Hard Questions: Where Do We Draw the Line on Free Expression?' (*Facebook Newsroom*, 9 August 2018) available at https://newsroom.fb.com/news/2018/08/hard-questions-free-expression.
[43] 'Community Standards' available at www.facebook.com/communitystandards.
[44] These categories were: Threats; Promoting Self-Harm; Bullying and Harassment; Hate Speech; Graphic Violence; Sex and Nudity; Theft, Vandalism, or Fraud; Identity and Privacy; Intellectual Property; Phishing and Spam. 'Facebook Community Standards' (22 February 2011) available at https://web.archive.org/web/20110222002817/https://www.facebook.com/communitystandards.
[45] For the role played by outside influence, see K Klonick, 'The Facebook Oversight Board: Creating an Independent Institution to Adjudicate Online Free Expression' (2020) 129 *The Yale Law Journal* 2418, 2439–47.
[46] See D Kirkpatrick, *The Facebook Effect: The Inside Story of the Company That Is Connecting the World* (New York, Simon & Schuster, 2011); Klonick, 'The Facebook Oversight Board' 2436.

of the moderation process was 'if it makes you feel bad in your gut, then go ahead and take it down'.[47] The first draft of the extensive internal standards for content moderation was created in 2009: the 15,000-word document translated the logic of the initial one-pager into objective rules with the ultimate goal of achieving a consistent and uniform approach towards content moderation.[48] As a subsequent step, the company published, for the first time, the Community Standards, a set of public rules for users.[49] The previous extensive standards were then transformed into operational *internal* rules for content moderators, the 'Abuse Standards', with the aim of clarifying the enforcement of the Community Standards.[50]

As we have seen, even though Facebook actively moderates content posted by its users, it has been eager to present itself as a neutral platform 'giving people a voice'. As noted by Suzor, this lack of transparency over content moderation is symptomatic of the paradox social media platforms seek to sustain: they 'want the absolute power to curate, moderate, and control their networks while not wanting to look like they're moderating'.[51] Accordingly, the original *public* Community Standards were short and vague, whereas the *private* 'Abuse Standards', which clarified how the Community Standards were to be enforced, were initially a 15,000-word document. It was not until April 2018 that a detailed version of the Community Standards was shared with the public.[52] While this move could be understood as revealing a progressive shift from an internal discourse of 'disavowal' to one rooted in a language of 'responsibility', the language of 'disavowal' has not been completely abandoned, albeit it is now framed as the idea that social media companies should not become 'arbiters of truth'.[53]

The policy on nudity can serve to illustrate the extent to which the Community Standards have evolved over time. This policy has been repeatedly criticised as a consequence of the very restrictive standards being applied.[54] A prominent example of this was the removal of the photo 'The Terror of War', depicting a naked nine-year-old girl running away from a napalm attack during the Vietnam War.[55] In 2011, the policy on nudity read: 'We have a strict "no nudity or pornography" policy. Any content that is inappropriately sexual will be removed. Before posting

---

[47] Klonick, 'The New Governors' 1631.
[48] ibid 1633–34.
[49] ibid 1634.
[50] ibid; Klonick, 'The Facebook Oversight Board' 2436.
[51] NP Suzor, *Lawless: The Secret Rules That Govern Our Digital Lives* (Cambridge, Cambridge University Press, 2019) 16.
[52] M Bickert, 'Publishing Our Internal Enforcement Guidelines and Expanding Our Appeals Process' (*Facebook Newsroom*, 24 April 2018) available at https://about.fb.com/news/2018/04/comprehensive-community-standards. The detailed Community Standards have since undergone frequent updates that are available at www.facebook.com/communitystandards/recentupdates.
[53] T McCarthy, 'Zuckerberg Says Facebook Won't Be "Arbiters of Truth" after Trump Threat' *The Guardian* (28 May 2020).
[54] See, eg, M Sweney, 'Mums Furious as Facebook Removes Breastfeeding Photos' *The Guardian* (30 December 2008).
[55] S Levin, JC Wong and L Harding, 'Facebook Backs down from "Napalm Girl" Censorship and Reinstates Photo' *The Guardian* (9 September 2016).

questionable content, be mindful of the consequences for you and your environment.'[56] In contrast, today the standard on nudity provides a list of content under the heading 'Do not post'; the list is preceded by a policy rationale clearly stating that the company's approach to nudity has become more nuanced over time and that it now allows nudity in certain circumstances, 'including as a form of protest, to raise awareness about a cause or for educational or medical reasons'.[57] The policy rationale also states that the company allows photographs of paintings, sculptures and other art that depicts nude figures. Incidentally, this specific issue was brought before a French court in 2011: a teacher sued Facebook on the grounds that it had violated his right to freedom of expression by deactivating his Facebook account after he posted a picture of the painting 'L'Origine du Monde' by Gustave Courbet.[58] Although the policy on nudity has since been expanded, the issue is still far from uncontroversial: one of the first six cases on which the Oversight Board has deliberated concerns the take-down of eight photographs depicting female breasts for the purposes of raising awareness of signs and symptoms of breast cancer.[59]

If the publication of a detailed version of the Community Standards was a welcome step towards transparency, it also revealed to what extent the platform was controlling speech and how much power it was exercising. As highlighted by Klonick:

> The public's discovery that a small cadre of people headquartered in Silicon Valley were the sole creators and deciders on rules governing this vital global platform for online speech and that, although rules existed, their operation lacked core ideas of procedure and process added fuel to long-standing comparisons between Facebook and a feudal state, kingdom, or dictatorship.[60]

Importantly, what emerged from the publication of the Community Standards is the fact that 'Facebook's governance of users' speech is an unchecked system' and 'the kind of arbitrary power that, unrestrained, can trample individual rights'.[61]

In 2018 Facebook also announced the establishment of an appeal system, administered by the company itself, allowing users to appeal its content decisions. Under this system, users can request a second review of content removed for violating the Community Standards.[62] If the appeals process can provide a weak

---

[56] 'Facebook Community Standards'.
[57] 'Community Standards'.
[58] CA Paris, February 2016, 15/08624; Tribunal de grande instance de Paris, 4e chambre 2e section, 15 March 2018, 12/12401.
[59] 'Announcing the Oversight Board's First Cases'. The platform concerned is Instagram, which is a Facebook service; 'Oversight Board Overturns Original Facebook Decision: Case 2020-004-IG-UA' (January 2021) available at www.oversightboard.com/news/682162975787757-oversight-board-overturns-original-facebook-decision-case-2020-004-ig-ua.
[60] Klonick, 'The Facebook Oversight Board' 2438.
[61] ibid 2476.
[62] 'Community Standards Enforcement' available at https://transparency.facebook.com/community-standards-enforcement/guide.

form of redress to Facebook's affected users, it has not helped boost the legitimacy of the company's content moderation policies. Since the appeals mechanism is still administered by Facebook and is still based on its Community Standards, which are perceived as an exercise of arbitrary power over freedom of expression, and as the company has continued to be condemned for its content decisions and governance, 'people are concerned that [Facebook] ha[s] so much control over how they communicate on [its] services'.[63]

The decision to establish an independent Oversight Board to review users' appeals of content moderation decisions comes in response to this problem. Douek has pointed out that this choice also entails some strategic benefits for Facebook: not only would the Oversight Board confer an aura of legitimacy to content moderation decisions and allow the company to potentially guide future governmental regulation, but, critically, it could outsource responsibility,[64] since '[a] more independent body set up by regulators would further distance Facebook from these [content moderation] choices'.[65]

III. An Independent Mechanism to Adjudicate Content Disputes

The purpose of the Facebook Oversight Board is 'to promote free expression by making principled, independent decisions regarding content on Facebook and Instagram and by issuing recommendations on the relevant Facebook company content policy'.[66] The decision to create such a mechanism is rooted in the idea that Facebook, as a company, should not be in charge of 'making so many decisions about speech and online safety on its own', and the Oversight Board is meant to 'help Facebook answer some of the most difficult questions around freedom of expression online: what to take down, what to leave up and why'.[67]

After Zuckerberg announced the idea of establishing this new institution, a draft Charter was released and a series of global workshops to discuss the board's design was announced.[68] The Global Consultation process started in February 2019 in Singapore, and the company held a total of 28 workshops and smaller

---

[63] Facebook, 'Mark Zuckerberg Stands for Voice and Free Expression' (*Facebook Newsroom*, 17 October 2019) available at https://about.fb.com/news/2019/10/mark-zuckerberg-stands-for-voice-and-free-expression. In this speech, Zuckerberg also stated 'Frankly, I don't think we should be making so many important decisions about speech on our own either'.
[64] Douek, 'Facebook's "Oversight Board"' 17–26.
[65] ibid 24.
[66] 'Ensuring respect for free expression, through independent judgment' available at https://oversightboard.com. For a detailed account of how the Facebook Oversight Board was created, see Klonick, 'The Facebook Oversight Board', on which this overview is based.
[67] 'Ensuring respect for free expression, through independent judgment'.
[68] Clegg, 'Charting a Course'.

roundtables, involving more than 2,000 stakeholders, to collect feedback on the Draft Charter as well as input on what the Oversight Board should do. Facebook has published the results of this process in a report and appendix,[69] which have been used in the development of the Charter that governs this body, released in September 2019.[70] In January 2020, the company also released a set of Bylaws establishing the rules for the board's operations and procedures.[71]

The Charter defines the collective powers of the Facebook Oversight Board:

> The board will have the following expressly defined authorities for content properly brought to the board for review:
> 1. Request that Facebook provide information reasonably required for board deliberations in a timely and transparent manner;
> 2. *Interpret Facebook's Community Standards* and other relevant policies (collectively referred to as 'content policies') *in light of Facebook's articulated values*;
> 3. Instruct Facebook to allow or remove content;
> 4. Instruct Facebook to uphold or reverse a designation that led to an enforcement outcome;
> 5. Issue prompt, written explanations of the board's decisions.
>
> In addition, the board can provide policy guidance, specific to a case decision or upon Facebook's request, on Facebook's content policies. The board will have no authority or powers beyond those expressly defined by this charter. (emphasis added)[72]

The role of the Facebook Oversight Board is twofold: to review content decisions that have been appealed by users; and to provide policy guidance to Facebook, either as a consequence of a case decision, or following a specific request from the company. The scope of the Oversight Board is further elucidated in article 2, paragraph 1, which establishes that users, provided they have exhausted internal appeals, can submit a request for content review to the board.[73] Facebook can also submit requests for review,[74] including requests for expedited reviews 'when content could result in urgent real-world consequences' and which will be accepted and reviewed by the board as quickly as possible.[75] Furthermore, Facebook can submit questions related to the treatment of content beyond the takedown/keep up paradigm.[76]

The board will not review every user request, but has discretion to choose cases having 'the greatest potential to guide future decisions and policies'.[77] Article 2, paragraph 1 establishes that 'a request for review can be submitted to the board

---

[69] Harris, 'Global Feedback and Input on the Facebook Oversight Board'.
[70] 'Oversight Board Charter' (2019). The Charter and the Bylaws constitute, together with an LLC Agreement, Trust Agreement, Member Contracts, Code of Conduct, and Facebook-LLC Service Provider Contract, the governing documents of the Oversight Board.
[71] Harris, 'Preparing the Way Forward for Facebook's Oversight Board'.
[72] 'Oversight Board Charter' art 1, para 4.
[73] ibid, art, 2 para 1.
[74] ibid.
[75] ibid, art, 3 para 7.2.
[76] ibid, art, 2 para 1.
[77] ibid.

by either the original poster of the content or a person who previously submitted the content for review',[78] implying that the board would be able to review content that has been *removed* but also content that has been *kept up* on the platform.[79] However, this jurisdiction appeared to be reduced by article 2, paragraph 1 in conjunction with article 3, paragraph 1.1.1 of the Bylaws, which establishes that the board can review 'content that has been *removed* for violations of content policies […] and currently within the scope for Facebook's appeals process'.[80] As envisaged by article 3, paragraph 1.1.2 of the Bylaws, this jurisdiction has been expanded to include 'content reviewed by Facebook for potential violations of content policies […] and ultimately allowed to remain on the platform' but not 'content rated "false" by third-party fact-checkers, on the basis that the content was not eligible for fact-checking'.[81] Currently 'content' only encompasses 'individual pieces of content, such as specific posts, photos, videos, and comments'[82] posted on Facebook or Instagram; though the board might eventually be able to review 'content such as groups, pages, profiles, and events, as well as advertisements',[83] these are, for the time being, excluded from its scope. Lastly, content that has received a valid report of illegality or whose reinstatement on the platform as a consequence of a board decision could lead to criminal liability for or adverse governmental action against Facebook is not eligible for the board to review.[84]

Article 2 paragraph 2 sets out the basis of the decision-making process:

> Facebook has a set of values that guide its content policies and decisions. The board will review content enforcement decisions and determine whether they were consistent with Facebook's content policies and values.
>
> For each decision, *any prior board decisions will have precedential value* and should be viewed as highly persuasive when the facts, applicable policies, or other factors are substantially similar.
>
> When reviewing decisions, the board will pay particular attention to the impact of removing content in light of human rights norms protecting free expression. (Emphasis added)[85]

The Bylaws indicate that the timeframe for a decision of the board and its implementation by Facebook is of maximum 90 days, starting from the date the case is selected for review.[86]

---

[78] ibid.
[79] Klonick, 'The Facebook Oversight Board' 2463.
[80] 'Oversight Board Bylaws' (2020) art 3, para 1.1.1.
[81] ibid, art 3, para 1.1.2; 'The Oversight Board Is Accepting User Appeals to Remove Content from Facebook and Instagram' (April 2021), available at www.oversightboard.com/news/267806285017646-the-oversight-board-is-accepting-user-appeals-to-remove-content-from-facebook-and-instagram.
[82] ibid, art 3, para 1.1.1.
[83] ibid, art 3, para 1.1.2.
[84] ibid, art 2, para 1.2.2.
[85] 'Oversight Board Charter' art 2, para 2.
[86] 'Oversight Board Bylaws' art 1, para 3.1; 'Announcing the Board's Next Cases and Changes to our Bylaws' (March 2021) available at www.oversightboard.com/news/288225579415246-announcing-the-board-s-next-cases-and-changes-to-our-bylaws.

Users who wish to submit a case are able to do so through the board's website,[87] provided they have exhausted the internal appeal processes.[88] The user is provided with an individualised identification number and is able to track the progress of the case, as well as view the final decision if the case if selected.[89] When submitting a case for review, users have the opportunity to explain why they believe Facebook has made an incorrect decision with respect to the content in question, why they believe their case should be selected for review by the board, why they originally posted the content, and how Facebook's decision could also impact others.[90] At the time of submission, users will also have the possibility to contextualise their case further by identifying the language(s) involved as well as the country or countries to which the content relates.[91] Lastly, users will also be able to express whether they consent to identifying details being included in the eventual final decision issued by the board.[92]

A case selection committee establishes a set of criteria for prioritising and selecting cases that will then be reviewed by the board;[93] the administration (the board's full-time staff) assists this committee by preparing case submissions based on those criteria.[94] Cases are then selected for review by a majority vote by the case selection committee and the concerned user and Facebook are promptly notified.[95] At this point, the case is assigned to a board panel of five anonymous members, of whom four are assigned randomly from the board as a whole and one is assigned randomly from the members who are from the region that the content primarily concerns.[96] The panellists have the possibility to request and receive additional information prior to case deliberation either from Facebook,[97] from outside experts on the subject (including academics, linguists, researchers on specific issues) and/or from advocacy and public interest organisations.[98] A case file is prepared for the panellists to review, containing (1) a statement by the person who submitted the case; (2) a case history (provided by Facebook); (3) a policy rationale (also provided by Facebook); (4) clarifying information (from Facebook) if the board so requires; (5) additional external information, if required by any member of the panel.[99] The panel then deliberates on the case privately, and all members must participate and vote, as abstentions are not allowed.[100] Once the

---

[87] ibid, art 3, para 1.2.
[88] ibid, art 3, para 1.1.
[89] ibid, art 3, para 1.2.1.
[90] ibid.
[91] ibid.
[92] ibid.
[93] ibid.
[94] ibid, art 1, para 3.1.1.
[95] ibid, art 1, para 3.1.2.
[96] ibid, art 1, para 3.1.3.
[97] ibid, art 1, para 3.1.3.
[98] ibid, art 1, para 3.1.4. The board has established a public comment process that allows interested parties to submit contributions. See 'Announcing the Oversight Board's First Cases'.
[99] ibid, art 1, para 3.1.5.
[100] ibid, art 1, para 3.1.6.

panel has deliberated, a draft decision is prepared that includes: (1) a determination of the content; (2) the rationale for the decision; (3) at their discretion, a policy advisory statement.[101] The decision can also include concurring or dissenting opinions from any member of the panel.[102] The draft decision is then reviewed by the board as a whole, and any member of the board can raise questions or provide comments.[103] The case can also be sent for another review, for which another panel will be convened.[104] Once a decision is approved, it will be publicly shared: the administration will approve its publication on the board's website,[105] notify the concerned user and Facebook, and translate the decision into the board's official languages.[106]

With respect to the implementation of the decisions taken by the board, article 4 of the Charter specifies that these are binding on Facebook and the company will implement them promptly, unless implementation would result in a violation of the law.[107] As soon as a final decision is issued by the board, Facebook will have seven days to implement it, and the company will also notify the user of the action(s) taken.[108] If Facebook identifies an identical piece of content in an analogous context to that on which the board has already deliberated, the company will consider whether it is possible to apply that same decision to that content.[109]

If the decisions of the board are binding on Facebook, policy guidance (which can be requested by Facebook) or policy opinions (that might be issued with a decision) are merely advisory: Facebook will, in this context, analyse 'the operational procedures required to implement the guidance, considering it in the formal policy development process of Facebook, and transparently communicating about actions taken as a result'.[110]

Article 5 of the Charter outlines the governance structure of the Oversight Board and the relationship between the Oversight Board's LLC, the Trust and Facebook.[111] The Oversight Board is administered by the Oversight Board LLC, a legal entity established by the Oversight Board Trust. The Oversight Board Trust carries out its purpose through the LLC.[112] The duties of the trustees include to 'formally appoint and, if necessary, remove members for breaches of the board's code of conduct [and] review and approve the board's operating budget, including

---

[101] ibid, art 1, para 3.1.7.
[102] ibid, art 1, para 3.1.7.
[103] ibid, art 1, para 3.1.8.
[104] ibid.
[105] ibid, art 1, para 3.1.9.
[106] ibid, art 1, para 3.2. As per art 1, para 4.3, whereas the board's working language is English, the board's website and the appeals submission portal are available in 18 languages.
[107] 'Oversight Board Charter' art 4.
[108] 'Oversight Board Bylaws' art 3, para 1.2.4.
[109] 'Oversight Board Charter' art 4.
[110] ibid.
[111] ibid, art 5.
[112] ibid, Introduction.

member compensation, administration and other needs'.[113] The creation of the trust finds its rationale in the need for the board to be financially independent from Facebook: if the compensation of board members came directly from Facebook, the company whose policies and decisions the board is tasked with reviewing, a strong conflict of interest would emerge.[114] The Oversight Board Trust Agreement[115] creates the trust which, through this agreement, accepts the 'Initial Trust Estate' from Facebook,[116] a sum of US$130 million which should cover operational costs and allow the board to operate for at least six years.[117] This gift is irrevocable.[118] The board, besides receiving funding from the trust, will also recommend members for appointment by the trust.

The board will consist of no fewer that eleven members and, fully staffed, is 'likely' to consist of 40 members.[119] The Charter establishes that members of the board must 'exhibit a broad range of knowledge, competencies, diversity, and expertise'.[120] They must also have

> demonstrated experience at deliberating thoughtfully and as an open-minded contributor on a team; be skilled at making and explaining decisions based on a set of policies or standards; and have familiarity with matters relating to digital content and governance, including free expression, civic discourse, safety, privacy and technology.[121]

In order to ensure geographic balance, membership of the Oversight Board should comprise the following regions: US and Canada; Latin America and the Caribbean; Europe; Sub-Saharan Africa; Middle East and North Africa; Central and South Asia; and Asia Pacific and Oceania.[122] Each member will serve for a term of three years, for a maximum of three terms.[123] Members can be removed by the trustees 'for violations of the code of conduct, but they may not [be] remove[d] due to content decisions they have made'.[124]

For the initial formation of the board, Facebook selected a group of four co-chairs, who then assumed the responsibility of interviewing and approving the candidates for the other board seats.[125] In the future, 'a committee of the board will select candidates to serve as board members based on a review of the candidates'

---

[113] 'Oversight Board Bylaws' art 4, para 2.
[114] Klonick, 'The Facebook Oversight Board' 2486.
[115] Facebook, 'Oversight Board Trust Agreement' (2019).
[116] Facebook, 'Oversight Board Trust Agreement' s 1.2.
[117] 'An Update on Building a Global Oversight Board' (*Facebook Newsroom*, 12 December 2019) available at https://about.fb.com/news/2019/12/oversight-board-update.
[118] Facebook, 'Oversight Board Trust Agreement' s 1.4.
[119] 'Oversight Board Charter' art 1. The Bylaws also indicate the 'ideal' size of the Board being of 40 people. 'Oversight Board Bylaws' art 1, para 1.4.
[120] 'Oversight Board Charter' art 1, para 2.
[121] ibid.
[122] 'Oversight Board Bylaws' art 1 para 1.4.1.
[123] ibid, art 1, para 1.4.2.
[124] 'Oversight Board Charter' art 1, para 8.
[125] 'Announcing the First Members of the Oversight Board' (May 2020) available at www.oversight-board.com/news/327923075055291-announcing-the-first-members-of-the-oversight-board.

qualifications and a screen for disqualifications'.¹²⁶ At this point, Facebook's role should be limited to proposing candidates to the board. Candidates can also be proposed by the public.¹²⁷

IV. The Facebook Oversight Board and the UN Guiding Principles on Business and Human Rights

Access to remedy constitutes a foundational pillar of the UN Guiding Principles on Business and Human Rights.¹²⁸ Facebook, as a company, has a responsibility, under the Guiding Principles, to respect human rights and also to provide access to effective remedy when individuals are adversely impacted by its activities.

The Facebook Oversight Board, as an adjudicatory mechanism for content decisions, could constitute a route for addressing Facebook's users' grievances and provide them with access to remedy. But to what extent is the design of the Facebook Oversight Board consistent with the Guiding Principles' framework? The rest of this chapter will investigate if and how the Oversight Board helps Facebook meet its human rights responsibilities.

A. The UN Guiding Principles on Business and Human Rights and the Corporate Responsibility to Respect and Remedy

The UN Guiding Principles on Business and Human Rights are a set of soft law standards for states and business enterprises adopted by the UN Human Rights Council in 2011. They do not create new international legal obligations, and they do not limit or undermine the obligations that states have undertaken under international law. Rather, they are to be understood

> as a coherent whole and should be read, individually and collectively, in terms of their objective of enhancing standards and practices with regard to business and human rights so as to achieve tangible results for affected individuals and communities, and thereby also contributing to a socially sustainable globalization.¹²⁹

Notably, the Guiding Principles do not define business enterprises as duty-bearers of international human rights law obligations, but they affirm that they have a *responsibility to respect human rights* according to which 'businesses should look

---

¹²⁶ 'Oversight Board Charter' art 1 para 8.
¹²⁷ ibid.
¹²⁸ UN OHCHR, 'Guiding Principles on Business and Human Rights: Implementing the United Nations "Protect, Respect and Remedy" Framework' (2011) UN Doc HR/PUB/11/04.
¹²⁹ ibid, p 1.

to currently internationally recognised rights for an authoritative enumeration, not of human rights *laws* that apply to them, but of human *rights* they should respect'.[130] This *responsibility to respect* is based on a near-universal recognition of a social norm (social expectations) that corporations have a responsibility to respect human rights.[131] The standards set out in the Guiding Principles rest on three pillars:

1. The state duty to protect against human rights abuses by third parties, including businesses, through appropriate policies, regulation, and adjudication.
2. An independent corporate responsibility to respect human rights, which means to avoid infringing on the rights of others and address adverse impacts with which companies are involved.
3. The need for greater access by victims to effective remedy, both judicial and non-judicial.[132]

These three pillars are rooted, respectively, on three general principles: states have existing obligations to respect, protect and fulfil human rights and fundamental freedoms; business enterprises, when fulfilling their role of specialised organs of society performing specialised functions, are required to comply with all applicable laws and to respect human rights; and rights and obligations have to be matched to appropriate and effective remedies when breached.[133]

The second pillar of the Guiding Principles outlines the standards that businesses should implement in order to meet their responsibility to respect human rights.

Guiding Principle 11, the first foundational principle of Pillar 2, affirms that '[b]usiness enterprises should respect human rights. This means that they should avoid infringing on the human rights of others and should address adverse human rights impacts with which they are involved'.[134] The responsibility to respect human rights is defined as a global standard of expected conduct:[135] this responsibility stands notwithstanding where business enterprises operate, 'independently of States' abilities and/or willingness to fulfil their own human rights obligations', and 'over and above compliance with national laws and regulations protecting human rights'.[136]

---

[130] JG Ruggie, 'The Social Construction of the UN Guiding Principles on Business & Human Rights', HKS Faculty Research Working Paper Series RWP17-030 (2017) 14 available at www.hks.harvard.edu/publications/social-construction-un-guiding-principles-business-human-rights.

[131] Ruggie, 'The Social Construction' 13–14: 'The corporate responsibility to respect human rights enjoys a near-universal recognition as a social norm in what I have elsewhere termed "the global public domain"'; 'We know that the corporate responsibility to respect human rights is a transnational social norm because the relevant actors acknowledge it as such, including businesses themselves in their corporate responsibility commitments'.

[132] JG Ruggie, 'Global Governance and "New Governance Theory": Lessons from Business and Human Rights' (2014) 20 *Global Governance: A Review of Multilateralism and International Organizations* 5, 7.

[133] UN OHCHR, 'Guiding Principles on Business and Human Rights' 1.

[134] UN OHCHR, 'Guiding Principles on Business and Human Rights' 13.

[135] See Ruggie, 'The Social Construction' 13–14.

[136] UN OHCHR, 'Guiding Principles on Business and Human Rights' 13.

Under Guiding Principle 12, the list of internationally recognised rights that should be respected by businesses includes, *at a minimum*, the rights listed in the International Bill of Human Rights (the Universal Declaration of Human Rights, International Covenant on Civil and Political Rights, herein ICCPR, and the International Covenant on Economic, Social and Cultural Rights), as well as the principles concerning fundamental rights set out in the International Labour Organisation's Declaration on Fundamental Principles and Rights at Work.[137] These instruments constitute 'the benchmarks against which other social actors assess the human rights impacts of business enterprises'.[138] However, it must be underscored that, in practice, some human rights may be subject to greater risk of violation according to particular industries or contexts, and these rights must therefore be paid particular attention and focus.[139]

In order to respect human rights, business enterprises are required to 'avoid causing or contributing to adverse human rights impacts through their own activities, and address such impacts when they occur' and 'seek to prevent or mitigate adverse human rights impacts that are directly linked to their operations, products or services by their business relationships, even if they have not contributed to those impacts'.[140]

While the corporate responsibility to respect human rights applies to all enterprises notwithstanding their size, sector, operational context, ownership and structure, the Guiding Principles recognise that 'the scale and complexity of the means through which enterprises meet that responsibility may vary according to these factors and with the severity of the enterprise's adverse human rights impacts'.[141] The rationale for this 'proportionality test' is grounded in the fact that small and medium-size enterprises might have less capacity and might also employ more informal processes and management structures in order to meet the requirements for complying with their human rights responsibility.[142] However, this latter category might still be responsible for adverse human rights impacts, and the corresponding measures required to address such concerns have to be taken regardless of their size.[143]

Among the policies and processes that a business enterprise should have in place in order to meet its responsibility to respect human rights, Guiding Principle 15 includes 'processes that enable the remediation of any adverse human rights impacts they cause or to which they contribute'.[144] The third pillar of the Guiding Principles focuses precisely on access to effective remedy for business-related human rights abuses. Under the Guiding Principles, access to effective remedy is

---

[137] ibid.
[138] ibid 14.
[139] ibid.
[140] ibid.
[141] ibid 15.
[142] ibid.
[143] ibid.
[144] ibid 15–16.

not limited to state-based judicial mechanisms, but also encompasses state-based non-judicial grievance mechanisms and non-state-based grievance mechanisms. This latter category includes company-based grievance mechanisms as well as mechanisms administered by an industry association or a multi-stakeholder group.[145] The establishment of an operational-level grievance mechanism would allow business enterprises to both support the identification of adverse human rights impacts within the framework of the enterprise's due diligence process, thus allowing the company to identify systemic problems and consequently adapt their practices, and to address grievances and remediate adverse impacts early and directly, potentially avoiding an escalation of said grievances.[146] It must be pointed out that a complaint or grievance does not need to amount to an alleged human rights abuse in order to be raised: the aim of the process would be to identify legitimate concerns which could, if not identified and addressed, escalate into major issues and human rights abuses.[147] For a non-judicial mechanism to be effective, it should be: (1) legitimate; (2) accessible; (3) predictable; (4) equitable; (5) transparent; (6) rights-compatible; and (7) a source of continuous learning.[148] Additionally, operational-level mechanisms should also be based on engagement and dialogue, as consulting with relevant stakeholders and intended users would ensure that the mechanism's design and performance meet their needs.[149] Whereas mechanisms should aim at resolving grievances through dialogue, in instances where adjudication is needed, the enterprise should make sure that these decisions are provided by a legitimate, independent third-party mechanism.[150]

B. A Missed Opportunity for Alignment?

The Oversight Board is a bold experiment that could have a meaningful impact on the governance of online speech. Indeed, its establishment makes Facebook 'a proactive player in the design of the future of Internet governance'.[151] An independent and binding review of content decisions taken by Facebook has the potential to increase Facebook's legitimacy with respect to such decisions while also mitigating the perception that the company exercises arbitrary power over freedom of expression online. As pointed out by certain commentators, the Oversight Board constitutes 'the largest, most powerful operational grievance mechanism established by any company'.[152]

---

[145] ibid 31.
[146] ibid 32.
[147] ibid.
[148] ibid 33–34.
[149] ibid 34.
[150] ibid 35.
[151] Douek, 'Facebook's "Oversight Board"' 24.
[152] G Casanova Carlos Lopez and S Zafiri, 'Some Questions Regarding Facebook's Oversight Board and Remediation of Human Rights Impacts (Part I)' (*Opinio Juris*, 3 March 2020).

As noted elsewhere, the design of this operational grievance mechanism presents some features that appear to be consistent with the standards outlined in the Guiding Principles, such as the conduct of global consultations and the creation of the trust to enhance the independence of the board from the company.[153] As we have seen, the Oversight Board is empowered to review content decisions that have been appealed by users and to provide policy recommendations to Facebook. These two objectives are in line with the purposes of an operational grievance mechanism identified in the Guiding Principles, namely the support of the identification of adverse human rights impacts with the aim of adapting business practices to human rights standards, and the remediation of users' grievances.

Although representing a noteworthy turn towards international human rights law in the company's discourse,[154] the design of the Oversight Board presents some features which are not fully aligned with the standards outlined in the Guiding Principles. The most glaring departure from the Guiding Principles is evident in both the collective powers bestowed on the board and the basis for decision-making. As we have seen, the board is empowered to *interpret Facebook's Community Standards* and to review content enforcement decisions in order to determine *whether they were consistent with Facebook's content policies and values*. The board is therefore not empowered to directly apply international human rights standards, and this constitutes a foundational issue for the proper functioning of the adjudicatory mechanism if it were to be aligned with the Guiding Principles.

As already mentioned, Facebook's values are deeply rooted in US values, and in particular US free speech values, and not international human rights standards.[155] The lack of content moderation policies firmly grounded in human rights standards has been deemed to 'have created unstable, unpredictable and unsafe environments for users and intensified government scrutiny'.[156] As highlighted by David Kaye, former UN Special Rapporteur on the promotion and protection of the right to freedom of opinion and expression, a *human rights by default* approach to content moderation policies would not only ensure that 'content-related actions will be guided by the same standards of legality, necessity and legitimacy that bind State regulation of expression',[157] but also offer 'a globally recognized framework

---

[153] D Kaye, 'Research Report by the Mandate of the Special Rapporteur on the Promotion and Protection of the Right to Freedom of Opinion and Expression, with the Support of the International Justice Clinic at the University of California, Irvine School of Law' (2020) available at www.ohchr.org/Documents/Issues/Opinion/ResearchPaper2020.pdf, 13–14.

[154] S Parmar, 'Facebook's Oversight Board: A Meaningful Turn Towards International Human Rights Standards?' (*Just Security*, 20 May 2020).

[155] This notion was reiterated by Zuckerberg in his speech given at Georgetown University on 17 October 2019: 'I'm proud that our values at Facebook are inspired by the American tradition, which is more supportive of free expression than anywhere else', Facebook, 'Mark Zuckerberg Stands for Voice and Free Expression'.

[156] UNHRC, 'Report of the Special Rapporteur on the Promotion and Protection of the Right to Freedom of Opinion and Expression' (2018) UN Doc A/HRC/38/35, 41.

[157] UNHRC, 'Report of the Special Rapporteur' 45.

for designing those tools and a common vocabulary for explaining their nature, purpose and application to users and States'.[158] While Facebook has stated that the company 'look[s] for guidance in documents like Article 19 of the International Covenant on Civil and Political Rights',[159] and that it looks at international human rights standards when making decisions about allowing content on their platform that would otherwise go against their Community Standards,[160] the board is not empowered to directly apply international human rights law. Instead, the board is merely required to 'pay particular attention' to human rights norms protecting free speech. This feeble approach to human rights law is also confirmed in the Introduction section of the Oversight Board Charter, which recognises freedom of expression as a fundamental right but does not guarantee it to Facebook's users: instead, it is a right to be balanced against Facebook's values. As noted by Klonick, '[t]hough this is a strong statement of company commitment to the *principle* of free expression, it too is not a *promise of rights* to users'.[161] While Guiding Principle 12 recognises that some human rights might be subject to greater risk in certain industries and specific contexts, it also states that the responsibility to respect human rights refers to the entire spectrum of internationally recognised human rights. Freedom of expression is indeed a human right to which social media companies, as an industry, should pay particular attention and focus, but it is not the only right that should be afforded protection and/or that is subject to greater risk.[162] As human rights are indivisible, interdependent and interrelated,[163] an approach that favours the protection of one specific human right over others is particularly problematic.

The fact that the board is not empowered to directly apply human rights also undermines the effectiveness of the operational grievance mechanism: when not even the protection of freedom of expression is clearly guaranteed by the governing instruments of the board, it might prove difficult to ensure that the mechanism's outcomes are rights-compatible (as provided by Guiding Principle 31) by simply 'paying attention' to human rights norms that protect free speech.[164] It is also unclear what would ultimately fall within such category: if a restrictive interpretative approach would confine 'human rights norms that protect free speech' to provisions that exclusively refer to the right to freedom of expression (such as article 19 ICCPR), it is important to acknowledge that other human rights provisions,

---

[158] ibid 43.
[159] R Allan, 'Hard Questions'.
[160] 'Community Standards'.
[161] Klonick, 'The Facebook Oversight Board' 2478.
[162] See D Allison-Hope, M Lee and J Lovatt, 'Human Rights Review: Facebook Oversight Board' (2019) available at www.bsr.org/reports/BSR_Facebook_Oversight_Board.pdf. The authors identify a wide range of relevant human rights harms (beyond just freedom of expression) that may result from content decisions and that should be identified by Facebook and the Oversight Board.
[163] World Conference on Human Rights, 'Vienna Declaration and Programme of Action' (1993) UN Doc A/CONF.157/23 Part I, para 5.
[164] Similar conclusions were reached in Kaye, 'Research Report by the Mandate of the Special Rapporteur on the Promotion and Protection of the Right to Freedom of Opinion and Expression'.

such as the right to freedom of religion, have a significant bearing on the right to freedom of expression itself. Similarly, human rights treaties other than the ICCPR, such as the International Convention on the Elimination of All Forms of Racial Discrimination, could also be instrumental in addressing crucial content moderation issues. An expansive interpretation of 'human rights norms that protect free speech' could therefore prove to be an important entry point to broaden the range of rights that are afforded protection, at least insofar as these rights are relevant for addressing content moderation disputes. Following the first decisions, the board seems to have taken an expansive approach in what has been labelled as the 'game of interpretation',[165] although it remains to be seen what would happen if the analysis under international human rights law conflicted with the Community Standards.

The lack of content decisions directly rooted in human rights law significantly weakens the Oversight Board's alignment with the Guiding Principles at its very foundations and can have significant repercussions with respect to both the legitimacy and transparency of the mechanism. The Community Standards and values, which are the benchmarks against which content is assessed by the board, are unilaterally created by Facebook and are outside the board's scope of control and amendment power.[166] Facebook is therefore in charge of determining the benchmark against which its decisions are assessed. If Facebook were to change its Community Standards and values, the board would be bound to apply the new rules. Rule-making transparency is also an issue that has been raised frequently in the context of content moderation; in particular, the former UN Special Rapporteur on freedom of opinion and expression has underscored that, given that companies often introduce amendments to their products and rules without conducting human rights due diligence or evaluating their impact, they should 'at least seek comment on their impact assessments from interested users and experts, in settings that guarantee the confidentiality of such assessments if necessary' and 'also clearly communicate to the public the rules and processes that produced them'.[167] By improving the legitimacy and transparency of its content moderation policies, Facebook could also strengthen the legitimacy and transparency of the Oversight Board.

Another key area of concern is the scope of the board's jurisdiction. Grievances that the board can address are quite limited: the board is empowered to review individual pieces of content (specific posts, photos, videos and comments) which have been or should be removed for violating content policies and which are currently

---

[165] A Bianchi, 'The Game of Interpretation in International Law: The Players, The Cards, and Why the Game Is Worth the Candle' in A Bianchi, D Peat and M Windsor (eds), *Interpretation in International Law* (Oxford, Oxford University Press, 2015).

[166] In contrast, the board has a role in the amendment process of the Charter. See art 6, para 1: 'This charter may only be amended with the approval of a majority of the individual trustees and with the agreement of Facebook and a majority of the board.'

[167] UNHRC, 'Report of the Special Rapporteur' 55.

within the scope for Facebook's appeal processes. It must be reiterated that content that has received a report of illegality or whose reinstatement would either violate criminal law or result in 'adverse governmental action' against Facebook in the national jurisdiction(s) concerned is outside the board's scope of review. As noted by Parmar, the exclusion of this type of content 'means that the board cannot consider cases that human rights activists care most deeply about: state censorship of content, particularly political speech, in flagrant violation of international human rights standards on freedom of expression'.[168] Furthermore, this bestows significant power on national governments: as underscored by Douek, 'a government can prevent the [Facebook Oversight Board] from giving an opinion on a matter if it makes a particular type of content illegal'.[169] As mentioned, however, the responsibility to respect human rights exists 'independently of States' abilities and/or willingness to fulfil their own human rights obligations', and 'over and above compliance with national laws and regulations protecting human rights'.[170] The Guiding Principles require that business enterprises address all adverse human rights impacts, but the board is empowered to merely 'pay attention' to human rights standards protecting freedom of expression specifically and within a limited range of cases in which adverse impacts on freedom of expression arise. Such a limited scope severely restricts Facebook's users' right to remedy.

At this stage, a clarification is to be made with respect to the responsibility to address *all adverse human rights impacts*. The board will not be able to hear every case brought by users, and it would be realistically impossible to do so: as explained by Klonick, given that in the second and third quarter of 2019 30.8 million pieces of content remained down even after appeal, this number of cases would translate into 1,700 cases per day that would be eligible for the board's review.[171] A pre-selection of cases, as envisaged by the board, which prioritises cases that present the most severe human rights harms, could therefore fall within the proportionality test envisioned by the Guiding Principles, whereby factors such as sector and operational context can be taken into account. In this sense, *all adverse human rights impacts* should not be read as 'every individual case in which human rights are adversely impacted', but would have to encompass, *at a minimum*, 'all cases that exemplify all potential adverse human rights impacts', and in this context the case selection criteria established by the board will play a pivotal role. Broadening the board's scope of review is thus necessary to meet the Guiding Principles' standards. Moreover, granted that such an approach should operate in conjunction with the idea that an operational grievance mechanism should be a source of continuous learning, this interplay could in fact be beneficial for preventing future grievances and harm. The Oversight Board is indeed also empowered to issue advisory policy

---

[168] Parmar, 'Facebook's Oversight Board'.
[169] Douek, 'Facebook's "Oversight Board"' 38.
[170] UN OHCHR, 'Guiding Principles on Business and Human Rights' 13.
[171] Klonick, 'The Facebook Oversight Board' 2490.

guidance to Facebook: while not bound to implement these recommendations, the company has nonetheless committed to 'analyzing the operational procedures required to implement the guidance, considering it in the formal policy development process of Facebook, and transparently communicating about actions taken as a result'.[172]

As far as remedies available to users are concerned, reinstatement of content seems to be the only available option. Given that the timeframe for a case decision to be adjudicated is 90 days, such a remedy might not be sufficient. As emphasised by Kaye:

> reinstatement of content would be an insufficient response if removal resulted in specific harm – such as reputational, physical, moral or financial – to the person posting. Similarly, account suspensions or content removals during public protest or debate could have significant impact on political rights and yet lack any company remedy.[173]

Lastly, with respect to the mechanism's accessibility and equity, we have seen that Facebook's users will have the opportunity to submit to the board the reasons for which they believe Facebook has made an incorrect decision on the incriminated content. The Guiding Principles specify that the aggrieved parties should be provided with adequate assistance if facing barriers to access, and should have reasonable access to sources of information, advice and expertise[174] in order to engage with the mechanism in a fair, informed and respectful manner. To bring a variety of perspectives into the decision-making process, the board has established a 'public comment process' open to third parties who wish to contribute by sharing relevant research and expertise.[175]

V. Conclusion

The establishment of the Oversight Board constitutes a promising effort to address important questions raised by content moderation. However, the current level of alignment with the Guiding Principles is unsatisfactory if the company is to positively fulfil its human rights responsibilities.

The current design of the board and the watered-down approach to international human rights law embedded in its governing documents raise legitimate questions about the genuineness of Facebook's commitment to the cause. As pointed out by certain commentators, since implementing a human-rights based

---

[172] 'Oversight Board Charter' art 4.
[173] UNHRC, 'Report of the Special Rapporteur' 38; see also Kaye, 'Research Report by the Mandate of the Special Rapporteur on the Promotion and Protection of the Right to Freedom of Opinion and Expression'.
[174] UN OHCHR, 'Guiding Principles on Business and Human Rights' 33.
[175] 'Announcing the Board's Next Cases and Changes to our Bylaws'.

approach to content moderation is not an easy task, there is an inevitable risk 'that online platforms may try to co-opt the vocabulary of human rights to legitimize minor reforms at the expense of undertaking more structural or systemic changes to their moderation processes'.[176] As things currently stand, a 'toothless' board[177] merely strengthens such a claim and reinforces the idea that '[t]he new Facebook review board will have no influence over anything that really matters in the world'.[178]

For the mechanism to be truly effective in a global operational context, the company's commitment to international human rights law needs to be stronger and, as a consequence, steps should be taken for the Oversight Board to be more aligned with the standards set out in the Guiding Principles. In particular, the board should be empowered to directly apply human rights standards in their content decisions. Although the range of human rights standards that inform the board's decision-making process has been broadened through an expansive interpretative approach, amending the Community Standards, the benchmarks against which decisions are taken, remains a prerogative of Facebook. A strong commitment to human rights in the company's Community Standards would therefore already represent an important step forward, even though it would not be a sufficient step on its own. For the board to prove an effective model for channels of redress, it would also be necessary to expand the board's scope of review, in order to address the full spectrum of instances in which users' grievances arise. An expansion of available remedies to users should also be envisaged.

A commitment to international human rights law should not merely serve as a rhetorical tool, but it necessarily needs to be coupled with effective implementation and access to effective remedy. By further aligning the mechanism with the Guiding Principles, the Oversight Board could not only be instrumental for Facebook to meet its human rights responsibilities but could also ensure greater access to remedy to the platform's global users when their rights are adversely impacted.

---

[176] Sander, 'Freedom of Expression' 1005. A similar argument has been made by E Douek, 'The Limits of International Law in Content Moderation' (*Social Science Research Network*, 2020).

[177] J Constine, 'Toothless: Facebook Proposes a Weak Oversight Board' (*TechCrunch*, 28 January 2020).

[178] S Vaidhyanathan, 'Facebook and the Folly of Self-Regulation' (*Wired*, 9 May 2020).

7
Privacy in the Workplace: A Human Rights Due Diligence Approach

ISABEL EBERT AND ISABELLE WILDHABER

I. Introduction

The workplace traditionally used to be a clearly defined physical place in which employees spent a considerable portion of their working day and has been acknowledged as a central place in which people form social relationships.[1] Despite the many opportunities for remote working provided by digitisation in a range of sectors, until the disruption of the Covid-19 pandemic, most employers required their staff to be physically present in the workplace. Parallel to this recent move towards remote work, business has developed an appetite for data-driven monitoring of work done on-site, from home and remotely. Workplace monitoring measures promise increased efficiency as well as more objective decision making when managing people.[2]

The analytical techniques applied rely on a phenomenon witnessed across a range of sectors, the datafication of the workplace:[3] vast amounts of data are available due to increasing data flows stemming from human activity, such as 'self-tracking' from mobile phone use as well as online browsing and purchasing histories.[4] Combined with the growing processing power of computers, analytical techniques are becoming cheaper and more widespread.[5] The datafication

---

[1] See, eg, European Court of Human Rights, *Niemitz v Germany*, no 13710/8816 (16 December 1992) 29.
[2] P Phan, M Wright and S-H Lee, 'Of Robots, Artificial Intelligence, and Work' (2017) 31 *Academy of Management Perspectives* 253.
[3] U Gasser and VA Almeida, 'A Layered Model for AI Governance' (2017) 21 *IEEE Internet Computing* 58.
[4] G Neff and D Nafus, *Self-Tracking* (Cambridge, MA, MIT Press, 2016).
[5] JA Kroll et al, 'Accountable Algorithms' (2016) 165 *University of Pennsylvania Law Review Online* 633.

extends to aspects of social life well beyond the workplace that previously were not quantified, such as people's movements or the frequency of communications between selected people.[6] Yet, while insights from people management analytics – analytics used to manage people – might deliver promising results to human resource managers, the change in management practices may also disrupt social patterns of interaction at work.[7] Managing people with data-driven technologies and increasingly applying algorithm-based decisions has the potential to challenge the traditional understandings of hierarchy, leadership and responsibility.[8]

Accelerated by the spread of Covid-19, people management analytics are not limited to the actual physical workplace. When people work from home, many monitoring practices permeate far into their private space. Consequently, it is only natural that a major concern with regard to automated decision-making,[9] such as in data-driven people management, relates to the right to privacy, in combination with structural issues for connected human rights. The concept of privacy protects the right to respect for private life, family life, home and correspondence.[10] Big Data analytics in human resource management can heavily impact employee privacy and lead to privacy harms and violations. The right to privacy underpins and is closely connected to other fundamental rights, at work and beyond, such as freedom of association and freedom of expression.[11]

In the first part of this chapter, we explore the ways in which privacy is put at risk when companies decide to use workplace monitoring facilitated by emerging technology, and we argue that this decision may result in opaque governance structures and that privacy protection will often be reliant on design-based protection and the data literacy of supervisors. Further, the first part of this chapter highlights how the low bargaining power of employees and workers weakens their ability to challenge the use of certain tools. Subsequently, we emphasise the tech-specific nature of risks arising from a combinatory logic of monitoring tools. Finally, we draw attention to the heightened risks for marginalised groups, people of colour and women from datafied workplace monitoring. In the second part of this chapter, we propose an approach drawing on Business and Human Rights and the UN Guiding Principles on Business and Human Rights to address the systemic challenges for privacy when workers and employees are confronted with vast tech-based monitoring techniques. Our human rights due diligence

---

[6] K Cukier and V Mayer-Schoenberger, 'The Rise of Big Data: How It's Changing the Way We Think About the World' (2013) 92 *Foreign Affairs* 27.
[7] KC Kellogg, MA Valentine and A Christin, 'Algorithms at Work: The New Contested Terrain of Control' (2020) 14 *Academy of Management Annals* 366; J Prassl, *Humans as a Service: The Promise and Perils of Work in the Gig Economy* (Oxford, Oxford University Press, 2018).
[8] J Prassl, 'What If your Boss Was an Algorithm? Economic Incentives, Legal Challenges, and the Rise of Artificial Intelligence at Work' (2019) 41 *Comparative Labor Law and Policy Journal* 123.
[9] ibid.
[10] European Convention on Human Rights, Art 8.
[11] ibid.

approach is tailored to address privacy issues and has four key features: impact assessments, 'techno-social' stakeholder engagement, avenues for grievance mechanisms and remedy, and oversight and accountability structures.

II. Data-Driven Workplace Monitoring and Privacy

Employee privacy is at stake throughout the entire life cycle of data recorded by workplace monitoring techniques. The workplace life cycle of data can be broken down into four phases.[12] (1) *Data collection*: employees experience surveillance, a lack of transparency and awareness about data collection taking place. Employees' freedom and autonomy to exercise adequate control over their privacy with respect to data collection might be limited or non-existent. (2) *Data analysis*: employees might not be informed about the analysing activities based on their data due to knowledge asymmetry. Also, the analysis might contain errors, or result in a misrepresentation of or bias against individual employees or groups. (3) *Data use*: decision-making based on employee data may lead to discrimination against a group of employees or individual employees, or a lack of autonomy about the implementation or use of data. (4) *Data erasure/deletion*: the importance of 'forgetting' employee data might be disregarded in an organisation and employees might lack autonomy, transparency and accountability over the right to be forgotten. This includes appropriate communication of the time span of data retention and the rights of the data subject to demand the deletion of personal data.

Some monitoring tools claim to be able to analyse interactions between employees to identify patterns of collaboration and combine these data sources with information from employee files in order to show which individuals in a company serve as 'key information holders'.[13] Other software measures how quickly an employee usually completes a range of tasks and might suggest ways to speed up. Some companies make their employees wear badges that record everything they see and hear, and then analyse the speech of the person wearing the device, ranging from voice volume and pitch to the length of time spent in one place and daily paths mapped by beacons installed throughout the office space.[14] While such monitoring practices might appeal with promises of increased efficiency and better staff performance, many methods are inherently invasive and can rarely be justified. In the following, we will explore five key areas of concern for privacy with regard to tech-based workplace monitoring.

---

[12] A Tamò-Larrieux, *Designing for Privacy and its Legal Framework* (Cham, Springer, 2018).
[13] SD Schafheitle et al, 'No Stone Left Unturned? Toward a Framework for the Impact of Datafication Technologies on Organizational Control' (2020) 6 *Academy of Management Discoveries* 455.
[14] C Steele, 'The Quantified Employee: How Companies Use Tech to Track Workers', *PC Mag* (14 February 2020).

A. Opacity of Governance Structures

From an employee's or worker's perspective, the ways in which workplace monitoring tools are governed and managed often resemble a 'black box'.[15] Pasquale defines the dual meaning of a 'black box' as a recording device, like a data monitoring system, and as a 'system whose workings are mysterious; we can observe its inputs and outputs, but we cannot tell how one becomes the other', making it possible 'to scrutinise the others while avoiding scrutiny oneself', which is 'one of the most important forms of power'.[16] Black boxes are characterised by real secrecy, establishing barriers to access (as a 'key' does for a 'door'), and legal secrecy, referring to laws that keep information secret. Through obfuscation, actors with the power over the governance of black boxes attempt to conceal their taking of influence in cases when real or legal secrecy have been compromised.[17]

The black box logic applies to many workplace monitoring systems.[18] Governing structures in automated decisions around hiring and recruiting, performance measurement and promotion schemes are often opaque. This lack of transparency risks having a negative impact on equal opportunity in employment as patterns of discrimination are concealed through opacity and/or obfuscation.[19] From a privacy point of view, the increased appetite for data collection to make the monitoring systems efficient is problematic. While big data analytics require large amounts of data to make their results accurate and precise, the principle of data minimisation to protect privacy requires the exact opposite: collect as little data as possible and in a targeted manner.

Some human resource departments, now sometimes called 'people management units', rely on data-driven algorithmic decision-making systems without informing the people concerned about the processes behind those systems.[20] At the same time, the workforce is increasingly required to disclose a high level of information about individual activities and behavioural patterns, without knowing precisely how such information (data) will inform employer decisions or subject workers to the control of algorithms.[21] For example, certain tools record employees' keyboard strokes, mouse movements, and visited websites. Another monitoring tool takes videos of employees' screens and/or photos through the webcam at regular intervals to check whether employees are at their desks.[22] The senior management in most cases decides which monitoring practices are necessary and justified. Key

---

[15] I Ajunwa, 'The "Black Box" at Work' (2020) 7 *Big Data & Society*.
[16] F Pasquale, *The Black Box Society* (Cambridge, MA, Harvard University Press, 2015) 3.
[17] ibid 6.
[18] Ajunwa, 'The "Black Box" at Work'.
[19] ibid.
[20] Pasquale, *The Black Box Society*; Prassl, *Humans as a Service*.
[21] Ajunwa, 'The "Black Box" at Work'.
[22] WD Heaven, 'This Startup Is Using AI to Give Workers a "Productivity Score"' *MIT Technology Review* (4 June 2020).

decisions may thus be taken somewhat arbitrarily without taking human rights or data protection requirements into account. From a privacy perspective, it is not tolerable to deduce political opinions, sexual orientation or information about an individual's health by analysing clicking and browsing patterns.

Automated management decision making changes social patterns in the workplace, turning it into an increasingly contested terrain of control.[23]

B. Limitations of Relying on Design-Based Protection and the Data Literacy of Supervisors

What makes the opacity in governance even more problematic is when managers accept the promise that design-based protections prevent all potential privacy risks stemming from data-driven workplace monitoring. Design-based solutions are claimed to complement the existing legal frameworks for the deployment of people analytics software. One of the most prominent such tech-based approaches is Privacy by Design.[24] It aims to provide better privacy protection by embedding design specifications of information technologies, accountable business practices, and networked infrastructures. A range of scholars describe Privacy by Design as a pragmatic compliance enabler to guarantee important elements of procedural regularity.[25] However, even if choices such as anonymisation of data sets are made ex ante to protect privacy, there is the risk that technological progress will outpace the protections. For example, studies have shown how re-identification can be achieved relatively easily in big data environments.[26]

Yet what design-based solutions cannot address is either the limited data literacy of supervisors or the human rights risks, in particular privacy risks, stemming from organisational embeddedness. Design-based privacy protection measures cannot address all circumstances of the organisational context, such as the proportionality of a monitoring measure that really requires a balance test between the potentially conflicting interests of employee and employer.[27] Added to this, design-based solutions cannot assist with the issue of whether consent was given in a free, prior and informed manner.[28] It may be difficult for employees to

---

[23] Kellogg, Valentine and Christin, 'Algorithms at Work'.
[24] I Ajunwa, K Crawford and J Schultz, 'Limitless Worker Surveillance' (2017) 105 *California Law Review* 735. See also A Cavoukian, 'Privacy by Design: Origins, Meaning, and Prospects for Assuring Privacy and Trust in the Information Era', in G Yee (ed), *Privacy Protection Measures and Technologies in Business Organizations: Aspects and Standards* (Hershey, PA, IGI Global, 2012).
[25] Neff and Nafus, *Self-Tracking*.
[26] L Rocher, JM Hendrickx and Y-A de Montjoye, 'Estimating the Success of Re-Identifications in Incomplete Datasets Using Generative Models' (2019) 10 *Nature Communications*.
[27] *Köpke v Germany*, no 420/07 (2010); *Bărbulescu v Romania*, no 61496/08 (2017); *López Ribalda and Others v Spain*, nos 1874/13 and 8567/13 (2019).
[28] EU General Data Protection Regulation (GDPR), Recital 43, Art 29 Working Party Guidelines on consent under Regulation 2016/679, 18.

give informed consent if their manager does not understand the functions of the monitoring tools being deployed and therefore fails to inform them properly about potential risks.

C. Low Bargaining Power of Employees to Challenge the Use of Certain Tools in the Workplace

Consent has a critical role to play in the processing of personal data. Consent has to be free, prior and informed. The weak bargaining power of employees in the employment context makes it questionable how 'free' their consent can be. This is particularly true in settings where there is a significant economic or other imbalance between the controller securing consent and the data subject providing it.[29] For instance, the recitals to the GDPR clearly state that consent 'should not provide a valid legal ground for the processing of personal data in a specific case where there is a clear imbalance between the data subject and the controller'.[30] Such a power asymmetry often exists between an employer and her employees. Consent to the processing of personal data might therefore be given even though the employee consenting might not have a 'real' choice. Hence, consent could still be seen as 'forced' in certain circumstances, even if it is perhaps prior and informed. If, moreover, the full spectrum of a people analytics technology has not been accurately communicated to the employee, their consent cannot be considered fully informed either. Ajunwa, Crawford and Schultz highlight the necessity of limiting workplace monitoring to its 'appropriate context – actual workplaces and actual work tasks', ring-fenced by an unbreachable boundary of 'notice-and-consent mechanisms'.[31]

An underlying issue when workplace monitoring practices are deployed is that the balancing of interests between employer and employee/worker might often be concluded in favour of the employer. Unequal bargaining power between the employee and employer strongly affects whether an employee consents to the terms of their employment contract. This can happen to the extent that the worker or employee has to decide between accepting vast monitoring practices or losing the job – scholars have criticised the potential trade-off between privacy rights and employment opportunities.[32]

Furthermore, even consent is not always a sufficient justification in data protection law to legitimise processing personal data and interfering in the right to privacy.

---

[29] European Union Agency for Fundamental Rights, *Handbook on European Data Protection Law* (Luxembourg, Publications Office of the European Union, 2018) 397.
[30] EU GDPR, Recital 4.
[31] Ajunwa, Crawford and Schultz, 'Limitless Worker Surveillance' 774.
[32] Pasquale, *The Black Box Society*.

D. Risks Arising from a Combinatory Logic of Monitoring Tools

Tech-based workplace monitoring often relies on technologies that are not developed by the company using them. Initial developers sell a range of off-the-shelf products to third parties who implement them within their respective unique organisational set-up. For example, certain providers offer internal communication platforms, similar to social media platforms, where users can post and reply to questions and are scored based on the pertinence of their questions and/or their ability to reply to questions from colleagues. From this, a user score is generated that feeds into the individual performance evaluation of an employee or worker. Issues can arise when the company selling the technological solutions does not inform the purchasing party about the pre-conditions and limitations of using a particular product.

While companies have an interest in ensuring employee productivity and preventing misconduct in the workplace, the measures used might employ a range of tools that, in combination, create 'cumulative risks' for the privacy of individuals. Cumulative risks refer to situations in which instances of abuse, when repeated many times, can have serious impacts on the privacy and related human rights of individuals or groups.[33] Cumulative risks are inherently more complex to anticipate than the risks from a single project, product or service. Unless the decision-makers overseeing workplace monitoring make the effort to assess and analyse potential cumulative risks, it will be difficult to prevent social disruption in the workplace, a social disruption that can have long-term impacts on privacy and related human rights. Also, data-driven models that quantify human behaviour are not immune to errors or false conclusions,[34] which makes a human assessment even more necessary to detect and mitigate potentially toxic combinations stemming from different business purposes and their respective uses of tech-based monitoring. For instance, data from health prevention schemes might be combined with data for performance monitoring and potentially create invasive insights into an employee's private life.[35] A critical factor here is the data literacy previously discussed. If the knowledge of the data models and/or algorithms on which the deployed technological tools are based is already limited, the knowledge

---

[33] UN OHCHR B-Tech, 'Access to Remedy and the Technology Sector: Understanding the Perspectives and Needs of Affected People and Groups' available at www.ohchr.org/Documents/Issues/Business/B-Tech/access-to-remedy-perspectives-needs-affected-people.pdf.

[34] B-J Koops and R Leenes, 'Privacy Regulation Cannot Be Hardcoded. A Critical Comment on the "Privacy by Design" Provision in Data-Protection Law' (2014) 28 *International Review of Law, Computers & Technology* 159.

[35] G Neff et al, 'Affordances, Technical Agency, and the Politics of Technologies of Cultural Production' (2012) 56 *Journal of Broadcasting & Electronic Media* 299; I Ajunwa, K Crawford and JS Ford, 'Health and Big Data: An Ethical Framework for Health Information Collection by Corporate Wellness Programs' (2016) 44 *The Journal of Law, Medicine & Ethics* 474.

of the potential consequences of simultaneously monitoring the same people with different tools will be all the more so.

Added to this, a range of service providers of tech-based monitoring tools require their client companies to use services that result in vendor-lock in. Supplier lock-in refers to a situation in which the costs of switching to another supplier are so high that the customer is essentially stuck with the original supplier. Due to financial pressure, inadequate staffing or the need to avoid interruptions to business, the customer is 'locked into' something that may be an inferior product or service for privacy protection. Such vendor lock-in forces a client company to accept design choices on data usage by default. This means that a company will have to accept 'bad design choices' from such a vendor, regardless of whether the client company has detected privacy violations stemming from these choices, for example, cumulative risks through combining different tools. A vendor lock-in gives the contracting party little room for manoeuvre to improve the organisational embedding in a more 'privacy-friendly' way.

E. Heightened Risks for Marginalised Groups, People of Colour and Women

Marginalised groups, people of colour and women are confronted with increased risks of privacy harms from the use of data-driven workplace monitoring. Scholars have highlighted that the gender data gap affects a plethora of contexts, including government policy and medical research, technology, workplaces, urban planning, and the media. Data sets that are collected based on male features can make the use of certain technologies dangerous to women due to blind spots regarding female representation.[36] In the workplace, occupational health and safety measures are often developed relying on data skewed towards men and risk neglecting the female physiognomy and consequential physical measures for the protection of women. In a similar fashion, machine-learning algorithms are trained to categorise and classify people into distinct groups that follow a binary logic, such as 'male/female'. This is problematic insofar as it remains questionable how the rights of people whose physiognomy or identity does not match these fixed categories could be respected when technology is literally blind to such important considerations.[37] Members of marginalised communities could be harmed and discouraged from entering the workforce of the digital economy as a result. Due to a mirroring and reinforcement of historic, societal biases in statistics and quantification of segments of society, the threat and reality of systemic discrimination

---

[36] Schafheitle et al, 'No Stone Left Unturned?'.

[37] C Criado Perez, *Invisible Women: Exposing Data Bias in a World Designed for Men* (London, Vintage, 2019); J Buolamwini and T Gebru, 'Gender Shades: Intersectional Accuracy Disparities in Commercial Gender Classification' (2018) 81 *Proceedings of Machine Learning Research* 77.

and racism through workplace monitoring is especially severe for women, gender minorities, people of colour, and other marginalised groups. Some of the worst outcomes of data-driven management failures are to be found in business implementation, when badly designed technology meets managers with a low level of digital literacy, leading to toxic effects on certain stakeholder groups,[38] for example, by creating systemic bias against marginalised groups in performance evaluation schemes.[39] Ensuring equality and diversity in workplace monitoring practices and their organisational embeddedness cannot be addressed without intervening in cultures of bullying and harassment that disproportionately impact and function to exclude these groups.[40]

If a company obtains personal data from data brokers to screen job candidates, it might do so without the data subject having had the chance to give consent. Resulting from such questionable access to personal data, an algorithm might infer that a female candidate or a candidate of colour is to be categorised as less qualified and screened out from the recruiting process.[41] Such algorithmic bias occurs when an algorithm has been trained using biased historical data. An example of biased historical data would be a data set that relates to the track record of a technology company that used to hire predominantly male, white staff. Based on this historical training data, the algorithm would classify white, male candidates as suitable staff members for the company and search for these characteristics within the pool of candidates. Consequently, women, people of colour or non-binary genders would be negatively impacted in the selection process, despite having the same professional qualifications as their white, male counterparts.

When companies neglect bias in data models and thereby create heightened risks for marginalised groups, people of colour and women, they might also fail to sufficiently understand the necessity of requesting the affected individuals' consent in a free, prior and informed manner and the corporate responsibility to ensure that they understand the risks involved.[42] Potentially negatively impacted individuals might not be aware of future proofing to protect themselves against human rights harms. They might also lack digital literacy and thus consent to a workplace monitoring practice without being fully aware of its potential negative consequences. This lack of awareness about future risks can be exacerbated by an absence of structural avenues for strategic engagement with individual rightsholders.

Despite the potential drawbacks for privacy, some workplace monitoring practices might be legitimate and necessary, for example, for health and safety

---

[38] Kellogg, Valentine and Christin, 'Algorithms at Work'.

[39] C DeBrusk, 'The Risk of Machine-Learning Bias (and How to Prevent It)' *MIT Sloan Management Review* (26 March 2018).

[40] S Costanza-Chock, *Design Justice: Community-Led Practices to Build the Worlds We Need* (Cambridge, MA, MIT Press, 2020).

[41] P Tambe, P Cappelli and V Yakubovich, 'Artificial Intelligence in Human Resources Management: Challenges and a Path Forward' (2019) 61 *California Management Review* 15.

[42] E Aizenberg and J van den Hoven, 'Designing for Human Rights in AI' (2020) 7 *Big Data & Society*.

reasons. To guarantee that such provisions for health and safety do not become a universal justification argument, there are managerial approaches that can assist in determining the actual necessity, proportionality and appropriateness of workplace monitoring tools.[43]

Employees who would like to raise grievances about privacy issues related to workplace monitoring practices, in particular those arising from technology products and services, face significant difficulties in identifying, accessing and navigating the mechanisms best placed to deal with the substance of their complaints.[44] The complexity of the potential cumulative risks of workplace monitoring measures, both in terms of the technical analytical capacity and of the business relationships with software/tool providers, might partially explain these difficulties. The lack of attention given to the perspectives and needs of actual and potential affected employees in remediation mechanisms for business-related human rights harms – both in the design and operation of these mechanisms – is a widespread problem, beyond digital workplace monitoring. Here one can think of the previously mentioned example of an internal communication platform that can be used voluntarily by employees, but an employee who does not might be disadvantaged in their performance evaluation. Another example can be virtual career planning assistants that offer emerging positions to internal candidates as they are planned within the human resources department, while candidates not using the career planning tool will not be considered.

III. Addressing Systemic Challenges for Privacy from a Business and Human Rights Perspective

The approach of Business and Human Rights, circling around the United Nations Guiding Principles on Business and Human Rights,[45] can offer a principled approach to ensuring that a company's technological advances in workplace monitoring are grounded in respect and dignity for all workers and employees. The Guiding Principles can serve as a tool for guiding company conduct because they are internationally agreed and supported by a diverse set of stakeholders including business, governments and civil society around the world.[46] Focusing on internationally recognised human rights, including privacy, helps companies and their stakeholders to pay attention to the most serious and important impacts on

---

[43] K Crawford and J Schultz, 'Big Data and Due Process. Toward a Framework to Redress Predictive Privacy Harms' (2014) 55 *Boston College Law Review* 93.
[44] UN OHCHR B-Tech, 'Access to Remedy and the Technology Sector'.
[45] UN OHCHR, 'Guiding Principles on Business and Human Rights: Implementing the United Nations "Protect, Respect and Remedy" Framework' (2011) UN Doc HR/PUB/11/04.
[46] F Wettstein, 'Normativity, Ethics, and the UN Guiding Principles on Business and Human Rights. A Critical Assessment' (2015) 14 *Journal of Human Rights* 162.

people that can result from monitoring. After all, respecting human rights is a societal undertaking, not purely a technical or procedural legal task. The Guiding Principles challenge companies to make affected individuals and groups an integral part of how a company understands and addresses the impacts of monitoring tools on employees and workers.

A range of recommendations for workplace monitoring can be deduced from a human rights-based approach as anchored in the Guiding Principles. In line with the corporate responsibility to respect human rights, all businesses need to identify, address and mitigate/remedy adverse human rights impacts stemming from their business activities.[47] In order to do that, they should carry out human rights due diligence, an ongoing process consisting of a set of measures to address all potential human rights risks that a business is involved in. Human rights due diligence requires different set-ups in different organisations and contexts: at its core it should involve assessing human rights impacts, integrating the lessons of the impact assessments and taking action based on them, tracking performance and communicating and documenting the results.[48] It is also fundamental that human rights due diligence should take place early in the decision-making process around workplace monitoring.

The Guiding Principles clarify what a company should do to address human rights risks based on whether it has caused, contributed or is linked to the harm, including privacy harms.[49] Companies need to apply a multidisciplinary approach involving a range of departments and expertise in order to take all reasonable steps to prevent contributing to privacy harms via acts or omissions related to product design, development, promotion, deployment, contracting, sales, licensing and use. When addressing privacy risks for certain individuals or groups, companies working with data-driven workplace monitoring techniques may need to devise ways to mitigate any unintended consequences on other human rights.

The effectiveness of the company's due diligence in identifying, preventing and mitigating privacy violations depends on those managing the workforce knowing that there is a privacy risk associated with the use of particular monitoring tools. Increasing the digital literacy of managers is important. For example, failing to require, encourage or support an impact assessment may create a permissive environment in which people could take actions that result in abuses. Departments responsible for managing people and deciding about workplace monitoring practices should engage stakeholders and relevant experts in their decision-making

---

[47] F Wettstein, 'From Side Show to Main Act: Can Business and Human Rights Save Corporate Responsibility?' in D Baumann-Pauly and J Nolan (eds), *Business and Human Rights: From Principles to Practice* (New York, Routledge, 2016) 77.
[48] UN OHCHR B-Tech, 'Key Characteristics of Business Respect for Human Rights' available at www.ohchr.org/Documents/Issues/Business/B-Tech/key-characteristics-business-respect.pdf.
[49] UN OHCHR B-Tech, 'Taking Action to Address Human Rights Risks Related to End-Use' available at www.ohchr.org/Documents/Issues/Business/B-Tech/taking-action-address-human-rights-risks.pdf.

processes and be prepared to explain their decisions and actions. Ultimately, using rights-based approaches to navigate these challenges may be a source of innovation and improvements in user experience.[50]

Within human rights due diligence, focusing on privacy violations of workplace monitoring technologies, impact assessments, 'techno-social' stakeholder engagement, avenues for grievance mechanisms and remedy, and oversight and accountability structures are of particular importance.

A. Assessing Impacts

There is an increased need to address the human rights challenges raised by digital technology and reemphasise the essential role of the human rights framework in ensuring that technology companies prevent potential negative impacts through risk management and identify, address and mitigate actual adverse impacts.[51] The United Nations Special Rapporteur on freedom of opinion and expression has called upon information and communications technology companies to conduct human rights impact assessments for their products and policies and to conduct ongoing assessments during operations, based on meaningful stakeholder engagement.[52]

The Guiding Principles emphasise the necessity for all businesses to identify, address and mitigate their negative human rights impacts. Yet guidance and methodologies for applying the Guiding Principles and also human rights impact assessments have generally focused on supply chains. Guidance for assessing and addressing the impacts of digital services, projects and products such as workplace monitoring tools is still nascent.[53]

The Guiding Principles provide guidance to companies on how to implement human rights due diligence in general terms. This can include to check whether the organisation has a risk assessment and escalation process for privacy and related human rights impacts stemming from the use of a product or practice, and determining all the potential privacy risks of the use of a certain technology. To address any potential human rights harms that tech-based workplace monitoring may cause, a company needs to carry out a risk assessment before integrating any new workplace monitoring technology and take into account the impacts of combining it with the technologies already in use in the company.

---

[50] ibid.
[51] UN High-Level Panel on Digital Cooperation, 2019.
[52] UN Human Rights Council, 'Surveillance and Human Rights: Report of the Special Rapporteur on the Promotion and Protection of the Right to Freedom of Opinion and Expression' (28 May 2019) UN Doc A/HRC/41/35.
[53] The Danish Institute for Human Rights, 'Guidance on Human Rights Impact Assessment of Digital Activities' (2020) available at www.humanrights.dk/publications/human-rights-impact-assessment-digital-activities.

New, holistic methods are required to identify, assess, prevent and mitigate negative impacts of workplace monitoring on privacy and connected human rights. The relationship between privacy, the technological life cycle and the corporate data ecosystem needs to be thoroughly reassessed in multidisciplinary teams.[54] In this way companies can more easily identify blind spots in automated systems and find systemic privacy violations in context-specific environments along all life cycle stages of automated systems, starting in product development.[55]

Privacy is an essential factor for upholding human rights in workplace monitoring: privacy has a gateway function for broader human rights protection in the workplace, meaning that adverse impacts on the right to privacy can lead to a wide variety of further human rights impacts. Indeed, virtually all human rights can be affected by data-driven workplace monitoring and need to be taken into account.

Upholding privacy helps to safeguard the private sphere from unjustified intrusion.[56] These further impacts might derive from the exploitation of data for purposes other than those agreed to. Moreover, even if a user might have withheld consent in the first place, data might still be reused for other means without consent, or one user might be impacting non-users by sharing their data on their behalf and without their consent. In network analysis, for example, the behaviour of key actors who have chosen not to take part can still be deduced from their interrelations with other key actors who have consented to the use of their own data. This is particularly true where tools make use of data derived from social media sources, such as Facebook or similar platforms. The interdependencies between the use of personal data and interlinkages between users in a data ecosystem demonstrate that the right to privacy is a cornerstone in the discussion about rights-respecting workplace monitoring practices, as an ever-increasing number of rights is influenced by digital contexts. Moreover, it is not only about one individual's privacy, but also about interconnected collective privacy effects, and how these relate to a wide range of related human rights.

Impact assessments need to integrate input from multiple stakeholders from the outset. Have labour unions or similar institutions and workers been consulted regarding the decisions to adopt, design, and integrate tech-based monitoring in the workplace? If so, there needs to be a transparent and clear process for workers and employees to reject or require changes for proposed rollouts and use of workplace monitoring technology. Not only workers and employees, but also other potentially affected stakeholders need to be heard in order to ensure design justice,[57] as workers might not be able to fully anticipate potential harm and/or lack

---

[54] I Ebert, T Busch and F Wettstein, *Business and Human Rights in the Data Economy: A Mapping and Research Study* (Berlin, German Institute for Human Rights, 2020).
[55] See the MIT Media Lab 'AI Blindspot Project' available at https://aiblindspot.media.mit.edu.
[56] P Bernal, 'Data Gathering, Surveillance and Human Rights: Recasting the Debate' (2016) 1 *Journal of Cyber Policy* 243.
[57] Costanza-Chock, *Design Justice*.

technological expertise. That is why a range of stakeholders should be consulted, such as community leaders, academics, policymakers and civil society.

B. 'Techno-social' Stakeholder Engagement

Strategic stakeholder engagement across the full life cycle of the monitoring tool is desirable from the development stage, but essential in the deployment and end-use stage in the actual workplace. Inspiration can be drawn from interdisciplinary projects aiming to detect unintended consequences of the use of automated systems, including a full assessment of risks, going beyond data impact assessments.[58] Recommendations include the dedicated training of a significant proportion of supervisors and employees on data models and the limitations of their insights. Such mainstreaming and capacity building should aim to raise digital literacy across the organisation and result in a more responsible use of workplace monitoring techniques. The involvement of dedicated worker representation around the use of technology in the workplace and how it can be used for monitoring is key.[59] Such groups need to be included in all strategic decision making around workplace monitoring technologies and their implementation. Diverse membership and composition in engagement bodies is of high importance so that all voices, including those of contracting workers, can be heard.

Engaging external experts and affected stakeholders in the assessment of human rights risks is important in order to ensure that actions taken to address those risks and tracking of their effectiveness are comprehensive.[60] If a company lacks internal diversity or existing mechanisms to engage affected groups, external stakeholder engagement is even more essential. The department in charge of people management needs to talk to software developers to better understand how the tools they are purchasing work in the individual context of a company. Those overseeing the embedding of workplace monitoring practices into the organisation need to establish ways of involving external experts even in the context of fast-paced innovation while taking into account legitimate concerns about intellectual property and commercial sensitivity. Just as 'translating' expectations and standards for internal stakeholders can be critical, external stakeholders can assist in making people management understand technical issues in workplace monitoring relevant to a company's efforts to respect privacy.

---

[58] MIT Media Lab, 'AI Blindspot Project'.
[59] Partnership on AI, 'Framework for Promoting Workforce Well-Being in the AI-Integrated Workplace' available at www.partnershiponai.org/workforce-wellbeing.
[60] UN OHCHR B-Tech, 'Key Characteristics of Business Respect for Human Rights' available at www.ohchr.org/Documents/Issues/Business/B-Tech/key-characteristics-business-respect.pdf.

C. Grievance Mechanisms and Remedy

To adequately address potential harms, companies need to have accessible and effective mechanisms in place that allow workers to question or seek remedy for decisions taken or supported by tech-based workplace monitoring. In line with the Guiding Principles, a grievance is understood as 'a perceived injustice evoking an individual's or a group's sense of entitlement, which may be based on law, contract, explicit or implicit promises, customary practice, or general notions of fairness of aggrieved communities'.[61] The term grievance mechanism can indicate a state-based or non-state-based, judicial or non-judicial process through which grievances concerning business-related human rights abuse can be addressed. This section focuses on 'operational-level grievance mechanisms', accessible directly to individuals and communities who may be adversely impacted by a business enterprise and administered by enterprises, alone or in collaboration with others, including relevant stakeholders. Company-led grievance mechanisms may assist in the identification of adverse privacy impacts as part of an enterprise's ongoing human rights due diligence, by providing a channel for those directly impacted and/or by analysing trends and patterns in complaints. Also, business enterprises can identify systemic privacy problems and adapt their practices accordingly. In this way, a business can ideally remediate adverse impacts early and directly, thereby preventing harms from compounding and grievances from escalating. Grievance mechanisms can include the possibility of requesting a human review of an automated decision or challenging potentially incorrect data inputs. A grievance mechanism in line with the Guiding Principles needs to be legitimate, accessible, predictable, equitable, transparent, rights compatible, a source of continuous learning, and based on engagement and dialogue. Principle 31 of the Guiding Principles defines a set of effectiveness criteria. Ways in which the adverse privacy impacts of technology can be remedied or redressed potentially take many different forms. While a range of harms may be addressed by a non-judicial, company-based grievance mechanism, some forms of harm might require judicial action.

Privacy violations stemming from the development and use of technologies are not always easy to articulate for rightsholders. Even in cases where employees are able to recognise the privacy harm and connected adverse impacts on their enjoyment of human rights, explaining them in privacy and/or human rights terms might not be straightforward. How should employees provide the necessary evidence to prove that promotions have been denied to certain individuals or groups based on discriminatory criteria? How can they demonstrate that personal data has been unlawfully disclosed? Often, there may be further, related impacts

---

[61] UN OHCHR, 'Guiding Principles on Business and Human Rights' 25.

(eg, risks to livelihoods in the case of firing) that might fall outside the mandates of company-based grievance mechanisms that would nevertheless be relevant.[62]

Furthermore, there are many contexts in which privacy violations may not be apparent to affected employees and/or workers at all. For instance, a group of employees might be unaware of having been subjected to tech-based workplace surveillance, or of the discriminatory effects of automated risk assessment software that result in less advantageous treatment in compensation schemes. The difficulties in identifying and analysing the adverse human rights impacts of business activities are even more pronounced in cases of 'collective' or 'cumulative' violations.

Being open with employees and workers about what a grievance mechanism can and cannot do, and what to expect at each stage of the process, is essential for users (potential and actual) of this mechanism. Expectation management is fundamental to gaining and retaining employee and worker trust. The workforce and its managers need accurate information, communicated in understandable formats, about timetables, decision-making methodologies and which steps they can take if they are not satisfied with the outcomes of decisions.[63] Often employees and workers might have to navigate extremely complex remediation systems. This can be due to limited resources within the people management department that do not allow for a user-friendly rollout of grievance mechanisms. As a result, a realistic assessment of what might be achievable from the viewpoint of the complainant through different company-led grievance mechanisms might not be a straightforward exercise. Information about the regulatory, law enforcement, alternative dispute resolution (eg, mediation or ombudsman services) or court-based processes may be available to assist employees or workers, also if she or he decides to take a grievance further because of dissatisfaction with the outcome of the previous process.

D. Oversight and Accountability

The departments deciding the ways in which workplace monitoring practices are implemented need to be transparent about if and how automated decision-making forms a part of grievance handling processes.[64] The Guiding Principles highlight the legitimacy and due process difficulties of company-based mechanisms being 'both the subject of complaints and unilaterally determining their outcome'.[65]

---

[62] UN OHCHR B-Tech, 'Designing and Implementing Effective Company-Based Grievance Mechanisms' available at www.ohchr.org/Documents/Issues/Business/B-Tech/access-to-remedy-company-based-grievance-mechanisms.pdf.

[63] See Accountability and Remedy Project (ARP) III, Main report, UN Doc A/HRC/44/32, Annex, 8 and 9; Explanatory Addendum A/HRC/44/32/Add.1, 50–58.

[64] UN OHCHR B-Tech, 'Designing and Implementing Effective Company-Based Grievance Mechanisms'.

[65] UN OHCHR, 'Guiding Principles on Business and Human Rights' 31(h), Commentary.

Nevertheless, in particular in the case of workplace monitoring, opportunities for independent review of decision-making and outcomes can considerably enhance the credibility of remediation mechanisms with affected people and groups. As well as helping to build trust, additional oversight safeguards for company-led grievance mechanisms create accountability for decision-making, helping to enhance the performance of the grievance mechanism overall.

The company and in particular a human resources department need to provide for accountability structures and avenues for grievance mechanisms in line with the Guiding Principles that go beyond participatory design and enable organisational learning. This should include targeted oversight boards and councils that ensure that employees' and workers' voices are heard by the leadership of the organisation when integrating technology for monitoring purposes. Such oversight structures need to provide accountability to affected individuals and make decisions in a transparent manner.[66] A clear process for internal participation and interaction increases the legitimacy of accountability structures and makes them effective. What happens when workers oppose a certain use of technology for monitoring? From a Guiding Principles perspective, there should be an emphasis on taking the voices of marginalised individuals and communities into account. With regard to technical expertise, it can be beneficial to work with advisory bodies that can provide expertise, for example, from an engineering perspective, in order to allow the company to think long term and strategically about impacts on workers and employees. Further, accountability can entail that the company reports on and keeps an inventory of decisions made with the support of monitoring technology.

IV. Conclusion

Data-driven workplace monitoring is an emerging field of practice in which rights-respecting strategies can assist in mitigating harm. By combining insights from multiple disciplines such as employment and data protection law, data science, human rights and privacy scholarship, innovative models for aligning basic human rights and privacy requirements and workplace monitoring practices will be possible. Some practices that companies might think about adopting may be privacy invasive and not appropriate to the individual context. Other practices exist that are necessary from a health and safety perspective, and that must be implemented in a way that allows for privacy protection.

The assessment of the effectiveness and the perception of the potentially intrusive nature of the use of big data technologies in human resources vary greatly depending on the group of employees.[67] Transparent communication about the

---

[66] Partnership on AI, 'Framework for Promoting Workforce Well-Being'.
[67] I Ebert, 'Big Data for People Management' (*BigData-Dialog*, 28 February 2020) available at https://bigdata-dialog.ch/big-data-for-people-management.

collected data and the right of participants to have a say plays an important role in the individual employee's perceptions. Human resources department can send out important signals here: processes have to be adapted in such a way that privacy is maintained, transparency and data control are guaranteed, employees have a secure say in strategic decisions (stakeholder engagement) and grievance systems are put in place. This is the only way employees can continue to have autonomy and 'agency' instead of being simple 'data objects'.

In order to ensure privacy-respecting data-driven workplace monitoring, a solid knowledge of the data models and how they feed into decision-making is necessary to overcome systemic risks to human rights, in combination with managerial actions. The business and human rights approach supports the identification of necessary measures and the implementation of a holistic business practice.

8

Freedom to Think and to Hold a Political Opinion: Digital Threats to Political Participation in Liberal Democracies

JÉRÔME DUBERRY

I. Introduction

Freedom of opinion is closely linked to both freedom of thought and freedom of expression: people need to be able to consider a wide range of media in order to form their own opinions. This is particularly important for citizens making political decisions, as a young Benjamin Franklin, under the moniker Silence Dogood, argued in 1722:

> Without freedom of thought, there can be no such thing as wisdom; and no such thing as public liberty. Freedom of speech is the right of every man, as far as by it, he does not hurt or control the right of others. And this is the only check it ought to suffer, and the only bounds it ought to know. This sacred privilege is so essential to free governments, that the security of property, and the freedom of speech always go together; and in those wretched countries where a man cannot call his tongue his own, he can scarce call anything else his own. Whoever would overthrow the liberty of a nation must begin by subduing the freeness of speech.[1]

With more and more information being shared online, it would seem that expression has never been so free and yet this abundance is strangely not benefitting freedom of thought or freedom of opinion. Indeed, the same technologies that opened up access to information and empowered civil society are now being used to harvest personal data and target people with disinformation, with grave consequences for democracy.

---

[1] B Franklin, 'Silence Dogood, No 8' in LW Labaree et al (eds), *The Papers of Benjamin Franklin*, vol 1 (New Haven, Yale University Press, 1959).

In November 2018, Nobel laureates Joseph Stiglitz, Shirin Ebadi and Mario Vargas Llosa were among 25 public figures calling for democratic guarantees on freedom of opinion.[2] The Information and Democracy Commission published an 'International Declaration on Information and Democracy' that could serve as a working basis for political leaders. The text lists the democratic guarantees necessary to ensuring the right to reliable information, privacy, and transparency of powers in a context of globalisation, digitisation and disruption of the public space. This International Declaration also challenges the large tech companies (often referred to as GAFAM: Google, Amazon, Facebook, Apple and Microsoft) to guarantee pluralism and put in place mechanisms to fight against massive online misinformation and political control over the press and the online media ecosystem.[3]

This is precisely what this chapter examines: how the widespread use of digital technologies challenges political participation in liberal democracies. It will first discuss notions of freedom of expression, freedom of thought, freedom of opinion, and political participation. It will then examine the threats to these core democratic principles in the digital age.

II. Freedom of Expression, Freedom of Thought and Freedom of Opinion

A well-functioning democracy is based on well-informed citizens. But it is also based on the premise that citizens are free to think and hold opinions. Thanks to these two freedoms, a citizen can make a political decision, whether it is voting for a policy, a party, or an individual. Information helps citizens to make well-informed decisions, but only when freedom of thought and freedom of opinion are respected.

The liberal tradition has extensively discussed freedom of thought and in particular its central influence on other liberties.[4] Wilhelm von Humboldt insisted on the importance of freedom of thought for the whole population, arguing that the process of thinking has more value and is more significant than the result it triggers. In his mind, society should agree to absolute freedom of thought.[5] For John Stuart Mill, freedom of thought was at the origin of human freedom,[6] and

---

[2] Information and Democracy Commission, 'International Declaration on Information and Democracy: Principles for the Global Information and Communication Space' (*Reporters Without Borders*, 2 November 2018) available at https://rsf.org/en/news/international-declaration-information-and-democracy-principles-global-information-and-communication.
[3] ibid.
[4] L Swaine, 'Freedom of Thought as a Basic Liberty' (2018) 46 *Political Theory* 405.
[5] W von Humboldt, *The Limits of State Action* (Cambridge, Cambridge University Press, 1969).
[6] JS Mill, *On Liberty* (Indianapolis, Hackett Publishing, 1978).

comprised of liberty of conscience in the broadest sense of the word, liberty of thought and feeling, complete freedom of opinion and sentiment on all topics.[7] He further distinguished how one thinks or feels about an issue from the opinion one holds on it and how one expresses it.[8] He also argued that freedom of thought is more essential than the freedom to express and publish opinions, but that they cannot be disconnected.[9] For John Rawls, freedom of thought was the first of the basic liberties, which also included freedom of speech, freedom of the press, and free association, and remained essential to the establishment of a just society.[10] He also contended that it must be guaranteed by the Constitution to ensure the free and informed exercise of political liberties.[11] He further stipulated that states should ensure liberty of conscience and freedom of thought for their populations at the national[12] and international levels since they are not limited to western traditions but should apply to all individuals on the planet.[13]

These views that closely associate freedom of thought with other liberties and rights can also be found in international human rights scholarship and international arrangements.[14] This approach highlights in particular two types of freedom that cannot be separated: freedom of thought and freedom of opinion. Article 18 of the Universal Declaration of Human Rights stipulates that:

> Everyone has the right to freedom of thought, conscience and religion; this right includes freedom to change his religion or belief, and freedom, either alone or in community with others and in public or private, to manifest his religion or belief in teaching, practice, worship and observance.

But, since freedom of thought must lead to the freedom to make a judgement and hold an opinion, as argued by some of the scholars presented previously, Article 19 of the Universal Declaration of Human Rights stipulates that: 'Everyone has the right to freedom of opinion and expression; this right includes freedom to hold opinions without interference and to seek, receive and impart information and ideas through any media and regardless of frontiers.' Moreover, Article 19 of the International Covenant on Civil and Political Rights (ICCPR) addresses the guarantees of freedom of opinion and expression, which are freedom of access to information and freedom of the media. The value of Article 19 of the ICCPR goes far beyond the rights it aims to protect, to enable the fulfilment of other fundamental rights, including the right to privacy (ICCPR Art 17), freedom of assembly (ICCPR Art 21) and association (ICCPR Art 22), and the exercise of political rights

---

[7] Swaine, 'Freedom of Thought'.
[8] Mill, *On Liberty*.
[9] Swaine, 'Freedom of Thought'; Mill, *On Liberty*.
[10] J Rawls, *Political Liberalism* (New York, Columbia University Press, 2005).
[11] ibid.
[12] ibid.
[13] J Rawls, *The Law of Peoples* (Cambridge, MA, Harvard University Press, 1999).
[14] Swaine, 'Freedom of Thought'.

(ICCPR Art 25).[15] As the Human Rights Committee argues in its General Comment No 34 (2011), the rights that Article 19 of the ICCPR stipulates are 'indispensable conditions for the full development of the person', 'essential for any society', and 'constitute the foundation stone for every free and democratic society'.[16] Similarly, the European Court of Human Rights has also affirmed that freedom of expression constitutes not only an essential foundation of a democratic society but also a basic condition for its progress in *Handyside v UK* (7 December 1976) and *Lingens v Austria* (8 July 1986). In other words, freedom of expression, freedom of thought and freedom of opinion are essential freedoms that must be protected, as they are the foundations of any well-functioning democracy.

III. Political Participation in Liberal Democracies

The very concept of political participation is at the core of the democratic state.[17] As Held argues:

> Within the history of the clash of positions lies the struggle to determine whether democracy will mean some kind of popular power (a form of life in which citizens are engaged in *self*-government and *self*-regulation) or an aid to decision-making (a means to legitimate the decisions of those voted into power).[18]

Lively proposes seven options to organise political equality concretely.[19] He contends that: (1) all citizens should govern, or that (2) they be involved in essential rule-making processes. The ones who are in position of power should be held accountable (3) towards those who are expected to apply the rules, or (4) towards the representatives of the latter. The ruled (5) or their representatives (6) should select the rulers, who should (7) act in the main interests of the ruled.

Political representation is based on the idea that some actors designate others 'to sign on [their] behalf, to act on [their] behalf, to speak on [their] behalf', and where the latter receives 'the power of a proxy'.[20] Marshall defines political citizen rights as the right to elect and to stand for election: 'By the political element (of citizenship) I mean the right to participate in the exercise of political power, as a member of a body invested with political power or as an elector of such a body.'[21]

---

[15] A Zayas and A Martín, 'Freedom of Opinion and Freedom of Expression: Some Reflections on General Comment No 34 of the UN Human Rights Committee' (2012) 59 *Netherlands International Law Review* 425.
[16] ibid.
[17] M Kaase and A Marsh, 'Political Action. A Theoretical Perspective' in S Barnes et al (eds) *Political Action: Mass Participation in Five Western Democracies* (Beverly Hills, Sage, 1979).
[18] D Held, *Models of Democracy* (Stanford, Stanford University Press, 2006) 3.
[19] J Lively, *Democracy* (Oxford, Blackwell, 1975) 30.
[20] P Bourdieu, *Language and Symbolic Power* (Cambridge, Polity Press, 1991) 203.
[21] TH Marshall, *Citizenship and Social Class and Other Essays* (Cambridge, Cambridge University Press, 1950) 10–11.

Teorell further distinguishes three aims of political participation: influencing policies, making a political decision, and contributing to political debates.[22]

According to the theories of participatory democracy, deliberative democracy, and social capital, the participation of citizens in designing policies has many advantages. It increases civic skills and virtues, enables deliberation and the emergence of more rational decisions, and increases the legitimacy of any decision-making processes.[23] Scholars have identified two main incentives for citizens to participate: (1) availability of resources; and (2) desire to participate.

Resources are either physical, human, or social capital.[24] Physical capital covers all material assets available to an individual, which includes financial capital, but also technologies and ICTs in particular. For instance, the use of web-based search engines to access information about a political party or a policy can reveal useful information to citizens before an election. Moreover, human capital implies the existence of skills and knowledge that allow action.[25] Indeed, participation requires some prior knowledge of political processes: 'Political knowledge is to democratic politics what money is to economics: it is the currency of citizenship.'[26] Verba, Schlozman and Brady talk about 'civic skills', which means linguistic proficiency, communication, and organisational capacity.[27] With more and more content and associated metadata produced every day, including 500 million tweets, 294 billion emails and 5 billion web searches daily,[28] these 'civic skills' are very necessary. However, they also need updating to include digital skills, meaning the 'abilities to use digital devices, communication applications, and networks to access and manage information'.[29] Lastly, social capital is a social resource, not an economic asset or a cognitive disposition: 'Unlike other forms of capital, social capital inheres in the structure of relations between persons and among persons. It is lodged neither in individuals nor in physical implements of production.'[30]

In terms of desire to participate, Olson focuses on material benefits and distinguishes between general and specific incentives. He argues that rational actors will not engage in activities oriented towards a common good as long as they can also reap the benefits of these general incentives without participating. However, they

---

[22] J Teorell, 'Political Participation and Three Theories of Democracy: A Research Inventory and Agenda' (2006) 45 *European Journal of Political Research* 787.

[23] A Michels and L De Graaf, 'Examining Citizen Participation: Local Participatory Policy Making and Democracy' (2010) 36 *Local Government Studies* 477.

[24] J Coleman, *Foundations of Social Theory* (Cambridge, MA, Belknap Press, 1990) 304.

[25] G Becker, *Human Capital* (New York, National Bureau of Economic Research, 1964).

[26] M Delli Carpini and S Keeter, *What Americans Know About Politics and Why It Matters* (New Haven, Yale University Press, 1996) 8.

[27] S Verba, KL Schlozman and H Brady, *Voice and Equality: Civic Voluntarism in American Politics* (Cambridge, MA, Harvard University Press, 1995) ch 11.

[28] J Desjardins, 'How Much Data Is Generated Each Day?' (*World Economic Forum*, 17 April 2019) available at www.weforum.org/agenda/2019/04/how-much-data-is-generated-each-day-cf4bddf29f.

[29] UNESCO, 'Digital Skills Critical for Jobs and Social Inclusion' (15 March 2018) available at https://en.unesco.org/news/digital-skills-critical-jobs-and-social-inclusion.

[30] Coleman, *Foundations of Social Theory* 302.

will participate if their benefits increase with their contribution to the outcome.[31] Other types of specific incentives, psychological and less tangible, have been considered.[32] For instance, 'expressive incentives' acknowledge the incentive for some people to join a process mainly to express their support or reaffirm their identity.[33] Another range of selective incentives are associated with social norms such as a sense of duty to the community, or the threat of social sanctions.[34]

Today, citizens are in fact exploring new forms of political participation. The traditional forms of political participation (eg, political elections) are in decline in many liberal democracies, while new social movements emerge thanks to the generalisation of digital technologies. ICTs are not the source of this change, but merely an enabler.

IV. Towards New Forms of Political Participation

Liberal democracies are based on the assumption that citizens can and will take part in the governance of the commons through elections, referendums, and votes.[35] Even if the objective of inclusive participation with a complete political integration of the working class has not been fully achieved in liberal democracies,[36] universal suffrage still enabled a large part of the population to participate in the design of public policies, and ended the conflict between labour and capital interests.[37] A consequence of this inclusion is the adoption of citizens' fundamental liberal basic rights and the generalisation of social welfare systems. This led to a high degree of contentment with representative democracy.[38]

However, levels of citizen participation have progressively declined for about two decades.[39] This disengagement is particularly illustrated by a reluctance to

---

[31] M Olson, *The Logic of Collective Action: Public Goods and the Theory of Groups* (Cambridge, MA, Harvard University Press, 1965) 51.

[32] S Rosenstone and JM Hansen, *Mobilization, Participation and Democracy in America* (New York, Macmillan, 1993) 16–20; Verba, Schlozman and Brady, *Voice and Equality* ch 4; P Whiteley, 'Rational Choice and Political Participation: Evaluating the Debate' (1995) 48 *Political Research Quarterly* 211; S Finkel and E Muller, 'Rational Choice and the Dynamics of Collective Political Action: Evaluating Alternative Models with Panel Data' (1998) 92 *American Political Science Review* 37.

[33] R Calvert, 'Identity, Expression and Rational Choice Theory' in I Katznelson and H Milner (eds), *Political Science: The State of the Discipline* (New York, Norton, 2002).

[34] J Elster, *Nuts and Bolts for the Social Sciences* (Cambridge, Cambridge University Press, 1989) ch 12; Coleman, *Foundations of Social Theory* chs 10–11; S Knack, 'Civic Norms, Social Sanctions and Voter Turnout' (1992) 4 *Rationality & Society* 133.

[35] P Parvin, 'Is Deliberative Democracy Feasible? Political Disengagement and Trust in Liberal Democratic States' (2015) 98 *The Monist* 407.

[36] N Bobbio, 'The Future of Democracy' (1984) 61 *Telos: Critical Theory of the Contemporary* 3.

[37] D Jörke, 'Political Participation, Social Inequalities, and Special Veto Powers' (2016) 19 *Critical Review of International Social and Political Philosophy* 320.

[38] Marshall, *Citizenship and Social Class*; C Crouch, *Post-Democracy* (Cambridge, Polity, 2004).

[39] Jörke, 'Political Participation'.

become an active member of political parties and abstention from voting.[40] Moreover, it is the poorest parts of the population that abstain from voting.[41] It has become evident that the decrease of participation corresponds mainly to the withdrawal of the most socially disadvantaged parts of the population[42] and is strongly related to inequalities in economic status and education level.[43] Hence, there is a social bias in the decline of political participation: it is primarily less-educated and low-income citizens who vote less often and show less interest in politics.[44] In other words, this political disengagement leads to 'a weakening of the political importance of ordinary working people'.[45]

This political disengagement is well illustrated by a study co-sponsored by the American Political Science Association and the Brookings Institution, which begins:

> American democracy is at risk. The risk comes not from some external threat but from disturbing internal trends: an erosion of the activities and capacities of citizenship. Americans have turned away from politics and the public sphere in large numbers, leaving our civic life impoverished. Citizens participate in public affairs less frequently, with less knowledge and enthusiasm, in fewer venues, and less equally than is healthy for a vibrant democratic polity.[46]

In his influential book entitled *Bowling Alone* Robert Putnam concludes:

> declining electoral participation is merely the most visible symptom of a broader disengagement from community life. Like a fever, electoral abstention is even more important as a sign of deeper trouble in the body politic than as a malady itself. It is not just from the voting booth that Americans are increasingly AWOL.[47]

Putnam is indeed probably one of the best-known contributors to the academic debate revolving around disengagement of citizens in post-industrial society,

---

[40] D Putnam and SJ Pharr, *Disaffected Democracies: What's Troubling the Trilateral Countries?* (Princeton, NJ, Princeton University Press, 2000); RJ Dalton, *Democratic Challenges, Democratic Choices. The Erosion of Political Support in Advanced Industrial Democracies* (Oxford, Oxford University Press, 2004).

[41] L Bartels, *Unequal Democracy: The Political Economy of the New Gilded Age* (Princeton, NJ, Princeton University Press, 2016); M Gilens, *Affluence and Influence: Economic Inequality and Political Power in America* (Princeton, NJ, Princeton University Press, 2014); F Solt, 'Economic Inequality and Democratic Political Engagement' (2008) 52 *American Journal of Political Science* 48.

[42] S Birch, *Full Participation: A Comparative Study of Compulsory Voting* (Manchester, Manchester University Press, 2009); A Schäfer, 'Republican Liberty and Compulsory Voting', Max-Planck-Institut für Gesellschaftsforschung Discussion Paper 11/17 (2011); A Schäfer, 'Liberalization, Inequality and Democracy's Discontent' in A Schäfer and W Streeck (eds), *Politics in the Age of Austerity* (Cambridge, Polity Press, 2013).

[43] A Lijphart, 'Unequal Participation: Democracy's Unresolved Dilemma' (1997) 91 *American Political Science Review* 1; L Hill, 'Turnout, Abstention and Democratic Legitimacy' in J Brennan and L Hill (eds) *Compulsory Voting: For and Against* (New York, Cambridge University Press, 2014).

[44] Jörke, 'Political Participation'.

[45] Crouch, *Post-Democracy* 29.

[46] S Macedo et al, *Democracy at Risk: How Political Choices Undermine Citizen Participation, and What We Can Do About It* (Washington, DC, Brookings Institution Press, 2005) 1.

[47] R Putnam, *Bowling Alone* (New York, Simon and Schuster, 2000) 35.

illustrated by decreasing levels of civic engagement, electoral turnout and higher distrust towards public institutions, political leaders and parties.[48]

The distrust in democratic institutions, and the lack of changes in political processes has led to an increasingly large gap between populations and their representatives, who are perceived as 'out of touch with the real world' and too far removed from 'normal' citizens' life-worlds,[49] which in turn feeds this vicious circle of reduced citizen participation. This distrust of political figures can also be associated with a rejection of democracy as a whole since it no longer succeeds in engaging, and consequently representing, all parts of society.[50]

The abstention from voting of one part of society is preoccupying for multiple reasons. First, due to the rise of economic inequalities in the world, this less privileged part of the population is growing and could eventually represent the majority in some countries. Second, this disengagement goes against the foundational principle of political equality.[51] This disregard for hard-won participation opportunities has some tangible impacts. In many liberal democracies today, the results of elections are more contested than ever, elected officials are viewed less and less as representative, and social movements emerge to bypass traditional democratic processes, which are perceived as only favouring the elite.

However, this political disengagement may be, in fact, only one side of the coin, and it is probably premature to assume the decline of civic engagement.[52] Low rates of political participation refer to a minimalist definition of political participation, which does not include all the new variations and actors that constitute civil society today. As Dalton mentions, 'the trends in political activity represent changes in the style of political action, and not just changes in the level of participation.'[53] Hence, if we include social movements such as the youth movement to denounce the inaction of politicians towards climate change 'Fridaysforfuture', political participation is not in decline but changing form. This leads Hay to state of political participation:

> those with the most restrictive and conventional conceptions of political participation identify a strong and consistent pattern of declining political participation and

---

[48] T Skocpol and MP Fiorina, 'Making Sense of the Civic Engagement Debate' in T Skocpol and MP Fiorina (eds), *Civic Engagement in American Democracy* (Washington, DC, The Brookings Institution, 1999).

[49] Jörke, 'Political Participation'.

[50] C Hay, *Why We Hate Politics* (Cambridge, Polity, 2007).

[51] T Christiano, *The Rule of the Many. Fundamental Issues in Democratic Theory* (Boulder, Westview, 1996); RA Dahl, *On Political Equality* (New Haven, Yale University Press, 2006).

[52] P Norris, *Democratic Phoenix: Reinventing Political Activism* (New York, Cambridge University Press, 2002) 5–7; D Stolle and M Hooghe, 'Shifting Inequalities: Patterns of Exclusion and Inclusion in Emerging Forms of Political Participation' (2011) 13 *European Societies* 119.

[53] RJ Dalton, 'Citizenship Norms and the Expansion of Political Participation' (2008) 56 *Political Studies* 76, 94.

engagement over time, whilst those with a more inclusive conception discern instead a change in the *mode* of political participation.[54]

By allowing information to propagate further and faster, digital technologies and, in particular, social media platforms have supported the rapid emergence of new forms of dissidence,[55] that compete with existing sources of authority to set the international agenda[56] or push politicians and business leaders in one direction or another. For instance, the anti-austerity 'Indignados' or 'Occupy' movements are prominent examples of such non-legislative and extra-judicial public arenas where citizens use online platforms to organise protests, coordinate their actions, debate societal and social issues, push for specific public policies, or defend a cultural identity.[57]

This new range of political activities has proliferated thanks to the generalisation of digital technologies. Indeed, digital technologies favour the dynamics of networking in any system or relation using these technologies.[58] They allow complex, global, and extensive interaction among individuals. A single post on Facebook can become viral and lead to millions of people taking to the streets or showing their support for a cause. For instance, it did not take long after the release of a new White House dress code for a backlash to be organised and the hashtag #DressLikeAWoman to go viral.[59] This network dynamic leads to flexible processes and organisations that can change shape and form rapidly.[60]

Thanks to social media platforms, citizens gained additional skills to coordinate their actions and have a say. The skill revolution enabled a new array of social movements and civil society organisations to emerge.[61] These new political forms of political activities provide a new source of political meaning to citizens, and digital technologies provide the means for their voices to be heard differently.

Moreover, these alternative forms of political participation are as subject to digital influence and disinformation campaigns as traditional forms of political participation. A social movement can also be influenced by private interests hiding behind social media platforms. All forms of political participation are vulnerable to the recent digital political communication instruments discussed below.

---

[54] Hay, *Why We Hate Politics* 23.
[55] M Castells, 'The New Public Sphere: Global Civil Society, Communication Networks, and Global Governance' (2008) 616 *The Annals of the American Academy of Political and Social Science* 78.
[56] H Anheier et al, *Global Civil Society 2006/7* (London, Sage, 2007).
[57] M Edwards, *Civil Society* (Cambridge, Polity, 2014).
[58] M Castells, *The Rise of the Network Society*, vol 1: *The Information Age: Economy, Society and Culture* (Oxford, Blackwell, 1996).
[59] E Cresci, '#DressLikeAWoman: Twitter Backlash Over Reports of Dress Code for Trump Staff' *The Guardian* (3 February 2017).
[60] Castells, *The Information Age*.
[61] J Rosenau, 'Distant Proximities: Dynamics Beyond Globalization' (Princeton, NJ, Princeton University Press, 2003); J Duberry, *Global Environmental Governance in the Information Age: Civil Society Organizations and Digital Media* (London, Routledge, 2019).

V. Digital and Data-Driven Political Communication Tools

The case of Cambridge Analytica revealed how contemporary political campaigns use advanced digital technologies to influence the vote of citizens in a democracy. But the influence of digital technologies on the political landscape extends far beyond the day of the vote. This is a world of perpetual communication and campaigning.

Politicians and other public figures have always used information to their advantage, whether it be to increase their support or to suppress any form of dissidence. Until the last century, politicians won elections thanks to so-called traditional communication tools: meetings, rallies, media relations, the printed press, etc. In the last century, broadcast communication enabled new forms of large-scale propaganda, including during wartime and in fascist regimes.[62] In the twenty-first century, social networking technologies have enhanced the scale, scope and precision of how information is transmitted.[63]

Personal data is at the heart of the big data phenomenon, where huge amounts of data, disclosed willingly or unwillingly, are collected, stored, processed, and traded between a myriad of private actors. Social media platforms allow users to interact, share information, produce content in the form of text, pictures and videos, and coordinate their activities worldwide. By offering these online services for free, they gain unprecedented access to large sets of personal data, which they analyse to better target their online ads and detect new trends.

Thanks to the data collected from citizens on social media platforms, political parties and their leaders can better understand citizens, tailor their messages based on this knowledge, and reach out to them individually and on a large scale during political campaigns. Data-driven politics encompasses activities such as outreach, persuasion and citizen mobilisation, which are now conducted thanks to the analysis of large datasets.[64] Data-driven marketing is now commonly used by businesses but also, and more recently, for political campaigns.

Previous online user activity, behavioural data, demographics, psychological attributes, and predictive analytics allow political campaign leaders to identify patterns and predict future outcomes and trends, including what-if scenarios and risk assessment.[65] In terms of data variety, political campaign leaders can

---

[62] J Carson and M Cogley, 'Fake News: What Exactly Is It – And How Can You Spot It?' *The Telegraph* (7 January 2021).

[63] S Bradshaw and PN Howard, 'The Global Disinformation Order: 2019 Global Inventory of Organised Social Media Manipulation' Working Paper 2019.3 (Oxford, Project on Computational Propaganda, 2019).

[64] Z Tufekci, 'Engineering the Public: Big Data, Surveillance and Computational Politics' (2014) 19 *First Monday*.

[65] KC Montgomery, J Chester and K Kopp, 'Health Wearable Devices in the Big Data Era: Ensuring Privacy, Security, and Consumer Protection' (*Center for Digital Democracy*, 2017) available at www.democraticmedia.org/sites/default/files/field/public/2016/aucdd_wearablesreport_final121516.pdf.

accumulate large amounts of information about individual citizens by using public voter files as well as commercial data from data brokers,[66] including from travel and supermarket loyalty cards, behaviours on social media and mobile phones, but also ethnicity, civil status, sexual orientation, political orientation, credit rating, among others.

To answer the thirst for data from political campaign leaders, Facebook and Google offer them bespoke services.[67] In order to identify potential voters, political campaign leaders can 'clone' their most valuable supporters and see if other individuals and segments of the population on social media platforms match the demographics, psychographics and interests of this clone.[68] Facebook offers this service under the name Lookalike Audiences. Another opportunity to garner more data is called data onboarding,[69] the transfer of offline data, such as pre-digital customer records, to an online environment, which expands the frontiers for understanding individuals, especially over time. To control all of the incoming and outgoing information, political campaign leaders use a Data Management Platform (DMP), which allows them to centralise all the information about their audience and about their campaign.[70]

Neuromarketing is increasingly used to understand human thought processes and to better determine the most impactful message for the right person. Messages are indeed designed to trigger specific emotions and subconscious answers.[71] It enables campaign leaders to better grasp the impact of their content on potential voters[72] and adapt the persuasion message to each psychological profile.[73]

Thanks to this new generation of political communication, political leaders can tailor information inputs at the individual level with ever-increasing accuracy. Micro-targeting refers to the ability to know how an audience processes information down to the level of the individual and, based on this knowledge, reach out to them with a highly individualised message. If emotions have always been used during political campaigns, neuromarketing and micro-targeting enable political campaign leaders to be much more effective.

---

[66] IS Rubinstein, 'Voter Privacy in the Age of Big Data' [2014] *Wisconsin Law Review* 861.
[67] S Bond, 'Google and Facebook Build Digital Ad Duopoly' *Financial Times* (14 March 2017).
[68] LiveRamp, 'Look-Alike Modeling: The What, Why, and How' (*LiveRamp*, 31 March 2020) available at http://liveramp.com/blog/look-alike-modeling-the-what-why-and-how.
[69] J Schulz, 'Did my Ad Really Work? Closing the Loop on Data Onboarding' (*Adweek*, 9 January 2015).
[70] BlueKai, 'Whitepaper: Data Management Platforms Demystified' (2011) available at https://web.archive.org/web/20200215224411/http://www.bluekai.com/files/DMP_Demystified_Whitepaper_BlueKai.pdf.
[71] C McEleny, 'Ford and Xaxis Score in Vietnam Using Emotional Triggers Around the UEFA Champions League' (*The Drum*, 18 October 2016) available at www.thedrum.com/news/2016/10/18/ford-and-xaxis-score-vietnam-using-emotional-triggers-around-the-uefa-champions.
[72] T Kelshaw, 'Emotion Analytics: A Powerful Tool to Augment Gut Instinct' (*Think with Google*, August 2017) available at www.thinkwithgoogle.com/nordics/article/emotion-analytics-a-powerful-tool-to-augment-gut-instinct.
[73] SC Matz et al, 'Psychological Targeting as an Effective Approach to Digital Mass Persuasion' (2017) 114 *Proceedings of the National Academy of Sciences* 12714.

In terms of ad placement, new forms of automation allow 24/7 service without human intervention. Traditionally, ad spaces were negotiated and placed by humans. Today, Programmatic Advertising allows political campaign leaders to delegate these tasks to software that purchases digital advertising in real-time online auctions.[74] Political campaign leaders can also use data profiling to identify who will certainly vote for an opponent and target them with messages to prevent them from going to vote. For example, the 2016 Trump campaign targeted idealistic white liberals, young women and African Americans.[75]

These new-generation political communication tools are not only used domestically: they also enable foreign governments to intervene digitally in the internal affairs of another state. In numerous speeches, Russian President Vladimir Putin has repeatedly presented digital technologies as a set of instruments to advance national interests on the international stage.[76]

As identified by the so-called Mueller report,[77] disinformation campaigns in 2016 stemming from Russia spread specific types of information on social media platforms through bots: promulgating extreme views from both ends of the political spectrum to exacerbate tensions, while at the same time fuelling conspiracy theories.[78] The use of bots to amplify a lie, a subject, or a division that already exist in a society, or to drown out another topic, is an efficient instrument to destabilise civil society and societal cohesion within a foreign country.

In this context, the use of digital technologies, either by certain political leaders and parties, or by foreign governments, threatens the freedom to access information and think and hold an opinion. Citizens must necessarily base their political decision on the information they can access. If most of the information they access is online, then it is possible to conclude that most of the information they access is tailored individually for two main purposes: profit and influence. On the one hand, GAFAM adapt the content so that users remain online the longest time possible. Indeed, they make substantial profit when an individual is online through data collection and advertising. On the other hand, political parties use the same channels to feed bespoke information to their targeted audience so that they can influence their vote. What is new is both the scope and the opacity of this influence. When it happens on social media platforms, personalised content can reach millions of individuals simultaneously, but without the necessary scrutiny of any public authority and traditional media.

---

[74] D Chaffey, 'What is Programmatic Marketing?' (*Smart Insights*, 21 May 2020) available at www.smart-insights.com/internet-advertising/internet-advertising-targeting/what-is-programmatic-marketing.

[75] J Green and S Issenberg, 'Inside the Trump Bunker, with Days to Go' (*Bloomberg Businessweek*, 27 October 2016).

[76] OS Adesina, 'Foreign Policy in an Era of Digital Diplomacy' (2017) 3 *Cogent Social Sciences*.

[77] RS Mueller III, 'Report on the Investigation into Russian Interference in the 2016 Presidential Election' (Washington, DC, US Department of Justice, 2019).

[78] N Bentzen, 'From Post-Truth to Post-Trust' (*European Parliamentary Research Service Blog*, 25 October 2018) available at http://epthinktank.eu/2018/10/25/from-post-truth-to-post-trust.

VI. Assessing the Veracity of News

In the digital age, access to information is a paradox. On the one hand, digital technologies provide an unprecedented access to numerous sources of information for a large part of the world's population. According to the Pew Research Center, in 2021, almost 70 per cent of adult US citizens have a Facebook account and 70 per cent of them consult the social network every day.[79] Citizens now have access to a large spectrum of information sources, and traditional media outlets such as newspapers have become just one out of the many. On the other hand, citizens are influenced as to how and what information they are exposed to: digital platforms select the information on their behalf.[80] Pariser described well how algorithms restrict access to diversity of information, and in particular to alternative views, in what he terms the 'filter bubble'. The algorithms of social media platforms and web browsers influence the choice of article, video or website people can consult online. Hence citizens are permanently confined to a bespoke online information space, governed by the criteria of algorithms.[81] This means that social media platforms and web browsers are simultaneously enhancing and restricting access to information for citizens. In other words, it is not possible to conclude that these technologies help to better inform citizens.

Freedom of thought and freedom to hold an opinion are not only threatened by the way information is produced and distributed on social media platforms, but also by people's ability to assess the veracity of what they read online and to retain that information.

If certain political leaders use the term 'fake news' to discredit those they disagree with – journalists and opponents – false news and disinformation campaigns are nonetheless a reality of our contemporary world. False news can be described as fabricated and often partisan content that is presented as factual.[82] Lewis and Luck distinguish several categories of false news.[83] First, state-sponsored disinformation aims to influence citizens to either win an election, influence public opinion, or propagate division among segments of the population, nationally or internationally. Second, highly partisan news sites spread information that is not necessarily factual but rather supportive of one political viewpoint or political party. Third, social media platforms enable the vast propagation of false news and

---

[79] B Auxier and M Anderson, 'Social Media Use in 2021' (*Pew Research Center*, 7 April 2021) available at www.pewresearch.org/internet/2021/04/07/social-media-use-in-2021.
[80] S Lindgren, *Digital Media and Society: Theories, Topics and Tools* (London, Sage, 2017).
[81] E Pariser, *The Filter Bubble: What the Internet Is Hiding from You* (New York, Penguin, 2012).
[82] G Pennycook et al, 'Prior Exposure Increases Perceived Accuracy of Fake News' (2018) 147 *Journal of Experimental Psychology: General* 1865.
[83] M Lewis and C Luck, 'Fake News and its Impact on SEO and Digital Marketing – Many-Minds Give It a Go' (*Slideshare.net*, 20 April 2018) available at www.slideshare.net/coraleva93/fake-news-and-its-impact-on-seo-many-minds-give-it-a-go.

emotional content at an unprecedented speed, scope and personalisation level. Lewis and Luck also added satire or parody as sources of false news.

False news is frequently juicy, sensational and crazy, which makes it highly attractive. On social media platforms, the most sensationalist and extreme content becomes viral by generating the most comments, shares and likes. In other words, the veracity of content is not the main criteria for virality. A 2018 MIT study found that fake news was 70 per cent more shared than real news on Twitter.[84] And the reason is users, not bots. Indeed, many users do not read social media posts in detail. The title, the image or the abstract are enough to 'like' and share them. In a context of infobesity, content itself loses some of its value. As Dean argued:

> [t]he message is simply part of a circulating data stream. Its particular content is irrelevant. Who sent it is irrelevant. Who receives it is irrelevant. That it need be responded to is irrelevant. The only thing that is relevant is circulation, the addition to the pool. Any particular contribution remains secondary to the fact of circulation.[85]

A piece of information is perceived as more believable when it has already been seen somewhere else some time before. Pennycook et al have shown how fake news headlines were perceived as more accurate when they had already been seen on Facebook, whether after a single exposure within the same session or after a week.[86] The fact that these headlines had a low level of overall believability, were contested by fact checkers and did not align with the user's political ideology did not reduce the accuracy perception. Prior exposure provided this 'illusory truth effect' and increased the believability of any type of news, with the exception of extreme implausible statements such as 'The earth is a perfect square'. This means that repetition is the key to increasing the impact of news on what people believe and is a more influential criteria than plausibility. Hence the capacity of political communication to cross-target and micro-target individuals everywhere anytime makes the filter bubble even more effective and increases the believability of any type of news, hence disinformation campaigns.

When a piece of news is revealed to be false, individuals adjust their judgement based on the new facts. In that sense, fact checking can help reduce the impact of disinformation campaigns. However, this re-evaluation depends on the cognitive ability of each individual. Indeed, De Keersmaecker and Roets have shown that citizens with lower levels of cognitive ability do not adjust their beliefs based on the new facts as much as others with higher levels of cognitive ability.[87] They tend

---

[84] S Vosoughi, D Roy and S Aral, 'The Spread of True and False News Online' (2018) 359 *Science* 1146.

[85] J Dean, *Publicity's Secret: How Technoculture Capitalizes on Democracy* (Ithaca, NY, Cornell University Press, 2002) 85.

[86] Pennycook et al, 'Prior Exposure'.

[87] J de Keersmaecker and A Roets, '"Fake News": Incorrect, But Hard to Correct. The Role of Cognitive Ability on the Impact of False Information on Social Impressions (2017) 65 *Intelligence* 107.

to keep believing that some part of this false news is probably true to a certain degree, even after the false information has been explicitly disproved.

Moreover, thanks to the unlimited – yet bespoke – access to content, online users do not need to make efforts to remember information anymore. They can easily find what they need to recall on Wikipedia, access news articles on Facebook, use an online map to find their way home, and browse the web for a definition or to find out about an upcoming event. Studies show that individuals have lower rates of recall when they know they can access the information online.[88] The danger is that citizens may have a very short-term memory of events and take different consecutive versions of the same reality for the truth.

Furthermore, individuals continuously evaluate the validity of their understanding of the world in a process called 'epistemic vigilance', checking that the information they believe to be true is accurate.[89] With this objective in mind, people can detect lies when they have the necessary time, resources, and motivation. Lies are often discovered through contradictory information from another source, or evidence that challenges a deceptive account. However, in our contemporary digital landscape, it is increasingly difficult for citizens to verify the source of information. Indeed, they rarely have the time, the motivation and the right skills to perform a thorough analysis of each piece of information they receive – in particular when the flow of information never stops.

This credulity is reinforced by a cognitive bias called the 'truth bias':[90] people tend to believe the information they receive. Although being biased towards the truth is usually the correct response, this is evidently not always the case. The difficulty in exercising epistemic vigilance, combined with the truth bias and the filter bubble, almost inevitably leads citizens to consume and believe the information they are presented with.

The overload of information, combined with the use of bots, trolls and fake accounts on social media platforms, has left the door open to disinformation campaigns, where false information is spread with the objective of blurring the line between fiction and reality: narratives, fiction and opinions have replaced reality and facts. The permeability of false news and the difficulty in countering it makes citizens vulnerable to online manipulation. By undermining traditional institutions, such as the traditional media, digital technologies have left a void that can then be filled with false news and propaganda.[91]

---

[88] B Sparrow, J Liu and DM Wegner, 'Google Effects on Memory: Cognitive Consequences of Having Information at our Fingertips' (2011) 333 *Science* 776.
[89] T Hancock, 'Psychological Principles for Public Diplomacy in an Evolving Information Ecosystem' in S Powers and M Kounalakis (eds), 'Can Public Diplomacy Survive the Internet? Bots, Echo Chambers, and Disinformation' (Washington, DC, US Advisory Commission on Public Diplomacy, 2016).
[90] ibid.
[91] N Persily, 'The 2016 U.S. Election: Can Democracy Survive the Internet?' (2017) 28(2) *Journal of Democracy* 63.

VII. Conclusion

The digital technologies described here threaten the 'right to hold opinions without interference', as stated in Article 19 of the ICCPR. Initially offering a space for free speech, digital technologies, and social media platforms in particular, have gradually become a space for disinformation to spread. The emergence of social bots, artificial intelligence, and computational propaganda contributes to a war of narratives. ICTs make persuasive techniques more extensive, more ubiquitous, and yet more difficult to identify because they are hidden under millions of other messages and behind multiple identities. As Fukuyama argues, the

> 'weaponization of information' is unprecedented. … The traditional answer to the spread of bad information has been to inject good information into the mix, on the assumption that the truth would rise to the top. But in a world of trolls and bots, where simple facts are instantly countered by automated agents, this strategy may not be adequate.[92]

Online, citizens are constrained in their filter bubbles and have difficulty in checking the veracity of information, which leads them to almost inevitably believing the information they are presented with. The challenge in distinguishing between interests and evidence, opinion, and fact are affecting not only citizens, but also journalism, academia, courts, law enforcement, science, and intelligence.[93] All sectors of society are vulnerable to disinformation and have their access to information restricted by algorithms, which presents a high risk for democratic institutions and can contribute to sharp domestic divisions, political paralysis, and deadlock.

This is of concern, in particular when a part of the population voluntarily excludes itself from taking part in the governance of their country, as democratic institutions become incredibly fragile. Indeed, political participation also has the role of preventing the capture of public institutions by elite power.[94] Democratically elected leaders gain their legitimacy thanks to their capacity to represent the largest part of their population. Without this legitimacy, democracy opens the floor to power struggles and power abuses. And as Jason Stanley notes, 'without truth, there is just power'.[95]

---

[92] F Fukuyama, 'Forward: Public Diplomacy in a Post-Truth Society' in S Powers and M Kounalakis (eds), 'Can Public Diplomacy Survive the Internet? Bots, Echo Chambers, and Disinformation' (Washington, DC, US Advisory Commission on Public Diplomacy, 2016) 1.

[93] Bentzen, 'From Post-Truth to Post-Trust'.

[94] P Parvin, 'Democracy Without Participation: A New Politics for a Disengaged Era' (2018) 24 *Res Publica* 31.

[95] J Stanley, 'In Defense of Truth, and the Threat of Disinformation' in S Powers and M Kounalakis (eds), 'Can Public Diplomacy Survive the Internet? Bots, Echo Chambers, and Disinformation' (Washington, DC, US Advisory Commission on Public Diplomacy, 2016) 71.

9

Is There a Human Rights Obligation to Protect Democratic Discourse in Cyberspace?

NULA FREI

I. Introduction

Discourse and deliberation are fundamental components of a functioning democracy and democratic theory stipulates that the public exchange of arguments is vital for political opinion-building. Concepts such as the Habermasian 'ideal speech situation' indicate that certain preconditions must be met in order to classify a public discourse as democratic. In recent years, more and more political discourses do not exclusively take place in classical media (such as newspapers, radio or TV broadcasting) anymore, but are increasingly held online. Political deliberations today also take place on blogs, vlogs, podcasts, in online discussion fora or on social media. On the one hand, new media technologies have promised further democratisation of society, ie, by providing easier access to information and by augmenting avenues for personal expression. On the other hand, critics lament that technologies induce fragmented and enraged discussion, and are thus far from guaranteeing a more democratic public sphere. Dangers associated with online manipulation (such as 'fake news' or opinion bots) and segmentation (due to 'echo chamber' and 'filter bubble' effects), coupled with the fact that information published online is able to circulate at unprecedented speed, raise doubts as to whether public discourse in cyberspace actually contributes to a democratic discourse in the sense of the Habermasian ideal.

This chapter looks at this problem from a human rights law perspective and specifically asks if there is an obligation under human rights law to protect democratic discourse in cyberspace. By analysing the case law of the European Court of Human Rights (ECtHR), it examines if and how far international human rights law mirrors the insights from democratic theory and translates them into legally binding standards. In legal terms, this means analysing whether there is a human rights obligation for states to guarantee, ensure and protect democratic discourse. In a first step, I will present the theoretical basis, that is the democratic theory of democratic deliberation and discourse. The second part analyses the extent to which the ECtHR has engaged with the quality of democratic discourse in its case law to date and whether a positive or negative obligation to protect democratic discourse can be derived from this. From there, I continue by describing the case law of the Court that specifically concerns online political discourse, which will allow me to answer the question whether we are currently witnessing the birth of a human rights obligation to protect democratic discourse in cyberspace. I end with concluding observations on the gaps and challenges posed by digital technology for democratic discourse and human rights.

II. The 'Public Space' in Democratic Theory

The contemporary democratic state bases the legitimacy of its political power usually on the consent given by public opinion. No matter what democratic theory we look at, all of them contain an element of public consent for the legitimisation of state power. The formation of rational public opinion is seen by many democratic theorists as central to a strong democracy.[1] The idea of the public is closely tied to democratic ideals that call for citizen participation in public affairs.[2] When thinking of the public, one envisions open exchanges of political thoughts and ideas, such as those in ancient Greek *agoras* or colonial-era town halls. For a public consent to be formed and expressed, the notion of 'public sphere' is critical in this regard. The most influential theory on the public sphere has certainly been Habermas's work and in particular his book on 'the structural transformation of the public sphere' (*Strukturwandel der Öffentlichkeit*), where he defines the public sphere as a realm of social life in which public opinion can be formed.[3]

The public sphere is the source of the public opinion needed to legitimise authority in a functioning democracy. For Habermas, the public sphere is a space in which all citizens can debate public policies critically, substantially and rationally. A space where private citizens interact and share information and ideas. Habermas believes that the public sphere can be constituted and maintained most effectively through dialogue, speeches, debate and discussion.

---

[1] See, eg, S Benhabib, 'Toward a Deliberative Model of Democratic Legitimacy' in S Benhabib (ed), *Democracy and Difference: Contesting the Boundaries of the Political* (Princeton, NJ, Princeton University Press, 1996).
[2] Z Papacharissi, 'The Virtual Sphere: The Internet as a Public Sphere' (2002) 4 *New Media & Society* 9.
[3] J Habermas, *The Structural Transformation of the Public Sphere: An Inquiry into a Category of Bourgeois Society* (reprinted, Cambridge, Polity Press, 2008) 27.

According to Habermasian theory, the ideal public sphere presents specific characteristics, namely:[4]

- *Reciprocity*: Citizens are engaged in conversation with each other, and their messages are reflected upon and discussed by others.
- *Justification*: Only if valid reasons are advanced may subjects be able to find common ground.
- *Reflexivity*: Participants critically examine their values, assumptions, and interests, as well as the larger social context.
- *Ideal role taking*: All positions, not just those immediately present in the forum but all affected by the question under consideration, are taken into account and listened to respectfully.
- *Sincerity*: Participants must make a sincere effort to make known all relevant information including their intentions, interests, needs, and desires.
- *Inclusion and discursive equality*: All those who are affected by the issues under discussion should be able to participate. Discursive equality concerns inclusion among those that are able to access a forum, where each participant should have an equal opportunity to introduce and question any assertion whatsoever and to express attitudes, desires, and needs.

The public sphere is not necessarily a geographical category. It can also be constituted by newspapers and other forms of public media. Habermas goes even further and asserts that public debate can take place in all kinds of opinion-forming associations, such as churches, sports clubs, grassroots movements, trade unions, etc, while he voices criticism on the commercialisation of the mass media in which the public sphere is produced top-down rather than bottom-up.

While the Habermasian model of 'public space' has been ground-breaking and remains one of the most important theoretical models to describe democratic opinion-building processes, it has also been criticised, most prominently from a postmodern-feminist angle. Fraser, for example, challenged the inclusivity and equality of the model, by pointing to the fact that the bourgeois public sphere excluded major sections of society (women, the working class, children),[5] a critique that was later accepted by Habermas himself.[6]

---

[4] L Dahlberg, 'The Habermasian Public Sphere: A Specification of the Idealized Conditions of Democratic Communication' [2004] *Studies in Social and Political Thought* 2.

[5] N Fraser, 'Rethinking the Public Sphere' in CJ Calhoun (ed), *Habermas and the Public Sphere* (Cambridge, MA, MIT Press, 2011) 66.

[6] J Habermas, 'Further Reflections on the Public Sphere and Concluding Remarks' in CJ Calhoun (ed), *Habermas and the Public Sphere* (Cambridge, MA, MIT Press, 2011) 422.

III. A Human Rights Obligation to Protect Democratic Discourse in the 'Offline' World

The theoretical model of democratic deliberation in the 'public space' has substantially influenced human rights discourse. This is most clearly visible in the fundamental role for democracy that is attributed to the guarantee of freedom of expression. The ECtHR, for example, consistently states that freedom of expression is a cornerstone of a functioning democracy. Already in its *Handyside* judgment from 1976, the Court stated that '[f]reedom of expression constitutes one of the essential foundations of such a [democratic] society, one of the basic conditions for its progress and for the development of every man'.[7] This is particularly true for free political debate and the freedom of political expression, to which the Court attaches 'a particular importance', as it stated for example in *Féret* in 2009.[8] The Court has also specifically pointed out the fundamental role of the press and its role for opinion-building and opinion communication:

> The press plays an essential role in a democratic society. Although it must not overstep certain bounds, in particular in respect of the reputation and rights of others and the need to prevent the disclosure of confidential information, its duty is nevertheless to impart – in a manner consistent with its obligations and responsibilities – information and ideas on all matters of public interest.[9]

And in *Centro Europa 7 SRL and Di Stefano* it stated:

> Freedom of the press and other news media affords the public one of the best means of discovering and forming an opinion of the ideas and attitudes of political leaders. It is incumbent on the press to impart information and ideas on political issues and on other subjects of public interest. Not only does the press have the task of imparting such information and ideas: the public also has a right to receive them.[10]

The Court thus acknowledges that public debate on political issues has a fundamental role for a functioning democracy. From a human rights perspective, the freedom of expression codified in Article 10 of the European Convention on Human Rights (ECHR) therefore becomes the guarantee that protects citizens' rights to take part in the public sphere and to contribute to the exchange of political arguments that are so important for democracy. Accordingly, the Court gives a heightened level of protection to forms of political expression, compared to other forms of expression such as commercial or artistic expressions.[11] Whether an expression or speech is 'political' will be determined by the Court with regard

---

[7] *Handyside v UK*, no 5493/72 (7 December 1976) 49.
[8] *Féret v Belgium*, no 15615/07 (16 July 2009) 63.
[9] *De Haes and Gijsels v Belgium*, no 19983/92 (24 February 1997) 37; *Fressoz and Roire v France*, no 29183/95 (21 January 1999) 45(ii).
[10] *Centro Europa 7 SRL and Di Stefano v Italy* [GC], no 38433/09 (7 June 2012) 131.
[11] See, eg, *Ayse Öztürk v Turkey*, no 24914/94 (15 October 2002) 67(iv).

to its content and the kind of terms employed.[12] The Court regularly gives a wide interpretation to the notion of 'political expression', and has considered as forms of political expression, for instance, paid political advertising in the media,[13] the display of symbols in order to express a political position,[14] the distribution of leaflets expressing the political position of a civil society organisation,[15] or the distribution of a newspaper to military personnel.[16]

A. The Negative Obligation to Abstain from Interfering in Political Speech

As a consequence of this heightened level of protection that is granted to the expression of political opinions, the Court allows only little scope for restrictions on political expression by governments and other public bodies.[17] While the Court acknowledges that certain restrictions on political expression might be necessary,[18] it clearly states that such exceptions must be interpreted narrowly.[19] The general rule is therefore one of non-interference: in order to guarantee a free and fair public sphere, governments have a negative obligation to abstain from interferiging in political communication, be it between private parties or mediated through the mass media, because restrictions of political communication would in principle distort the ideal speech situation.

The Court thus acknowledges in its settled case law the important role that political expression plays for democracy. Even though the Court has – to our knowledge – never explicitly referred to democratic theory, the fact that the Court emphasises the importance of political expression and the mass media for democratic opinion-building and opinion communication, and ultimately for the formulation of consent to political authority, is a clear reflection of this theory.

B. The Positive Obligation to Protect Democratic Discourse

The human rights obligations of states are not confined to negative obligations, however. As I will show in the following paragraphs, it follows from the Court's

---

[12] *Ceylan v Turkey*, no 23556/94 (8 July 1999) 33; *TV Vest As & Rogaland Pensjonistparti v Norway*, no 21132/05 (11 December 2008) 64.
[13] *VgT Verein gegen Tierfabriken v Switzerland*, no 24699/94 (28 June 2001); *TV Vest As & Rogaland Pensjonistparti v Norway*; *Animal Defenders International v UK*, no 48876/08 (22 April 2013).
[14] *Fáber v Hungary*, no 40721/08 (24 July 2012).
[15] *Bowman v UK*, no 24839/94 (19 February 1998); *Brosa v Germany*, no 5709/09 (17 April 2014).
[16] *Vereinigung demokratischer Soldaten Österreichs and Gubi v Austria*, no 15153/89 (19 December 1994).
[17] *Perinçek v Switzerland*, no 27510/08 (15 October 2015) 197; *Wingrove v UK*, no 17419/90 (25 November 1996) 58; *Ceylan v Turkey* 34; *Animal Defenders International v UK* 102.
[18] See, eg, *Incal v Turkey*, no 22678/93 (9 June 1998) 53.
[19] *Ayse Öztürk v Turkey* 49.

case law that there is also a positive obligation to guarantee an effective democratic discourse and to take active steps in that regard. Those positive obligations flow from Article 10 ECHR as well as from Article 3 of Additional Protocol No 1.

i. Under Article 10 of the ECHR

Under Article 10, we can distinguish two constellations. First, the Court has consistently accepted that measures that aim to protect democratic processes constitute a legitimate aim for restrictions of Article 10 of the Convention, in that they fall under the legitimate aim of the 'protection of rights of others'. Although not a 'positive obligation' per se, this case law shows us that the protection of democratic discourse is a legitimate aim and can thus justify interferences in the freedom of expression and even in political expression that benefits from a higher degree of protection. For example, in *Ahmed and Others*, the Court considered that restrictions on the involvement of senior local government officers in certain types of political activity (such as standing for, and holding, public elected office, holding office in a political party, or speaking in public in a way that might be regarded as engaging in party political debate) were justified because they intended to protect the rights of others to effective political democracy.[20] It explicitly rejected the argument of the applicants that the protection of effective democracy could only be invoked where there was a threat to the stability of the constitutional or political order. The Court stated:

> To limit this notion to [a context where there was a direct threat to the constitutional or political order] would be to overlook both the interests served by democratic institutions such as local authorities and the need to make provision to secure their proper functioning where this is considered necessary to safeguard those interests.[21]

In the Court's view, therefore, the proper functioning of democracy, and democratic discourse, must be protected at all times and on a daily basis. In its case law, the Court has also given indications as to what is to be understood by the protection of democratic processes. In *VgT Verein gegen Tierfabriken*, it accepted that specific measures served

> to ensure the *independence of broadcasters*, spare the political process from undue commercial influence, provide for a degree of *equality of opportunity among the different forces of society* and to *support the press*, which remained free to publish political advertisements. (Emphases added)[22]

And in *Orlovskaya Iskra*, the Court acknowledged that the limitations found in the Russian Electoral Rights Act in force at the time of application were 'aimed at *transparency of elections*, including *campaign finances*, as well as at enforcing the

---

[20] *Ahmed and Others v UK*, no 22954/93 (2 September 1998) 49.
[21] ibid 52.
[22] *VgT Verein gegen Tierfabriken v Switzerland* 6.

voters' right to *impartial, truthful and balanced information via mass media outlets* and the *formation of their informed choices in an election*' (emphases added).²³

This case law gives us indications as to what elements of the public sphere are considered so important by the Court that their protection even justifies restrictions of political expression: the independence of the press, a certain balance or equality of opportunity among the different forces of society, transparency of elections, including campaign finances, as well as the impartiality and truthfulness of mass media information. While there might certainly be many more elements of a democratic public sphere that merit active protection by the state, and it is not excluded that the Court could acknowledge further elements in future cases, the ones already established do align to a substantial extent with the characteristics of an ideal public sphere in the Habermasian sense, such as justification, sincerity and inclusion.

Second, in specific cases, the Court has also found a clear positive obligation to guarantee elements of democratic discourse. This has particularly been the case with content pluralism in the audio-visual media. In *Informationsverein Lentia and Others*, the Court stressed, once more, the fundamental role of freedom of expression in a democratic society, in particular where, through the press, it serves to impart information and ideas of general interest. It stated that such an undertaking 'cannot be successfully accomplished unless it is grounded in the principle of pluralism, of which the state is the ultimate guarantor. This observation is especially valid in relation to audio-visual media, whose programmes are often broadcast very widely.'²⁴ Furthermore, in *Centro Europa 7 SRL and Di Stefano*, the Grand Chamber of the Court, after having stated that there can be no democracy without pluralism and that it is of the essence of democracy to allow diverse political programmes to be proposed and debated,²⁵ went on to observe 'that in such a sensitive sector as the audio-visual media, in addition to its negative duty of non-interference the state has a positive obligation to put in place an appropriate legislative and administrative framework to guarantee effective pluralism'.²⁶

To sum up, with regard to the right to freedom of expression, the Court has acknowledged a positive duty to protect specific aspects of democratic discourse such as the independence of the press, a certain balance or equality of opportunity among the different forces of society, transparency of elections, as well as the impartiality and truthfulness of mass media information, and has, in view of the wide reach of audio-visual media, stipulated a clear obligation to put in place a legislative and administrative framework to protect pluralism in those specific media.

---

²³ *Orlovskaya Iskra v Russia*, no 42911/08 (21 February 2017) 104.
²⁴ *Informationsverein Lentia and Others v Austria*, nos 13914/88; 15041/89; 15717/89; 15779/89; 17207/90 (24 November 1993) 38.
²⁵ *Centro Europa 7 SRL and Di Stefano v Italy* 129.
²⁶ ibid 134.

ii. Under Article 3 of Protocol No 1

Article 10 of the Convention is not the only article that covers activities in the context of democratic processes. The right to free elections, as enshrined in Article 3 of Protocol No 1, obliges Member States to hold free elections at reasonable intervals by secret ballot, under conditions which will ensure the free expression of the opinion of the people in the choice of the legislature. Article 3 of Protocol No 1 differs from the other substantive provisions of the Convention and the Protocols as it is phrased in terms of the obligation of the High Contracting Party to hold elections which ensure the free expression of the opinion of the people rather than in terms of a particular right or freedom.[27] From its wording, Article 3 concerns only the choice of the legislature. The Court and the Commission have consistently held that Article 3 is limited to elections concerning the choice of the legislature and does not apply to referendums.[28] However, the Court has indicated that under certain circumstances, a process described as a referendum could also fall within the ambit of Article 3 of Protocol No 1, if the process takes place 'at reasonable intervals by secret ballot, under conditions which will ensure the free expression of the opinion of the people in the choice of the legislature'.[29]

In a number of cases concerning Article 10 of the Convention, the Court has emphasised the close relationship between the right to free elections and freedom of expression. This interplay between the Article 10 and Article 3 of Protocol No 1 rights was first defined in the case of *Mathieu-Mohin and Clerfayt*[30] and then further elaborated in the *Bowman* case.[31] The relevant principles in this context were recently extensively set out in the *Orlovskaya Iskra* case, which concerned a regional newspaper that had been sanctioned for publishing articles criticising a candidate in national elections.[32] In this case, the Court stressed the following:

> the rights guaranteed by Article 3 of Protocol No. 1 are crucial to establishing and maintaining the foundations of an effective and meaningful democracy governed by the rule of law. Free elections and freedom of expression, particularly freedom of political debate, together form the bedrock of any democratic system. The two rights are inter-related and operate to reinforce each other: for example, freedom of expression is one of the 'conditions' necessary to 'ensure the free expression of the opinion of the people in the choice of the legislature'. For this reason, it is particularly important in the period preceding an election that opinions and information of all kinds are permitted to circulate freely. In the context of election debates, the unhindered exercise of freedom of speech by candidates has particular significance.[33]

---

[27] ECtHR, Guide on Article 3 of Protocol No 1 (30 April 2019) 6.
[28] See *Bader v Austria*, no 26633/95 (15 May 1996); *Nurminen v Finland*, no 27881/95 (26 February 1997); *Castelli and Others v Italy*, nos 35790/97 and 38438/97 (14 September 1998); *McLean and Cole v UK*, nos 12626/13 and 2522/12 (11 June 2016) 32.
[29] *McLean and Cole v UK* 33; *Moohan and Gillon v UK*, nos 22962/15 and 23345/15 (13 June 2017) 42.
[30] *Mathieu-Mohin and Clerfayt v Belgium*, no 9267/81 (2 March 1987).
[31] *Bowman v UK*, no 24839/94 (19 February 1998).
[32] *Orlovskaya Iskra v Russia*, no 42911/08 (21 February 2017).
[33] *Orlovskaya Iskra v Russia* 110 (citations omitted).

In order for the rights guaranteed by Article 3 of Protocol No 1 to be effective, their protection cannot remain confined to the candidature itself. The election campaign thus also falls within the scope of the provision.[34] While numerous cases concerning election campaigns have been examined under Article 10,[35] we also find cases that have been treated under Article 3 of Protocol No 1, where positive obligations, such as an equal distribution of airtime during pre-election campaigns, have been discussed. For example, in *Partija 'Jaunie Demokrāti' and Partija 'Mūsu Zeme'*, the Court stated that, while Article 3 of Protocol No 1 enshrined the principle of equal treatment of all citizens in the exercise of their electoral rights, it did not guarantee, as such, any right for a political party to be granted airtime on radio or television during the pre-election campaign. However, an issue may indeed arise in exceptional circumstances, for example, if in the run-up to an election one party were denied any kind of party political broadcast whilst other parties were granted slots for that purpose.[36] In the case of *Communist Party of Russia and Others*, the Court acknowledged the existence of a positive obligation under Article 3 of Protocol No 1 to ensure that coverage by regulated media was objective and compatible with the spirit of 'free elections' and secured de facto equality between different candidates.[37] In a different sense, in the *Oran* case, the Court held that the applicant, an unaffiliated independent candidate who was not granted airtime on national television for electioneering purposes, unlike the political parties, had not suffered a breach of his rights under Article 3 of Protocol No 1. The impugned measure, as applied to the applicant, did not disproportionately undermine the very substance of free expression of the opinion of the people or of the applicant's right to stand in elections for the purposes of Article 3 of Protocol No 1.[38]

To sum up, the duty to protect democratic discourse applies both in 'normal' times as well as in the period preceding elections and manifests itself in a negative and in a positive obligation. On the negative side, the state must refrain from interfering in free political debates, while on the positive side, a duty for the state to take action so as to guarantee free political deliberation and discourse can arise. The intensity of this positive obligation depends on the impact and reach of the particular form of expression, with audio-visual media raising stronger concerns in this regard. This jurisprudence was developed with regards to 'traditional' forms of public discourse, in particular print

---

[34] ECtHR, Guide on Article 3 of Protocol No 1, 85.
[35] See, eg, *TV Vest As & Rogaland Pensjonistparti v Norway* (violation of Article 10 on account of a fine imposed on a television channel for broadcasting an advertisement for a small political party, in breach of legislation prohibiting any political advertising on television); *Vitrenko and Others v Ukraine*, no 23510/02 (16 December 2008) (no violation of Article 10 for a case where a warning had been issued by an electoral commission to a female politician for describing a rival candidate as a 'thief' in her absence on live television in the run-up to the election).
[36] *Partija 'Jaunie Demokrāti' and Partija 'Mūsu Zeme' v Latvia*, nos 10547/07 and 34049/07 (29 November 2007).
[37] *Communist Party of Russia and Others v Russia*, no 29400/05 (19 June 2012).
[38] *Oran v Turkey*, 28881/07 and 37920/07 (15 April 2014) 77.

media such as newspapers, political leaflets or brochures, and audio-visual media (television and radio). Furthermore, the Court to date has only examined cases that concerned actions by government entities or government-controlled media. Even the cases where 'clear' positive obligations were recognised (for example the obligation to grant equal distribution of TV airtime) concerned national public TV stations, and there does not seem to be any case law regarding private media.

IV. Democratic Discourse in Cyberspace

A. Another Structural Transformation of the Public Sphere?

In recent years, with the rise of electronic communication, a shift in public discourse from 'analogue' to 'digital' discursive fora can be witnessed. News and relevant information are no longer selected, commented on and conveyed solely by journalistic media such as television, press and radio, but are selected, algorithmically structured and made searchable and accessible by specific online offerings such as search engines, social networks and microblogging services, also known as the new intermediaries. Studies show a loss of importance of traditional journalistic media while at the same time digital and social media offerings are being used as a central source of information for more and more people.[39] The new intermediaries are thus considered a significant influencing factor in modern opinion-forming processes, especially in the run-up to elections and votes.[40]

The rise of the internet has brought about a resurgence of scholars applying theories of the public sphere to internet technologies.[41] 'Enthusiasts' advance the argument that online media offer an expectation of improved democratic structures by increasing the opportunities for participation – even for previously marginalised groups – who can communicate past journalistic gatekeepers.[42] 'Sceptics', on the other hand, have argued that not everyone has the same degree of access or the competence and understanding to actively participate in the debate (the so-called digital divide).[43] Online intermediaries would merely reflect or even

---

[39] See Reuters Institute for the Study of Journalism, 'Digital News Report 2020' available at www.digitalnewsreport.org.

[40] See, eg, F Oehmer, L Udris and M Eisenegger, 'Zur Wirkung von Tech-Informations-Intermediären Auf Die (Schweizer) Öffentlichkeit – Chancen Und Risiken' (Swiss Federal Office of Communications, 2020).

[41] See, eg, D Janssen and R Kies, 'Online Forums and Deliberative Democracy' (2005) 40 *Acta Politica* 317; L Dahlberg, 'The Internet, Deliberative Democracy, and Power: Radicalizing the Public Sphere' (2007) 3 *International Journal of Media & Cultural Politics*; Papacharissi, 'The Virtual Sphere'.

[42] See, among many others, HS Christensen, 'Political Activities on the Internet: Slacktivism or Political Participation by Other Means?' (2011) 16 *First Monday*; Papacharissi, 'The Virtual Sphere'; Oehmer, Udris and Eisenegger, 'Zur Wirkung'.

[43] See E Hargittai and YP Hsieh, 'Digital Inequality' in WH Dutton (ed), *The Oxford Handbook of Internet Studies*, vol 1 (Oxford, Oxford University Press, 2013).

reinforce the existing power imbalances and inequalities.[44] In addition, wealthy actors have an advantage in actively participating in public discourse in that they can increase the probability of perception of their communication content by exploiting algorithmic selection logics[45] – for example, by buying likes, followers, using social bots and trolls, creating fake accounts or employing strategies of search engine optimisation.

In selecting, curating and promoting content, intermediaries generally follow neither journalistic rules nor operational logics oriented to the common good or democratic maxims: their goal is usually to increase the length of time and duration of use as well as the reach of their offerings through attention-grabbing content in order to do justice to their business models – which are financed primarily by advertising. Even though in (western) European democracies there is little evidence of fragmentation of users due to filter bubbles or echo chambers and the existing findings in this regard usually refer to the US context, which is characterised by a strongly polarised political and social climate, researchers and activists still point to the worrying fact that the selection of or attention to persons with similar views and opinions can be strengthened by algorithmic selection in an unrecognisable and non-transparent manner.[46]

Despite the comprehensive research already conducted on the subject, it has to be said that knowledge about the functioning and effects and thus about the opportunities and risks of intermediaries is still incomplete.[47]

B. Case Law of the Court

In this last section, I will analyse whether and how those structural changes to the public sphere have been reflected by the ECtHR.

The Court has recognised in its case law under Article 10 that the internet today plays an important role in enhancing the public's access to news and facilitating the dissemination of information, due to its accessibility and its capacity to store and communicate vast amounts of information.[48] The Court has also observed that an increasing amount of services and information is no longer available in

---

[44] AL Kavanaugh, 'Community Networks and Civic Engagement: A Social Network Approach' (2002) 11 *The Good Society* 17; P Norris, *Digital Divide: Civic Engagement, Information Poverty, and the Internet Worldwide* (Cambridge, Cambridge University Press, 2001).
[45] RK Nielsen and C Vaccari, 'Do People "Like" Politicians on Facebook? Not Really. Large-Scale Direct Candidate-to-Voter Online Communication as an Outlier Phenomenon' (2013) 7 *International Journal of Communication* 2333; J Van Dijck and T Poell, 'Understanding Social Media Logic' (2013) 1 *Media and Communication* 2.
[46] Oehmer, Udris and Eisenegger, 'Zur Wirkung' 3; Democracy Reporting International, 'Online Threats to Democratic Debate', Briefing Paper 100 (2019).
[47] Oehmer, Udris and Eisenegger, 'Zur Wirkung' 28.
[48] *Times Newspapers Ltd v UK (nos 1 and 2)*, nos 3002/03 and 23676/03 (10 March 2009) 27.

analogue media, but exclusively on the internet.⁴⁹ In its judgment in the *Kalda* case, which concerned access to internet services, the Court stated:

> The Court cannot overlook the fact that in a number of Council of Europe and other international instruments the public-service value of the Internet and its importance for the enjoyment of a range of human rights has been recognised. Internet access has increasingly been understood as a right, and calls have been made to develop effective policies to attain universal access to the Internet and to overcome the 'digital divide'. The Court considers that these developments reflect the important role the Internet plays in people's everyday lives.⁵⁰

Different forms of expression on the internet have been accepted by the Court as falling under Article 10 of the Convention. Cases treated by the Court have concerned, inter alia, internet archives of importance for the operation of the internet site at issue;⁵¹ publication of photographs for commercial purposes or free use;⁵² publication of political statements in various forms, such as party programmes and messages, or artistic material with a political message;⁵³ managing and use, including for commercial purposes, of internet platforms;⁵⁴ or blogging and vlogging with political content.⁵⁵

The findings of the Court's case law generally follow the principle of 'what applies offline, also applies online', which was developed by the United Nations Human Rights Council in its 2012 Resolution concerning human rights and the internet.⁵⁶ In that sense, the standards regarding the heightened level of protection afforded to political expression under Article 10 are more or less equally applied to the expression and advertising of political positions on internet platforms.⁵⁷ For example, in the case of *Rebechenko*, the Court found in 2019 that the applicant, a YouTube vlogger who had published a video comment on the relations between Russia and the Ukraine, had suffered a violation of his freedom of expression by his conviction for defamation and the obligation to take down his video from YouTube.⁵⁸ Similarly, in its judgment in *Savva Terentyev* in 2018, the Court

---

⁴⁹ *Kalda v Estonia*, no 17429/10 (19 January 2016) 52; *Jankovskis v Lithuania*, no 21575/08 (17 January 2017) 49.

⁵⁰ *Kalda v Estonia* 52 (cross-reference to earlier paragraphs omitted).

⁵¹ *Times Newspapers Ltd v UK (nos 1 and 2)* 27 and 45; *ML and WW v Germany*, nos 60798/10 and 65599/10 (28 June 2018) 90.

⁵² *Ashby Donald and Others v France*, no 36769/08 (10 January 2013) 34.

⁵³ *Féret v Belgium* 66–71; *Willem v France*, no 10883/05 (16 July 2009) 36–38; *Mariya Alekhina v Russia*, no 38004/12 (17 July 2018).

⁵⁴ *Ahmet Yıldırım v Turkey*, no 3111/10 (18 December 2012) 49; *Delfi AS v Estonia* [GC], no 64569/09 (16 June 2015) 115–16; *Cengiz and Others v Turkey*, nos 48226/10 and 14027/11 (1 December 2015) 51–52; *Magyar Tartalomszolgáltatók Egyesülete and Index.hu Zrt v Hungary*, no 22947/13 (2 February 2016). See also, from the perspective of Art 8, *Phil v Sweden*, no 74742/14 (7 February 2017).

⁵⁵ *Rebechenko v Russia*, no 10257/17 (16 April 2019).

⁵⁶ United Nations Human Rights Council, 'The Promotion, Protection and Enjoyment of Human Rights on the Internet' (5 July 2012) UN Doc A/HRC/RES/20/8.

⁵⁷ See, eg, *Renaud v France*, no 13290/07 (25 February 2010); *Tierbefreier eV v Germany*, no 45192/09 (16 January 2014) 56; *De Lesquen du Plessis-Casso v France (no 2)*, no 34400/10 (30 January 2014) 35.

⁵⁸ *Rebechenko v Russia*, no 10257/17 (16 April 2019).

A Human Rights Obligation to Protect Democratic Discourse in Cyberspace? 163

had recognised a very high level of protection of freedom of speech concerning insulting comments about police officers published on a blog.[59] It seems thus that in the context of negative obligations, there is no difference between online and offline political expressions. State interference into political discourse is in principle as equally reprehensible in analogue as in digital communication channels because it has the potential to distort the ideal speech situation.

When it comes to positive obligations of the state, the Court also takes into account the special features of expression on the internet such as its capacities of diffusion of information. In the case of *Willem* for example, it considered that a discriminatory – and therefore reprehensible – nature of a political message, first delivered orally and then published in a newspaper outlet, was exacerbated by its publication on the internet.[60] In this connection, it held that the risk of harm posed by content and communications on the internet to the exercise and enjoyment of other human rights and freedoms is certainly higher than that posed by the press. State policies governing reproduction of material from print media and the internet may therefore differ. The latter, undeniably, have to be adjusted according to the technology's specific features in order to secure the protection and promotion of the rights and freedoms concerned.[61]

On the other hand, and in a somewhat contradictory finding, the Court has considered that the impact of the expression of information via the internet is much more limited than the impact which the traditional audio-visual media are capable of producing. In *Schweizerische Radio- und Fernsehgesellschaft SRG*, which concerned the limitation on a radio and television broadcasting company to film inside a prison to prepare a television programme and interview one of the detainees, the Court addressed the issue of viable alternatives for the publication of the information that the applicant company wanted to convey. The Court reasoned as follows:

> [T]he fact that a telephone interview with A. was included in the applicant company's 'Schweiz aktuell' programme on 19 August 2004, available on its Internet site, is not in itself relevant as it used different techniques and means, had a less direct impact on viewers and was broadcast in a different programme.[62]

In the particular context of political expression, this principle was further elaborated in the *Animal Defenders International* case. The Court explained the relevance of newer media, such as the internet, in comparison to the traditional audio-visual media concerning the expression and advertising of political position in the following manner:

> the Court considers coherent a distinction based on the particular influence of the broadcast media. In particular, the Court recognises the immediate and powerful effect

---

[59] *Savva Terentyev v Russia*, no 10692/09 (28 August 2018).
[60] *Willem v France*, no 10883/05 (16 July 2009).
[61] *Editorial Board of* Pravoye Delo *and Shtekel v Ukraine*, no 33014/05 (5 May 2011) 63; *Cicad v Switzerland*, no 17676/09 (7 June 2016) 59.
[62] *Schweizerische Radio- und Fernsehgesellschaft SRG v Switzerland*, no 34124/06 (21 June 2012) 64.

of the broadcast media, an impact reinforced by the continuing function of radio and television as familiar sources of entertainment in the intimacy of the home. ... In addition, the choices inherent in the use of the internet and social media mean that the information emerging therefrom does not have the same synchronicity or impact as broadcasted information. Notwithstanding therefore the significant development of the internet and social media in recent years, there is no evidence of a sufficiently serious shift in the respective influences of the new and of the broadcast media in the respondent State to undermine the need for special measures for the latter.[63]

C. Protecting Democratic Discourse in Cyberspace?

The case law of the ECtHR on political expression on the internet reveals that the Court makes a distinction between the capacity for diffusion on the one side and the importance or influence of specific media on the other side. While the Court recognises the special importance of internet platforms as a means of diffusion of political expression, which seems to be much greater than that of the traditional press, the Court has so far not been ready to attribute the same importance to the internet as to the traditional audio-visual media, the latter still being considered to have a more immediate and powerful impact on the diffusion of information to the general public.[64]

While the Court has accepted different public interests as legitimate aims for injunctions against certain internet postings, such as the protection of personality,[65] the protection of whistle-blowers[66] and the protection of morals, particularly with regards to sexualised content,[67] no case law exists yet on the question of whether a state measure limiting expression on the internet would also be legitimate if it aimed at the protection of democratic processes. According to the principle of 'what applies offline, also applies online', one could imagine at first sight that the Court would apply the same principles in such a case as the ones developed with regards to 'offline' media. However, at a second glance, it seems less than clear which elements of democratic opinion-building online are so important that they justify an interference in political expression online. This is mainly due to the lack of conclusive evidence about the functioning and effects of digital discourses on democratic opinion-building. It seems almost impossible to determine at which point a state is not only allowed to take action (and thus possibly restrict expression online), but might even be obliged to take proactive measures to prevent distortions of the democratic opinion-building process, if there is no evidence about the real influence of online discursive practices on democratic opinion-building.

---

[63] *Animal Defenders International v UK* 119.
[64] ECtHR, 'Article 10: Expression and Advertising of Political Positions Through the Media/Internet in the Context of Elections/Referendums' (22 August 2018) 21.
[65] *PETA Deutschland v Germany*, no 43481/09 (8 November 2012) 49.
[66] *Růžový panter, o.s. v the Czech Republic*, no 20240/08 (2 February 2012) 33.
[67] *Akdaş v Turkey*, no 41056/04 (16 February 2010) 29.

There have not yet been cases where a clear positive obligation to take measures to protect democratic discourse in cyberspace was in question. However, according to the case law on 'traditional' media, one can assume that the Court would only recognise positive obligations if the medium in question is as sensitive as the 'traditional' audio-visual media. While the Court, in *Informationsverein Lentia and Others*, qualified audio-visual media as sensitive due to the fact that its programmes 'are often broadcast very widely',[68] the newly introduced distinction in the context of internet communication between capacity of diffusion on the one side and influence on the other side seems to add further confusion and to erect barriers to the recognition of positive obligations in cyberspace.

To summarise, it remains open whether there is not only a duty to not interfere in political discourse online, but also a state obligation to ensure democratic deliberation according to the fairness criteria developed by Habermas – reciprocity, justification, reflexivity, ideal role taking, sincerity, inclusion and discursive equality.

V. Conclusion

This chapter asked whether there is an obligation under human rights law to protect democratic discourse in cyberspace. By looking at the case law of the ECtHR, I observed that at least for the 'traditional' or 'offline' forms of political discourse in analogue settings, both during as well as between elections, the Court has accepted not only a negative duty for states not to interfere in political deliberations, but also, under certain circumstances, a positive obligation to take specific measures to protect the cornerstones of democratic deliberation in the public sphere, such as content pluralism in the audio-visual media, the independence of the press, a certain balance or equality of opportunity among the different forces of society, transparency of elections, as well as the impartiality and truthfulness of mass media information.

The case is less clear, however, for political expression in cyberspace, such as blogs, vlogs, podcasts, social media and others, even though researchers and activists have long been warning about potential dangers to democracy which arise from online manipulation such as 'fake news' or opinion bots and segmentation due to 'echo chamber' and 'filter bubble' effects.[69] Considering these risks, it seems logical to call for a state obligation to guarantee at least the minimum prerequisites of democratic discourse online. However, the formulation of positive obligation is confronted with several obstacles, most importantly, the absence of empirical evidence about the influence of political discourses in cyberspace. Other than with

---

[68] *Informationsverein Lentia and Others v Austria* 38.
[69] See, eg, Democracy Reporting International, 'Online Threats to Democratic Debate'.

national radio or TV channels, it seems less likely that a single platform in the fragmented discursive cyberspace would have a clear and decisive influence over an election or a referendum. State measures to guarantee, for example, content pluralism in online discourses or an equal distribution between the different forces of society, are therefore much harder to impose, also because of the transnational business models of platforms. The 'what applies offline, also applies online' logic, which is advanced by the Court, therefore has its limitations. Online deliberations have attained new qualities and not all threats to democracy are the same online as offline.

This finding aligns with the general impression that there is not yet a European consensus on how to regulate intermediaries and platforms, and how to regulate speech in cyberspace generally. This chapter has shown that the case law of the European Court of Human Rights cannot serve as a reference for national or European discussions on the regulation of platforms to date. More empirical research on the actual impact of cyber-deliberations is necessary, which could help courts and legal researchers to identify the cornerstones of democratic discourse in the sense of the Habermasian ideal speech situation and to make propositions for the formulation of positive obligations.

10

The European Approach to Governing Harmful Speech Online

FRÉDÉRIC BERNARD AND VIERA PEJCHAL

'When the looting starts, the shooting starts' will be remembered as one of the world's most powerful leaders' most polemical tweets.[1] At the time, Twitter decided to hide it because it 'glorified violence' and thus violated community rules, but kept it accessible because it 'may be in the public's interest'. Facebook, whose founder has claimed that the 'values at Facebook are inspired by the American tradition',[2] decided to keep it available without attaching any sort of warning to it. In fact, though Facebook is the biggest social media platform operating worldwide,[3] only around seven per cent of its users actually live under US jurisdiction.[4] What is meant by free speech and hate speech differs greatly among nations and depends on the context.[5] Thus, in another setting but still within Facebook's sphere of influence, the United Nations Independent International Fact-Finding Mission on Myanmar concluded that there was 'a serious risk that genocidal actions may occur or recur, and that Myanmar is failing in its obligation to prevent genocide' of the Rohingya[6] and called on 'Facebook and other social media to enhance

---

[1] D Trump [@realDonaldTrump], '… These THUGS are dishonoring the memory of George Floyd, and I won't let that happen. Just spoke to Governor Tim Walz' (29 May 2020) available at https://twitter.com/realDonaldTrump/status/1266231100780744704. See also M Wines, '"Looting" Comment from Trump Dates Back to Racial Unrest of the 1960s' *The New York Times* (29 May 2020).

[2] M Zuckerberg, 'Standing for Voice and Free Expression' (speech given at Georgetown University on 17 October 2019) available at https://about.fb.com/news/2019/10/mark-zuckerberg-stands-for-voice-and-free-expression.

[3] In August 2020, there were 2.7 billion Facebook users worldwide. See 'Number of Monthly Active Facebook Users Worldwide as of 3rd Quarter 2020' (*Statista*, 24 November 2020) available at www.statista.com/statistics/264810/number-of-monthly-active-facebook-users-worldwide.

[4] In October 2020, there were 190 million Facebook users in the US. See 'Leading Countries Based on Facebook Audience Size as of October 2020' (*Statista*, 24 November 2020) available at www.statista.com/statistics/268136/top-15-countries-based-on-number-of-facebook-users.

[5] M Herz and P Molnar, *The Content and Context of Hate Speech: Rethinking Regulation and Responses* (Cambridge, Cambridge University Press, 2012).

[6] 'Detailed Findings of the Independent International Fact-Finding Mission on Myanmar', UN Doc A/HRC/42/CRP.5 (9–27 September 2019) 9.

their capacity to combat the use of their platforms for the spread and promotion of threats and of hate speech and for the incitement to violence, hostility and discrimination'.[7]

There is no doubt that the internet provides new possibilities of communication and has become vital to the exchange of information and to different forms of political participation.[8] But it has also become a platform where likeminded individuals can easily connect and create groups that remain in their echo chambers – online fora, pages, chats – where the audience already agrees with the opinions expressed. This is true for all sorts of groups. However, cyber extremism, by inciting crime and spreading violence, poses a threat to offline societies. Cohen-Amalgor has described hate speech as speech 'intended to injure, dehumanise, harass, intimidate, debase, degrade and victimise the targeted groups, and to foment insensitivity and brutality against them'.[9] Even when hate speech does not immediately lead to physical violence, victims may still internalise insults, suffer from emotional distress and feel isolated, which leads to reinforcement of social stratification.[10] Their social standing is attacked and they may become less engaged in democratic processes.[11] Many victims do not feel empowered enough to stand up for their rights and protect themselves from online or offline hatred.

The question of how to regulate hate speech online does not have a uniform solution. There are those for whom existing regulations suffice and 'cyberlibertarians' who argue that the harm caused by regulating online hate speech is greater than that caused by online hate speech itself.[12] Even though there is no global consensus on how to address hate speech, it is nevertheless vital to reach a common understanding of the public goods that democratic communities want to protect. Public goods should be understood as values that society enshrines and shields as legal rights from any infringement because its members individually and as a whole recognise their essentiality in the proper functioning of a social and political community. When private actors decide which public goods are given priority and what speech is permitted without any overview from independent judges, they influence the understanding of fundamental freedoms and democratic mechanisms. Companies not only have to comply with the laws of the states

---

[7] A/HRC/42/CRP.5, 466. See also 'Report of the detailed findings of the Independent International Fact-Finding Mission on Myanmar', A/HRC/39/CRP.2 (10–28 September 2018) 1312–60, in particular 1342–54.

[8] See D Joyce, 'Internet Freedom and Human Rights' (2015) 26 *The European Journal of International Law* 493.

[9] R Cohen-Amalgor, 'Fighting Hate and Bigotry on the Internet' (2011) 3(3) *Policy and Internet* 1, 1–2.

[10] R Delgado, 'Words That Wound: A Tort Action for Racial Insults, Epithets and Name-Calling' (1982) 17 *Harvard Civil Rights-Civil Liberties Law Review* 133.

[11] J Waldron, 'Dignity and Defamation: The Visibility of Hate' (2010) 123 *Harvard Law Review* 1596.

[12] I Nemes, 'Regulating Hate Speech in Cyberspace: Issues of Desirability and Efficacy' (2002) 11 *Information & Communications Technology Law* 193.

in which they operate, but also with the international human rights framework, which outlaws incitement to violence, discrimination and hatred, and at the same time refers to protection of security, freedom and equality, and human dignity as the protected legal goods with special focus on minority groups and their members. Certainly in Europe, there is a growing consensus that hate speech is damaging to individuals and societies as a whole and that the absence of adequate means of prevention and response goes against the EU's core values, notably human dignity, freedom, democracy, equality, the rule of law and respect for human rights.[13]

This chapter explores first what public goods should be protected from hate speech. It argues that protection of these public goods by a variety of public and private actors is needed in a democracy. Second, it considers the state of the European Court of Human Rights' (ECtHR) case law regarding hate speech and the recognition of online platforms' responsibility in governing harmful speech. Third, it discusses to what extent European case law fits with a larger global framework deriving from UN documents, in particular the UN Guiding Principles on Business and Human Rights and recent reports by the Special Rapporteur on freedom of expression.

I. Hate Speech, Harm and the Threat to Democracy

There is no internationally agreed definition of hate speech, despite many efforts to provide one.[14] When Molnar asked Robert Post about the possibility of having a universal definition of 'hate speech', Post questioned whether such a definition would be useful.[15] It might facilitate the adoption of a clear legal framework, but it could not, alone, erase hatred from society altogether.

There is however a consensus that some speech can cause 'harm' and 'wrong'[16] because it attacks 'goods'. JS Mill's notion of harm has been used as a guiding principle for criminalising harmful behaviour based on a principled line that follows values or ideas of a just society.[17] In this context, the role of a just (democratic) society is to prevent harm and punish those who infringe values (public goods). However, those who have been in power and governed others have often imposed

---

[13] J Bayer and P Bárd, 'Hate Speech and Hate Crime in the EU and the Evaluation of Online Content Regulation Approaches' (European Parliament, Policy Department for Citizens' Rights and Constitutional Affairs, 2020) available at www.europarl.europa.eu/RegData/etudes/STUD/2020/655135/IPOL_STU(2020)655135_EN.pdf.
[14] E Heinze, 'Viewpoint Absolutism and Hate Speech' (2006) 69 *The Modern Law Review* 543.
[15] Interview with Robert Post in M Herz and P Molnar (eds), *The Content and Context of Hate Speech: Rethinking Regulation and Responses* (Cambridge, Cambridge University Press, 2012) 31.
[16] Legal philosophers prefer the term 'harm' and legal moralist the term 'wrong'. See C Bakalis, 'Regulating Hate Crime in the Digital Age' in J Schweppe and MA Walters (eds), *The Globalization of Hate: Internationalizing Hate Crime?* (Oxford, Oxford University Press, 2016).
[17] See G Dworkin, 'The Limits of the Criminal Law' in J Deigh and D Dolinko (eds), *The Oxford Handbook of Philosophy of Criminal Law* (Oxford, Oxford University Press, 2011) 4–6.

their own ideas of a just society and have been reluctant to acknowledge the harm that some actions, though not illegal at the time, can cause. Therefore, a contextual and historical analysis of the legacy of power, oppression and inequalities forms an inherent part of addressing wrongs and preventing harm. Hate speech regulation raises constitutional issues and issues of public political morality.[18] Tsesis has referred to the likelihood of causing harm by 'antisocial oratory that is intended to incite persecution against people because of their race, colour, religion, ethnic group, or nationality'.[19] Democratic society should protect its most vulnerable members from this harm.

When the social contract's core values are attacked, its essence is breached and democracy, which is underpinned by citizen participation, is infringed. A long-standing principle is that freedom of expression plays a crucial role in the proper functioning of democracy, therefore any restriction to speech has historically been seen with suspicion and as potentially undermining democracy. Nevertheless, limiting speech in order to protect vulnerable groups from violence, discrimination and hatred is necessary to ensure participation in a properly functioning democracy. Hate speech and censorship both directly impact democracy and the social contract, but the harm of hate speech outweighs the cost of interference with free speech.[20] Even if hate speech laws alone might not eliminate hatred from society, it is of cardinal importance for any democratic regime to govern by protecting agreed public goods both offline and online.

The Additional Protocol to the Council of Europe Convention on Cybercrime, an international treaty regulating substantive, procedural and international cooperation against racist or xenophobic propaganda which entered into force in 2006, acknowledges the threat hate speech represents for a democracy. It states that 'acts of a racist and xenophobic nature constitute a violation of human rights and a threat to the rule of law and democratic stability'.[21] The main concern of the Protocol with protecting democracy relates to protecting ethnic and national minorities. Religion is used only as an additional factor of hate speech, and minority groups relating to sexual orientation are not mentioned in the Protocol.

In the absence of a satisfactory definition of hate speech, the three-pronged theory considers that it can simultaneously be understood as: (1) incitement to violence; (2) incitement to discrimination; or (3) incitement to hatred.[22] This being

---

[18] J Feinberg, *The Moral Limits of the Criminal Law*, vol 4 (New York, Oxford University Press, 1990) 12.

[19] A Tsesis, *Destructive Messages: How Hate Speech Paves the Way for Harmful Social Movements* (New York, NYU Press, 2002) 211.

[20] LW Sunner, 'Criminalizing Expression: Hate Speech and Obscenity', in J Deigh and D Dolinko, *The Oxford Handbook of Philosophy of Criminal Law* (reprint, New York, Oxford University Press, 2019) 20.

[21] Council of Europe, 'Additional Protocol to the Convention on Cybercrime, Concerning the Criminalisation of Acts of a Racist and Xenophobic Nature Committed Through Computer Systems', Treaty No 189, preamble.

[22] V Pejchal, *Hate Speech and Human Rights in Eastern Europe: Legislating for Divergent Values* (Abingdon, Routledge, 2020).

said, it should be noted that hate speech is highly contextual and evolves over time: 'what one society accepts as a domain of regulation might in another time and place stand at the core of protected speech'.[23] This theory allows for a deeper apprehension of harm and the values that a democratic society wants to protect.

Despite the differences between online and offline hate speech, in particular the capacity to spread and incite violence in different physical locations or the speed with which speech can be disseminated, the most recent cases at the ECtHR confirm that the existing legal framework on offline hate speech can be applied to cyberhate cases: the internet cannot be separated from the realm of the law.[24]

II. The European Court of Human Rights' Case Law on Hate Speech

Mendel has observed that international law provides standards in relation to the criminal prohibition of hate speech. However, he has also admitted that 'international courts have in key respects failed to provide a clear interpretative framework for the hate speech rules'.[25] We have chosen to concentrate on the ECtHR, which delivers a high number of judgments that are binding for Member States.[26]

European case law, together with soft law instruments, clarifies European values and strategies to combat hate speech. Prior to the Additional Protocol to the Convention on Cybercrime, the Council of Europe's Committee of Ministers adopted in 1997 one of the few existing international definitions of hate speech, according to which,

> the term 'hate speech' shall be understood as covering all forms of expression which spread, incite, promote or justify racial hatred, xenophobia, anti-Semitism or other forms of hatred based on intolerance, including: intolerance expressed by aggressive nationalism and ethnocentrism, discrimination and hostility against minorities, migrants and people of immigrant origin.[27]

In 2018, the Committee of Ministers also adopted a 'Recommendation on the Roles and Responsibilities of Internet Intermediaries'.[28] To this recommendation

---

[23] RA Kahn, 'Holocaust Denial and Hate Speech' in L Hennebel and T Hochmann (eds), *Genocide Denials and the Law* (New York, Oxford University Press, 2011) 79.
[24] I Gagliardone et al, 'Countering Online Hate Speech' (Paris, United Nations Educational, Scientific and Cultural Organization, 2015) 6.
[25] T Mendel, 'Does International Law Provide for Consistent Rules on Hate Speech?' in M Herz and P Molnar (eds), *The Content and Context of Hate Speech: Rethinking Regulation and Responses* (Cambridge, Cambridge University Press, 2012) 417.
[26] J-P Costa, *La Cour européenne des droits de l'homme: des juges pour la liberté* (Paris, Dalloz, 2013) 52–53.
[27] Council of Europe Committee of Ministers, 'Recommendation No R (97) 20 on "Hate Speech"' (30 October 1997).
[28] Council of Europe Committee of Ministers, 'Recommendation CM/Rec(2018)2 on the Roles and Responsibilities of Internet Intermediaries' (7 March 2018).

are annexed 'Guidelines for States on Actions to Be Taken vis-à-vis Internet Intermediaries with Due Regard to their Roles and Responsibilities', whose section 2 is entirely dedicated to the responsibilities of internet intermediaries with respect to human rights and fundamental freedoms.

In this section, we will briefly recap the main tenets of the Court's position regarding freedom of speech (A). We will then address its case law concerning hate speech (B), before delving into the obligations of Member States (B.iii) and how the Court's case law has been transferred to online cases (C).

A. The Main Tenets of the European Court of Human Rights' Case Law on Freedom of Expression

Freedom of expression is protected in Article 10, paragraph 1 of the European Convention on Human Rights (ECHR). The ECtHR has always interpreted this provision as protecting in particular information and ideas 'that offend, shock or disturb the State or any sector of the population. Such are the demands of that pluralism, tolerance and broadmindedness without which there is no "democratic society"'.[29] Like other 'freedoms' in a technical sense (eg, freedom of religion, association or assembly), freedom of expression is not absolute and may be restricted by governments, provided that certain criteria enunciated in Article 10, paragraph 2 ECHR (legal basis, legitimate public interest and proportionality) are complied with. Governing or limiting hate speech entails a restriction to freedom of expression, since its effect is that some speech will remain unprotected in the name of other values.[30] Among the values protected by the Convention, the Court has identified, based on the Convention's preamble, democracy[31] as well as tolerance, social peace, non-discrimination, justice and peace.[32] The Court has also repeated on many occasions a statement first made in its 1994 *Jersild* judgment, which addressed racist statements in a television documentary, according to which 'it is particularly conscious of the vital importance of combating racial

---

[29] *Handyside v UK*, no 5493/72 (7 December 1976) 49.

[30] AK Struth, *Hassrede und Freiheit der Meinungsäußerung* (Heidelberg, Springer, 2018). The very idea of judging speech based on its content is resisted in some legal traditions, in particular in the US. See, for instance, E Chemerinsky, *Constitutional Law: Principles and Policies*, 4th edn (New York, Aspen, 2011) 960–69, and, specifically on hate speech, 1046: '[T]he Supreme Court's decision in *R.A.V. v. City of St. Paul* makes it difficult for hate speech codes to survive judicial analysis; if they prohibit only some forms of hate, they will be invalidated as impermissible content-based discrimination. But if the codes are more expansive and general, they likely will fail on vagueness and overbreadth grounds.'

[31] *United Communist Party of Turkey and Others v Turkey*, no 19392/92 (30 January 1998) 45.

[32] *Roger Garaudy v France* (decision), no 65831/01 (24 June 2003) 29 (in French); *Pavel Ivanov v Russia* (decision), no 35222/04 (20 February 2007).

discrimination in all its forms and manifestations'.³³ Thus, the Court considers that some forms of expression, in particular those that spread, incite, promote or justify hatred based on intolerance (including religious intolerance), may be sanctioned or even prevented.³⁴

At this point, we should note that Article 10, paragraph 2 ECHR is the only provision in the Convention that mentions that the exercise of the freedom it guarantees 'carries with it duties and responsibilities',³⁵ an element that has been put to use by the Court in the context of online hate speech (see C below).

To deal with speech contrary to the Convention's values, the Convention provides the exclusion scheme of Article 17 ECHR. According to this provision:

> [n]othing in this Convention may be interpreted as implying for any State, group or person any right to engage in any activity or perform any act aimed at the destruction of any of the rights and freedoms set forth herein or at their limitation to a greater extent than is provided for in the Convention.

When Article 17 ECHR applies, its effect is radical, since it means that some behaviours will fall outside of the protection offered by the Convention.³⁶ In this context, there is no 'relativity of truth perspective': democracy and fundamental rights are the values that must be protected even at the expense of limiting speech.³⁷

It should be noted that the Universal Declaration of Human Rights has a similar wording.³⁸ It shows that, after the Second World War, an international consensus emerged on limiting fundamental freedoms when their exercise poses a threat to fundamental values.³⁹ According to the Court, such values may be justice and peace, effective political democracy, gender equality and the coexistence of members of society free from racial segregation.⁴⁰ They should all be considered as public goods as defined earlier and, as such, worthy of being protected from hate speech.

---

[33] *Jersild v Denmark*, no 15890/89 (23 September 1994) 30. See, eg, ECtHR, *Sigma Radio Television LTD v Cyprus*, no 32181/04 and 35122/05 (21 July 2011) 208.

[34] *Erbakan v Turkey*, no 59405/00 (6 July 2006) 56 (in French).

[35] P van Dijk et al, *Theory and Practice of the European Convention on Human Rights*, 4th edn (Antwerp, Intersentia, 2006) 801–02.

[36] DJ Harris et al, *Harris, O'Boyle & Warbrick: Law of the European Convention on Human Rights*, 2nd edn (Oxford, Oxford University Press, 2009) 650.

[37] M van Noorloos, *Hate Speech Revisited: A Comparative and Historical Perspective on Hate Speech Law in the Netherlands and England & Wales* (Antwerp, Intersentia, 2011) 65.

[38] Art 30 UDHR: 'Nothing in this Declaration may be interpreted as implying for any State, group or person any right to engage in any activity or to perform any act aimed at the destruction of any of the rights and freedoms set forth herein.'

[39] AWB Simpson, *Human Rights and the End of Empire: Britain and the Genesis of the European Convention* (Oxford, Oxford University Press, 2001) 487.

[40] ECtHR, 'Guide on Article 17 of the European Convention on Human Rights' available at www.echr.coe.int/Documents/Guide_Art_17_ENG.pdf.

B. Hate Speech's Degree of Illegitimacy

Hate speech may be subject to Article 17 or Article 10 ECHR, depending on its level of illegitimacy (i). The Court may also enrich its reasoning by invoking other provisions of the Convention (ii). We will end this section by assessing states' responsibilities in this context (iii).

i. Article 17 or Article 10 ECHR?

If the Court judges that the defending state has not breached the Convention in limiting freedom of speech in a given case, it may ground its reasoning either on Article 10 or Article 17 ECHR, which essentially yield similar results. But the Court's choice of the relevant provision has strong symbolic value because it characterises the degree of (il-)legitimacy of the speech under consideration as well as the relevant public goods.[41] The application of Article 17 ECHR involves the affirmation of values, not merely a balancing of competing interests.

In its 1979 *Glimmerveen and Hagenbeek v the Netherlands*, the European Commission on Human Rights stated that Article 17 could be seen as a stronger expression of the duties and responsibilities referred to in Article 10 ECHR.[42] But the crux of the matter lies in determining when the speech in question requires the radical intervention of the Court through Article 17 ECHR.

To deal with this issue, the Court has, in fact, distinguished between two levels of hate speech, an approach recently summarised in the 2020 *Lilliendahl* decision:[43]

> 'Hate speech', as this concept has been construed in the Court's case-law, falls into two categories. […]
>
> The first category of the Court's case-law on 'hate speech' is comprised of the gravest forms of 'hate speech', which the Court has considered to fall under Article 17 and thus excluded entirely from the protection of Article 10 […]
>
> The second category is comprised of 'less grave' forms of 'hate speech' which the Court has not considered to fall entirely outside the protection of Article 10, but which it has considered permissible for the Contracting States to restrict[44]

In other words, the Court has recognised the existence of two types of hate speech, a 'regular' one and a 'heightened' one, with only the latter subject to the full consequences of Article 17 ECHR. This distinction is helpfully enriched

---

[41] F Sudre, *Droit européen et international des droits de l'homme*, 11th edn (Paris, 2012) 218–20.

[42] European Commission on Human Rights (Plenary), *Glimmerveen and Hagenbeek v the Netherlands* (decision), no 8348/78 (11 October 1979) 194.

[43] See also European Court of Human Rights Press Unit, 'Factsheet – Hate Speech' available at www.echr.coe.int/Documents/FS_Hate_speech_ENG.pdf.

[44] *Lilliendahl v Iceland*, no 29297/18 (12 May 2020) 33–35 (references omitted).

with considerations drawn from the 2019 *Pastörs* case, in which the Court insisted that:

> Article 17 is only applicable on an exceptional basis and in extreme cases and should, in cases concerning Article 10 of the Convention, only be resorted to if it is immediately clear that the impugned statements sought to deflect this Article from its real purpose by employing the right to freedom of expression for ends clearly contrary to the values of the Convention. The decisive point when assessing whether statements, verbal or non-verbal, are removed from the protection of Article 10 by Article 17, is whether those statements are directed against the Convention's underlying values, for example by stirring up hatred or violence, or whether by making the statement, the author attempted to rely on the Convention to engage in an activity or perform acts aimed at the destruction of the rights and freedoms laid down in it.[45]

There is thus a line of cases applying Article 17 ECHR to speech denying the Holocaust or the role Hitler played in it,[46] and to speech inciting to ethnic hatred against (religious) communities.[47] The Court has taken a clear stake in protecting human dignity as an essential democratic value.

But there is another line of cases, where, since Article 17's 'effect is to negate the exercise of the Convention right that the applicant seeks to vindicate in the proceedings before the Court',[48] the Court has preferred to apply Article 10 ECHR.[49] To give only one example, in its 2015 *Perinçek* decision, the Court controversially refused to apply Article 17 ECHR to speech denying that the events that took place in Turkey in 1915 could be classified as genocide.[50] When it addresses a

---

[45] *Pastörs v Germany*, no 55225/14 (3 October 2019) 37.

[46] *Roger Garaudy v France* (decision), no 65831/01 (24 June 2003) 29 (in French); *Witzsch v Germany* (decision), no 7485/03 (13 December 2005). The Court has reached a similar conclusion in many decisions. See, eg, *M'Bala M'Bala v France* (decision), no 25239/13 (20 October 2015) 36–40 (blatant display of a hateful and anti-Semitic position disguised as an artistic production).

[47] *Pavel Ivanov v Russia* (decision), no 35222/04 (20 February 2007); *Fouad Belkacem v Belgium* (decision), no 34367/14 (27 June 2017) (in French); ECtHR, *Mark Anthony Norwood v UK* (decision), no 23131/03 (16 November 2004). See also *WP and Others v Poland* (decision), no 42264/97 (2 September 2004) (statements alleging the persecution of Poles by the Jewish minority and the existence of inequality between them that can be seen as reviving anti-Semitism).

[48] *Ibragim Ibragimov and Others v Russia*, no 1413/08 and 28621/11 (28 August 2018) 62.

[49] *Šimunić v Croatia*, no 20373/17 (22 January 2019) 37–38 (use of an expression symbolising the official greeting of the totalitarian regime of the Independent State of Croatia and thus manifesting a racist ideology and contempt towards others on the basis of their religious and ethnic identity). See also *Williamson v Germany* (decision), no 64496/17 (8 January 2019) (denial of the existence of gas chambers and of the killing of Jews in those gas chambers under the Nazi regime).

[50] *Perinçek v Switzerland*, no 27510/08 (15 October 2015), confirming the Chamber judgment in *Perinçek v Switzerland*, no 27510/08 (17 December 2013). See also, eg, *Lehideux and Isorni v France*, no 24662/94 (23 September 1998) 47 (statements describing the Vichy policy of Philippe Pétain as 'supremely skilful'); *Gündüz v Turkey*, no 35071/97 (4 December 2003) 51–52. See also *Balsytė-Lideikienė v Lithuania*, no 72596/01 (4 November 2008) (statements expressing aggressive nationalism and ethnocentrism, while referring to the Jews and the Poles as perpetrators of war crimes and genocide against the Lithuanians). See also the long 'Le Pen v France' saga: *Le Pen v France* (decision), no 18788/09 (20 April 2010) (statements depicting Muslims as a threat to the French people); *Le Pen v France* (decision), no 52672/13 (13 September 2016) (statements according to which

case by applying Article 10 ECHR, the Court will look at, among other things, the nature and severity of the sanction inflicted[51] as well as confer to national jurisdictions a 'margin of appreciation'.[52]

These principles may seem clear, but their implementation is much more difficult, as evidenced by the relatively frequent dissenting opinions issued by individual judges. Thus, in the 2012 *Vejdeland* judgment, the Court judged that the dissemination of leaflets that presented homosexuality as '"a deviant sexual proclivity" that had "a morally destructive effect on the substance of society"' and alleged that 'homosexuality was one of the main reasons why HIV and AIDS had gained a foothold' constituted 'serious and prejudicial allegations' that did not amount to heightened hate speech.[53] Judge Ganna Yudkivska, joined by Judge Mark Villiger, argued in her concurring opinion that, based on the Committee of Ministers' 1997 recommendation, this case was a clear instance of heightened hate speech that should not have been protected at all (ie, subject to Article 17 ECHR).[54]

In sum, there is a long-established case law of the ECtHR dealing with the appropriate coexistence between freedom of expression and the other values protected by the Convention.[55] But it is not always easy to discern if the Court will apply Article 17 ECHR, thus symbolically bringing a strong rebuttal to the speaker, or if it will prefer to enter the substance of the application through a discussion of Article 10 ECHR.

ii. *The Invocation of Other Provisions*

In the context of hate speech, the Court may also resort to another provision of the Convention, for instance Article 8 ECHR, which protects the right to respect for private and family life. Thus, after having excluded the application of Article 17 ECHR in the above-mentioned *Perinçek* case, the Grand Chamber analysed the case as an instance in which 'the right to freedom of expression under Article 10 of the Convention has to be balanced against the right to respect for private life under Article 8 of the Convention'.[56]

---

the Nazi occupation of France had not been 'particularly inhumane'); *Le Pen v France* (decision), no 45416/16 (28 February 2017) (statement using a pun based on the double meaning, in French, of the verb 'voler' – to fly and to steal – applied to Roma people).

[51] See, eg, *Perinçek* [GC] 273.
[52] See, eg, *Soulas and Others v France*, no 15948/03 (10 July 2008) 44 (in French).
[53] *Vejdeland and Others v Sweden*, no 1813/07 (9 February 2012) 54.
[54] *Vejdeland and Others v Sweden*, concurring opinion of Judge Yudkivska joined by Judge Villiger. See also the dissenting opinion of Judge Elisabeth Steiner in *Erbakan v Turkey*, no 59405/00 (6 July 2006) (in French), arguing that statements disseminating religious intolerance in a sensitive region should not benefit from the protection of Art 10 ECHR; the dissent of Judge Helen Keller in *Fáber v Hungary*, no 40721/08 (24 July 2012) 56; the dissent of Judges Nebojša Vučinić and Paulo Pinto de Albuquerque in the *Perinçek* Chamber judgment.
[55] See European Court of Human Rights Press Unit, 'Factsheet – Hate Speech'.
[56] *Perinçek* 198.

Technically, the reliance on two different provisions produces a conflict of rights:[57] freedom of speech, protected by Article 10 ECHR, versus the right to privacy enshrined in Article 8 ECHR. In its long-standing case law, the Court has repeatedly asserted that the analysis of the case must be identical whether it comes from the point of view of Article 8 ECHR (the 'target' of the speech complaining of the lack or insufficiency of national sanctions) or Article 10 ECHR (the 'author' complaining of having being sanctioned).[58]

The question then becomes one of balancing the two competing rights and the values they enshrine and, while acknowledging that they are interdependent and connected, deciding which one should prevail in a specific case.[59] In order to provide consistency to the way this conflict is solved, the Court has developed multiple criteria to balance the two rights.[60] Did the speech contribute to a debate of general interest? To what extent does the person concerned belong to the public sphere (hence is expected to have to accept more criticism)? What was the subject of the report? How did the person concerned behave before the speech? What were the content, form and consequences of the speech?

Similarly, the Court may resort to Article 9 ECHR protecting freedom of thought, conscience and religion, which will also create a conflict of rights with Article 10 ECHR, as shown in the 2019 *Tagiyev and Huseynov* judgment, which dealt with the publication of an article comparing western and eastern values and containing attacks on the Prophet Muhammad and on Muslims.[61]

iii. The Role of the State

The relevance of the inclusion of Articles 8 and 9 ECHR in the analysis of the interference with freedom of speech cannot be overstated, since it has implications on the nature of Member States' obligations. Indeed, there is a crucial difference between applying Article 10, paragraph 2 ECHR alone and resorting to another of the Convention's protected rights. In the first hypothesis, the protection of the rights of others only comes as a justification for state interference into freedom of expression, when it has chosen to restrict speech based on that aim. In the second one, Articles 8 and 9 ECHR create a positive obligation for the state to take measures to prevent or stop the harm to someone's private and family life or religion.

---

[57] O De Schutter, *International Human Rights Law*, 2nd edn (Cambridge, Cambridge University Press, 2014) 511–22.
[58] *Von Hannover v Germany (No 2)*, no 40660/08 and 60641/08 (7 February 2012) 106.
[59] See Art IV of the French Declaration of the Rights of Man and Citizen of 1789: 'Liberty consists in being able to do whatever does not harm another. Thus, the exercise of each man's natural rights has no limits other than those which guarantee to the other members of society the enjoyment of these same rights; those limits can only be determined by the law' (translation A Lentin).
[60] See *Von Hannover* 108–13. See also S Smet, 'Conflicts between Human Rights and the ECtHR: Towards a Structured Balancing Test' in S Smet and E Brems (eds), *When Human Rights Clash at the European Court of Human Rights: Conflict or Harmony?* (Oxford, Oxford University Press, 2017).
[61] *Tagiyev and Huseynov v Azerbaijan*, no 13274/08 (5 December 2019).

The Court said so in its 2020 *Atamanchuk* judgment, in which it reiterated that states

> may be *obliged, by their positive obligations under Article 8 of the Convention*, to regulate the exercise of freedom of expression so as to ensure adequate protection by law in such circumstances and/or where fundamental rights of others have been seriously impaired (emphasis added).[62]

This positive obligation may, in particular, involve 'the adoption of measures designed to secure respect for private life even in the sphere of the relations of individuals between themselves'.[63]

C. Online Hate Speech

The topic of online hate speech combines 'classic' questions and new challenges, which will be addressed in turn below.

When the author of the speech is directly implicated by the victim – because his or her identity is known – the fact that the speech took place online does not present any additional theoretical difficulty, even if there is clearly a difference in the speed and extent with which the relevant speech can be disseminated. The principles enunciated above can therefore simply be transplanted.[64]

But the internet also presents new challenges, in particular because 'online hate speech often involves unknown speakers, with coordinated bot threats, disinformation and so-called deep fakes and mob attacks'.[65] Therefore, it is tempting to place increased responsibility on the provider that makes the publication or dissemination of the speech possible, called 'the intermediary'.[66] The notion of intermediary includes a wide range of service providers that facilitate interactions

---

[62] *Atamanchuk v Russia*, no 4493/11 (11 February 2020) 70 (a referral to the Grand Chamber is currently pending).

[63] *Pihl v Sweden* (decision), no 74742/14 (7 February 2017) 26. See also on Art 2 ICCPR, UN Human Rights Committee, General Comment No 31, 'Nature of the General Legal Obligation Imposed on States Parties to the Covenant' (26 May 2004), UN Doc CCPR/C/21/Rev.1/Add.13, 8.

[64] See, eg, *Savva Terentyev v Russia*, no 10692/09 (28 August 2018) (conviction for having posted online a statement inciting hatred and enmity against police officers as a 'social group' and calling for their 'physical extermination'); *Smajić v Bosnia and Herzegovina* (decision), no 48657/16 (16 January 2018) (statements posted on a publicly accessible internet forum that described military action to be undertaken against Serb villages and neighbourhoods in the Brčko District region in the event of war caused by the Republika Srpska's secession); *Nix v Germany* (decision), no 35285/16 (13 March 2018) (conviction of the applicant for having used the symbols of unconstitutional organisations – a picture of Himmler in SS uniform wearing a swastika armband – in a post on his blog); *Beizaras and Levickas v Lithuania*, no 41288/15 (14 January 2020) (homophobic statements posted on the applicant's Facebook page).

[65] UN General Assembly, 'Report of the Special Rapporteur on the Promotion and Protection of the Right to Freedom of Opinion and Expression' (9 October 2019) UN Doc A/74/486, 40.

[66] On this notion, see G Frosio, *The Oxford Handbook of Online Intermediary Liability* (Oxford, Oxford University Press, 2020); R Spano, 'Intermediary Liability for Online User Comments under the European Convention on Human Rights' (2017) 17 *Human Rights Law Review* 665.

on the internet between natural and legal persons (by connecting users to the internet, hosting web-based services, gathering information, etc).[67]

The first and foremost case in which the Strasbourg Court established the principles governing intermediaries' responsibility was the 2015 *Delfi* Grand Chamber judgment.[68] Delfi AS, a commercial entity running a large news portal, complained that its condemnation for having let third parties publish defamatory (and antisemitic) comments on its portal breached Article 10 ECHR.

The Court transposed its Article 8 and 10 conflict scheme into the digital arena,[69] stressing that the case concerned 'the "duties and responsibilities" of Internet news portals, under Article 10 para. 2 of the Convention'.[70] It then recalled that the freedom of speech of the comments' authors was not at stake, but that it had to address the issue of whether the fact of holding Delfi AS liable for the comments posted by third parties on its website respected the Convention. The Court then took note of the difficulties frequently associated with identifying the authors of online comments and judged that it was not a disproportionate interference with the right to freedom of speech to shift the possibility to obtain redress in defamation proceedings to the intermediary.[71] The Court then declared that the speech involved constituted hate speech, so that internet news portals needed 'to take measures to remove clearly unlawful comments without delay, even without notice from the alleged victim or from third parties'.[72] The Court thus concluded that the sanction imposed on Delfi AS remained within the margin of appreciation afforded to Member States and that there had been no violation of Article 10 ECHR.[73]

In the following 2016 *MTE and Index.hu v Hungary* judgment,[74] the Court refined its position by incorporating the distinction between the ordinary and heightened levels of hate speech (see II.B.i above). It noted that the comments under examination in this case were not hate speech, but value judgements. It also observed that the applicant, a non-commercial entity, had taken measures to prevent defamatory comments, among which the publication of 'general terms and conditions' and a 'notice-and-take-down' system,[75] therefore concluding that the sanction of MTE amounted to a violation of Article 10 ECHR. To prevent anyone

---

[67] See Council of Europe, 'Brief Overview of the Council of Europe's Standards on the Roles and Responsibilities of Internet Intermediaries' (2018) available at https://rm.coe.int/leaflet-internet-intermediaries-en/168089e572.
[68] *Delfi AS v Estonia*, no 64569/09 (16 June 2015).
[69] ibid 110.
[70] ibid 115.
[71] ibid 151.
[72] ibid 159.
[73] ibid 162 (the result was reached by a clear vote of 15 to 2).
[74] *Magyar Tartalomszolgáltatók Egyesülete and Index.Hu Zrt v Hungary*, no 22947/13 (2 February 2016).
[75] ibid 86. In *Høiness v Norway*, no 43624/14 (19 March 2019) 67, the Court added that it would include, in the proportionality analysis, the liability of the actual authors of the comments as an alternative to the intermediary's liability.

from thinking that *MTE* had somehow overruled *Delfi*, Lithuanian Judge Egidijus Kūris wrote a concurring opinion, in which he insisted that the difference between the two cases was to be found in the level of hate speech involved.

From the combination of these two judgments, it follows that, in the case of 'simple' offensive comments – which constitute, according to the Court, many, if not most, cases[76] – it is enough for internet portals to set up a system of deletion upon notification. However, if the speech is deemed 'clearly unlawful' (ie, constitutes heightened hate speech such as incitement to violence), internet portals need to remove comments automatically, on their own initiative.[77] In addition to this, the fact that an intermediary is a non-commercial entity will speak in favour of leniency.

This balance was confirmed in the 2017 *Pihl* decision, in which the Court considered that the Convention had not been breached, because the speech in question, although offensive, did not amount to hate speech, that the blog was run by a non-profit association and that the litigious post was removed, on demand, nine days after its publication.[78]

III. Assessment

To conclude, we will assess the Court's case law in the light of the three-pronged approach and the role companies play in online hate speech.

A. The Three-Pronged Approach

The Court's decisions show engagement with cases involving incitement to violence, incitement to discrimination and incitement to hatred, so that the Court's approach seems broad enough to affirm consensus about European values.

---

[76] See also Spano, *Intermediary Liability* 678.

[77] If, theoretically, the distinction makes sense, it should be noted that it is not certain that it is genuine in practice. As Ombelet and Kuczerawy have observed, to identify comments that amount to hate speech, there is no real alternative to general monitoring. P-J Ombelet and A Kuczerawy, 'Delfi Revisited: The MTE-Index.hu v Hungary Case', (*LSE Media Policy Project blog*, 19 February 2016).

[78] *Pihl v Sweden* (decision), no 74742/14 (7 February 2017). See also *Tamiz v UK*, no 3877/14 (19 September 2017) (information society service providers, 'ISSPs', which store information provided by a recipient of their service, in respect of an Art 8 complaint and in line with the standards on international law, should not be held responsible for content emanating from third parties unless they failed to act expeditiously in removing or disabling access to it once they became aware of its illegality); *Magyar Jeti Zrt v Hungary*, no 11257/16 (4 December 2018) (extension of this line of reasoning to the 'duties and responsibilities' of internet news portals, for the purposes of Art 10 ECHR, when an online article includes a hyperlink leading to content, available on the internet, which is later held to be defamatory).

The application of Article 17 ECHR typically involves responding to the question of which values are worth safeguarding in a democracy. In several cases, it is the value of human dignity or that of democracy that is deemed as the most prized and, thus, has to be protected.

One may, however, question the relevance of the Court's distinction between two degrees of hate speech ('regular' and 'heightened'). Does it really make sense not to apply Article 17 ECHR in cases involving denial of the Holocaust and of the existence of gas chambers, as in the 2019 *Williamson v Germany* decision? While it does not necessarily incite violence or invite to discrimination, does this speech not also attack human dignity? The Court should stand firm and remind European society more often that '[t]olerance and respect for the equal dignity of all human beings constitute the foundations of a democratic, pluralistic society'.[79] It could qualify the notion of pluralism required by a democratic society so that it does not extend to political ideologies that are liberticidal and construct their discourse on racist, extremist, homophobic or xenophobic theories, thus taking into account the potential harm these produce to both vulnerable individuals and democratic society.[80]

Whereas the Court, as a part of its evolving interpretation of the Convention,[81] frequently refers to other treaties and soft law documents, notably adopted by the Council of Europe or UN bodies, its case law does not, for example, seriously engage with the Additional Protocol to the Convention on Cybercrime in cases related to online harmful speech.[82] We believe that the Court's judges could use more actively the legal tools that are at their direct disposal: for instance the recent 2018 Committee of Ministers' 'Recommendation on the Roles and Responsibilities of Internet Intermediaries', and engage with stakeholders and affected communities to further develop the notion of democratic pluralism and protected values of a just society – all important public goods.

B. The Role of Companies

The Strasbourg Court has confirmed principles laid down by UN soft law: online companies have human rights responsibilities. As private actors they operate to maximise their profits through the use of artificial intelligence and automation,

---

[79] *Erbakan v Turkey*, no 59405/00 (6 July 2006) 56 (in French; our translation).
[80] Pejchal, *Hate Speech and Human Rights* 164.
[81] *Tyrer v UK*, no 5856/72 (25 April 1978) 31. For more on this model of interpretation, see E Bates, *The Evolution of the European Convention on Human Rights: From its Inception to the Creation of a Permanent Court of Human Rights* (Oxford, Oxford University Press, 2010) 328–30.
[82] The Additional Protocol is mentioned in the *Perinçek* GC judgment, but exclusively under the angle of the denial of a genocide (Art 6).

but they do not act only as gatekeepers, deciding on what content they allow, but also as content organisers, tailoring the content to individual users.[83]

In 2019, the Special Rapporteur on freedom of expression presented a report on online hate speech in which he noted that:

> internet companies have enormous impact on human rights, particularly but not only in places where they are the predominant form of public and private expression, where a limitation of speech can amount to public silencing or a failure to deal with incitement can facilitate offline violence and discrimination.[84]

When online hate speech is inadequately regulated, the consequences can be tragic:[85] parallels can be drawn between certain parties' use of the Facebook social media platform in Myanmar and the poisonous invective shared on *Radio Télévision Libre des Mille Collines* in Rwanda.[86]

International human rights law provides guidelines for companies which can be encapsulated as: identify, prevent, mitigate and account for human rights impacts and remediate harm when it occurs.[87] It is striking how similar these duties are to the ones exercised by states. However, there are also important differences. Democracies adopt constitutions in which they usually set the values framework which lasts generations. They adopt laws and implement international human rights conventions with the view to ensure the universality of fundamental freedoms and human dignity as they consider them public goods. Companies, on the other hand, are based on their founders' values and implement the 'corporate philosophy'.[88] Nevertheless, the international human rights law framework requires them to adopt the due diligence policy and to periodically review its rules.

Companies should conduct 'meaningful consultation with potentially affected groups and other relevant stakeholders'.[89] In the constantly evolving understanding of hate speech, it is vital to pay attention to the context and content of harmful online speech.[90] In this regard, the three-pronged theory offers a clear framework through which companies can understand harm and what actions are needed to avoid it. Banning incitement to *violence* and *discrimination* is universally

---

[83] EB Laidlaw, *Regulating Speech in Cyberspace: Gatekeepers, Human Rights and Corporate Responsibilities* (Cambridge, Cambridge University Press, 2015) 2.
[84] A/74/486, 41.
[85] ibid.
[86] See K Ndahiro, 'In Rwanda, We Know All About Dehumanizing Language' *The Atlantic* (13 April 2019).
[87] See, eg, A/74/486, 42.
[88] K Klonick, 'The New Governors: The People, Rules, and Processes Governing Online Speech' (2018) 131 *Harvard Law Review* 1598; D Kaye, *Speech Police: The Global Struggle to Govern the Internet* (New York, Columbia Global Reports, 2019).
[89] UN OHCHR, 'Guiding Principles on Business and Human Rights: Implementing the United Nations "Protect, Respect and Remedy" Framework' (2011) UN Doc HR/PUB/11/04, principle 18.
[90] ibid, principle 20 on regular evaluation and effectiveness of approaches to human rights harms.

understood as legitimate prevention of harm and thus such incitement should be prevented regardless of the speaker.[91] Preventing incitement to *hatred* requires a better understanding of the context, history and likelihood of committing more serious acts of violence.[92] Twitter, once branded 'the free speech wing of the free speech party',[93] has gradually adapted its rules and realised that 'some groups of people are disproportionately targeted with abuse online'.[94] This is an important shift in values and towards accepting responsibility for building the social contract rather than promoting violence and hatred.

The Strasbourg Court's means of action towards companies are necessarily limited, since the Convention does not apply directly between private entities and individuals (the so-called '*Drittwirkung*'): '[i]nsofar as the Convention touches the conduct of private persons, it does so only indirectly through such positive obligations as it imposes upon a state'.[95] Despite the fact that its action is indirect, the Court possesses the necessary tools to push states towards adopting new legislation designed to ensure better respect of human rights by private online companies, for instance by requiring states, under their positive obligations, to incorporate the UN Guiding Principles on Business and Human Rights or their equivalent into domestic law.[96] In fact, it has already started to do so by indicating that, in order to comply with individual rights, online companies should set a 'deletion upon notification' system.[97] Even if mistakes are unavoidable, citizens conversant with human rights law, and who understand the context and evolution of values in society, are more capable of assessing how hatred should be banned from online speech better than any algorithm or AI.

---

[91] This affirmation should be qualified as far as elected officials are concerned. The ECtHR has always maintained that 'freedom of political debate is at the very core of the concept of a democratic society which prevails throughout the Convention'. See *Lingens v Austria*, no 9815/82 (8 July 1986) 42. Therefore, '[f]reedom of speech is especially valuable for an elected official, who represents his or her constituents, signals their concerns and defends their interests'. See *Féret v Belgium*, no 15615/07 (10 December 2009) 65. But this heightened protection does not extend to hate speech. Ibid 64.

[92] UNHRC, 'Report of the United Nations High Commissioner for Human Rights on the Expert Workshops on the Prohibition of Incitement to National, Racial or Religious Hatred' (11 January 2013) UN Doc A/HRC/22/17/Add.4, Appendix, 'Rabat Plan of Action on the Prohibition of Advocacy of National, Racial or Religious Hatred that Constitutes Incitement to Discrimination, Hostility or Violence'.

[93] J Halliday, 'Twitter's Tony Wang: "We Are the Free Speech Wing of the Free Speech Party"' *The Guardian* (22 March 2012).

[94] 'Hateful conduct policy' available at https://help.twitter.com/en/rules-and-policies/hateful-conduct-policy.

[95] Harris et al, *Law of the European Convention on Human Rights* 20.

[96] See also A/74/486 fn 42.

[97] See 'The EU Code of Conduct on Countering Illegal Hate Speech Online' (2016) available at ec.europa.eu/info/policies/justice-and-fundamental-rights/combatting-discrimination/racism-and-xenophobia/eu-code-conduct-countering-illegal-hate-speech-online_en.

11
Hate Speech and Journalism: Challenges and Strategies

GUIDO KEEL

I. Introduction

It is part of the journalistic mission not only to inform the audience and to allow for the forming of opinions, but also to criticise powerful actors in society. Journalism is understood to be an institution in society, the fourth estate, whose power counterbalances the powers of the government, the legislature and the courts.

As the media are invested with a certain power, it comes as no surprise that critical journalists become the object of criticism themselves. This has always been part of their reality, and, for some journalists, to be criticised is testament to the relevance of their work. However, criticism of individual journalists, their work, media organisations, and journalism in general has in recent years become more hateful. This hate speech stems from all kind of actors: from heads of states around the world, their governments and allies, to groups in society who organise around a common interest or against a shared supposed threat, to dissatisfied individuals who feel the media do not adequately respect their needs and views.

Traditional journalism faces the difficult task not just of finding ways to deal with the outrageous statements of rogue politicians, but also to handle the coverage of even more unscrupulous players, such as extremists and terrorists.[1] As part of their function, the media, like no other institution in society, have the means and power to continually reach large audiences. Even with the internet and social media, it is still the news media which shape and influence the public discourse and opinions more than anything else.[2] Various actors use the reach and influence of the media in

---

[1] A White, 'Journalism, Hate-Speech and Terrorism' (*Ethical Journalism Network*) available at https://ethicaljournalismnetwork.org/resources/publications/ethical-journalism/case-study.

[2] M Djerf-Pierre and A Shehata, 'Still an Agenda Setter: Traditional News Media and Public Opinion During the Transition from Low to High Choice Media Environments' (2017) 67 *Journal of Communication* 733; R Fletcher, and RK Nielsen, 'Are News Audiences Increasingly Fragmented? A Cross-National Comparative Analysis of Cross-Platform News Audience Fragmentation and Duplication' (2017) 67 *Journal of Communication* 476; U Gleich, 'Medienwirkungen auf den Prozess der öffentlichen Meinungsbildung' (2018) 12 *Media Perspektiven* 608.

order to spread their messages of hate. Journalists sometimes become inadvertent victims of political manipulation and spreaders of prejudice, when a lack of time or knowledge leads to a lack of appreciation of different cultures and beliefs, to a reinforcement of stereotypes and racial attitudes or other discriminatory views.[3] It is a daily challenge for journalists to prevent discriminatory content from spreading through their channels, be it in the form of news content or of online comments.

This outline shows that the issue of hate speech impacts journalism and journalists on several levels. In this chapter, I first look at the technological and economic changes that have made hate speech a more pressing issue in journalism. Next, I reflect on the dilemmas journalists face when trying to stop or counter hate speech – both on an abstract level as well as in their everyday work. When describing the various manifestations of hate speech that affect journalism and journalists in their daily practice, I also discuss the various options that journalists have for dealing with hate speech.

This chapter seeks to show that hate speech is not only a threat to minorities and disadvantaged people, but is also highly relevant for journalism in the digital context. It should thus not be left to the individual journalist to deal with hate speech; rather, it is the duty of media organisations and the profession as a whole to actively prevent hate speech in and against journalism.

II. Journalism Under Pressure

Digital technologies have been playing a role in journalistic production for about 25 years, since newspapers first adopted digital editorial systems. Since then, new journalistic forms, such as multimedia journalism, have emerged as a result of technological change. The relationship between journalists and the audience has also changed,[4] with their interaction becoming much more immediate. First, new technology allowed journalists to have a much better idea of what stories the audience were reading, how much time was spent on which article, and even how different headlines could change the attention an article was getting. Second, thanks to online comments, journalists received substantially more feedback to their reporting – whether this feedback was substantial in quality is still open to debate, but where journalists had been receiving an occasional letter to the editor in pre-digital times, a single article could now easily trigger a hundred comments if it hit a nerve. And these comments not only responded to the original article, but also to other comments, creating a conversation in which the journalist was only one participant among many, if at all.

---

[3] A White, 'Ethical Challenges for Journalists in Dealing with Hate Speech' (2012) available at www.ohchr.org/documents/issues/expression/iccpr/vienna/crp8white.pdf.

[4] V Lilienthal and I Neverla, *Lügenpresse: Anatomie eines politischen Kampfbegriffs* (Köln, Kiepenheuer & Witsch, 2017).

When it first became technologically possible to include the audience, around the turn of the millennium, there was great hope that this would emancipate the media from outdated traditions and routines. Not only would the audience be given a voice, their participation offered radically new forms of storytelling[5] – at a time when numbers of readers and viewers had started to decline, and revenues from sales and advertising were stagnating.[6] Furthermore, media managers were having 'economic fantasies of a willing, free workforce' that would lower production costs while at the same time enriching the journalistic content thanks to the contributions of active readers and users.[7] As an additional benefit, the individual media user's closer relationship with the media product would increase consumer loyalty. This had become a major concern of media managers as – again thanks to the internet – countless new sources of information had become easily available and often free of charge.

Audience empowerment went well beyond the news websites of journalistic media organisations though. Thanks to blogs and social media, anyone with access to the internet and minimal online skills was now not only able to publish their news and views to a potentially worldwide audience, but could also easily find like-minded people and build up an online network with them. Where in the past the relationships in public communication had been mainly between a few moderating media organisations on the one side, and selected actors and the general audience on the other, these actors and the audience now had various means to shortcut the debate, bypassing the media and creating their own information platforms and networks.

All in all, while these developments were originally seen to be the salvation of or at least a great new opportunity for journalism, they led to what is now widely seen as a shift in power away from journalism and towards the audience.

Digital technologies also had an economic impact on journalism, and this was just as fundamental: traditional business models of journalistic media organisations no longer worked. As revenue streams dried up, the pressure on time – already higher due to real-time online reporting and social media reports by on-site witnesses – and on the productivity of journalists increased. As has been noted among academics and journalists themselves, this poses a real threat to journalistic quality.[8]

As a consequence, journalism is, more than ever, under pressure to prove its legitimacy and its raison d'être. Journalists used to enjoy a monopoly in society: they were traditionally the gatekeeper which decided which information from which actors and which ways of life would reach the audience.[9] The journalists at

---

[5] M Deuze, 'Towards Professional Participatory Storytelling in Journalism and Advertising' (2005) 10 *First Monday*.

[6] M Deuze, A Bruns and C Neuberger, 'Preparing for an Age of Participatory News' (2007) 1 *Journalism Practice* 322.

[7] T Quandz, 'Dark Participation' (2018) 6 *Media and Communication* 36, 37.

[8] M Schröder and A Schwanebeck, *Qualität unter Druck* (Baden-Baden, Nomos, 2011).

[9] DM White, 'The "Gate Keeper": A Case Study in the Selection of News' (1950) 27 *Journalism Bulletin* 383.

the gate controlled the public discourse by selecting the information which seemed relevant and suitable for it. In its ideal form, journalism did so with society's best interests in mind, putting them above other interests such as the government's or those of individual groups or actors.

In today's world, journalism no longer holds this privileged position as the gatekeeper of public information and discourse.[10] The question arises: if news is ubiquitous and if journalism is no longer able to play the role of the gatekeeper that sets the stage and the agenda for public discourse, what is its role? And what is it still good for?

With alternative sources and actors bypassing and replacing the news media, the criticism of journalists has become louder. Already in 2002, it was noted that 'racialist [sic] extremist organizations' distrusted not only governments, but also popular media outlets, and thus discovered the internet as an alternative communication space.[11] Recently, catch phrases like 'fake news' or 'lying press' ('Lügenpresse') in Germany sum up this wave of criticism and distrust of the media.[12] New channels through which these critical views can be voiced and heard are one reason for this phenomenon. Another is a general distrust of societal institutions, be they the traditional political parties, science, religious organisations, or others. It is remarkable that despite the loud criticism of the news media, public trust in journalism remains relatively high, or at least stable.[13] Nevertheless, the media and journalists have increasingly become the target of public criticism. While it can generally be considered healthy for a democracy to be sceptical of all institutions, interviews with journalists have shown that this criticism is taking on a different quality, where the legitimacy of news media is denied altogether. Hate speech against journalists is only one form of radical criticism of journalism.

III. The Concept of Hate Speech from a Journalist's Perspective

While hate speech is a phenomenon that is discussed around the globe, its definition is not clear at all. Different countries, different judicial systems and different groups in civil society define hate speech differently. The term is shaped and interpreted by political and public discourse.

---

[10] SH Lee, 'The End of the Traditional Gatekeeper' (2012) 12(2) *Gnovis Journal*; T Vos and F Heinderyckx, *Gatekeeping in Transition* (London, Routledge, 2015).

[11] JA Schafer, 'Spinning the Web of Hate: Web-Based Hate Propagation by Extremist Organizations' (2002) 9 *Journal of Criminal Justice and Popular Culture* 69, 72.

[12] Lilienthal and Neverla, *Lügenpresse*.

[13] C Reinemann, N Fawzi and MK Obermaier, 'Die "Vertrauenskrise" der Medien – Fakt oder Fiktion? Zu Entwicklung, Stand und Ursachen des Medienvertrauens in Deutschland' in I Neverla and V Lilienthal (eds), *Lügenpresse: Anatomie eines politischen Kampfbegriffs* (Köln, Kiepenheuer & Witsch, 2017).

The Merriam Dictionary defines hate speech quite generally as 'speech expressing hatred of a particular group of people'. This definition requires further clarification as to what kind of people. It is generally agreed that hate speech expresses prejudice and discrimination against minorities and disadvantaged groups, but what constitutes a minority and especially a disadvantaged group is and needs to be constantly debated. In the definition of the Council of Europe, these groups are identified more clearly:

> the term 'hate speech' shall be understood as covering all forms of expression which spread, incite, promote or justify racial hatred, xenophobia, anti-Semitism or other forms of hatred based on intolerance, including: intolerance expressed by aggressive nationalism and ethnocentrism, discrimination and hostility against minorities, migrants and people of immigrant origin.[14]

However, as the German government agency Wissenschaftliche Dienste Deutscher Bundestag noted, this definition is more a collection of politically charged terms, which need further interpretation.[15] The point can be made that this perspective on who is a minority or disadvantaged group has a political bias – it focuses on hate speech against groups that are commonly associated with the political left. The argument can thus be made that the concept of hate speech has a political bias.

Countries around the world, with their different histories and cultures of public discourse, have their own unique debates about what constitutes hate speech and where the line should be drawn. In Germany, Article 130 of the criminal code states that is a punishable offence to incite violence against groups based on nationality, race, religious or ethnic heritage, or to violate a person's dignity by insulting a group or person based on their being part of a certain group within society. In Switzerland, a law was passed in 1995 which criminalised the distribution of materials promoting an ideology that discriminates against people or groups based on their race, ethnicity or religion. However, this law has been the object of controversy ever since, as it is seen to violate freedom of expression. Some European countries, such as Austria, Belgium, France, Germany and Switzerland, explicitly outlaw Holocaust denial, based on their historic memory of fascism in World War II.[16]

In legal debates in the US, freedom of speech and expression has generally been favoured over the criminalisation of hate speech. While speech that calls for imminent violence against a person or a group is not protected by the freedom of speech amendment to the constitution, hate speech is widely tolerated in

---

[14] Council of Europe, 'Recommendation No R (97) 20 of the Committee of Ministers to Member States on "Hate Speech"' (adopted by the Committee of Ministers on 30 October 1997).
[15] Deutscher Bundestag, 'Hassrede (hate speech) und Holocaust-Leugnung in der menschenrechtlichen Spruchpraxis' (2016) 4.
[16] White, 'Ethical Challenges for Journalists'.

a society that – maybe because of this legal situation – has an extensive discourse on the political correctness of public speech. As the US Supreme Court stated in a decision in 2017:

> Speech that demeans on the basis of race, ethnicity, gender, religion, age, disability, or any other similar ground is hateful; but the proudest boast of our free speech jurisprudence is that we protect the freedom to express 'the thought that we hate'.[17]

It has been noted that hate speech laws have usually been implemented to protect vulnerable groups from discrimination or violence, but that in some countries, they go beyond that, prohibiting any statement perceived as offensive.[18] Journalistic codes in Rwanda, for example, are filled with warnings to guard against speech that degrades, intimidates, or incites violence – understandably, considering the role of the media in the 1994 genocide.[19] While the new penal code that was passed by the Parliament in June 2018 slightly revised these strict measures, it 'retained its worryingly extensive restrictions on freedom of expression'.[20] For example, it is still a crime to defame the country's president, or to 'humiliate' a government official 'verbally, by gestures or threats, in writings or cartoons'.[21]

The spread of the internet as a platform for immediate and personal public discourse has added a new dimension to the issue. As early as 1995, a watchdog website, later renamed HateWatch, was founded to monitor the threat of hate groups on the internet. HateWatch defined those they were monitoring as:

> an organization or individual that advocates violence against or unreasonable hostility toward those persons or organizations identified by their race, religion, national origin, sexual orientation, gender or disability. Also including organizations or individuals that disseminate historically inaccurate information with regards to these persons or organizations for the purpose of vilification.[22]

Hate speech online was not limited to websites with extremist ideologies, but included a wide range of online activities: from direct text messages aimed at individuals to blogs and forums and comments on social media and on news websites.[23]

What does this mean for journalism? If hate speech is less a legal and more a political term, dealing with hate speech is less of a legal issue and more a matter of public discourse and ethics. And this poses several dilemmas for journalism and journalists.

---

[17] *Matal v Tam*, 582 U.S. __ (2017).
[18] White, 'Ethical Challenges for Journalists'.
[19] R Dallaire and K Annan, 'The Media Dichotomy' in A Thompson (ed), *The Media and the Rwanda Genocide* (London, Pluto Press, 2007).
[20] Article 19, 'Rwanda: Analysis of the Penal Code' (10 September 2018) available at www.article19.org/resources/rwanda-analysis-of-penal-code.
[21] M Sobel and K McIntyre, '"A Fragile Period": Journalism in Rwanda, 25 Years After the Genocide' (*Columbia Journalism Review*, 4 April 2019) available at www.cjr.org/watchdog/journalism-rwanda-25-years-after-genocide.php.
[22] Schafer, 'Spinning the Web of Hate' 73.
[23] T Quandt and R Festl, 'Cyberhate' in P Rössler (ed), *The International Encyclopedia of Media Effects*, vol 1 (Chichester, Wiley Blackwell, 2017).

One of the main functions of journalism is to enable and ensure a public discourse on the issues relevant to society. Journalism not only serves as an institution which informs the public and sorts this information to allow the audience to form an opinion, it also serves as a forum in which all members of a society – those in power and those without a voice, those with more or less laudable motives – can contribute to the public discourse. Journalism should therefore include all views, even those it does not agree with, and it should specifically support the public discourse on what constitutes hate speech. At the same time, it is supposed to respect social norms, and if a norm prevents sharing hate speech publicly, journalists as part of society are supposed to uphold this norm in their reporting.

To put it another way: as part of society, news media have to respect social norms. One of these norms may well be to avoid giving hate speech a platform. Here journalism sees itself in a passive role, upholding and reinforcing a social norm – the norm of treating people equally, of avoiding discrimination against certain groups in society. At the same time, journalism has an active role in forming and changing social norms. Journalism is still the main institution in society to set the stage for public discourse. Even though it is not the gatekeeper it used to be, public perception is still largely influenced by news media. Whether a norm needs to be reinforced or questioned, whether the violation of a norm becomes the object of reporting and public debate is still to a large degree in the hands of the media. There are new phenomena like #metoo, where the public debate was triggered on social media and gained momentum through the viral spread of the hashtag and associated reports. However, even in that case, it can be argued that while initially it could have been of value for the women directly affected by the abuse to see the spread on Twitter, it was when the movement was picked up by news media that it became relevant for the general public. In short, journalism is influenced by the shared understanding of what constitutes hate speech, and at the same time, it plays a crucial role in shaping the perception of what constitutes hate speech.

Another dilemma can be seen in relation to the right of free speech versus the ban on hate speech. Arguments in favour of limiting free speech and expression in order to impede hate speech are highly critical for journalism, as briefly illustrated by the Rwandan case mentioned above. Freedom of speech and expression is not an absolute right – no right is. But the discussion as to where the limits lie is of high relevance for journalism, because this freedom is essential for journalism to be able to play its assigned role in society. Only media that are free to publish what they deem to be relevant can comprehensively inform and educate the general public. Only media that are free from excessive state or market regulations, from government or corporate influences, can fulfil the role of a critical watchdog vis-à-vis the government and other powerful actors in society.

And it goes without saying that the emergence of the internet, cyber hate, or hate speech online, has become an even more serious issue in journalism, since the internet enabled most people with a computer and access to the internet to participate or at least have an impact on journalistic production. The discussion about hate speech must thus find answers to several dilemmas on an abstract level. At the same time, journalists are confronted with hate speech in their everyday work, in at least three different ways.

IV. Journalists Writing about, Witnessing and Receiving Hate Speech

A. Journalistic Routines: Writing about Hate Speech

Journalistic reporting follows rules and routines that have emerged over many decades. Journalists report on events as they are happening, on 'snapshots in time'.[24] And journalists select stories based on certain 'qualities' or 'news values'.[25] The more of these qualities an event has, the more likely it is to be covered by journalists. For example, an event that includes a celebrity or a public figure is more likely to be in the news than one that deals with an ordinary person. Or an event that is unambiguous is more likely to make the next day's newspaper than one that leaves a lot of room for interpretation and has multiple meanings. Journalists like to tell stories to make sense of the world, and stories require a clear attribution of roles and qualities. There are different lists and understandings of what these qualities or news values are.

Strategic actors who aim to make use of the wide reach of news media have learned to work with these news values in order to spread their messages. This lies at the core of media relations practices in public relations: a company that wants journalistic news media to report on a story in the company's interest will write a press release that contains as many news values as possible. This practice is not limited to public relations though. Politicians have learned that their statements are more likely to be picked up by journalists if they, for example, break with norms and expectations – another news value. Donald Trump famously showed how breaking with the norms and standards guaranteed him a lot of media attention. But one does not have to look to the US to find evidence for the application of this logic. Ueli Maurer, then President of the Swiss People's Party who later became a minister of the Swiss Government, once remarked: 'As long as I say "nigger", the cameras stay with me.'[26]

---

[24] R Wijnberg, 'This Is How We Can Fight Donald Trump's Attack on Democracy' (*The Correspondent*, 3 February 2017) available at https://thecorrespondent.com/6150/this-is-how-we-can-fight-donald-trumps-attack-on-democracy.
[25] T Harcup, *Journalism: Principles and Practice* (London, Sage, 2015) 37–41.
[26] D Bühler, 'Ueli, der Staatsmann' (*Republik*, 20 December 2018) available at www.republik.ch/2018/12/20/vom-knecht-zum-staatsmann.

This poses a new challenge for journalism and journalists. Donald Trump's presidency is just one example that has made journalists realise that they have to rethink their passive role of simply reporting what is happening in the world; because as simple chroniclers, they can easily be manipulated by people who know that they will get all the attention as long as they say outrageous things.

Uttering hateful messages tends to fit well into the logic of news values. They are direct, often personal, they deal with issues close to the audience's interests, and they break with social norms. As a consequence, if journalists do not reflect on their practice regarding news values, they not only risk being manipulated by the actors they cover in their reporting, they are also prone to pointing their microphones and cameras towards individuals making hateful messages, offering them a stage from which they can address a large audience.

Journalists must realise that they have to take a more active stance instead. As former journalist and journalism scholar Barbie Zelizer states: 'Journalists are going by professional cues that make them ill-equipped to deal with the situation today. That includes deference and moderation, objectivity and balance.'[27] At the same time, they have to avoid the trap of having their own agenda and thus delivering biased news, or of self-righteously breaking with social norms, because they put their role of reporting freely above all other considerations.

Recent examples show that more and more journalists have started to learn the lessons. In the discussion of the media's role in Trump's first election campaign, journalists realised self-critically that with their passive 'he-said-she-said' journalism, they had neglected their active role as critical watchdogs.[28] As the executive of a German journalists' association writes: 'Journalists have learned: They become accomplices of populists and agitators if they jump through every hoop that is put in front of them.'[29] And she goes on: 'Today's gatekeepers have to expose this Trojan horse.'

Furthermore, over the last decades, objectivity has become a basic quality of journalism, both in the eyes of the audience and of the journalists themselves. While there is a tradition of scepticism towards the concept of objectivity in the academic world,[30] journalism surveys around the world show that the role that

---

[27] MW Berger, 'Political Intimidation, At-Risk Media, and the Future of Journalism' (*Penn Today*, 19 October 2018) available at https://penntoday.upenn.edu/news/discussing-political-intimidation-at-risk-media-journalism-future-with-barbie-zelizer.

[28] M Massing, 'Journalism in the Age of Trump' *Le Monde diplomatique* (2 August 2018).

[29] I Dippmann, 'Journalisten als Zielscheibe von Hass' in Die Medienanstalten, *Der Ton wird härter. Hass, Mobbing und Extremismus* (Judith Zimmermann und Thomas Köhler GbR, Berlin, 2019) 20.

[30] B McNair, 'Trust, Truth and Objectivity. Sustaining Quality Journalism in the Era of the Content-Generating User' in C Peters and MJ Broersma (eds), *Rethinking Journalism: Trust and Participation in a Transformed News Landscape* (Abingdon, Routledge, 2013); G Tuchman, 'Objectivity as Strategic Ritual: An Examination of Newsmen's Notions of Objectivity' (1972) 77 *American Journal of Sociology* 660.

journalists usually identify with most is that of the objective reporter.[31] In a recent survey in Switzerland, journalists considered the duty to 'report things as they are' and 'be a detached observer' as the two most important aspects of their role.[32]

The role of the media is to stay neutral, not to take a position, 'to be independent of ideology'.[33] However, not taking a position is problematic when dealing with hate speech. To merely be an objective observer who lets the world and its actors set the agenda and claim a voice leads to becoming a platform for sinister voices as well as legitimate ones. According to McNair: 'Objective journalism does not imply neutral, value-free or impartial journalism or journalists.'[34] However, in everyday practical journalism, there is a thin line between being an impartial journalist who treats each voice and each argument as equally valid, and objective reporting, which 'takes pains to represent fairly each leading side'.[35] To be in a passive role of a neutral observer delivering a well-balanced report would mean to treat any position as equally legitimate – a position no ethical journalist would seek.

The phrase 'journalism of attachment' has been coined to describe a journalism 'that is aware of the moral ground on which it operates, that cares as well as knows, and that will not stand neutrally between good and evil'.[36] This helps to define the role of a journalist towards hate speech: to be seeking the truth, to take into consideration all positions on an issue, but also to allow for judgement, while subjecting that judgement to public scrutiny. To take a stand against evil does not contradict the standards of objective journalism, as long as journalists subject their reports to objective controls, by applying measures such as the careful presentation of facts, the consultation of expert opinion, the provision of accurate references and a fair representation of major viewpoints.[37] Objectivity is then more a matter of journalistic method than of the journalist's position.

B. Dealing with User-Generated Hate Speech

Second, digital technologies have allowed new forms of journalistic presentation, which allow for a much more immediate and visible audience participation. Twenty years ago, a newspaper article might have triggered a letter to the editor – a letter which took time and effort to write, and which would take at least a day to reach the newsroom and then at least another day to be published, if it was

---

[31] DH Weaver and L Wilnat, *The Global Journalist in the 21st Century* (New York, Routledge, 2012) 536.

[32] F Dingerkus et al, 'Journalists in Switzerland: Structures and Attitudes Revisited' (2018) 18 *Studies in Communication Sciences* 117, 125.

[33] McNair, 'Trust, Truth and Objectivity' 84.

[34] ibid.

[35] M Schudson, 'The Objectivity Norm in American Journalism' (2001) 2 *Journalism* 149, 150.

[36] M Bell, 'The Truth Is Our Currency' (1998) 3 *Harvard International Journal of Press/Politics* 102, 103.

[37] SJ Ward, 'An Answer to Martin Bell: Objectivity and Attachment in Journalism' (1998) 3 *Harvard International Journal of Press/Politics* 121.

published at all. Nowadays, readers of most news websites are invited to post their comment right below a published article. And readers use this opportunity. The New York Times has counted an average of about 12,000 comments a day since 2007 on its website, even though only selected stories offer the option to leave a comment.[38] These comments sometimes contain well-thought-out arguments, but more often spontaneous reactions to an article. Interviews with journalists about the value of the comments for their daily work and as a contribution to the public discourse show that they view them rather negatively.[39] Most see very little substance in these comments, and a shocking amount of aggression and hate. As a reaction, some online newspapers started to restrict audience participation and shut down their comments sections. Reputable titles and media organisations such as *The Guardian*, *Reuters*, *Bloomberg*, *Stern*, *De Volkskrant* or *The Moscow Times* limit the opportunities to comment online, or have closed down the comment function altogether.[40] In 2017, the *Neue Zürcher Zeitung*, the flagship quality newspaper in Switzerland, decided to remove its comment section in their web edition. They explained: 'The mood has become more hateful. Where readers used to debate, they increasingly insult each other. We are increasingly called "system press" or "propaganda catapult", instead of being notified of mistakes in our reporting.'[41] It was not an easy decision for those in charge at *Neue Zürcher Zeitung*, and it disappointed many readers – the last thing a media house wants to do, especially at a time when print media are facing massive losses in readership.

The reasons and motivations for this cyber hate vary. While some writers of hateful messages may do this in order to express their frustration and general hatred against others or 'the system', others might simply enjoy the attention they get by causing turmoil ('trolling'). Their goal is to annoy and provoke other readers and they enjoy seeing them unnerved by aggressive or sometimes simply nonsensical comments.[42] The aggression ranges from insults against people, both journalists and others, to mean-spirited comments on ideas, plans, policies or behaviours. They are sometimes uttered by frustrated individuals who use the anonymity of the internet to let out their anger, but sometimes by groups or even states running strategic campaigns.[43]

---

[38] K Long, 'Keeping The Times Civil, 16 Million Comments and Counting' *The New York Times* (1 July 2017).
[39] See, eg, D Allemann, I Messerli and G Keel, *IAM-Bernet Studie Journalisten im Web 2017: Recherchieren, Publizieren, Diskutieren: Ausgewählte Einblicke in den Social-Media-Alltag von Schweizer Journalisten* (Zürich, buch & netz, 2017); A Hermida et al, 'The Active Recipient: Participatory Journalism Through the Lens of the Dewey-Lippmann Debate' (International Symposium on Online Journalism, University of Texas, Austin, April 2011); G Keel and V Wyss, 'Journalistische Praxis und Internet' in M Leonarz (ed), *Aktuelle Studien Zur Leistungsfähigkeit von Presse, Radio Und Fernsehen in Der Schweiz: Im Auftrag des BAKOM* (Zürich, SwissGIS, 2012).
[40] Quandt, 'Dark Participation' 37.
[41] O Fuchs, 'Warum wir unsere Kommentarspalte umbauen' *Neue Zürcher Zeitung* (4 February 2017).
[42] Quandt, 'Dark Participation' 41.
[43] C Elliott, 'The Readers' Editor on … the Pro-Russia Trolls Below the Line on Ukraine Stories' *The Guardian* (4 May 2014).

In general, user participation in online journalism never fulfilled the hope that it would render journalism more democratic and more inclusive. What was once seen as a great new opportunity for journalism[44] had turned into a nightmare. This is in line with the finding that communication in the media, especially on social media, has seen a remarkable increase of hateful speech in general.[45] A group of researchers has confirmed these findings for the world of journalism in Germany.[46] They found that new roles, such as mediators and community managers, have emerged in newsrooms specifically in reaction to such comments. Journalists have also learned that while they can gain in acceptance and legitimacy if they give the audience a voice, this can also be a risky strategy, because agitators can use the attention and reach they get to spread hateful messages.[47]

While academic research found the picture to be less bleak than sometimes described by journalists,[48] newsrooms still felt a need to come up with strategies to counter what has been described as 'dark participation'.[49] And since there are no clear legal definitions of what constitutes hate speech and there is only a limited legal framework to which a newsroom can refer, it is the responsibility of each newsroom to come up with its standards and practices regarding hate speech. Editorial teams have to decide, often on a case-by-case or comment-by-comment basis, if a certain act of speech constitutes hate speech or not. The support news media can expect from regulatory bodies in the form of laws against hate speech are generally limited, because state regulation fundamentally conflicts with the principle of freedom of the media and might be seen as inappropriate censorship.[50] Thus, the question remains how journalists as a profession and individual newsrooms should react to hate speech on their websites.

To identify hate speech and counter it is a difficult task of self-regulation for journalists and editorial teams. There are several questions linked to this problem. What is the responsibility of a news organisation when it comes to user-generated hate speech on their websites? To what extent is a media organisation liable for the content on its website? What is the legal, but – just as important – the ethical role

---

[44] D Gillmor, *We the Media: Grassroots Journalism by the People, for the People* (Cambridge, O'Reilly, 2004).

[45] Die Medienanstalten, *Der Ton wird härter. Hass, Mobbing und Extremismus* (Judith Zimmermann und Thomas Köhler GbR, Berlin, 2019).

[46] L Frischlich, S Boberg and T Quandt, 'Comment Sections as Targets of Dark Participation? Journalists' Evaluation and Moderation of Deviant User Comments' (2019) 20 *Journalism Studies* 2014.

[47] K Coe, K Kenski and SA Rains, 'Online and Uncivil? Patterns and Determinants of Incivility in Newspaper Website Comments' (2014) 64 *Journal of Communication* 658.

[48] T Graham and S Wright, 'A Tale of Two Stories from "Below the Line": Comment Fields at the Guardian' (2015) 20 *The International Journal of Press/Politics* 317; Z Papacharissi, 'Democracy Online: Civility, Politeness, and the Democratic Potential of Online Political Discussion Groups' (2004) 6 *New Media & Society* 259.

[49] Quandt, 'Dark Participation'.

[50] V Wyss and G Keel, 'Media Governance and Media Quality Management: Theoretical Concepts and an Empirical Example from Switzerland' in A Czepek, E Nowak and M Hellwig (eds), *Press Freedom and Pluralism in Europe: Concepts and Conditions* (Bristol, Intellect, 2009).

of a media organisation? Is it just a platform that allows for the mass publication of content, including hate speech? Or do other standards apply, since journalism and journalistic organisations fulfil a unique role in society and are thus provided with unique rights compared to other types of organisations and individuals?

When the freedom of the press is explicitly guaranteed, this comes with a moral and sometimes even a constitutional and legal obligation for the media, as for example for radio and TV in Switzerland. The Swiss Constitution states in Article 93.2, for electronic media: 'They shall present events accurately and allow a diversity of opinions to be expressed appropriately.' At the same time, Swiss radio and TV law protects journalistic media organisations from external pressure, especially from the pressure of having to publish anything. In Article 6, it is stated: 'No-one may demand that a broadcaster broadcast specific presentations and information.' And it is stated in the Swiss professional journalistic code of conduct under the self-declared rights of journalists: 'They cannot be forced to do or say something in their professional role which contradicts their professional norms or their conscience.' Thus, journalists and the media in Switzerland are free to publish whatever they consider to be in line with their professional standards. However, they also have the moral obligation to allow opinions that they do not share in their coverage. If they do not, they not only disrespect the normative goal to be comprehensive in their coverage, they are quickly considered by a critical audience to be biased, to censor views and opinions. The current discussions on so-called fake news or the Lügenpresse are evidence for this increasing lack of trust in the media, based on the perception that journalists only publish what is in line with their world view and their interests.

Thus, how to deal with hate speech in their comments sections is a delicate topic for a newsroom. This is even more the case at a time when media are seen as having an agenda, or as the lying press. As for the decision to stop comments altogether on the *Neue Zürcher Zeitung* website, the audience reacted negatively. One reader commented on that decision as follows: 'The comments showed me the range of public opinion. I don't need filtered and censored debates. We have a lot to learn from the US and its take on free speech.' Another reader stated: 'For a liberal flagship like NZZ, there should be nothing more sacred than its role as a platform of free speech.' And yet another reader quoted Benjamin Franklin: 'If all printers were determined not to print anything till they were sure it would offend nobody, there would be very little printed.'

Legal action and the blocking of comments are but two strategies journalists and newsrooms apply when fighting hate speech in audience comments. Two journalism scholars have tried to identify and evaluate the various strategies used in German newsrooms against hate speech.[51] They distinguish between empowering and disempowering strategies. A disempowering strategy denies the agitator

---

[51] L Kramp and S Weichert, *Hass im Netz: Steuerungsstrategien für Redaktionen, Schriftenreihe Medienforschung der Landesanstalt für Medien Nordrhein-Westfalen* (Leipzig, Vistas Verlag, 2018).

attention and power to influence the public discourse, while an empowering strategy encourages that person to participate in a dialogue and, hopefully, revise their hateful attitudes and positions.

The authors then identified ten strategies, which can be categorised according to their empowering/disempowering potential and the level of journalistic engagement required. These options all have implications for the media's reputation and their ability to perform their normative function. Furthermore, given the limited resources at the media's disposal, these options are not all equally feasible.

i. Disempowering Strategies

a. Deleting and Blocking

The authors of the study on strategies against hateful comments found the strategy of deleting and/or blocking to be widespread in German media, as it requires few resources.[52] However, it has not proven to be very effective, as providers of hate speech learn to overcome blocking and have been shown to come back and try again. Furthermore, this strategy reinforces the perception, or at least the narrative of such agitators, that the media is silencing dissonant voices, only allowing views that are in line with the accepted 'mainstream'.

b. Legal Action

Libel, slander, or inciting violence are civil or even criminal offences in many countries. Journalists and journalistic organisations may have the means to take people who publish such comments to court. While the most effective against hate speech, this option requires considerable effort on the part of journalists. Recently, media organisations and law enforcement agencies in Germany have joined together to facilitate the prosecution of user-generated hate speech on news platforms.[53] Their approach of 'prosecute rather than just delete' has been noted in other EU countries and could thus gain traction elsewhere. However, prosecuting people for posting hateful comments means that journalism is relying on the state and its instruments to influence the public discourse, contradicting liberal ideals, and can therefore be found questionable by advocates of a free press. For conspiracy theorists and agitators behind hateful comments, legal action is likely to be seen as yet another way in which the elite suppresses divergent voices.

c. Ignoring Hate Speech

Ignoring hate speech also requires few resources and is less aggressive against those producing it. However, this strategy carries the risk that a debate on a

---

[52] ibid 21.
[53] M de Groot, 'Verfolgen statt nur Löschen' in Die Medienanstalten, *Der Ton wird härter. Hass, Mobbing und Extremismus* (Judith Zimmermann und Thomas Köhler GbR, Berlin, 2019) 83.

media platform will get out of hand. Furthermore, new ethical issues arise:[54] if the audience is invited to comment freely, who is responsible for the quality, the legality and the legitimacy of the content? The audience's contributions may violate basic quality standards or laws, for which the media company can then be held at least partly responsible. Overall, to simply ignore hateful comments on one's own website is a surrender to hate speech. Such a passive position contradicts journalists' mission to contribute to a meaningful and constructive public discourse and thus to society's self-observation.[55]

d. Countering Speech

Arguing against hate speech is a laborious strategy, requiring a high degree of attention and communication on the part of the journalist. It therefore requires resources that are increasingly scarce in today's newsrooms. It is also doubtful that a purely confrontational reaction from a journalist will succeed in convincing someone producing the hate speech to change their mind. However, counter speech signals to both the author of a hateful comment and the audience in general that hate speech is not accepted.

e. Deconstructing Hate Speech

Deconstructing the reasoning behind hate speech also requires a lot of resources. However, it seems to be more promising and effective than counter speech when it comes to changing the views of someone disseminating hate speech, as it is not purely confrontational. When countering or deconstructing hate speech, journalists find themselves in a new role – not that of a reporter or researcher, but that of a moderator and interlocutor. This entails either a change in the role of a journalist, or specialised staff such as community managers. Since deconstruction demands an in-depth understanding of an issue, this new role requires experts in mediation as well as in the details of the particular issue.

ii. *Empowering Strategies*

a. Irony

Research has shown that journalists turn to irony, cynicism or sarcasm when they feel frustrated or helpless in the face of hateful comments. Their hope may be that by using humour and irony, they might be able to turn hate speech into something less aggressive. However, in writing, irony often gets lost, and what is meant as a

---

[54] JB Singer, 'Taking Responsibility' in *Participatory Journalism* (Oxford, Wiley Blackwell, 2011).
[55] N Luhmann, *Die Realität der Massenmedien* (Wiesbaden, Springer, 2017) 118.

humorous reaction can be fundamentally misunderstood, adding fuel to the fire. Therefore, the effectiveness of this strategy remains doubtful.

b. Questioning the Haters

By asking why someone shares such a hateful view, or for factual arguments rather than just opinions, a journalist can question and counter that person and their hateful opinions without starting an open confrontation. By doing so, the bitterness in a discussion can be moderated. This is a strategy that requires considerable editorial resources and skilled moderators who keep calm in heated debates.

c. Mediated Dialogue

The goal here is to engage the person producing hate speech in a factual, constructive debate. While the questioning strategy sees the moderator interacting with the person behind the hate speech in a one-to-one situation to change that person's views, in the dialogue strategy the moderator mediates among and engages the commentators. This strategy requires even more resources, skills and patience than the questioning strategy and the result can be disappointing. However, when the journalist succeeds in engaging the aggressor in a constructive dialogue, this strategy can have a lasting effect.

d. Solidarity

With this strategy, moderators or journalists try to team up with the targets of hate speech or the opponents of the person spreading hateful messages. As has been discussed above, the ideal of the objective reporter prohibits a journalist from taking sides. However, this strategy has the potential not only to stop hate speech, it can also create strong communities who are active for a good cause and against hate speech – an effect media managers had in mind when they initially hoped that audience participation would help improve journalism. Compared to the following strategy referred to as 'embracing', this strategy sees the journalist in a more passive role, where he or she expresses sympathy without providing facts or arguments.

e. Embracing

With this last strategy option, journalists and moderators actively support the targets of hate speech and the opponents of the person producing hate speech by providing them with arguments and moral support. It is a more active form of solidarity with the good forces in the debates against hate speech. Unlike the solidarity strategy, this strategy does not ignore those producing hate speech, but it primarily addresses their opponents.

As can be seen, media organisations and journalists have various strategies for dealing with hate speech in their comments section. As this overview has also shown, some of them come with serious drawbacks, as they are not very successful at stopping hate speech or at preventing future attacks. Other strategy options require a rethinking of traditional journalistic norms and roles. And yet other strategies require resources both in terms of time and skills that are unlikely to be found in abundance in today's newsrooms.

Which option to recommend depends on various factors. The frequency of hateful comments and thus the urgency of the issue should be taken into consideration, as well as the resources and staff available to deal with the problem. Furthermore, the comments of a frustrated individual whose hate or rage is authentic should be distinguished from those that may be part of a tactical or even strategic campaign by a group. Finally, it is also relevant to adapt the response to the target of the hateful comment. Depending on the target's resources and the motive for the attack, the suitable response is different.

These considerations show that there is no simple method to counter hateful online comments. However, the range of possible options should allow journalists to tackle them more consciously.

C. Journalists as Victims of Hate Speech

As well as the issues of how to report on hate speech, and how to respond to hate speech in online comments, hate speech can also address journalists directly. This can be in the form of online comments, but is not limited to that channel. As the 2019 report from Reporters Without Borders states: 'hatred of journalists has degenerated into violence, contributing to an increase in fear'.[56] Attacks range from insults in comments sections and on social media to intimidation, letter bombs and physical violence.[57] A study in Germany found that almost one in two journalists had experienced hate speech in the previous 12 months, and that more than a quarter had experienced it several times.[58] Furthermore, the survey showed that over the previous 12 months, two thirds of all interviewed journalists felt that hateful responses to articles had increased, compared to roughly one fifth who denied such an increase.[59] Eighty-five per cent of the journalists who had faced hate speech felt that they had been attacked in their role as a journalist, and not

---

[56] Reporters Without Borders, '2019 World Press Freedom Index – A Cycle of Fear' available at https://rsf.org/en/2019-world-press-freedom-index-cycle-fear.
[57] Dippmann, 'Journalisten als Zielscheibe von Hass'.
[58] M Preuss, F Tetzlaff and A Zick, '"Publizieren wird zur Mutprobe". Studie zur Wahrnehmung von und Erfahrungen mit Angriffen unter Journalist_innen' (*Mediendienst Integration*, 2017) available at https://mediendienst-integration.de/fileadmin/Dateien/Studie-hatespeech.pdf.
[59] ibid 7.

because of personal characteristics. From 2015 to 2018, the European Centre for Press and Media Freedom (ECPMF) registered 109 cases of violence against journalists that had been reported to the police.[60] The true number is no doubt even higher.

This hate speech has consequences: for example, journalists decide not to take part in and report on protests because they are tired of being yelled at and intimidated. One out of two journalists stated that they felt that hate speech had a restraining impact on their work, whether they had been the target of it or not. Furthermore – and this affects the core of journalism – 24 per cent of journalists stated that they felt constrained in their work as a result of hate speech attacks. For example, they considered not covering a topic at all, or covering it in a way that offered no reason for hateful reactions, in order to avoid being the target of hate speech.[61]

The reasons for the hatred directed at journalists and journalism are likely to lie too deep to be easily countered. Instead, journalists must find ways to cope with these attacks. A study among German journalists found that journalists often resort to emotion-focused coping strategies such as discussing hate speech with colleagues, friends or family, but that problem-focused strategies such as taking legal action or seeking psychological support are less common.[62] An international study has shown that female journalists have developed various strategies to deal with online harassment, such as limiting what they post online, changing what stories they report on, and using technological tools to prevent people from posting offensive words on the journalists' public social media pages.[63] As the authors of this study discovered, media organisations rarely offer their journalists psychological or legal support, because up until fairly recently, there was no need to do so. In another survey in Germany, the authors found that in a majority of newsrooms, hate speech had never been openly dealt with, and in two thirds of cases, incidents involving hate speech against journalists were not taken seriously.[64] However, journalists stated that it was important to them that media organisations and executives take responsibility for protecting their journalists and their products from hate and aggression.

These three aspects show that hate speech is thus both a challenge and a threat to journalism on a personal and institutional level. It affects individual journalists and it has a negative effect on the performance of journalism. It impedes or even prevents the inclusion of the audience and of the citizens into the journalistic process.

---

[60] Dippmann, 'Journalisten als Zielscheibe von Hass' 17.

[61] Preuss, Tetzlaff and Zick, 'Publizieren wird zur Mutprobe' 15f.

[62] M Obermaier, M Hofbauer and C Reinemann, 'Journalists as Targets of Hate Speech. How German Journalists Perceive the Consequences for Themselves and How They Cope with It' (2018) 7 *SCM Studies in Communication and Media* 499, 513.

[63] GM Chen et al, '"You Really Have to Have a Thick Skin": A Cross-Cultural Perspective on How Online Harassment Influences Female Journalists' (2020) 21 *Journalism* 877.

[64] Preuss, Tetzlaff and Zick, 'Publizieren wird zur Mutprobe' 19f.

Journalists and media organisations thus need to find ways to report on what is happening in the world without becoming a megaphone for those who try to disseminate hateful messages. Second, they have to make sure their wide reach and their credibility is not being abused for the spread of hateful messages, not least because they can be held accountable for hate speech that is published on their websites. And third, they have to come up with strategies to protect themselves against hate speech aimed directly at them.

V. Conclusion

Economic and technological changes have led to new forms of journalism and new forms of public discourse. One consequence is that journalists are left more exposed to aggression and hate speech than ever. Journalists and media organisations are confronted with hate speech on different levels, and they play a key role in confronting hate speech in society. In doing so, they have to face this challenge themselves, as part of their professional responsibility.

Journalists need to rethink long-held standards and practices to avoid becoming platforms for hate speech. When it comes to the handling of hateful messages in reaction to their work, journalists have various strategic options at their disposal. However, some of these strategies require a great deal of effort and thus resources, which are not easily obtainable in today's media world, while others seek the support and power of the state, which compromises the media's independence. More promising strategy options to counter hate speech sometimes necessitate a rethinking of the journalist's role, with journalists assuming a more active and even activist role. Finally, journalists and media organisations need to raise their awareness of the fact that hate speech has become part of their trade and have to come up with strategies to help themselves, their colleagues and their employees.

The news media enjoy a unique role in society, and they are given special means to fulfil their function. Hate speech poses not only a threat to minorities and disadvantaged people, but also to journalism. Thus journalistic actors – media managers, editors-in-chief, journalists – need to rethink their professional roles and ethics, and it is imperative that journalists are provided with the necessary resources to become active and successful in the fight against hate speech.

12
Digital Technologies for Sustainable Development

CLAUDIA ABREU LOPES AND MARCUS ERRIDGE

I. Introduction

The rise of new information and communication technologies (ICTs) has had a profound effect on areas where communication, access to information, learning, research and innovation play a key role in driving social and economic development.[1] A broad definition of ICTs is a 'set of activities that facilitate, by electronic means, the capturing, storage, processing, transmission and display of information',[2] encompassing traditional technologies, such as TV and radio broadcasting, and digital technologies, such as mobile phones, mobile internet and the internet of things.

In September 2015, Member States of the United Nations adopted the 2030 Agenda for Sustainable Development. The 17 sustainable development goals (SDGs) and 169 targets contained in the 2030 Agenda constitute a transformative plan for people, planet, prosperity, partnerships and peace.[3] Achieving the SDGs by 2030 depends in part on the universal adoption of ICT solutions, for example, in healthcare, financial inclusion, agriculture and education. More specifically, SDG 17 seeks to strengthen capacity and the means of implementation for partner countries. This includes enhancing the use of ICTs as 'enabling technology' and improving country-level data, with specific targets aimed at increasing the proportion of the population with access to the internet (indicator 17.8.1), full data disaggregation (indicator 17.18.1), and the presence of a national statistics plans (indicator 17.18.3).

---

[1] D Jorgenson and K Vu, 'The ICT Revolution, World Economic Growth, and Policy Issues' (2016) 40 *Telecommunications Policy* 383.

[2] F Rodriguez and E Wilson, 'Are Poor Countries Losing the Information Revolution?', InfoDev working paper (Washington DC, The World Bank, 2000).

[3] See Annex IV of the 'Report of the Inter-Agency and Expert Group on Sustainable Development Goal Indicators' (2016) available at https://sustainabledevelopment.un.org/content/documents/11803Official-List-of-Proposed-SDG-Indicators.pdf.

The adoption of new technologies is spreading to all corners of the globe, but it is still far from being universal. Mobile phone subscriptions amounted to 67 per cent of the world's population (5.1 billion people) by the end of 2018.[4] The previous four years showed considerable growth in the adoption of mobile phones, with a total of one billion new subscribers gained (average annual growth rate of 5 per cent).[5] Although the rate of growth is decelerating, it is estimated that 71 per cent of the global population (5.8 billion) will have a mobile phone subscription and 60 per cent (5 billion people) will be mobile internet subscribers by 2025.[6] In this period (2018–25), smartphone connections in Sub-Saharan Africa will more than double (from 39 per cent to 66 per cent of all subscriptions) and millions of people will start using mobile internet for the first time.[7]

Notwithstanding the progress on ICT infrastructure and affordable prices of devices and subscriptions, more than four billion people will remain offline by 2025. Of these, around one billion do not live within the reach of a mobile broadband network, being 'coverage excluded'. The other three billion live within the reach of a network but do not access mobile internet services, being 'usage excluded'.[8] In this chapter, we will discuss how ICTs can be leveraged to achieve and monitor the SDGs, weighing both the opportunities and the threats such as exclusions and breaches of privacy that these technologies entail.

II. The Role of ICTs for Achieving the SDGs

Mobile phones have transformed the delivery and implementation of development projects by enabling exchanges with target groups and coordination between teams. For many people, owning a mobile phone means that they are able to access health information or new farming techniques; they can use banking services, including applying for micro-loans to start a business; they are able to vote in and monitor elections; they can seek help during pandemics or natural disasters, and receive humanitarian assistance.

Two general positions highlight the benefits and downsides of ICTs. On one side there are 'ICT optimists, who believe that the new technologies have largely positive impacts such as wealth creation and improved service delivery'. Conversely, there are 'ICT pessimists, who associate ICTs largely with negative impacts such

---

[4] J Stryjak and M Sivakumaran, 'The Mobile Economy 2019' (GSMA Intelligence, London, 2019) 4. For further related internet penetration and digital growth data, see S Kemp, 'Digital 2019: Global Digital Overview' (*Datareportal*, 31 January 2019) available at https://datareportal.com/reports/digital-2019-global-digital-overview.
[5] Stryjak and Sivakumaran, 'The Mobile Economy' 4.
[6] ibid.
[7] ibid 15.
[8] ibid 24.

as unemployment and growing social exclusion'.[9] As May, Waema and Bjåstad suggest, one view is theoretically grounded in modernisation, the other rooted in dependency theory.[10]

Among the earliest uses of ICT tools are mobile health (mHealth) projects, which utilise mobile communication technologies to support the delivery of healthcare information, patient observation and provision of care. For example, the project Mobile Kunji ('mobile guide' in Hindi) by BBC Media Action helps community health workers to promote health messages about maternal health, child health, family planning and immunisation to families in rural areas of Jharkhand, a state in Eastern India with very high rates of child mortality. A fictional doctor called Dr Anita delivers voice messages in Hindi and in Santhali, the most widely spoken languages in that state, via mobile phones (interactive voice response) supplemented by an illustrated deck of cards.[11]

A systematic review of literature regarding what works in mHealth projects in several African countries acknowledged that interventions may fail due to low literacy levels and/or user preference for making voice calls or face-to-face interactions (particularly when SMS is used).[12] Successful mHealth projects have operationalised two-way data information processes, utilising ICTs to serve health monitoring purposes, whilst providing information and choice for patients. The successful rollout of mHealth initiatives is heavily reliant on technology that is characterised by low cost, ease of use and widespread availability.

In what can be seen as a progression of earlier mHealth technologies with a citizen participation component, Schaaf et al explored comparative case studies of SMS-based reporting relating to healthcare accountability interventions in Guatemala and India, for low-income women.[13] A number of supportive offline activities sought to engage volunteers in rights and entitlement consciousness-raising and communicate the purpose and value of reporting. For example, SAHAYOG in India deployed a 'conscientisation component' in the implementation of an ICT tool-enabled health evaluation project that was intended to create conditions for the women to learn about human rights in order to understand that these rights apply to them so that they were motivated to make reports. Access

---

[9] J May, TM Waema and E Bjåstad, 'Introduction: The ICT/Poverty Nexus in Africa' in EO Adera et al (eds), *ICT Pathways to Poverty Reduction: Empirical Evidence from East and Southern Africa* (Practical Action Publishing, Rugby, 2014) 3, referring to R Heeks, 'Information and Communication Technologies, Poverty and Development' Development Informatics Working Paper Series, Paper no 5 (1999) 13.

[10] May, Waema and Bjåstad, 'Introduction' 4.

[11] See BBC Media Action, 'Empowering Community Health Workers in India: Mobile Academy and Mobile Kunji' available at www.bbc.co.uk/mediaaction/where-we-work/asia/india/sdp-ma-mk.

[12] CB Aranda-Jan, N Mohutsiwa-Dibe and S Loukanova, 'Systematic Review on What Works, What Does Not Work and Why of Implementation of Mobile Health (mHealth) Projects in Africa' (2014) 14 *BMC Public Health* 188.

[13] M Schaaf et al, 'Does Information and Communication Technology Add Value to Citizen-Led Accountability Initiatives in Health? Experiences from India and Guatemala' (2019) 20(2) *Health and Human Rights Journal* 169, 176–79.

barriers identified by female participants in Uttar Pradesh included poor phone networks, lack of access to electricity (to charge the phone), and gender norms around phone use. The Guatemala-based organisation CEGSS sought to mitigate the problem posed by low tech literacy by giving communities a role in the design of the technology. Citizen data volunteers helped design a healthcare access complaints platform, associated survey forms and project website, and helped field-test ICT tools. However, despite their best efforts at recruitment, CEGSS found that the poorest and most marginalised were often not present and/or able to take part. Crucially, Schaaf et al suggest that technical support is unique to ICT whereas the challenge of providing feedback to community members and volunteers making reports as part of health system monitoring projects is not.[14] This research highlights efforts to address technological literacy and close the 'digital divide' in access to and use of ICTs with a gender equality focus.

A different example from the private sector is M-PESA, a widely used mobile-based money transfer platform launched in Kenya in 2007. Eleven years later, M-PESA had more than 30 million active users across ten countries, having expanded their services to offer international transactions, savings, loans, overdraft and insurance products. M-PESA has dramatically changed the way that people access financial services, particularly among unbanked households (96 per cent of households outside Nairobi use M-PESA).[15] By facilitating quick, secure and cheap transactions from a registered mobile phone, M-PESA enables informal networks of geographically dispersed family and friends to act as a form of insurance, and this has been proven to make a difference in supporting households when they experience negative income shocks, such as illness, unemployment or agricultural losses.[16]

Grassroot movements such as #MeToo and #NiUnaMenos were also instigated through the use of ICTs, sparking global interest on issues relating to sexual harassment, gender-based violence and femicide. By the end of 2018, the hashtag #MeToo had been used more than 20 million times, with 29 per cent of tweets non-English, written mainly in Afrikaans (7 per cent of the total), Somali (4 per cent) and Spanish (3 per cent).[17] In Brazil, 'Mete a Colher' ('Put the spoon' in Portuguese) is an app designed by a collective of women for other women in abusive or violent relationships to connect with others who can provide help – from lawyers and psychologists to other female victims of domestic violence. The idea is to encourage women to recognise signs of physical or emotional abuse and leave violent or

---

[14] ibid 179.

[15] F de Soyres et al, 'What Kenya's Mobile Money Success Could Mean for the Arab World' (*The World Bank*, 3 October 2018) available at www.worldbank.org/en/news/feature/2018/10/03/what-kenya-s-mobile-money-success-could-mean-for-the-arab-world.

[16] J William and S Tavneet, 'Risk Sharing and Transactions Costs: Evidence from Kenya's Mobile Money Revolution' (2014) 104 *The American Economic Review* 183.

[17] M Anderson and S Toor, 'How Social Media Users Have Discussed Sexual Harassment Since #MeToo Went Viral' (*Fact Tank*, 11 October 2018) available at www.pewresearch.org/fact-tank/2018/10/11/how-social-media-users-have-discussed-sexual-harassment-since-metoo-went-viral.

abusive relationships before they escalate. The app has a security function where conversations are regularly deleted, a plus for women who fear repercussions from violent partners if their conversations are discovered. In 2018, the app connected over 13,000 women across 63 cities in Brazil and has helped 2,000 women to find support and to escape violence.[18]

As these examples demonstrate, successful ICT-based interventions need to be suited to people's needs (eg, informal transactions), to their context (eg, domestic violence), to be inclusive (eg, allowing different languages and levels of literacy), easy to scale up to other contexts if they relate to global issues and affordable (to access, use and maintain), in order to have a sustainable positive impact on people's lives. The potential of ICTs transcends sectors. It has been recognised that they stimulate economic prosperity and potentially good governance by increasing accountability, transparency, security and citizen participation.[19] However, there is limited evidence that ICT tools are delivering promised governance outcomes, particularly in low income and conflict-affected regions.

A review of evidence on the use of 23 ICT platforms to project citizen voice in order to improve public service delivery in the Global South considers that the relationship between citizen uptake and the degree to which public service providers respond to expressions of citizen voice operates through different mechanisms.[20] On the one hand, upward accountability delineates from service providers to managers and policymakers, by identifying problems and triggering administrative action; while on the other hand, accountability can radiate downward, from the public sector to society, by generating external political pressure on decision-makers. A dual accountability mechanism such as this mirrors theoretical frameworks of norms socialisation, such as Keck and Sikkink's Boomerang Model[21] and Risse, Ropp and Sikkink's Spiral Model,[22] which suggest that political will is produced as a reaction to pressure, and that pressure is brought about by a combination of advocacy and activism from 'above' and 'below'. Peixoto and Fox found that the existence of ICT-enabled platforms alone is not sufficient to trigger institutional responsiveness.[23] These platforms can only be effective if there is willingness or motivation from policymakers to respond, related to a sense of mission or potential risk associated with dissatisfied citizens.

Gagliardone et al, referring to the role of ICTs in peacebuilding, state-building, and governance in Africa, consider that the discourse of the transformative

---

[18] See https://meteacolher.org.

[19] G Relhan, K Ionkova and R Huque, 'Good Urban Governance through ICT: Issues, Analysis, and Strategies, African Urban and Water Sector' (Washington DC, World Bank Group, 2012).

[20] T Peixoto and J Fox, 'When Does ICT-Enabled Citizen Voice Lead to Government Responsiveness?' (2016) 47(1) *IDS Bulletin* 23.

[21] ME Keck and K Sikkink, *Activists Beyond Borders* (Ithaca, Cornell University Press, 1998).

[22] T Risse, SC Ropp and K Sikkink, *The Power of Human Rights: International Norms and Domestic Change* (Cambridge, Cambridge University Press, 1999).

[23] Peixoto and Fox, 'When Does ICT-Enabled Citizen Voice'.

potential of ICTs, endorsed mainly by actors from the Global North,[24] is marked by normative assumptions of how ICTs ought to work.[25] The over-emphasis on the technology prevents learning about patterns of failure of ICT initiatives. Some common obstacles are: (i) the lack of adequate technological infrastructure to guarantee not only widespread access, but also a stable electricity supply and technical maintenance; and (ii) a reluctance of individuals to use ICTs in the ways they are intended to, because they do not fit in their lives/culture and/or they cannot solve an immediate problem. These points can be illustrated by the challenges with the biometric voter registration system during the 2013 Kenyan elections, marked by technical failures and poor public mobilisation.[26] In parallel, there are successful examples of tech initiatives by community-based organisations that are under the radar of the main funding bodies and mainstream media. Gagliardone et al suggest exploring ways in which new and old practices and technologies coexist and integrate, learning from what users actually do with ICTs and how they combine them with other, more traditional forms of communication.[27] Therefore, leveraging ICTs to achieve development outcomes implies both learning from failures and what is already working and supporting initiatives that have stood the test of time, ensuring that they are accessible and of benefit to all.

A complementary view of the role of ICTs in development considers a more systemic and holistic way of understanding how ICTs contribute to developing the freedom of individuals, framed in Amartya Sen's capabilities approach.[28] Rather than ICTs contributing to development outcomes, ICTs can be thought of as tools to expand people's capabilities (or freedoms) to make choices that will enable them to live their lives the way they value, which cannot be equated with economic growth. However, people may have restricted agency to make these choices, for example, due to their gender or ethnicity or due to formal and informal structures of opportunity and power relations (such as laws, social norms or customs). In this way, unequal access to ICTs can be thought of as limiting the opportunities for some individuals to live the lives they want.

III. The Role of ICTs for Monitoring the SDGs

Monitoring and achieving the SDGs are intertwined processes. Progress needs to be recorded to understand what is working, while the process of monitoring SDGs'

---

[24] Referring to richer countries, largely those above the World GDP per capita.
[25] I Gagliardone et al, 'In Search of Local Knowledge on ICTs in Africa' (2015) 4(1) *Stability: International Journal of Security and Development*, 35.
[26] 'Report of the Commonwealth Observer Group' (*Commonwealth Secretariat*, 4 March 2013) available at http://thecommonwealth.org/sites/default/files/news-items/documents/130411.pdf.
[27] Gagliardone et al, 'In Search of Local Knowledge'.
[28] See D Kleine, 'ICT4WHAT? Using the Choice Framework to Operationalise the Capability Approach to Development' (2010) 22 *Journal of International Development* 674.

indicators can, in itself, also create awareness among governments and citizens about certain issues, contributing to government responsiveness and collective action. Data collection and monitoring of progress towards 169 targets measured by 231 SDG indicators[29] across all countries is a massive undertaking with deep-rooted capacity challenges, including the enlargement of the data divide – the gap between those who have ready access to data and information, and those who do not.[30] Clark et al acknowledge that 'the resources to measure and report on 231 indicators means the government can't go it alone' with participation needed 'from all sectors' to 'generate, analyse, and report on the SDGs at the national and local levels'.[31] A range of digital tools, data platforms, and methodologies are used to generate data for the SDGs, aligned with monitoring and implementation guides that aim to support data gathering and validation processes.

The data revolution in development followed the exponential increase in the volume and types of data captured by digital technologies, adding the possibility of real-time data collection and transfer. However, the recognition of the value these new data types have for designing, monitoring and evaluating policies needs to be balanced with caution regarding inequalities in collection, access and opportunities to develop the required skills to use these data.[32] The expression that 'data is the new oil' does not hold true for development.[33] Development data needs to be shared and re-used, and linked to other data to have value. The quality of insights derived from the data are related more with the quality of the measurements and data linkages, than to the volume, variety and velocity of the data. Data is widely fungible, in that it is not consumed, but rather, it can be shared without depletion (unlike oil). The SDGs emphasise the interconnected nature of data, but not all targets are equally measurable or attainable. Indicators for the SDGs are divided into three tiers: Tier I contains agreed statistical methods for data collection with available data for at least 50 per cent of countries; Tier II has clear statistical methodologies, but little data; Tier III lacks agreed standards, methodology, and data.[34] Across the three tiers, where metrics may bisect different SDG targets, it is not always possible to analyse links between certain sets of indicator variables, due to gaps in data.

---

[29] There are 247 total indicators, of which 12 cross different targets, with 231 individual indicators (https://unstats.un.org/sdgs/indicators/indicators-list).

[30] I Marcovecchio et al, 'Capability Maturity Models Towards Improved Quality of the Sustainable Development Goals Indicators Data' (Challenges for a Data-Driven Society ITU Kaleidoscope academic conference, Nanjing, China, 27–29 November 2017).

[31] C Clark et al, 'Open Mapping for the SDGs: A Practical Guide to Launching and Growing Open Mapping Initiatives at the National and Local Levels' (2016) 6 available at http://documents1.worldbank.org/curated/en/967511563521548873/pdf/Open-Mapping-for-the-SDGs-A-Practical-Guide-to-Launching-and-Growing-Open-Mapping-Initiatives-at-the-National-and-Local-Levels.pdf.

[32] See, eg, Independent Expert Advisory Group on a Data Revolution for Sustainable Development, 'A World that Counts: Mobilising the Data Revolution for Sustainable Development' (2014) available at www.undatarevolution.org/report.

[33] A Schlosser, 'You May Have Heard Data is the New Oil. It's Not' (*World Economic Forum*, 10 January 2018) available at www.weforum.org/agenda/2018/01/data-is-not-the-new-oil.

[34] Marcovecchio et al, 'Capability Maturity Models' 1.

Building on the Millennium Development Goals (MDGs), the SDGs offer many better-defined indicators, including those associated with improving global access to water and sanitation. Data pertaining to the Water, Sanitation and Hygiene (WASH)-related MDG and SDG targets from the year 2000 onwards are available online and can be drilled down by region and country.[35] Under SDG 6, Target 6.2 seeks access to adequate and equitable sanitation and hygiene for all by 2030, focusing on the needs of women and girls and those in vulnerable situations. According to UN Water there exists a 'dynamic, two-way interdependence' between SDG 6 and every other goal.[36] Attaining SDG 6 can be seen to help reduce poverty (Targets 1.1, 1.2 and 1.4) and gender inequality (Targets 5.1, 5.2, 5.4, 5.5 and 10.1–10.3), while increasing access to education (Targets 4.1–4.5) and workforce productivity (Targets 8.5 and 8.8). For example, Hanchett notes how 'problems associated with menstrual hygiene can obstruct, or even stop, adolescent girls' educational progress, unless their schools' facilities are set up to help meet this need'.[37] These links between the human rights to sanitation, education, and gender equality highlight specific intersections between SDG 6 and SDG 3, healthy lives and well-being for all at all ages, as well as the gender equality and empowerment aims of SDG 5.

SDG target 6a focuses on expanding international cooperation and capacity-building support for WASH activities, while SDG 6b focuses on the participation of local communities in improving water and sanitation management. In a discussion paper produced by the University of Queensland's Global Change Institute, Hall et al explored participatory approaches in some 60 WASH projects in Pacific Island countries that occurred between 2005 and 2015.[38] The authors note the relevance of participatory target SDG 6b, which 'recognises that community involvement is a key influence on the long-term sustainability of water, sanitation and hygiene (WASH) initiatives',[39] while noting that '[t]he current UN indicator tends toward the old approach of a managerial or "top-down" approach, which contrasts with the more recent shift to an emphasis on government and community engagement'.[40] According to Hall et al, there has been a recent shift in participatory approaches, due to 'documented limitations of top-down community participation approaches, including the SDG 6b indicator, it is now more common to consider

---

[35] See the Global SDG Indicators Database available at https://unstats.un.org/sdgs/indicators/database.
[36] UN Water, 'Water and Sanitation Interlinkages Across the 2030 Agenda for Sustainable Development' (Geneva, 2016) 6 available at www.unwater.org/publications/water-sanitation-interlinkages-across-2030-agenda-sustainable-development.
[37] S Hanchett, 'Sanitation in Bangladesh: Revolution, Evolution, and New Challenges', CLTS Knowledge Hub Learning Paper (Institute of Development Studies, Brighton, 2016) 17.
[38] N Hall et al, 'Strengthening Community Participation in Meeting UN Sustainable Development Goal 6 for Water, Sanitation and Hygiene', Discussion Paper (Global Change Institute, The University of Queensland, Brisbane, 2016) 15.
[39] ibid 7.
[40] ibid 11 for this and following quotations.

bottom-up or demand-driven strategies'. These alternative 'bottom-up' approaches to community participation seek to increase the 'technical and economic sustainability of projects, as well as a sense of ownership by the community members'. An important point relating to the potential role of ICT tools is made by the authors, in that 'the transfer of technology or services is not considered the ultimate goal; rather, the goal is positive development of the community'.

As data gaps tend to overlap with lack of digital coverage and usage exclusions, some groups of people, certain dimensions of people's lives, or aspects of the environment are often missing from data produced by digital technologies. Good-quality data needs to be actionable and to ensure that 'no one is left behind'. Exclusions are linked to marginalisation processes that can occur across the full length of an indicator's value chain. Thinyane proposed a typology of reasons why individuals can be left behind in ICT contexts: from unknown voices (eg, isolated communities), silent voices (eg, elderly people living in institutions), muted voices (eg, refugees), unheard voices (eg, digitally unconnected), to ignored voices (eg, historically marginalised minority groups).[41] For different reasons, these voices are often absent from official data sources. A Sanitation Action Summit held in Mumbai in 2016 looked at ways to ensure no-one was left behind in achieving the 2014–19 Swacch Bharat Mission (Clean India Project) of ending open defecation, in line with the aims of SDG 6, by focusing on including the voices of 'invisible and unheard' stakeholders.[42] For example, transgender participants reported being stigmatised and not allowed to use sanitation facilities, suggesting a need to 'sensitize the public, service providers and policy makers and build their understanding of transgender issues'.[43]

Programmes and policy that are informed by incomplete aggregated data only serve to reinforce existing exclusions, by ignoring the realities of those more vulnerable. Acknowledging this risk, the Cape Town Global Action Plan for Sustainable Development Data calls for facilitating the application of new technologies and new data sources into mainstream statistical activities (Objective 2.3) while strengthening and expanding data on all groups of population to ensure that no one is left behind (Objective 3.5).[44] The Dubai Declaration that supported the implementation of the Cape Town Global Action Plan for Sustainable Development Data stresses that the full ambition of the 2030 Agenda cannot be realised without 'quality, timely, relevant, open' data that is also disaggregated 'by income, sex, age, race, ethnicity, migratory status, disability and geographic location'

---

[41] M Thinyane, 'Engaging Citizens for Sustainable Development: A Data Perspective' (Macau, United Nations University Institute on Computing and Society, 2018).

[42] Water Supply and Sanitation Collaborative Council (WSSCC), 'Changing Hearts and Minds to Leave No One Behind' (Geneva, WSSCC, 2016) 13.

[43] ibid 17.

[44] 'Cape Town Global Action Plan for Sustainable Development Data' (2017) 5, 6 available at https://unstats.un.org/sdgs/hlg/Cape_Town_Global_Action_Plan_for_Sustainable_Development_Data.pdf.

(urban/rural), to ensure that no one is left behind.[45] Such data demands require solutions that leverage the power of new data sources and technologies, through partnerships between national statistical authorities and the private sector, civil society and academia.

Good-quality data should capture the lived realities of all people. For example, gender-specific data is needed to monitor and advance progress on gender-related SDGs, and beyond the central gender equality targets of SDG 5, roughly a quarter of all SDG indicators (54 out of 232) explicitly or implicitly address gender equality. However, there remains a general lack of gender-disaggregated data in these areas. A recent systematic analysis of all indicators revealed that 48 per cent of gender-relevant indicators were missing (26 per cent) or lacking (22 per cent) gender-disaggregated data in the study countries.[46]

ICT tools, such as mobile survey tools (MSTs) to facilitate field data collection, are commonly used by global monitoring bodies. An example of a large-scale programme reliant on ICT tools is U-Report, a global crowdsourcing SMS platform managed by UNICEF that seeks to amplify the voices of youth, serving over 7 million members in more than 50 countries.[47] The U-Report tool is a two-way SMS platform, through which, users (U-reporters) can send unsolicited messages sharing relevant information about their communities and answer targeted polls that inform UN strategy. Fuelling concerns about equitable access and use of mobile technologies, U-reporters emerge as the better-educated and more tech-literate part of the youth population.[48]

Digital footprints derived from the use of ICTs such as social media, online transactions, mobile phone data and other digital data can be leveraged to derive insights to develop better policies, particularly for countries where other data sources are scarce or non-existent. For example, call detail records provided by the primary mobile operator in Rwanda were used to predict wealth indices and rates of electrification for the districts in the country with a high degree of precision.[49]

The potential of big data and data analytics to offer rapid feedback on a large scale also holds great promise in the context of humanitarian crisis. For example, a project by the ITU in Liberia, Guinea and Sierra Leone showcased the potential of big data to facilitate the timely exchange of information to combat the Ebola

---

[45] 'Dubai Declaration Supporting the Implementation of the Cape Town Global Action Plan for Sustainable Development Data' (2018) arts 2 and 13 available at https://unstats.un.org/sdgs/hlg/dubai-declaration.

[46] Open Data Watch, 'Bridging the Gap: Mapping Gender Data Availability in Africa' (2019) available at https://opendatawatch.com/monitoring-reporting/bridging-gender-data-gaps-in-africa.

[47] See https://ureport.in/about.

[48] E Berdou and C Abreu Lopes, 'The Case of UNICEF's U-Report (Uganda)' in T Peixoto and ML Sifry (eds), *Civic Tech in the Global South: Assessing Technology for the Public Good* (Washington DC, The World Bank and Personal Democracy Press, 2017).

[49] J Blumenstok, G Cadamuro and R On, 'Predicting Poverty and Wealth from Mobile Phone Metadata' (2015) 350 *Science* 1073.

epidemic. Call detail records from mobile operators can provide information to governments and to humanitarian aid agencies on human mobility, including cross-border movement, and the spatiotemporal distribution of people, while being aggregated to safeguard individual privacy. However, big data analytics has its limitations and risks, such as lack of representativeness, self-selection bias, and spurious correlations.[50]

A type of data that is more commonly associated with hard-to-reach populations is citizen-generated data (CGD), defined as 'data that people or their organisations produce to directly monitor, demand or drive change on issues that affect them'.[51] It is actively given by citizens, providing direct representations of their perspectives and an alternative to datasets collected by governments or international institutions.[52] In theory, CGD can feed citizen's views into policy debates and help to validate or challenge official narratives.

CGD is not necessarily produced by new technologies, as it can be collected by household surveys or community scorecards. Tools or technologies that produce CGD can include online or mobile surveys, crowdsourcing apps and other engagement formats using mobile phones. For example, Humanitarian OpenStreetMap Team (HOT) employs a method where the public can access maps from satellite imagery through their mobile phones and annotate them with reference points, such as buildings, parks and street names. These types of maps are particularly useful for disaster response and crisis management, but they may also be used for monitoring the SDGs. For example, OpenStreetMap was used in a project for malaria elimination, mapping buildings using malaria Indoor Residual Spray (IRS) in several African countries.[53] This type of data can be used to inform malaria prediction models, but also to demand IRS in malaria-affected areas. Working with USAID, YouthMappers operating in Mozambique and Kenya mapped malaria-preventative insecticide spraying locations with HOT, producing data that was pertinent to health targets of SDG 3, which was made available to other actors under a Share Alike Open Data License.[54] Through collection and access, CGD empowers citizens to participate in accountability efforts. For governments and multilateral organisations, CGD has the potential to address data gaps or improve data representation, for example reaching marginalised population groups to ensure that 'no one is left behind'.

---

[50] J Meltcalf and K Crawford, 'Where Are Human Subjects in Big Data Research? The Emerging Ethics Divide' (2016) 3(1) *Big Data & Society* 1.

[51] www.civicus.org/thedatashift/about.

[52] S Jameson, D Lämmerhirt and E Prasetyo, 'Acting Locally, Monitoring Globally? How to Link Citizen-Generated Data to SDG Monitoring' (Datashift and Open Knowledge International, 2016).

[53] See www.hotosm.org/projects/malaria_elimination_campaign.

[54] P Solis et al, 'Engaging Global Youth in Participatory Spatial Data Creation for the UN Sustainable Development Goals: The Case of Open Mapping for Malaria Prevention' (2018) 98 *Applied Geography* 143, 146.

IV. The Inequality Threats Posed by ICTs

ICTs can be understood as 'multi-purpose artefacts whose social meanings change depending on places of use and origin through sustained dialogical encounters'.[55] As such, access to and application of ICTs are subject to inherent inequalities. 'Digital poverty' is a term that encompasses the inequitable costs, skills and infrastructure that determine access to digital technologies,[56] while often inequitable access to ICTs also reflects other forms of marginalisation, such as gender inequality. For example, the gender gap in internet access is more pronounced in countries where general access is low, such as Malawi and Niger, where women are three times less likely to use the internet.[57]

The gender digital divide has been explained by financial constraints, ICT skills, interest and perceived relevance of ICTs, safety and security, and sociocultural and institutional contexts.[58] Social norms and gender roles can also be exclusionary factors. For example, a study by Girl Effect and Vodafone Foundation of mobile phone use in 25 countries found evidence of gendered access, with boys twice as likely to own a phone than girls.[59] In some communities, discriminatory social norms prevent girls from having mobile phones as they can be stigmatised as 'bad girls' who use phones to talk with boys or for prostitution. In some contexts, girls can enter transactional relationships with older men in exchange for mobile phones, which can expose them to a range of physical and mental health risk factors, such as HIV/AIDS transmission, unwanted pregnancies, school dropout and intimate partner violence.

Ownership is not everything, as sometimes access to devices, data or electricity still needs to be negotiated. Technologies can be restricted for women due to issues related to power and control. For example, in contexts of domestic violence, access to social media platforms are often monitored and sometimes prohibited. Access in certain contexts can also create or exacerbate vulnerabilities for groups exposed to cyberbullying and unwanted contacts. As noted by Sey and Hafkin, intersectional identities related to sexuality, poverty, class, disability and other factors have been ignored by the discourse of ICT exclusions that frame issues in terms of gender only.[60] Inequalities related to technology go beyond ownership and access. How and when technology is used can determine not only how people benefit

---

[55] C Abreu Lopes and S Srinivasan, *'Africa's Voices*: Using Mobile Phones and Radio to Foster Mediated Public Discussion and to Gather Public Opinions in Africa', CGHR Working Paper 9 (Cambridge, University of Cambridge Centre of Governance and Human Rights, 2014) 3.

[56] May, Waema and Bjåstad, 'Introduction' 19.

[57] See www.itu.int/en/ITU-D/Statistics/Pages/stat/default.aspx.

[58] A Sey and N Hafkin, 'Taking Stock: Data and Evidence on Gender Equality in Digital Access, Skills, and Leadership' (Macau, United Nations University, 2019).

[59] Girl Effect and Vodafone Foundation, 'Real Girls, Real Lives, Connected' (2018) available at www.girleffect.org/stories/real-girls-real-lives-connected.

[60] Sey and Hafkin, 'Taking Stock'.

from technologies, but also their digital footprint. Phenomena linked to social media, like cyber bullying, trolling (making a deliberately offensive or provocative online post with the aim of upsetting someone), flaming (making personal attacks on someone online) and threats against certain groups are prevalent. These threats do not need to be directed at users to affect the way people interact on social media platforms, as attitudes and behaviours prevalent in a negative environment can affect all those in the environment.[61] At the more extreme end of the spectrum, online hate incidents threaten to undermine the human rights of citizens, including their right to privacy.

Irresponsible data use needs to be addressed with reference to sustainable development. Those who provide data might not always be in a position to make informed choices or provide consent. They might not be aware of the implications of their data being collected or used, have little or no awareness of their digital rights, and have even less power to influence the process of data gathering.[62] Discussions on how data are managed or used, and whether access to or collection of said data will benefit communities, should be aligned with responsible data frameworks that include: (i) transparency and education about the possible risks and benefits of data use (and non-use); (ii) conducting risk assessments of the use of data in a given context; and (iii) well-informed consent.[63]

Restricted access and use of technologies are associated with the risk of 'black holes' of data where entire demographics can be missed. For example, evaluating a programme solely based on social media data risks 'elite capture' and skewed representation.[64] But discriminatory data collection practices also lead to the exclusion of groups of people.[65] As Khan points out, 'who is being counted, and who is not, is more than an issue of numbers and data. It is deeply political and fundamental to the struggle to end poverty'.[66] For example, the Indigenous Peoples Major Group (IPMG) considers that official data, such as that produced by National Statistical Offices (NSOs) 'should be complemented by citizen-generated data and shadow reporting produced directly by individuals and Indigenous Peoples organisations and institutions'.[67] While NSOs are seen as important to measuring the SDGs, in their absence or ineffectiveness, it is also possible to see spaces where greater participation from civil society can support data gathering and validation processes.

---

[61] C Abreu Lopes, S Bailur and G Barton-Owen, *Can Big Data Be Used for Evaluation? A UN Women Feasibility Study* (New York, UN Women, 2018).

[62] See K Antin et al, 'Shooting Our Hard Drive Into Space and Other Ways to Practise Responsible Development Data' (2014) available at https://responsibledata.io/wp-content/uploads/2014/10/responsible-development-data-book.pdf.

[63] Abreu Lopes, Bailur and Barton-Owen, *Can Big Data Be Used for Evaluation?* 19.

[64] ibid 18.

[65] Thinyane, 'Engaging Citizens for Sustainable Development'.

[66] I Khan, *The Unheard Truth: Poverty and Human Rights* (New York, Amnesty International, 2009) 61.

[67] Indigenous Peoples Major Group, 'High Level Political Forum (HLPF): "Ensuring that No One is Left Behind"' (2016) available at https://sustainabledevelopment.un.org/content/documents/10135IPMG.HLPF.pdf.

Incomplete or biased data may perpetuate exclusions, particularly as artificial intelligence (AI) systems become more central to all domains of society. Opportunities related to employment and education, immigration policies, national security, social benefits or access to credit are all based on algorithms which can discriminate against individuals or groups. Fairness of AI systems depends on the quality of data available for training, testing and validation, as well as the initial development of the algorithm. Poor indicators, black holes for certain time-periods and groups, plus failures to include necessary contextual information, can lead to inaccurate predictions that perpetuate inequalities.[68] Where general trends can underline dominant patterns of behaviour, this can obscure other patterns that reflect existing economic and social vulnerabilities. For example, gaps in internet usage result in algorithms that generalise based on biased and insufficient data from non-connected groups. Automatic processes based on biased data mimic the cognitive processes that lead to human discrimination of individuals or groups, driven by stigmas and stereotypes. As O'Neil puts it:

> Racism, at the individual level, can be seen as a predictive model [...] built from faulty, incomplete, or generalised data. Whether it comes from experience or hearsay, the data indicates that certain types of people have behaved badly. That generates a binary prediction that all people of that race will behave that same way.[69]

V. Conclusion

Discussions about the harms related to misuse of digital technologies and data for sustainable development need also to acknowledge the lost opportunities or missed uses.[70] Unshared data contributes to missed opportunities. For a number of reasons, from data ethics to data illiteracy, sharing data with on-the-ground stakeholders, including those who produced the data, is not yet the default practice in development. Shared data not only empowers people who can use it for monitoring and accountability purposes, but it also produces better data insights when validated through inclusive and participatory processes. However, 'even with a robust conceptual framework using the highest quality, complete data, identified as having utmost utility, the process of moving towards better decision-making is not automatically guaranteed'.[71] Citizen-generated data initiatives need to be supported to reduce data gaps and to provide meaning and context to data produced organically by new technologies. To reduce multiple inequalities,

---

[68] C O'Neil, *Weapons of Math Destruction: How Big Data Increases Inequality and Threatens Democracy* (New York, Crown Books, 2016).
[69] ibid 23.
[70] R Kirkpatrick, 'Unpacking the Issue of Missed Use and Misuse of Data' (*UN Global Pulse Blog*, 2019) available at www.unglobalpulse.org/news/unpacking-issue-missed-use-and-misuse-data.
[71] Solis et al, 'Engaging Global Youth' 151.

data for sustainable development should also move from binary disaggregation (eg, male vs female) towards finer degrees of multiple and interacting identities, taking an intersectionality approach.[72] If, as Schlosser indicates, data is not the 'new oil' and a finite resource,[73] then perhaps we can instead think of data as an unrefined resource. New technologies may bring new societal risks and reinforce existing inequalities, but they can also be used to understand and correct marginalising processes to ensure that no one is left behind.

---

[72] Sey and Hafkin, 'Taking Stock'.
[73] Schlosser, 'You May Have Heard Data is the New Oil'.

13
Digital Technologies and the Rights of Children in Europe

REZVAN KASEB AND ELIZABETH MILOVIDOV

I. Children and Young People in the Digital Environment

For a long time, children were perceived as humans who lacked agency and were in constant need of support and protection by adults around them. Policies and regulations largely focused on protecting children as a vulnerable and dependent group. In recent years, however, a shift has occurred in perceiving children as individual holders of rights who deserve respect for their autonomy and voice as well as protection.[1] With the evolution of the internet and new technologies, the focus has shifted towards children's agency in using technologies to enjoy their rights.[2]

Many children and young people around the world are using technology to exercise a wide range of their rights, including their right to information, to education, to play, to expression, to association and to have a voice on issues that resonate for them – issues such as climate change, bullying, equality, identity, social justice and more. However, the online world also replicates and amplifies the offline barriers children face in exercising their rights, for instance, due to a lack of access to technology for children living in poverty, in the reinforcement of norms and stereotypes for girls and children with disabilities and through the proliferation of online hate speech.[3] Children with disabilities and learning challenges may

---

[1] See, eg, J Fortin, *Children's Rights and the Developing Law* (Cambridge, Cambridge University Press, 2009); KC Montgomery, 'Balancing the Needs of Young People in the Digital Marketplace' (2011) 5 *Journal of Children and Media* 334.

[2] See J Byrne and P Burton, 'Children as Internet Users: How Can Evidence Better Inform Policy Debate?' (2017) 2 *Journal of Cyber Policy* 39.

[3] See, eg, S Livingstone and B O'Neill, 'Children's Rights Online: Challenges, Dilemmas and Emerging Directions' in S van der Hof, B van den Berg and B Schermer (eds), *Minding Minors Wandering the Web: Regulating Online Child Safety* (Berlin, Springer, 2014); JH Graafland, 'New Technologies and 21st Century Children: Recent Trends and Outcomes' (2018) OECD Education Working Papers No 179 available at www.oecd-ilibrary.org/education/new-technologies-and-21st-century-children_e071a505-en.

be more vulnerable to online risks.[4] The digital environment may also be used by those who seek to groom, abuse and exploit children, often beyond local and national boundaries.[5] Although enhancing children's digital skills may help to limit potential harm, concerns remain around children's internet use and especially social media, because of their exposure to unsuitable content and people, such as scammers or paedophiles, as well as issues such as online bullying.[6] Moreover, excessive technology use by children may interfere with their development, 'with too much screen time affecting concentration levels and keeping them away from traditional, "creative" play and education'.[7]

In Europe, children are exposed to digital technologies, be they electronic toys, smartphones or tablets, from a very early age.[8] Parents and caregivers rely on these technologies for soothing and monitoring newborns, entertaining children, teaching and socialising young people. Babies, children and young people also use these technologies, either with help and supervision or independently. This access is not limited to the family setting, but extends to day-care and kindergarten, and later to school where the skills developed at home have important implications for learning.[9] Teenagers aged 15 and 16 are likely to use smartphones on a daily basis and to spend about twice as much time online as 9- to 11-year-olds.[10] But the possibility of going online from a young age involves risks as well as new developmental and learning opportunities.[11]

---

[4] S Livingstone and D Zhang, 'Children with Special Educational Needs and Disabilities More Likely to Encounter Harm Online, Say Parents' (*LSE Parenting for a Digital Future*, 4 February 2019) available at https://blogs.lse.ac.uk/parenting4digitalfuture/2019/02/04/children-with-special-educational-needs-and-disabilities-more-likely-to-encounter-harm-online-parents-say.

[5] See E Milovidov, 'Children's Rights in the Digital Environment: Paper for the European Network of Ombudspersons for Children (ENOC) on the Evidence Supporting the Drafting of a Statement on Children's Rights in the Digital Environment' (2019) 6 available at http://enoc.eu/wp-content/uploads/2019/10/FINAL-ENOC-Evidence-Paper-Sept-2019.pdf.

[6] See, eg, S Livingstone et al, 'Children's Online Activities, Risks and Safety: A Literature Review by the UKCCIS Evidence Group' (2017) available at www.lse.ac.uk/business-and-consultancy/consulting/assets/documents/childrens-online-activities-risks-and-safety.pdf.

[7] GJ Matsumoto et al, 'A Day in the Digital Lives of Children Aged 0–3' (2019) available at http://digilitey.eu/wp-content/uploads/2018/06/DigiLitEY-A-Day-in-the-Digital-Lives-FINAL.pdf. See also A Blum-Ross et al, 'Looking Forward: Technological and Social Change in the Lives of European Children and Young People' (Brussels, ICT Coalition, 2018) available at www.coface-eu.org/wp-content/uploads/2019/01/ICT-REPORT_2018_WEB.pdf.

[8] Matsumoto et al, 'A Day in the Digital Lives of Children Aged 0–3'. See also S Chaudron, *Young Children (0–8) and Digital Technology: A Qualitative Exploratory Study Across Seven Countries* (Luxembourg, Publications Office of the European Union, 2015); S Chaudron, R Di Gioia and M Gemo, *Young Children (0–8) and Digital Technology: A Qualitative Study Across Europe* (Luxembourg, Publications Office of the European Union, 2018); J Sefton-Green et al, 'Establishing a Research Agenda for the Digital Literacy Practices of Young Children' (2016) available at http://digilitey.eu/wp-content/uploads/2015/09/DigiLitEYWP.pdf; J Marsh et al, 'Digital Play: A New Classification' (2016) 36 *Early Years* 242.

[9] Matsumoto, 'A Day in the Digital Lives' 4. See also Sefton-Green et al, 'Establishing a Research Agenda'.

[10] D Smahel et al, 'EU Kids Online 2020: Survey Results from 19 Countries' (2020) available at www.eukidsonline.ch/files/Eu-kids-online-2020-international-report.pdf.

[11] S Livingstone et al, 'EU Kids Online: Final Report 2011' (2011) available at http://eprints.lse.ac.uk/39351/1/EU_kids_online_final_report_%5BLSERO%5D.pdf.

This chapter begins by giving a brief overview of the European legal framework on children's rights that may be at greater risk in the digital environment. It goes on to examine relevant policies in Europe and ends by suggesting considerations for further buttressing the rights of all children under the United Nations Convention of the Rights of the Child (CRC) through a more holistic approach to the division of responsibility among stakeholders, from parents, caregivers and educators to industry and the state, not forgetting children themselves.

II. The European Legal Framework on Children's Rights in the Digital Environment

Since the adoption of the European Convention on Human Rights (ECHR)[12] and later the CRC,[13] to which all European countries are parties, children's rights law in Europe has been developed by the Council of Europe and the European Union.[14] As an underlying notion, children – 'every human being below the age of eighteen years'[15] – are recognised as full-fledged holders of human and fundamental rights under European law, who, given their special status as vulnerable members of society, have become subjects of further special safeguards and regulations.[16]

A. United Nations Convention on the Rights of the Child

The development of European children's rights law has been predominantly based on the provisions of the CRC, the most complete statement of children's rights produced to date. Its 54 articles are designed to apply to every aspect of children's lives – their survival and well-being, their development, their protection and participation in social life. Because the CRC imposes the same obligations on all state parties, it has had a significant effect on European institutions' approaches to developing and applying children's rights. The importance of the CRC's provisions and principles has been acknowledged not only by the European Union and the Council of Europe, but also in the case law of the European Court of Human Rights and the Court of Justice of the European Union.

---

[12] Council of Europe, European Convention for the Protection of Human Rights and Fundamental Freedoms, as amended by Protocols Nos 11 and 14 (4 November 1950) ETS 5, 213 UNTS 221.
[13] United Nations General Assembly (UNGA), Convention on the Rights of the Child (20 November 1989) United Nations, Treaty Series, 1577, 3.
[14] For a more detailed overview of the development of children's rights law in Europe, see European Union Agency for Fundamental Rights, *Handbook on European Law Relating to the Rights of the Child* (Luxembourg, Publications Office of the European Union, 2017).
[15] Art 1, CRC; For more information on the definition of 'child' in Europe, see European Union Agency for Fundamental Rights, *Handbook* 17–19.
[16] Council of Europe, Convention on Action Against Trafficking in Human Beings (16 May 2005) CETS 197; Council of Europe, Convention on the Protection of Children Against Sexual Exploitation and Sexual Abuse (12 July 2007) CETS No 201 (Lanzarote Convention).

B. The Treaty on European Union, the Charter of Fundamental Rights and the European Convention on Human Rights

Within the EU, the Treaty on European Union (TEU) sets forth the 'protection of the rights of the child' as one of the EU's general objectives and core obligations, not only at the Union level but also at the international level.[17] The Treaty of Lisbon, which came into force in 2009 as an amendment to the TEU, also includes an explicit reference to the EU's commitment to promote the protection of the rights of the child in its internal and external action.[18] The EU's adherence to the provisions and principles of the CRC has been reiterated in the Charter of Fundamental Rights (the Charter),[19] with explicit mentions of the CRC's principles, notably 'non-discrimination',[20] 'the best interests of the child',[21] 'the child participation principle'[22] and the child's right to live with and/or enjoy a relationship with his or her parents.[23] In its Agenda for the Rights of the Child, the European Commission has emphasised that 'the standards and principles of the UNCRC must continue to guide EU policies and actions that have an impact on the rights of the child'.[24]

The Council of Europe has also been greatly influenced in its policy-making and standard-setting by the provisions and principles of the CRC, based on its primary objective to protect and promote human rights, including the rights of children, under the ECHR.[25] Since all state parties to the ECHR are parties to the CRC, the interpretation of their obligations under the ECHR are made in the light of all applicable principles of international law, most notably the principles of the CRC with respect to states' obligations in the area of children's rights. As well as the general references to children's rights in the Council of Europe's two main human rights treaties, the ECHR and the European Social Charter,[26] the protection of the rights of the child is enhanced through the adoption of a number of conventions that focus on specific aspects of the protection granted to children, such as

---

[17] Consolidated Version of the Treaty on European Union [2008] OJ C115/13, arts 3(3) and 3(5).
[18] European Union, Treaty of Lisbon Amending the Treaty on European Union and the Treaty Establishing the European Community (13 December 2007) [2007] C306/01.
[19] European Union, Charter of Fundamental Rights of the European Union, [2012] OJ C326.
[20] Art 21 of the Charter; Art 2 CRC.
[21] Art 24 of the Charter; Art 3 CRC.
[22] Art 24 of the Charter; Art 12 CRC.
[23] Art 24 of the Charter; Art 9 CRC.
[24] European Commission, An EU Agenda for the Rights of the Child, COM(2011)0060 final.
[25] Although there is no direct reference to children's rights in the ECHR, the Convention is still essentially relevant to children's rights protection based on the interpretation of Art 1 ECHR which guarantees Convention rights and freedoms to 'everyone' in conjunction with Art 14 ECHR prohibiting discrimination in the enjoyment of Convention rights on different grounds, including age, though it has not been specifically enumerated in the provision. See U Kilkelly, 'The Best of Both for Children's Rights? Interpreting the European Convention on Human Rights in the Light of the UN Convention on the Rights of the Child' (2011) 23 *Human Rights Quarterly* 308.
[26] Council of Europe, European Social Charter (revised) (3 May 1996) CETS No 163.

the Convention on Cybercrime,[27] the Convention on the Protection of Children against Sexual Exploitation and Sexual Abuse (Lanzarote Convention)[28] and the Convention for the Protection of Individuals with regard to Automatic Processing of Personal Data.[29]

C. General Data Protection Regulation

Before the adoption of the EU's General Data Protection Regulation (GDPR) in 2018,[30] the main instrument regulating the data protection of individuals was the EU Data Protection Directive adopted in 1995.[31] Although the Directive was intended to grant protection to the processing of personal data of all individuals, including children, within the EU, there was no explicit reference to children as data subjects holding the rights enshrined in the Directive. Inspired by the principles of the CRC, the GDPR focuses not only on the protection and privacy rights of children, but on their participation rights, including their right to information. Recital 38 of the GDPR explicitly asserts that: 'Children merit specific protection with regard to their personal data, as they may be less aware of the risks, consequences and safeguards concerned and their rights in relation to the processing of personal data.' Moreover, Article 8(1) sets the applicable conditions to a child's consent in relation to information society services:

> in relation to the offer of information society services directly to a child, the processing of the personal data of a child shall be lawful where the child is at least 16 years old. Where the child is below the age of 16 years, such processing shall be lawful only if and to the extent that consent is given or authorised by the holder of parental responsibility over the child.

Further, the introduction of the 'right to be forgotten' in Article 17 provides for the right of the data subject to ask for 'the erasure of personal data concerning him or her without undue delay', and in this spirit, the GDPR emphasises the relevance and importance of this right 'in particular where the data subject has given his or her consent as a child and is not fully aware of the risks involved by the processing,

---

[27] Council of Europe, Convention on Cybercrime (2001) CETS No 185.
[28] Council of Europe, Convention on the Protection of Children against Sexual Exploitation and Sexual Abuse, CETS No 201.
[29] Council of Europe, Convention for the Protection of Individuals with Regard to the Automatic Processing of Individual Data (28 January 1981) ETS 108.
[30] Regulation (EU) 2016/679 of the European Parliament and of the Council of 27 April 2016 on the protection of natural persons with regard to the processing of personal data and on the free movement of such data, and repealing Directive 95/46/EC (General Data Protection Regulation), [2016] OJ L119/1.
[31] Directive 95/46/EC of the European Parliament and of the Council of 24 October 1995 on the protection of individuals with regard to the processing of personal data and on the free movement of such data, [1995] OJ L281/31.

and later wants to remove such personal data, especially on the internet'.[32] The significance of the GDPR is, further, in its risk-based approach towards obligations and the fact that it incorporates rules for policy-making with an emphasis on the importance of cooperation and sector-specific codes of conduct.[33] On several occasions such rules are accompanied by specific references to children.[34]

III. The European Policy Framework on Children's Rights in the Digital Environment

Informed by the principles of international treaties, most importantly the CRC, in the European legal system, the Council of the European Union, the Council of Europe, the Organisation for Economic Co-operation and Development (OECD), along with the United Nations Committee on the Rights of the Child, have contributed to the realisation of the rights of children in a wide range of areas through guidelines, recommendations and general comments. The case law of the European Court of Human Rights and the Court of Justice of the European Union has also been of great importance in setting policies to address children's rights protection. While these bodies play different roles in the European legal system, from standard-setting to applying and interpreting European human rights laws in the light of common international principles, at the core of the policy framework are the rights of children as a vulnerable, oft-forgotten group who can play an important role in the policy- and law-making discourse. The emphasis of such policy actions is on the human rights of all children, not only their protection rights but increasingly their participation rights, as well as the responsibility of those involved to support and promote children's rights. Through these policy actions, children are allotted an equal status as individuals while still being granted the protection they need. Some of the most important and relevant policy principles which are informed by the rights of children in the digital environment and have helped guide the policy recommendations in this area are, on the one hand, respect for dignity and privacy online; control over personal data; and protection against harassment, bullying and sexual exploitation, and, on the other hand, education through the internet; access and use of a secure and open internet;

---

[32] Recital 65 GDPR.
[33] Art 40 GDPR. See, eg, G Maldoff, 'The Risk-Based Approach in the GDPR: Interpretation and Implications' (IAPP, 2016) available at https://iapp.org/media/pdf/resource_center/GDPR_Study_Maldoff.pdf.
[34] Recital 58 and Art 12 GDPR (provision of information 'in a concise, transparent, intelligible and easily accessible form, using clear and plain language, in particular for any information addressed specifically to a child'); Recital 65 GDPR (specific implications of 'the right to be forgotten' for children); Recital 71 GDPR (no commercial data profiling of children); Recital 75 and Art 57(b) GDPR (identification and promotion of 'public awareness and understanding of the risks, rules, safeguards and rights' specially regarding children); Art 8 GDPR (verified parental consent for children under 16).

and the ability to seek, receive and impart information, as well as to communicate freely with others for social and other purposes.

A. European Union Guidelines

At the level of the EU, the Council has adopted the 'EU Human Rights Guidelines on Freedom of Expression Online and Offline' providing that '[a]ll human rights that exist offline must also be protected online, in particular the right to freedom of opinion and expression and the right to privacy, which also includes the protection of personal data'.[35] The aim of these guidelines is to address the EU's mandate to 'promote awareness raising and media and internet literacy and its importance for the safe and responsible use of the Internet, especially for children and young people, in the context of programmes of education and training on human rights'.[36]

The 'EU Guidelines for the Promotion and Protection of the Rights of the Child', adopted by the Council in 2017, reaffirm the EU's 'commitment to comprehensively protect and promote the rights of the child in its external human rights policy'[37] and provide practical guidance to Member States and institutions by emphasising the principles of the child-rights-based approach as the basis of every action and policy.[38]

B. Council of Europe Recommendations

'Building a Europe for and with Children' is a programme the Council of Europe launched in 2006 to address issues arising from children's rights and as a plan of action to guide policy-making in a range of areas.[39] The programme aimed to support the implementation of children's rights based on international standards, with four key objectives of promoting child-friendly services and systems; eliminating all forms of violence against children; guaranteeing the rights of children in vulnerable situations; and promoting child participation.[40] In pursuing these objectives, the programme provided practical guidance and recommendations for

---

[35] Council of the European Union, 'EU Human Rights Guidelines on Freedom of Expression Online and Offline' (12 May 2014) para 6 available at https://data.consilium.europa.eu/doc/document/ST-9647-2014-INIT/en/pdf.
[36] Council of the European Union, 'EU Human Rights Guidelines' 66.
[37] Council of the European Union, 'Revision of the EU Guidelines for the Promotion and Protection of the Rights of the Child' (Brussels, 6 March 2017) 3 available at https://data.consilium.europa.eu/doc/document/ST-6846-2017-INIT/en/pdf (this is the revised version of the 2007 Guidelines).
[38] Council of the European Union, 'Revision of the EU Guidelines' 9–10.
[39] See Council of Europe, 'Building a Europe for and with Children' available at www.coe.int/t/dg3/children/BriefDescription/Default_en.asp.
[40] For the final strategy, see Council of Europe, 'Strategy for the Rights of the Child (2012–2015)', CM (2011)171 final (15 February 2012) available at www.coe.int/t/dg3/children/StrategySept2012_en.pdf.

the adoption of measures which ensure the promotion of children's rights – particularly their participation rights, including their right to be heard under Article 12 CRC – in the 'Recommendation on Participation of Children and Young People under the Age of 18' adopted by the Council of Europe in 2012.[41]

The 'Guide to Human Rights for Internet Users' aims to provide direct guidance to internet users, including children, on learning about their human rights online and aspects of internet use which may limit their ability to manage their rights and freedoms on the internet, in particular their privacy and personal data.[42] The guide was prepared as a draft for the Council of Europe 'Recommendation on a Guide to Human Rights for Internet Users' which addresses Member States' obligation to foster the exercise and protection of human rights and fundamental freedoms of individuals and communities on the internet by empowering them through access to the internet and best use of it.[43] The guide also has valuable information for anyone whose rights and freedoms are restricted or violated on the internet on how to seek an effective remedy, as enshrined in Article 13 of the ECHR.[44]

The Council of Europe 'Guidelines to Respect, Protect and Fulfil the Rights of the Child in the Digital Environment' contain recommendations for states and other relevant stakeholders on the adoption of a comprehensive approach to ensure children's rights and safety in the digital environment, especially with respect to 'the protection of personal data, provision of child-friendly content adapted to their evolving capacities, [...] vulnerability and resilience as well as the role and responsibility of business enterprises'.[45] The guidelines emphasise the importance of children's voices as well as best interests in states' decision- and policy-making processes to ensure an adequate reference to the full range of children's rights. They also draw on states' obligation to ensure that businesses along with other stakeholders meet their human rights responsibilities or are held accountable.

'The Internet Governance Strategy (2016–2019)' of the Council of Europe is a 'people-centred' policy guideline with the overall objectives of 'building democracy online, protecting internet users, and ensuring the protection and respect for human rights online'.[46] With several direct references to children and young

---

[41] Council of Europe, 'Recommendation Rec(2012)2 on the Participation of Children and Young People under the Age of 18' (28 March 2012) available at https://rm.coe.int/168046c478.

[42] Council of Europe, 'Guide to Human Rights for Internet Users' (16 April 2014) available at www.coe.int/en/web/freedom-expression/guide-to-human-rights-for-internet-users.

[43] Council of Europe, 'Recommendation Rec(2014)6 on a Guide to Human Rights for Internet Users' (16 April 2014) available at https://rm.coe.int/CoERMPublicCommonSearchServices/DisplayDCTMContent?documentId=09000016804d5b31.

[44] ibid 26.

[45] Council of Europe, 'Guidelines to Respect, Protect and Fulfil the Rights of the Child in the Digital Environment', Recommendation CM/Rec(2018)7 of the Committee of Ministers (4 July 2018) available at https://edoc.coe.int/en/children-and-the-internet/7921-guidelines-to-respect-protect-and-fulfil-the-rights-of-the-child-in-the-digital-environment-recommendation-cmrec20187-of-the-committee-of-ministers.html.

[46] Council of Europe, 'The Internet Governance Strategy (2016–2019)' (30 March 2016) 5 available at https://rm.coe.int/internet-governance-strategy-2016-2019-updated-version-06-mar-2018/1680790ebe.

people, the strategy provides guidance on the respect and protection of human rights of everyone in the digital world by 'rais[ing] awareness of legitimate expectations and restrictions when using Internet services, and how to seek redress and remedies when human rights have been violated'.[47]

Further, the Council of Europe has developed the 'Strategy for the Rights of the Child (2016–2021)', which incorporates five priority areas for Member States, including equal opportunities, participation, a life free from violence, child-friendly justice and children's rights in the digital environment.[48] The strategy has been developed to help Member States face challenges in providing practical knowledge to children on how to be online and stay safe, through a remarkably participatory approach involving not only governments and international organisations, but civil society, experts and, most importantly, children.[49]

C. Organisation for Economic Co-operation and Development Recommendations

The OECD is a unique forum for governments, policymakers and citizens to address new challenges and developments in a wide range of economic, social and environmental matters. In addressing issues relating to the impacts of the internet and new technologies on children, the OECD has provided a setting for collaborative efforts among governments, the private sector and civil society to discuss common problems, compare policies, identify good practices and work to coordinate domestic and international policies for the protection of children's rights when using the internet.

In 2011, the OECD Committee for Information, Computer and Communications Policy Working Party on Information Security and Privacy released a report on risks faced by children on the internet and the existing policies to protect them.[50] Based on the findings of this report, the OECD's Council developed the 'Recommendation on the Protection of Children Online' in 2012 with the participation of business, civil society and the internet technical community.[51] The recommendation includes principles which assist governments in protecting

---

[47] ibid 11.
[48] Council of Europe, 'Strategy for the Rights of the Child 2016–2021' (March 2016) 3 available at https://rm.coe.int/CoERMPublicCommonSearchServices/DisplayDCTMContent?documentId=090000168066cff8.
[49] See A Daly, S Ruxton and M Schuurman, 'Challenges to Children's Rights Today: What Do Children Think? A Desktop Study on Children's Views and Priorities to Inform the Council of Europe Strategy for the Rights of the Child' (Council of Europe, March 2016) available at https://rm.coe.int/1680643ded.
[50] OECD, 'The Protection of Children Online: Risks Faced by Children Online and Policies to Protect Them', OECD Digital Economy Papers No 179 (2011) available at http://dx.doi.org/10.1787/5kgcjf71pl28-en.
[51] OECD, 'Recommendation on the Protection of Children Online', OECD Council, C(2011)155 (16 February 2012) available at www.oecd.org/sti/ieconomy/childrenonline_with_cover.pdf.

children online through policies which both reduce risks and enable children to protect themselves from such risks through a more responsible use of the internet. Such policies are meant to be made through an evidence-based approach and enhanced policy coordination, as well as international cooperation and information-sharing to improve the efficiency of national policy frameworks.[52]

D. Committee on the Rights of the Child General Comments

One of the main points of reference for policy guidance are the documents of the Committee on the Rights of the Child. Since the adoption of the CRC, the Committee has been mandated to monitor and give guidance on the implementation of the provisions of the CRC and its Optional Protocols[53] through its guidelines and general comments,[54] including in relation to changes and developments that arise, such as technological advances and their impacts on children's rights.[55] The Committee's recommendations to Member States are aimed at ensuring children's participation, protection and provision rights in the digital environment, that is to enable '[a]ll children […] to safely access ICTs and digital media, and be empowered to fully participate, express themselves, seek information and enjoy all the rights enshrined in the Convention on the Rights of the Child and its Optional Protocols without discrimination of any kind'.[56] In this spirit, the Committee has recently adopted, through an international consultation with children along with other stakeholders, General Comment No 25 on children's rights in relation to the digital environment.[57] With the aim of addressing the application of all children's

---

[52] ibid. For information about updates of the Recommendation, see E Ronchi and L Robinson, 'Child Protection Online' in T Burns and F Gottschalk (eds), *Educating 21st Century Children: Emotional Well-Being in the Digital Age* (Paris, OECD Publishing, 2019); OECD, 'Policy Note on Growing up Online' (February 2020) available at www.oecd.org/sti/ieconomy/growing-up-online.pdf; OECD, 'Protecting Children Online: An Overview of Recent Developments in Legal Frameworks and Policies', OECD Digital Economy Papers No 295 (2020) available at www.oecd-ilibrary.org/docserver/9e0e49a9-en.pdf. For pandemic implications for children in the digital environment, see OECD, 'Combatting Covid-19's Effect on Children' (11 August 2020) available at https://read.oecd-ilibrary.org/view/?ref=132_132643-m91j2scsyh&title=Combatting-COVID-19-s-effect-on-children.

[53] UNGA, Optional Protocol to the Convention on the Rights of the Child on the Sale of Children, Child Prostitution and Child Pornography (16 March 2001) UN Doc A/RES/54/263; UNGA, Optional Protocol to the Convention on the Rights of the Child on the Involvement of Children in Armed Conflict (25 May 2000) UN Doc A/RES/54/263; UN Human Rights Council, Optional Protocol to the Convention on the Rights of the Child on a Communications Procedure (14 July 2011) UN Doc A/HRC/RES/17/18.

[54] UN Committee on the Rights of the Child, General Comment No 12, 'The Right of the Child to Be Heard' (1 July 2009) UN Doc CRC/C/GC/12; UN Committee on the Rights of the Child, General Comment No 14, 'The Right of the Child to Have His or Her Best Interest Taken as a Primary Consideration' (Art 3, para 1) (29 May 2013) UN Doc CRC/C/GC/14.

[55] UN Committee on the Rights of the Child, 'Report of the 2014 Day of General Discussion on "Digital Media and Children's Rights"' (May 2015) available at www.ohchr.org/Documents/Issues/Women/WRGS/GenderDigital/CRC_3.pdf.

[56] ibid 24.

[57] UN Committee on the Rights of the Child, General Comment No 25, 'Children's Rights in Relation to the Digital Environment' (2 March 2021) UN Doc CRC/C/GC/25.

rights online as well as offline and taking into account the positive and negative impacts of technologies on children's rights, this General Comment stresses the respective obligations of states as the primary duty bearers and of non-state actors, particularly businesses, in the realisation of children's rights through a safe and equal access to the internet and digital technologies.[58] The objective of the General Comment is to provide states with 'guidance on relevant legislative, policy and other measures to ensure full compliance with their obligations under the Convention and the Optional Protocols thereto in the light of the opportunities, risks and challenges in promoting, respecting, protecting and fulfilling all children's rights in the digital environment'.[59]

E. European Courts' Jurisprudence

i. European Court of Human Rights

Within the system of the Council of Europe, the European Court of Human Rights has played an important role in ensuring the realisation and promotion of children's rights in its case law with frequent references to the provisions of the CRC as well as the ECHR.[60] The Court has delivered judgments with important implications for children's rights in the digital environment, in particular for their right to respect for private life under Article 8 ECHR, though in some cases that right has been balanced against other rights, for example freedom of expression and other persons' right to privacy. It has emphasised the particular vulnerability of children, especially in the context of the internet, with various consequences as to whether or not there has been a violation of the child's rights, especially where a state has failed to meet its positive obligation to provide adequate protective and legislative measures.

In the Court's landmark decision in *KU v Finland* concerning the Finnish authorities' failure to provide adequate protection to a 12-year-old boy's right under Article 8 ECHR to respect for private life following an advertisement of a sexual nature being posted about him on an internet dating site with detailed information about his physical appearance as well as other personal information, including date of birth and contact details, the Court asserted that the applicant's Article 8 right had been violated because of the failure of the state to meet its positive obligations under the ECHR to provide effective measures for the protection of the applicant's private life, having regard to the potential threat resulting from the impugned act to the applicant's physical and mental integrity and to his vulnerability in view of his young age.[61]

---

[58] See UN Committee on the Rights of the Child, General Comment No 25, paras 22 and 32–39.
[59] UN Committee on the Rights of the Child, General Comment No 25, para 7.
[60] See European Union Agency for Fundamental Rights, *Handbook* 30–31.
[61] *KU v Finland* (13 November 2008) no 2872/02.

Moreover, the Court has considered the impact of children's data being accessible and the positive obligations of states to secure children's Article 8 right, even where it conflicts with the freedom of expression of others. *Mouvement raëlien Suisse v Switzerland* concerned a billboard campaign by the applicant and its activities which include the promotion of human cloning and sensual meditation which may expose children to the risk of sexual abuse by adults.[62] *Aleksey Ovchinnikov v Russia* concerned the publication of an article by a journalist on the subject of a child subjected to sexual abuse by other children at a summer camp resulting in harms to the moral and psychological development of a minor involved.[63] To protect children's right to private life, the Court has also given due account to states' obligation to criminalise acts of covert filming of a child naked in her home and without her knowledge, even where no physical violence or abuse has been endured by the child.[64]

It is worth noting, however, that in *Trabajo Rueda v Spain*, the Court held that the police's seizure of the applicant's computer containing child pornography material[65] amounted to an interference with his right to respect for private life, though the Court also asserted that the impugned interference had pursued the legitimate aim of preventing crime and protecting the rights of children who are entitled to the state's special protection measures. The Court found, however, that the seizure and inspection of the computer files by the police as effected in the present case was disproportionate to the legitimate aims pursued and had therefore not been 'necessary in a democratic society'.[66]

ii. Court of Justice of the European Union

In contrast with the European Court of Human Rights, the jurisprudence of the Court of Justice of the European Union in the area of children's rights is still relatively limited. In the *Dynamic Medien Vertriebs GmbH v Avides Media AG* case, the Court directly referred to the provisions of the CRC in the interpretation of EU law in relation to children.[67] The case concerned the lawfulness of German restrictions on the sale of imported DVDs of Japanese cartoons on the internet in Germany where they were considered inappropriate for children below 15 years of age according to the relevant national law. In determining whether these restrictions were lawful based on the EU's free movement of goods provisions, the Court concluded that they were, given that they aimed to protect the welfare of children against content which may be detrimental to them. The Court supported its

---

[62] *Movement raëlien Suisse v Switzerland* [GC] (13 July 2012) no 16354/06.
[63] *Aleksey Ovchinnikov v Russia* (16 December 2010) no 24061/04.
[64] *Söderman v Sweden* [GC] (12 November 2013) no 5786/08.
[65] See Council of Europe, Convention on Cybercrime (2001) CETS No 185, Art 9.
[66] *Trabajo Rueda v Spain* (30 May 2017) no 32600/12. For an English summary, see www.globalgovernancewatch.org/library/doclib/20170801_ECtHRTrabajoRuedavSpain.pdf.
[67] *Dynamic Medien Vertriebs GmbH v Avides Media AG* (14 February 2008) C-244/06.

decision by reference to Article 17 of the CRC and the obligation of Member States to encourage 'the development of appropriate guidelines for the protection of the child from information and material injurious to their well-being'.[68]

IV. Responsibilities Towards Children in the Digital Environment

The United Nations' comprehensive 'respect, protect and fulfil' framework addresses the negative and positive obligations of states and other actors in the realisation of the objectives of human rights treaties, including the CRC.[69] The obligation to 'respect' requires states along with other actors to refrain from interfering with the rights of the child. The obligations to 'protect' and to 'fulfil' on the other hand require them to take positive steps to protect children against the interference with and violation of their rights, and to make sure by all means that children enjoy their rights to the utmost.[70]

A. Parents and Caregivers

Many children's rights, including their digital rights, are heavily dependent on their age and evolving capacities. For example, not all children are capable enough to exercise their rights and yet, until they come of age, those rights shall be respected and protected.[71] The role of parents and caregivers is significant in this respect, as they bear the primary responsibility of guardianship towards their children and may be best situated to decide about matters relating to them, including matters linked to the use of technology.[72] In conjunction, Articles 3, 5 and 18(1) CRC provide that parental responsibilities need to be exercised 'in a manner consistent with the evolving capacities of the child' and with the 'best interests of the child' as the primary consideration.[73] In the context of the digital environment, the

---

[68] ibid 42, 52.
[69] See 'The UN "Protect, Respect and Remedy" Framework for Business and Human Rights' (September 2010); UN Office of the High Commissioner for Human Rights, 'Guiding Principles on Business and Human Rights: Implementing the United Nations "Protect, Respect and Remedy" Framework' (2011).
[70] Council of Europe, 'Guidelines to Respect, Protect and Fulfil' 8.
[71] UN Committee on the Rights of the Child, General Comment No 7, 'Implementing Child Rights in Early Childhood' (20 September 2006) UN Doc CRC/C/GC/7/Rev.1.
[72] OA Khazova, 'International Children's Rights Law: Child and the Family' in U Kilkelly and T Liefaard (eds), *International Human Rights of Children* (Singapore, Springer, 2019) 167, 169–170.
[73] See BC Hafen and JO Hafen, 'Abandoning Children to Their Autonomy: The United Nations Convention on the Rights of the Child' (1996) 37 *Harvard International Law Journal* 449, 458; NV Sahovic, JE Doek and J Zermatten, *The Right of the Child in International Law* (Bern, Stämpfli, 2012) 160.

meaning of the 'best interest' principle has undergone change.[74] Given children's status as rights-holders, the 'best interest' principle must take into consideration not just need, derived from children's lack of capability, but also their agency in order to enhance their opportunities to exercise their rights and their coping skills and resilience to potential harm.[75] To this end, parents and caregivers must responsibly support children's exploration of the internet from an early age and inform themselves about the benefits and the risks that the internet offers by raising their own and their children's awareness of digital technology in order to understand quality screen time[76] as well as to 'identify ways in which [they] can use digital technology to benefit their child in terms of learning, play and developing skills'.[77] Parents and caregivers must regularly communicate with children about what they may find problematic online while creating positive content.[78] They must, further, be clear about expectations and rules relating to online behaviour and treat media coverage concerning online risks critically.[79]

However, parents and caregivers face many challenges in meeting their responsibilities towards children, for different reasons, including their own lack of necessary knowledge and experience in using digital technologies,[80] as well as the fact that they themselves may also violate their children's rights while exercising their own.[81] This is particularly apparent in cases where parents and caregivers enjoy their own digital rights, such as the right to freedom of online expression, which may conflict with their role as guardians of their child's seemingly competing rights in the digital environment, most importantly their right to privacy.[82]

---

[74] See M Freeman, 'Article 3: The Best Interests of the Child' in A Alen et al (eds), *A Commentary on the United Nations Convention on the Rights of the Child* (Leiden, Nijhoff, 2007).
[75] See General Comment No 14, 4; M Freeman, 'Why It Remains Important to Take Children's Rights Seriously' (2007) 15 *International Journal of Child Rights* 5; S McLaughlin, 'Rights v. Restrictions: Recognising Children's Participation in the Digital Age' in B O'Neill, E Staksrud and S McLaughlin (eds), *Towards a Better Internet for Children? Policy Pillars, Players and Paradoxes* (Goteborg, Nordicom, 2013); S Livingstone et al, 'Towards a Better Internet for Children: Findings and Recommendations from EU Kids Online to Inform the CEO Coalition' (2012) available at http://eprints.lse.ac.uk/44213/1/Towards%20a%20better%20internet%20for%20children%28LSERO%29.pdf.
[76] See, eg, E Lievens et al, 'Children's Rights and Digital Technologies' in U Kilkelly and T Liefaard (eds), *International Human Rights of Children* (Singapore, Springer, 2019).
[77] See D Kernaghan, 'Connections: Parenting Infants in a Digital World' (Barnardo's Northern Ireland, 2018) 10 available at https://getactiveabc.com/wp-content/uploads/2018/06/Connections_FullReport.pdf.
[78] See S Livingstone et al, 'Maximizing Opportunities and Minimizing Risks for Children Online: The Role of Digital Skills in Emerging Strategies of Parental Mediation' (2017) 67 *Journal of Communication* 82.
[79] See S Livingstone et al, 'Children's Online Risks and Opportunities: Comparative Findings from EU Kids Online and Net Children Go Mobile' (2014) available at www.eukidsonline.net and www.netchildrengomobile.eu.
[80] S Livingstone and J Byrne, 'Challenges of Parental Responsibility in the Digital Age: A Global Perspective' (*UNICEF Connect*, 11 December 2017) available at https://blogs.unicef.org/evidence-for-action/challenges-of-parental-responsibility-in-the-digital-age-a-global-perspective/.
[81] See, eg, LS Clark, *The Parent App: Understanding Families in the Digital Age* (Oxford, Oxford University Press, 2013).
[82] See, eg, SB Steinberg, 'Sharenting: Children's Privacy in the Age of Social Media' (2016) 66 *Emory Law Journal* 839.

There are ambiguities around the role of the state in cases where the issue is a matter related to parental responsibilities.[83] The responsibility that is borne by the state in these cases is often restrictively interpreted as providing parents and caregivers with necessary means to fulfil their responsibilities towards children (Article 18(2) CRC) and it is only in extreme cases of harm, maltreatment or negligence, where the health and wellbeing of the child is significantly at risk, that the state may intervene.[84]

B. Educators

As digital technologies are constantly evolving, competence building is essential and digital citizenship education should begin from earliest childhood at home and continue to other learning environments.[85] Efforts must be made by education providers to promote positive, safe, and effective use of technology by children in both formal and non-formal educational contexts, as well as to ensure that the benefits of digital technologies reach all children to avoid new digital divides.[86] Online safety awareness and digital skills must be integrated across the curriculum and partnerships must be formed with trusted providers and sources of expertise in the delivery of internet safety education.[87] Educators in all educational contexts must ensure the provision of digital skills development for teachers and students, supported by awareness-raising about risks and safety for young people online.[88]

On the one hand, educators must develop whole-school policies regarding positive uses of technology as well as protocols to deal with instances of online bullying and harassment.[89] On the other hand, the benefits of non-formal, outside

---

[83] See S Livingstone and A Third, 'Children and Young People's Rights in the Digital Age: An Emerging Agenda' (2017) 19 *New Media & Society* 657. See also JE Doek, 'The Human Rights of Children: An Introduction' in U Kilkelly and T Liefaard (eds), *International Human Rights of Children* (Singapore, Springer, 2019) 14–15.

[84] See J Bridgeman, 'Parental Responsibility, Responsible Parenting and Legal Regulations' in J Bridgeman and C Lind (eds), *Responsibility, Law and the Family* (Aldershot, Ashgate, 2008); C Bessant, 'Sharenting: Balancing the Conflicting Rights of Parents and Children' (2018) 23 *Communications Law* 7; General Comment No 7, 20.

[85] See Council of Europe, 'What is Digital Citizenship Education?' available at www.coe.int/en/web/digital-citizenship-education/what-is-dce.

[86] Y Toom, 'Draft Report on Education in the Digital Era: Challenges, Opportunities and Lessons for EU Policy Design', European Parliament Committee on Culture and Education, 2018/2090(INI) (4 September 2018). See also JN Amin, 'Redefining the Role of Teachers in the Digital Era' (2016) 3(6) *International Journal of Indian Psychology* 40.

[87] See European Commission, 'Boosting Children's Digital Literacy: An Urgent Task for Schools' (11 July 2018) available at https://ec.europa.eu/jrc/en/news/boosting-children-s-digital-literacy-urgent-task-schools.

[88] European Commission, 'Boosting Children's Digital Literacy'. See Chaudron et al, *Young Children (0–8) and Digital Technology: A Qualitative Study Across Europe*; J Richardson, E Milovidov and M Schmalzried, 'Internet Literacy Handbook: Supporting Users in the Online World' (Council of Europe, 2017) available at https://rm.coe.int/1680766c85.

[89] Richardson, Milovidov and Schmalzried, 'Internet Literacy Handbook' 137.

school education for acquiring digital skills and competencies by children should not be overlooked. As an alternative gateway to learning, non-formal education, which can be in the form of leisure-time training activities,[90] provided by schools or other public and private institutions as well as non-governmental organisations,[91] can effectively contribute to filling the gaps in school systems' ability to follow the pace of technological developments by providing children with tailored and context-specific skills and competencies they require in the digital world.[92] The participatory nature of digital media and technologies makes it possible for children to learn as part of their highly motivated engagement in networking, content creation and sharing, and even online playing.[93]

C. Industry

Due to the complexities of the online world, the responsibility and the role of industry in regulating its own activities are of great importance in protecting and promoting children's rights online.[94] According to the 'Children's Rights and Business Principles', 'respecting and supporting children's rights requires business to both prevent harm and actively safeguard children's interests'.[95]

Providers of social media and interactive services must ensure the implementation of 'safety by design' and 'safety by default',[96] whereby customisable, easy-to-use safety features are enabled and accessible to those with only basic digital literacy.[97] Simplified terms and conditions on social media, gaming and other platforms remain to be achieved, so that children and young people can actually agree to legal conditions which are updated annually.[98] Industry must further

---

[90] See D Buckingham, *Media Education: Literacy, Learning and Contemporary Culture* (Cambridge, Polity Press, 2003).

[91] See UNESCO Institute for Statistics, *International Standard Classification of Education: ISCED 2011* (Montréal, UNESCO Institute for Statistics, 2012) 292.

[92] See F Nascimbeni and S Vosloo, 'Digital Literacy for Children: Exploring Definitions and Frameworks' (UNICEF, New York, 2019).

[93] H Jenkins et al, *Confronting the Challenges of Participatory Culture: Media Education for the 21st Century* (Cambridge, MA, MIT Press, 2009).

[94] See E Lievens, *Protecting Children in the Digital Era: The Use of Alternative Regulatory Instruments* (Leiden, Nijhoff, 2010).

[95] UNICEF, Save the Children, United Nations Global Compact, 'Children's Rights and Business Principles' (2012) available at www.unicef.org/csr/12.htm.

[96] Art 25 and Recital 78 GDPR. See Council of Europe, 'What Does Data Protection 'by Design' and 'by Default' Mean?' available at https://ec.europa.eu/info/law/law-topic/data-protection/reform/rules-business-and-organisations/obligations/what-does-data-protection-design-and-default-mean_en; S van der Hof and E Lievens, 'The Importance of Privacy by Design and Data Protection Impact Assessments in Strengthening Protection of Children's Personal Data under the GDPR' (2018) 23 *Communications Law* 33.

[97] S Livingstone et al, 'Children's Online Risks and Opportunities'.

[98] See UK Children's Commissioner, 'Simplified Social Media Terms and Conditions for Facebook, Instagram, Snapchat, YouTube and WhatsApp' (29 September 2017) available at www.childrenscommissioner.gov.uk/publication/simplified-social-media-terms-and-conditions-for-facebook-instagram-snapchat-youtube-and-whatsapp.

develop a toolkit for children's online privacy and freedom of expression,[99] '[r]estricting access to products and services that are not suitable for children or that may cause them harm, while ensuring that all such actions align with international standards, including non-discrimination, freedom of expression and access to information'.[100] Confusion in the application of the GDPR's provisions on the digital age of consent must be addressed and effective standards on data protection need to be set, so that young people – often with parents' knowledge and support – do not circumvent age restrictions.[101] To this end, industry must promote greater standardisation in classification and advisory labels to guide parents and must ensure age limits are genuine and effective, using appropriate methods of age verification where possible, and accompanied by sufficient safety information.[102] Moreover, service providers must implement tools so that under-18s can remove content, including personal information shared by them, that may be damaging to their reputation or personal integrity based on their rights under the GDPR.[103]

Emerging technologies that will be used by children need to be based on principles of privacy by design, and oversight measures need to be implemented for services, platforms and physical devices used by children.[104] In this respect, cybersecurity in family homes through hacking, surveillance of webcams and home assistants must be properly addressed.[105] Commercial content must be clearly distinguishable, age-appropriate, ethical and sensitive to local cultural values, gender and race.[106] Independent evaluation and testing of all specified safety tools and features must be supported by the industry and a shared resource of standardised industry data regarding the reporting of risks must be properly developed.[107]

D. Government

Under human rights treaties, including the CRC, the primary responsibility of safeguarding children's rights is borne by governments providing appropriate and

---

[99] Designing for Children's Rights, 'Designing for Children's Rights Guide' (2018) available at https://childrensdesignguide.org.

[100] UNICEF, Save the Children, United Nations Global Compact, 'Children's Rights and Business Principles'.

[101] See Blum-Ross et al, 'Looking Forward'.

[102] See P Pointer, 'Protecting Minors Online: Why It's Time to Take a Risk-Based Approach to Age Verification' (*ITProPortal*, 20 July 2020) available at www.itproportal.com/features/protecting-minors-online-why-its-time-to-take-a-risk-based-approach-to-age-verification.

[103] A Bunn, 'Children and the "Right to be Forgotten": What the Right to Erasure Means for European Children, and Why Australian Children Should Be Afforded a Similar Right' (2019) 170 *Media International Australia* 37.

[104] Blum-Ross et al, 'Looking Forward'.

[105] S Hessel and A Rebmann, 'Regulation of Internet-of-Things Cybersecurity in Europe and Germany as Exemplified by Devices for Children' [2020] *International Cybersecurity Law Review*.

[106] See Lievens et al, 'Children's Rights and Digital Technologies'; UN Committee on the Rights of the Child, General Comment No 16, 'State Obligations Regarding the Impact of the Business Sector on Children's Rights' (17 April 2013) UN Doc CRC/C/GC/16.

[107] Livingstone et al, 'Children's Online Risks and Opportunities'.

adequate legislation, also with respect to digital technologies.[108] Based on Article 18(2) CRC, the state is obliged to provide parents with necessary assistance and adequate information about children's technology use and the associated risks and opportunities. Provision of digital literacy and education must be at the forefront of such undertakings.[109] Governments' efforts in providing resources must continue to support digital inclusion of all citizens while providing support for socially disadvantaged parents and households.[110] States should encourage broadcasters, content developers and entrepreneurs to develop content tailored to the needs of different age groups,[111] and ensure that private companies meet their responsibilities to respect children's rights.[112] Governments should take a more interventionist role in matters which may put children at significant risks in the digital world, not only by businesses and third-party individuals, but also increasingly by those who bear the responsibility to care for and safeguard children in the first place.[113] Since the internet and new technologies have blurred the borders between public and private spheres of life, an appropriate intervention by the government would be justified in the light of its primary responsibility to protect children from new risks and challenges.[114]

States must ensure that effective mechanisms are in place in case of violation of children's rights by providing for 'effective, child-sensitive procedures available to children and their representatives. These should include the provision of child-friendly information, advice, advocacy, including support for self-advocacy, and access to independent complaints procedures and to the courts with necessary legal and other assistance.'[115] This applies to the violation of children's rights in the digital environment where data protection authorities, children's rights commissioners or ombudspersons can play an important role.[116]

Moreover, governments are responsible for coordinating multi-stakeholder efforts to bring about greater levels of internet safety and ensure there is

---

[108] Art 4 CRC; UN Committee on the Rights of the Child, General Comment No 5, 'General Measures of Implementation of the Convention on the Rights of the Child' (27 November 2003) UN Doc CRC/GC/2003/5.

[109] UN Committee on the Rights of the Child, 'Report of the 2014 Day of General Discussion' p 20. See also Lievens et al, 'Children's Rights and Digital Technologies'.

[110] See, eg, S Livingstone and E Helsper 'Gradations in Digital Inclusion: Children, Young People and the Digital Divide' (2007) 9 *New Media & Society* 671.

[111] See Livingstone et al, 'Children's Online Risks and Opportunities'; General Comment No 7, 35.

[112] General Comment No 16.

[113] See Livingstone and O'Neill, 'Children's Rights Online'; Bessant, 'Sharenting: Balancing the Conflicting Rights of Parents and Children'.

[114] See, eg, C Bessant, 'Determining the Boundaries of the Public and Private Spheres' (SLSA Annual Conference, Warwick, 2015).

[115] General Comment No 5, 24.

[116] Lievens et al, 'Children's Rights and Digital Technologies' 504. See also Council of Europe, 'Guidelines of the Committee of Ministers of the Council of Europe on Child Friendly Justice' (2010) available at https://search.coe.int/cm/Pages/result_details.aspx?ObjectID=09000016804b2cf3.

meaningful youth participation in all relevant multi-stakeholder groupings.[117] This includes cooperation with all those who work with children, from industry to parents, carers and civil society.[118] Addressing the different roles and responsibilities of different stakeholders in a cohesive manner will allow governments, in partnership with industry and other stakeholders, to deliver complementary policy actions through, for instance, the promotion of industry codes of conduct or self-regulatory mechanisms.[119]

E. Children and Young People

Last but not least, children and young people have the right to say what they think should happen and have their opinions taken into account with respect to their online world. Children's active participation, as set out in Article 12 of the CRC, has positive impacts for them as they offer their perspectives on decisions that will affect them and their online lives.[120] Children can become responsible users of the internet and other technologies by being encouraged to maximise the benefits of the internet through diverse activities that expand their digital skills to more participative and creative uses.[121] They should learn to share responsibility for their own online safety and welfare and those of others, particularly in contexts of online bullying and harassment where, as bystanders or participants, they can have a decisive impact.[122] They should respect age limits for online services[123] and seek advice from parents and teachers about the suitability of services and content they would like to access. Moreover, children should develop proactive coping strategies such as deleting messages, blocking unwanted contacts and using reporting tools.[124] They should seek help from a parent, trusted adult or friend if they have

---

[117] UN Committee on the Rights of the Child, 'Report of the 2014 Day of General Discussion' p 19, 21–22; General Comment No 5, 37, 56.
[118] General Comment No 5, 53. See also Ronchi and Robinson, 'Child Protection Online' 196.
[119] See Ronchi and Robinson, 'Child Protection Online'; Livingstone and O'Neill, 'Children's Rights Online'; General Comment No 5, 58.
[120] See A Third et al, *Children's Rights in the Digital Age: A Download from Children Around the World* (Melbourne, Young and Well Cooperative Research Centre, 2014).
[121] See, eg, SHL Chen, 'Safe and Responsible Online Behaviors for Children' (2003) 40 *Journal of Educational Media & Library Sciences* 439.
[122] See UNICEF, 'Cyberbullying: What Is It and How to Stop It' available at www.unicef.org/end-violence/how-to-stop-cyberbullying.
[123] See I Milkaite and E Lievens, 'Status Quo Regarding the Child's Article 8 GDPR Age of Consent for Data Processing Across the EU' (*Better Internet for Kids*, 20 December 2019) available at www.betterinternetforkids.eu/web/portal/practice/awareness/detail?articleId=3017751.
[124] See L d'Haenens, S Vandoninck and V Donoso, 'How to Cope and Build Online Resilience?' (*EU Kids Online*, January 2013) available at http://eprints.lse.ac.uk/48115/1/How%20to%20cope%20and%20build%20online%20resilience%20(lsero).pdf; S Vandoninck, L d'Haenens and K Segers, 'Coping and Resilience: Children's Responses to Online Risks' in S Livingstone, L Haddon and A Görzig (eds), *Children, Risk and Safety on the Internet: Research and Policy Challenges in Comparative Perspective* (Bristol, Policy Press, 2012).

been bullied or encounter something problematic online, review online privacy settings on a regular basis, share personal information only with friends, and never post another's personal information, including pictures, without consent.

V. Conclusion

Various policymakers across Europe, including the Council of the European Union, the Council of Europe and the Organisation for Economic Co-operation and Development, continue to contribute, along with the Committee on the Rights of the Child at the wider international level, to the further realisation of the rights of children in the digital environment in Europe through the development of multi-stakeholder policies. Such policies are centred around a 'child rights' approach that aims to develop the capacity of responsibility-bearers to meet their obligations to respect, protect and fulfil children's rights, while enhancing the capacity of children rights-holders to claim their rights embedded in the CRC and other international and European instruments. This child rights approach is holistic and places emphasis on the responsibilities of all actors who are charged with protecting children's rights, including parents, caregivers, educators, industry, government and children themselves.

Parents are the primary guardians of their children and may be best situated to decide about matters relating to them, including matters linked to technology use. In meeting their obligations though, parents may face many challenges for the lack of necessary resources, knowledge and education, as well as the fact that they themselves may also violate their children's rights while exercising their own. To mitigate such challenges, educators play an important role in promoting positive and safe technology use by integrating technologies in educational contexts and providing children and parents as well as teachers with the necessary digital skills. Along with parents and educators, industry bears the responsibility to protect and promote children's rights by regulating its own activities with a view to the complexities of technologies and the risks that they may pose to children's lives considering their lack of internet literacy and digital skills. This includes the application of the principles and rules enshrined in the relevant laws, notably data protection and privacy laws. Governments are obliged to provide the necessary resources and infrastructure for the development of cohesive policy actions by other actors to meet their obligations towards children. Governments are also responsible for coordinating and aiding the cooperation between themselves and other actors, so that all rights of all children are addressed and remedies are available should a violation occurs. Finally, children's participation in policy-making is a key principle which has positive implications for children's more responsible and safer use of technology.

14

Conclusion

FRÉDÉRIC BERNARD

On 6 January 2021, a violent mob attacked the US Capitol, occupying the building for several hours while trying to locate members of Congress, who had to interrupt their joint session in the midst of formalising the presidential election's results.[1] In the context of this book, this tragic event has interesting digital ramifications.

Thus, on 7 January 2021, Mark Zuckerberg, Facebook's CEO, published a post announcing an indefinite block of US President Donald Trump's Facebook and Instagram accounts. He explained that the platform had been used to 'incite violent insurrection against a democratically elected government' and that 'the risks of allowing the President to continue to use our service during this period are simply too great'.[2] The following day, Twitter, which had been intensively used by the President during his mandate as a means of communication,[3] permanently suspended his account. The company explained that tweets posted on 6 January by the President were in violation of its 'Glorification of Violence' policy, since they could be interpreted as encouragement and support for those having participated in the riot and presented 'the risk of further incitement of violence'.[4]

These bans, which had been regularly discussed during Trump's presidency, were generally met with popular approval.[5] However, they also drew criticism. One of these was based on freedom of expression. Thus, German Chancellor Angela Merkel criticised the fact that the President's freedom of expression had been restricted by a private company: 'rights like the freedom of speech "can be

---

[1] See 'Woman Dies After Shooting in U.S. Capitol; D.C. National Guard Activated After Mob Breaches Building' *The Washington Post* (6 January 2021).
[2] M Zuckerberg, 'The Shocking Events of the Last 24 Hours' (7 January 2021) available at www.facebook.com/zuck/posts/10112681480907401.
[3] M Ingram, 'The 140-Character President' [2017] *Columbia Journalism Review*.
[4] Twitter Inc, 'Permanent Suspension of @realDonaldTrump' (8 January 2021) available at https://blog.twitter.com/en_us/topics/company/2020/suspension.html. For more details on the process that led to this decision, see E Dwoskin and N Tiku, 'How Twitter, on the Front Lines of History, Finally Decided to Ban Trump' *The Washington Post* (17 January 2021).
[5] J Guynn, 'Twitter's Trump Ban After Capitol Attack Supported by Most Americans But Not Most Republicans, Harris Poll Says' *USA Today* (12 January 2021).

interfered with, but by law and within the framework defined by the legislature – not according to a corporate decision".[6] Another criticism was grounded on an evaluation of whether a ban was really in the public interest. The American Civil Liberties Union explained that keeping President Trump on Twitter during his term had clearly been in the public interest, since it had provided the ACLU and other associations with important evidence in lawsuits brought against him.[7]

The digital ramifications of the Capitol attack are not limited to the question of access to social media. In the days that followed, the authorities gathered a wide array of digital information in order to identify the rioters: from GPS location tracking, social media posts, emails, selfies, dating sites, Airbnb bookings, etc.[8] The same sources of information may well also serve later as evidence in criminal proceedings brought against the perpetrators.[9]

These events provide a vivid illustration of the ramifications of digital technologies in our world and of the difficulties involved in assessing human rights responsibilities. Indeed, if most people agree that the current situation is not (entirely) satisfactory, they differ widely on the nature of the problems, their causes and the solutions available.

Therefore, as a conclusion to this edited collection, I propose to briefly summarise some of its findings and lessons by breaking down the issue into three categories: observations, current flaws (with potential solutions) and, finally, open questions.

Let us begin with two observations.

The first one is that technological changes, which bring about a growing and uninterrupted digitisation of the world,[10] are inevitable. It is therefore useless to dream about restoring some form of pre-digital world. As Justice William Brennan famously said, '[w]e must meet the challenge rather than wish it were not before us'.[11]

The second observation is that technological advances are per se not exclusively good or bad. Their nature is intrinsically mixed. It is in their nature to simultaneously offer new possibilities and create new risks. We therefore must find a way to embrace the progress that new technologies make possible while trying to avoid or reduce their dangers.

---

[6] B Jennen and A Nussbaum, 'Germany and France Oppose Trump's Twitter Exile' (*Bloomberg*, 11 January 2021).

[7] P Noor, 'Should We Celebrate Trump's Twitter Ban? Five Free Speech Experts Weigh In' *The Guardian* (17 January 2021).

[8] DM West, 'Digital Fingerprints Are Identifying Capitol Rioters' (*Brookings Techtank blog*, 19 January 2021).

[9] ibid.

[10] See, eg, the recent study on dating apps and couple life by G Potarca, 'The Demography of Swiping Right. An Overview of Couples Who Met Through Dating Apps in Switzerland' (2020) 15(12) *PLoS ONE*.

[11] WJ Brennan Jr, 'The Great Debate', Speech at Georgetown University (12 October 1985) available at https://fedsoc.org/commentary/publications/the-great-debate-justice-william-j-brennan-jr-october-12-1985.

With these observations in mind, let us now turn to some flaws of the current system and possible solutions that may help fix them.

The first flaw derives indirectly from the new technologies, more precisely from their ubiquity in today's world, a trend that has been reinforced by the various lockdowns imposed since early 2020 to fight the Covid-19 pandemic. Because of unequal access to the internet, there exists a serious risk of digital exclusion that may aggravate existing inequalities and discriminations.[12] The solution to this problem is technically relatively easy – it consists in building the equipment necessary to expand and improve internet coverage – but has important financial implications.

The second shortcoming is knowledge asymmetry. As many chapters in this collection note, the 'digital marketplace' is characterised by a fundamental inequality between tech companies and individuals. This asymmetry concerns the value of the information electronically transferred and shared as well as knowledge about the risks of harm. Historically, in similar unequal relationships, for instance in labour or lease relationships, states have sought to adopt laws providing additional protection to the party considered to be in a weaker position. To a certain extent, the European Union's General Data Protection Regulation proceeds along those lines in reinforcing the rights of individuals over their personal data (right of access, right to rectification, right to erasure, etc).

The third deficiency is linked to the previous one and resides in the opacity of the new technologies' inner workings. Which algorithms are used by the different programmes and applications to advise and orientate their users? What kind of (personal) data is gathered and what uses are made of them by computer software? The new technologies' functioning is so mysterious that scholars such as Pasquale have argued that these technologies are part of a 'black box society'.[13] To remedy opacity, it is essential to require greater transparency from the actors involved in devising and using new technologies, in particular companies and governments.[14] This request for greater transparency would be part of a larger trend that permeates many legal areas, for example the development of 'global administrative law'.[15]

Finally, the fourth defect is the absence of sufficient and adequate means of contestation and redress when individual rights are affected. Given the large scope of these rights, many aspects of the new technologies are concerned here. To name but a few, one can think of the secret gathering of data that breaches the right to privacy, the (mis-)use of personal data or the treatment of hate speech online. The

---

[12] B Chakravorti, 'Antitrust Isn't the Solution to America's Biggest Tech Problem' (*Harvard Business Review*, 2 October 2020): 'The United States' most serious tech problem is that half of Americans struggle to reliably get online at all'.

[13] F Pasquale, *The Black Box Society: The Secret Algorithms That Control Money and Information* (Cambridge, MA, Harvard University Press, 2015).

[14] IDI-Yad Vashem, 'Recommendations for Reducing Online Hate Speech' (Israel Democracy Institute, 2019).

[15] B Kingsbury, N Krisch and RB Stewart, 'The Emergence of Global Administrative Law' (2005) 68 *Law and Contemporary Problems* 15.

third pillar of the United Nations' Guiding Principles on Business and Human Rights (aka 'Ruggie Principles') is precisely dedicated to access to remedy.[16] The creation by Facebook of an independent Oversight Board appears, despite its shortcomings, to reflect this growing concern regarding the lack of available remedies in the case of human rights infringements.[17] The strengthening and expansion of grievance mechanisms are directly linked to the request for greater transparency, since only transparency can make public oversight possible and meaningful.[18]

Finally, we must address two important open questions that need answers.

The first question is the one of agency (who acts?). It is relevant on at least two levels. First, who is responsible for triggering a human rights issue? The situation is obviously different depending on whether states themselves are at the helm – for instance, because they are trying to identify rioters, expand the digitisation of health services or develop smart cities – or the primary actors are private companies. Whereas, in the first hypothesis, the relationship is mainly bilateral (state–individual), it becomes trilateral in the second (private company–individual–state). Likewise, who is responsible for promoting, respecting and monitoring human rights? In a dual relationship, the answer is relatively straightforward. The state, as the classic addressee of human rights obligations, will be responsible. But in a trilateral relationship the question becomes trickier (which is why it has been used as the skeleton of this book's table of contents). Should states be generally entrusted with the responsibility to guarantee respect of human rights in the digital sphere? Should companies also be involved and share part of the responsibility, by adopting the necessary rules and mechanisms? Or should even individuals be empowered to make and assume their own choices (for instance, by using a messaging app that is more respectful of their right to privacy)?[19] We should note, at this point, that this latter hypothesis could become credible only if the knowledge asymmetry identified above is corrected.

The second question concerns the relevant legal framework. First of all, should we simply apply to the digital sphere the rules and solutions that pre-existed it: 'the same rights that people have offline must also be protected online'.[20] Or do we need

---

[16] UN OHCHR, 'Guiding Principles on Business and Human Rights: Implementing the United Nations "Protect, Respect and Remedy" Framework' (2011) UN Doc HR/PUB/11/04, 27–35.

[17] On 21 January 2021, Nick Clegg, Facebook's Vice-President for Global Affairs and Communications, announced that the company had referred its decision to suspend President Trump's access to Facebook and Instagram to the Oversight Board, explaining that 'We believe our decision was necessary and right. Given its significance, we think it is important for the board to review it and reach an independent judgment on whether it should be upheld.' See N Clegg, 'Referring Former President Trump's Suspension from Facebook to the Oversight Board' (*Facebook Newsroom*, 21 January 2021) available at https://about.fb.com/news/2021/01/referring-trump-suspension-to-oversight-board.

[18] Un General Assembly, 'Report of the Special Rapporteur on the Promotion and Protection of the Right to Freedom of Opinion and Expression' (9 October 2019) UN Doc A/74/486.

[19] C Page, 'WhatsApp Clarifies Facebook Data-Sharing as Users Flock to Rival Signal' *Forbes* (13 January 2021).

[20] UN Human Rights Council, 'The Promotion, Protection and Enjoyment of Human Rights on the Internet' (5 July 2012) UN Doc A/HRC/RES/20/8, 1.

to amend existing frameworks or even devise new ones in order to fully account for the new technologies' specificities? As mentioned above, the human rights framework was built on the idea that the state is the main bearer of responsibility, which works well in a bilateral relationship, but it is less clear that it remains adequate when the actors involved are predominantly of a private and transnational nature. The doubts caused by social media companies' decision to ban the US President from using their services illustrate this difficulty.

Actually, the question of the relevant legal framework may be even more radical. Is human rights law the right framework to deal with these issues at all? Or, as exemplified by procedures initiated in the EU and in the US,[21] should antitrust laws be used to break the monopolies of large social media companies? For its supporters, this method avoids freedom of speech issues by prohibiting private companies from acquiring such a large share of the market that it somehow becomes a public forum.[22]

Because the issues involved are multiple and highly complex, it is likely that any meaningful solution will have to be nuanced and will involve different actors as well as multiple legal fields. What is essential is that the devising of mechanisms, algorithms and rules be subject, in the words of the former Special Rapporteur on freedom of expression, on 'robust public participation'.[23]

---

[21] See F Yun Chee, 'Facebook in EU Antitrust Crosshairs Over Data Collection' *Reuters* (2 December 2019); Federal Trade Commission, 'FTC Sues Facebook for Illegal Monopolization' (9 December 2020) available at www.ftc.gov/news-events/press-releases/2020/12/ftc-sues-facebook-illegal-monopolization.
[22] Noor, 'Should We Celebrate Trump's Twitter Ban?'.
[23] A/74/486, 22.

INDEX

4chan, 70
7amleh, 86, 88
8chan, 70

Abreu Lopes, Claudia, 16, 205–19
access to information, 52, 115, 135, 137, 139, 146, 147, 149, 150, 151, 160, 161–2, 206, 211, 237, 243
access to internet, 1, 4, 7, 82, 83, 205–6, 208, 226, 228, 230–1, 243
Adalah, 82–3
Addameer, 85
agency, 9, 134, 210, 221, 234, 244
Agenda 2030, 205, 212, 213
Airbnb, 10, 242
Ajunwa, I, 120, 122
Al Qassan, 89
Albano, R, 49–50
algorithms
 see also artificial intelligence
 disinformation and, 147
 marginalised people and, 124–5
 neutrality issue, 78–9
 opacity, 243
 predictive policing, 77
 social media, 68–9, 147
Allan, R, 98
Amazon, 10, 90, 136
American Civil Liberties Union (ACLU), 242
American Political Science Association, 141
Andrew, Jonathan, 1–17, 61–74
Animal Crossing, 69
Apple, 28, 39, 136
Arab Spring, 68, 86
artificial general intelligence (AGI), 78
artificial intelligence:
 accuracy, 79
 algorithms, 78–80
 biases, 79–81, 218
  workplace, 124–6
 due diligence, 12
 human rights and, 75–81, 89–91
 Israeli-Palestine conflict, 75–6
 legitimacy, 79

 meaning, 78
 Narrow AI, 78
 neutrality issue, 79–81
 opacity, 76, 81, 243
 privacy and, 81
 social media and, 68–9, 81, 147
 state obligations, 8
 surveillance, 6, 75–91
 Toronto Declaration, 90
 unaccountability, 76
asymmetric knowledge, 119, 243, 244
Australia: Five Eyes, 28
Austria: Holocaust denial, 189

Baldwin, D, 24, 25, 26
Barak, A, 33
Barlow, John Perry, 21
BBC Media Action, 207
Belgium: Holocaust denial, 189
Berkman Klein Center for Internet & Society, 78
Bernard, Frédéric, 13, 167–83, 241–5
big data, 39, 44, 47, 56, 72, 76–7, 79, 118, 120, 121, 133, 144, 214–15
biometrics, 11, 40, 42, 43, 44, 47, 210
Bjåstad, E, 207
black box society, 120, 243
Bloomberg, 195
Bluetooth, 62
bots, 146, 149, 150, 151, 161, 165
Brady, H, 139
Brazil, 45, 208–9
Brennan, William, 242
Brookings Institution, 141

Cambridge Analytica, 22–3, 94, 144
Canada, 28, 33
Cape Town Global Action Plan for Sustainable Development Data, 213
CEGSS, 208
Change.org, 68
children:
 abuse of, 222
 age verification, 237
 best interest principle, 234

digital environment, 221–3
disabled children, 221–2
opinions, 239–40
responsibilities to, 233–40
   children's opinions, 239–40
   educators, 235–6
   industry, 236–7
   parents and carers, 233–5
   state obligations, 237–39
rights *see* children's rights
children's rights:
Council of Europe: Recommendations, 227–9
ECtHR case law: privacy, 231–2
Europe, 226–33
European Union, 224, 226–7
   CJEU case law, 232–3
   data protection, 225–6, 237
OECD and, 229–30
positive obligations, 231–2
privacy, 234, 237
UN Committee on the Rights of the Child, 230–1
UN Convention, 223, 232–3, 235, 238, 239
China:
China International Telecommunications and Construction Corporation, 57
data protection and, 59
health information exchange, 43
Philippines and, 57
predictive policing, 76
SIM cards, 44
smart cities, 44, 47, 47–8
Social Credit System, 43
territorial disputes, 57
Xinjiang, 76
citizen-generated data, 215, 217, 218
citizenship:
digital communication tools, 144–6
Global South, 209–10
liberal democracies, 138–40
new forms, 140–3
Clark, C, 211
Clean India Project, 213
Clearview AI, 41
climate change, 142, 221
cloud computing, 31, 62
Cohen-Amalgor, R, 168
Cold War, 24
companies *see* **corporations**
COMPAS, 79
Convention on the Rights of the Child (CRC, 1989), 223, 232–3, 235, 238, 239

corporate responsibility:
children and, 236–7
human rights, 9–12
scope, 244
UN Guiding Principles *see* Ruggie Principles
corporations
see also workplace
abuse of dominance, 10
democracy and, 10
due diligence, 10–11, 12, 110, 113, 118–19, 127–8, 131, 182
hate speech and, 181–3
tax liabilities, 7
UN Guidelines *see* Ruggie Principles
Council of Europe:
children's rights, 227–9
Cybercrime Convention, 225
   Additional Protocol, 170, 181
data protection, 58
hate speech and, 171–2, 189
Internet Governance Strategy, 228–9
internet intermediaries, 12–15, 171–2, 181
Lanzarote Convention, 225
Covid-19, 31, 71, 117, 118, 243
Crawford, K, 122
credit scoring, 41
crime:
organised crime, 8, 64, 70
predictive policing, 73, 75–7, 80–1
profiling, 73
unequal treatment, 80–1
Croatia: privacy, 4
cybersecurity:
defining, 20–6, 35
   contested definition of security, 24–6
   parsimonious definition, 26, 34
human rights and, 19–20, 27–35
   proportionality of restrictions, 33–4
   trade-offs, 27–32
Israel, 86
privacy and, 6
state obligations, 8
vulnerable persons and, 34–5

Dalton, RJ, 142
data-intensive systems:
Asia, 37–8, 41–5
assessment, 57–9
data-driven world, 38–41
impact, 45–50
meaning, 37

Philippines, 38, 50–7
surveillance, 47–8
data management platforms (DMPs), 145
data mining, 6, 62
data protection:
European Convention, 58
European Union, 122, 243
children's rights, 225–6, 237
OECD Guidelines, 58
right to be forgotten, 225
UN Guidelines, 58–9
workplace, 121–2
De Keersmaecker, J, 148
Dean, J, 148
democracy:
access to information, 151, 160, 161–2
corporations and, 10
cyberspace discourse, 160–5
data-intensive systems and, 59
digital space and, 68
disinformation and, 135, 150
distrust in institutions, 142
ECtHR case law, 151–2, 154–60, 161–5
encryption and, 31
free elections, 31–2, 158–61
free expression and, 154–7
free information and, 136–38
hate speech threat to, 168, 169–71
human rights to, 151–2, 154–60
ideal speech situation, 151, 155, 163, 166
majoritarianism, 16
political participation, 138–40
public space, 152–3, 157
social media disinformation and, 15
Denmark, 77
Di Stefano, Stefania, 9, 11, 93–116
digital divide, 1, 160, 162, 208, 211, 214, 216–18, 221–2, 235, 243
digital exclusion, 68, 213, 216, 217–18, 243
digital platforms:
content moderation, 95–8
definition, 96
private norms, 95–101
Dippman, J, 193
disinformation, 8, 15, 135, 147–9, 150, 151, 165, 188, 197
dissidents, 35, 143, 144
distributed denial of service attacks, 16
domestic violence, 208–9, 216
Douek, E, 95, 101, 114
Dubai Declaration, 213
Duberry, Jérôme, 10, 15, 135–50

due diligence, 10–11, 12, 110, 113, 118–19, 127–8, 131, 182
Duterte, Rodrigo, 51, 53, 55, 57

Easterbrook, Frank, 21
Ebadi, Shirin, 136
Ebert, Isabel, 9, 11, 117–34
Ebola, 214–15
ECG monitoring, 62
ecommerce:
Asia, 42
growth, 38–9
Philippines, 50, 51
Ecuador: SIM cards, 46
education:
digital literacy, 7
responsibilities of educators to children, 235–6
state obligations, 7
Egypt: SIM cards, 45
election rights, 31–2, 158–61
emergency derogations: ICCPR, 32–3
employment *see* **workplace**
encryption, 6, 19, 28, 29, 30–1, 34, 43, 46
Erdan, Gilad, 82
Erridge, Marcus, 16, 205–19
Estonia: Personal Identification Code, 40, 45, 46
European Centre for Press and Media Freedom (ECPMF), 202
European Charter of Human Rights:
children's rights, 224
free expression, 65
privacy, 65
European Convention on Human Rights:
Article 17, 173, 174–6, 181
children's rights, 224, 231–2
free elections, 158–61
free expression and thought, 138, 154–7
hate speech and, 171–80
living instrument, 2
privacy, 2–6, 63, 176–7
children, 231–2
remedy rights, 63–4
European Cybercrime Convention:
Additional Protocol, 170, 181
children's rights, 225
European Social Charter, 224
European Union:
children's rights, 224, 226–7
CJEU case law, 232–3
competition law, 245

cybersecurity: definition, 20–1
data protection, 122, 243
    children's rights, 225–6, 237
    free expression: Guidelines, 226
    human rights: Internet users, 228
    mobile sensing and, 71
    privacy, 3
extremism, 53, 67, 70, 146, 148, 168, 181, 185, 188, 190

Facebook:
    2016 US presidential election and, 22–3
    algorithms, 68
    appeal system, 100–1
    Asia, 42
    ban on Trump, 241–2
    Cambridge Analytica and, 94
    Community Standards, 98–101, 111, 112, 113, 116
    democracy and, 68
    disinformation, 31, 148
    dominance, 10, 57, 93, 147, 149
    ethics and, 90
    free speech, 98, 100, 111–12, 114
    GAFAM, 136
    impact, 143
    Israel, 75, 82, 85, 86, 88–9
    location data, 71
    Lookalike Audiences, 145
    mission, 95
    nudity policy, 99–100
    Oversight Board, 11, 95, 244
        assessment, 115–16
        case selection, 103–4
        consultation, 101–2
        implementation of decisions, 105, 111
        introduction, 94–5
        missed opportunity, 110–15
        objectives, 101, 111
        powers and procedures, 101–7
        role, 102
        Ruggie Principles and, 9, 11, 107–15
        scope, 113–14
        structure, 105–6
        transparency, 113
    political data, 145
    regulation of speech, 98–101
    Sudan, 68
    translation mistakes, 75, 76, 85
    values, 98, 111–12, 167
facial recognition, 40, 41, 79–80, 89, 90
fair trial: ICCPR, 31

fake news, 147–9, 151, 165, 188, 197
Farid, Hany, 79
Fatafta, Marwa, 6, 8, 9, 12, 75–91
Fatah, 82, 86
feminism, 153
filter bubbles, 69, 147, 148, 149, 150, 151, 161, 165
Finland, 40, 231
fintech, 39, 41, 53, 208
Five Eyes, 28
flaming, 217
Foursquare, 70–1
Fox, J, 209
France, 40, 49–50, 189
Frankling, Benjamin, 135, 197
Fraser, N, 153
Freedom House, 51
freedom of assembly:
    development, 66–71
    digital space, 67–71
    ICCPR, 31, 66, 137
    ICESCR, 66
    mobile sensing and, 71–4
    UDHR, 66
freedom of expression/thought:
    corporate responsibilities, 9
    democracy and, 136–8, 154–7
    ECHR, 65
        case law, 138, 154–7, 161–5
        hate speech, 171–2, 179–80
        negative obligations, 154
        positive obligations, 154–7, 163–4, 165, 177–8
    European Union: Guidelines, 226
    Facebook, 98, 100, 111–12, 114
    fake news and, 147
    free elections and, 158
    hate speech and, 171–2, 179–80, 182–3, 189, 190–1
    Holocaust denial and, 189
    ICCPR, 31, 32, 112, 137, 138, 150
    Israel, 83, 88–9
    rationale, 135
    social media, 93, 97, 241–2
    state obligations, 6–7
    UDHR, 137
    whistleblowers, 164
Frei, Nula, 10, 151–66
Fukuyama, Francis, 150

GAFAM, 136, 146
Gagliardone, J, 209–10

gaming, 69, 70
genocide, 167, 175, 190
Germany:
  datasets, 81
  hate speech, 189, 197–8, 201–2
  journalism, 196
  victims of hate speech, 201–2
  Lügenpress, 188, 197
  public emergency derogations from basic rights, 33
  surveillance, 63
Gillespie, T, 95, 96
Girl Effect, 216
GitHub, 69
'going dark', 28–32, 34
Google, 9, 39, 80, 82, 90, 136, 145
Gorwa, R, 96
GPS, 62, 65, 242
Grewal, P, 22
Guardian, 195
Guatemala, 207–8
Guinea, 214–15

Habermas, Jürgen, 151, 152–3, 166
hacking, 49, 237
Hafkin, N, 216
Hall, N, 212
Hamas, 82, 83, 86, 89
Hanchett, S, 212
harassment, 34, 47, 54, 67, 70, 94, 125, 168, 202, 208, 226, 235, 239
hate speech:
  corporate responsibility, 181–3
  definition, 168, 171, 188–92
  ECtHR case law, 171–80
    Article 17, 173, 174–6, 181
    degree of illegitimacy, 174–80
    freedom of expression, 171–2
    internet intermediaries, 178–80
    privacy, 176–7
  free expression and, 171–2, 189, 190–1
  internet intermediaries and, 178–80
  journalism and, 185–203
    blocking, 198
    countering, 199
    deconstructing, 199
    deleting, 198
    disempowering strategies, 198–9
    embracing strategy, 200–1
    empowering strategies, 199–201
    ignoring, 198–9
    irony strategy, 199–200

  journalists as targets, 186, 188, 201–3
  legal action, 198
  mediated dialogue, 200
  questioning haters, 200
  solidarity strategy, 200
  user-generated, 194–201
  writing about hate speech, 192–4
  regulation, 168–9
  social media, 167–8, 190
  state obligations, 177–8, 183
  technological development and, 186
  threat to democracy, 168, 169–71
  three-pronged approach, 180–1, 182–3
HateWatch, 190
Hay, C, 142–3
health and safety, 124, 125–6
health apps, 76
health information exchanges (HIEs), 40, 43, 48, 52
healthcare, 207
Held, David, 138
HIV/AIDS, 176, 216
Hizbollah, 89
Holocaust denial, 189
Human Rights Committee, 8, 15–16, 30, 138
Human Rights Council, 1, 10–11, 107, 162, 244
human rights in digital age:
  civic duties, 15–16
  companies *see* corporate responsibility; corporations
  evolution, 1–5
  fair apportionment, 12–15
  impact assessments, 11–12
  regulating, 16–17
  state obligations *see* state obligations
human security, 24–5
Humanitarian OpenStreetMap Team (HOT), 215
Humboldt, Wilhelm von, 136

IBM, 90
ICERD, 113
ID cards, 39–40, 45, 47–8, 49
ideal speech situation, 151, 155, 163, 166
inciting violence, 76, 82, 84–6, 94, 168–71, 173, 175, 180–3, 189–90, 198, 241
India:
  Clean India Project, 213
  health information exchange, 43
  mobile health projects, 207–8
  national ID system, 42, 47, 48
  predictive policing, 77

public emergency derogations from basic rights, 33
smart cities, 44
Indigenous Peoples Major Group (IPMG), 217
Indignados, 143
Indonesia, 42, 43, 44–5, 48
information and communication technologies (ICT):
definition, 205
growth, 206
ICT optimists, 206
ICT pessimists, 206–7
inequality threats, 216–18
SDG 17, 205
SDG monitoring, 210–15
sustainable development and, 205–19
role of ICT in achieving, 206–10
Information and Democracy Commission, 136
Instagram, 88, 101, 241
intermediaries *see* internet intermediaries
International Commission on Intervention and State Sovereignty, 24
International Covenant on Civil and Political Rights:
fair trial, 31
free assembly, 31, 66, 137
free expression, 31, 32, 112, 137, 138, 150
political participation rights, 137–8
privacy, 30, 32–3, 137
proportionality of right restrictions, 33–4
public emergency derogations, 32–3
right to liberty and security, 30
right to life, 30, 32
voting right, 31–2
International Covenant on Economic, Social and Cultural Rights (ICESCR), 32, 66
International Organization for Standardization: definition of cybersecurity, 21
International Telecommunications Union (ITU), 38, 50, 214–15
internet intermediaries
see also specific intermediaries
Council of Europe on, 12–15, 171–2, 181
data protection, 58
hate speech and, 178–80
new intermediaries, 160
objectives, 161
responsibilities, 8, 10
state obligations, 13–15
Ireland, 64–5
Islamic Jihad, 83

Israel:
cybersecurity, 86
illegal settlements, 81–2
Oslo Peace Agreement, 87
Palestinian conflict, 75–6, 77, 81–9
predictive policing, 75–6, 77, 81–91
social media, 75–6, 77, 82–3, 85–9
surveillance methods, 86–7
voters' registry, 48

Jacob, Jamael, 7–8, 37–59
Jaradat, Hiran, 88
Jihad, 89
journalism:
function, 191
hate speech and, 185–203
blocking, 198
concept, 188–92
countering, 199
deconstructing, 199
deleting, 198
disempowering strategies, 198–9
embracing strategy, 200–1
empowering strategies, 199–201
ignoring, 198–9
irony strategy, 199–200
journalists as targets, 186, 188, 201–3
legal action, 198
mediated dialogue, 200
questioning haters, 200
solidarity strategy, 200
user-generated, 194–201
writing about hate speech, 192–4
influence, 185–6
journalism of attachment, 194
objectivity, 193–4, 200
public discourse and, 191
technological impact on, 186–8

Kaseb, Rezvan, 7, 221–40
Kaye, David, 6, 81, 111, 115
Keck, ME, 209
Keel, Guido, 10, 185–203
Kenya, 46, 47, 208, 210, 215
Khan, I, 217
King, Martin Luther, 35
Klonick, K, 97, 98–9, 100, 112
Kogan, Aleksander, 22
Krishnamurthy, Vivek, 6, 8, 12, 19–35

Laos, 44
Lanzarote Convention, 225

Lehr, Amy, 6, 8, 12, 19–35
Lewis, M, 147
libel, 198
Liberia, 214–15
LinkedIn, 68
Lithuania, 3–4
location monitoring, 62, 70–1
Luck, C, 147
Lyft, 47

M-PESA, 208
McCarthy, John, 78
Macedo, S, 141
McNair, B, 194
majoritarianism, 16
malaria, 215
Malawi, 216
Malaysia, 43–4
Marshall, TH, 138
Maurer, Ueli, 192
May, J, 207
Mendel, T, 171
Mendel, Yonathan, 85
Merkel, Angela, 241–2
'Mete a Colher', 208–9
#MeToo, 191, 208
Mexico: SIM cards, 49
mHealth projects, 207
micro-targeting, 145, 148
Microsoft, 70, 90, 136
Mill, John Stuart, 136–7, 169
Millennium Development Goals (MDGs), 212
Milovidov, Elizabeth, 7, 221–40
Mobile Kunji, 207
mobile phones, 38, 40, 42, 45–6, 55, 62, 117, 145, 206, 207, 208, 214, 215, 216
mobile sensing, 71–4
mobile survey tools, 214
Molnar, P, 169
monitoring *see* surveillance
Moscow Times, 195
Mozambique, 215
Mueller Report (2019), 146
Myanmar, 167–8, 182

national identity systems, 39–40, 42–3, 45, 47–8, 49, 53–5
national security
   see also terrorism
   artificial intelligence and, 218
   concepts, 28–9
   human rights and, 33, 59

   Israel, 85, 90
   Philippines, 51, 53–4
   surveillance and, 35, 63, 64
Netanyahu, Benjamin, 87
Netherlands: predictive policing, 77
Neue Zürcher Zeitung, 195, 197
neuromarketing, 145
New America, 22
New York Times, 195
New Zealand, 28
Niger, 216
Nigeria, 45–6, 48–9
#NiUnaMenos, 208

Obermaier, M, 202
Occupy movement, 143
OECD, 58, 229–30
Olson, M, 139–40
O'Neil, C, 218
organised crime, 8, 64, 70

Pakistan, 44, 49
Palantir Technologies, 77
Pariser, E, 147
Parmar, S, 114
Pasquale, F, 120, 243
peacebuilding, 209–10
Peixoto, T, 209
Pejchal, Viera, 13, 167–83
Pennycook, G, 148
Philippines:
   armed conflicts, 50
   China and, 57
   corruption, 54
   data-intensive systems, 38, 50–7
   data protection, 51
   ecommerce, 50, 51
   ePassports, 52
   extrajudicial killings, 51
   health information exchange, 52
   human rights instruments, 50–1
   ICT regulation, 51
   internet use, 50
   National Big Data Center, 56
   national ID programme, 53–5
   national security, 51, 53–4
   SIM cards, 55
   voter registration, 52
platforms *see* digital platforms
political participation:
   decline, 140–3
   definition, 142

digital communication tools, 144–6
ICCPR, 137–8
liberal democracies, 138–40
new forms, 140–3
social media and, 143, 144–6
veracity of news, 147–9
political parties, 139, 141, 144, 145–6, 159, 188
populism, 51, 193
portals, 179–80
Post, Robert, 169
predictive policing, 6, 9, 46, 73, 75–7, 80–91
privacy:
  artificial intelligence and, 81
  children, 234, 237
  concept, 118
  cybersecurity and, 6
  data minimisation, 120
  diversity of perceptions, 2
  due diligence, 118–19
  ECtHR, 2–6, 63, 176–7
    children, 231–2
  European Union, 3
  evolution of concept, 4
  hate speech and, 176–7
  ICCPR, 30, 32–3, 137
  Philippines, 54–5, 56
  positive obligations, 231–2
  privacy by design, 121, 237
  proportionality, 3
  public emergency derogations, 32–3
  security and, 27–9
  SIM cards and, 47
  surveillance and, 3, 5, 63–6
  workplace monitoring and, 118, 119–33
Privacy International, 49
programmatic advertising, 146
public sphere, 152–3, 157, 160–1
Putin, Vladimir, 146
Putnam, Robert, 141

Quora, 69

racism:
  Additional Protocol to European Cybercrime Convention, 170
  artificial intelligence and, 80, 218
  hate speech, 192
  ICERD, 113
  Israel, 86
  online examples, 70
  social media, 86, 113, 188
  workplace monitoring and, 125

Rawls, John, 137
Reddit, 70
religious freedom, 11, 62, 113, 137, 177
remedy rights:
  ECHR, 63–4
  effectiveness criteria, 131
  Facebook, 114
  inadequacy, 243–4
  Ruggie Principles, 108, 109–10, 244
  workplace monitoring grievances, 131–2
Reporters Without Borders, 201
Reuters, 195
right to be forgotten, 225
right to liberty and security: ICCPR, 30
right to life, 30, 32
Risse, T, 209
Roets, A, 148
Ropp, SC, 209
Ruggie, John, 10
Ruggie Principles:
  Facebook Oversight Board and, 9, 11, 95, 110–15
  hate speech and, 183
  impact, 10–11
  obligations, 108–10
  remedy rights, 108, 109–10, 244
  soft law, 107
  workplace privacy and, 118, 126–33
Russia, 22–3, 146, 156–7, 162–3, 232
Rwanda, 182, 190, 191, 214

Sada Social, 89
SAHAYOG, 207
Sander, B, 97–8
Sanitation Action Summit (2016), 213
sarcasm, 89, 199
Schaaf, M, 207–8
Schlosser, A, 211, 219
Schlozman, KL, 139
Schmidt, Devony, 6, 8, 12, 19–35
Schneier, B, 26
Schultz, J, 122
search engines, 56, 76, 81, 139, 160, 161
security: defining, 24–6
self-driving cars, 76
sexism, 79–80
Sey, A, 216
Shaked, Ayelet, 82
Share Alike Open Data License, 215
Sikkink, K, 209
SIM cards, 39–40, 44, 45–6, 47, 49, 55
Singapore, 43, 44, 56

slander, 198
smart cities, 39–40, 41, 44, 45, 47, 49, 56, 72, 244
smartphones, 65, 206, 222
SMS, 207, 214
Snowden, Edward, 28
social capital, 139
social credit scoring, 43
social media
  see also specific networks
  2016 US presidential election and, 22–3
  artificial intelligence and, 68–9, 81, 147
  content moderation, 95–8
  corporate responsibility, 97
  democracy and, 68–9
  disinformation, 8, 15, 147–9
  dominance, 10, 38, 245
  finances, 39
  free expression, 93, 97
    Trump suspensions, 241–2
  hate speech, 167–8, 190
  Israeli-Palestinian conflict, 75–6, 77, 82–3, 85–9
  journalism and, 186–8
  location data, 70–1, 72
  Philippines, 50
  political participation and, 143, 144–6
  racism, 86, 113, 188
  responsibilities to children, 236
  source of information, 242
  trend, 61
  vulnerable people and, 12
  workplace and, 129
social movements, 140, 142, 143
South Africa, 33, 213
South Korea, 44, 49
Soviet Union: Cold War, 24
Stanley, Jason, 150
state-building, 209–10
state obligations:
  children's rights, 237–39
  data-intensive systems, 37–59
  digital age, 5–8
  free expression, 154–7, 163–4, 165
  hate speech and, 177–8, 183
  internet intermediaries, 13–15
  privacy, 231–2
  Ruggie Principles, 108
  scope, 244–5
Stern, 195
Stiglitz, Joseph, 136
Sudan, 68

surveillance:
  artificial intelligence and, 6
  children, 237
  cybersecurity and, 34–5
  data-intensive systems and, 47–8
  ECtHR case law, 63–5
  location monitoring, 62, 70–4
  predictive policing, 73, 75–7, 80–1
  privacy and, 3, 5, 63–6
  smart cities, 47
  surveillance capitalism, 41
  US case law, 65–6
sustainable development: SDGs:
  Agenda 2030, 205
  ICT monitoring, 210–15
  ICT role in achieving, 206–10
  indicators, 211
  SDG 3, 212, 215
  SDG 5, 214
  SDG 6, 212, 213
  SDG 17, 205
Switzerland, 189, 192, 194, 195, 197, 232

Taipei: smart cities, 44
Tatour, Dareen, 85
taxation: companies, 7
Teorell, J, 139
terrorism, 8, 28–31, 49, 53, 63, 64, 70, 77, 83–5, 88, 185
Thailand: ecommerce, 42
Toronto Declaration, 90
trolls, 149, 150, 161, 195, 217
Trump, Donald, 22, 146, 192, 193, 241–2
truth bias, 149
Turkey: genocide, 175
Twitch, 70
Twitter, 68, 71, 97, 148, 167, 183, 191, 241, 242

U-Report, 214
Uber, 10, 47, 76
UNICEF, 214, 236
United Nations
  see also specific instruments
  Committee on the Rights of the Child, 230–1
  Convention on the Rights of the child, 223, 232–3, 235, 238, 239
  data protection, 58–9
  freedom of expression and, 81
  Guiding Principles on Business and Human Rights *see* Ruggie Principles
  human rights in digital age, 1, 6
  human rights instruments, 109

ICERD, 113
MDGs, 212
'respect, protect and fulfil', 233
SDGs, 205, 210–15
United States:
  2016 presidential election, 22–3, 146
  antitrust laws, 245
  artificial intelligence, 79
  Capitol attack (2021), 241–2
  Cold War, 24
  cybersecurity: definition, 20
  datasets, 81
  Facebook accounts, 147
  FBI, 35
  Five Eyes, 28
  free speech, 97, 189–90, 197
  hate speech, 189–90
  Mueller Report (2019), 146
  National Institute of Science and Technology (NIST), 20
  Philippines and, 56
  predictive policing, 77, 80
  racism, 80
  surveillance case law, 65–6
Universal Declaration of Human Rights, 1, 50, 66, 137, 173

Vargas Llosa, Mario, 136
Verba, S, 139
Vietnam, 59
Vietnam War, 99
Vodafone Foundation, 216
Volkskrant, 195
Vosoughi, S, 148
voting decline, 141
voting right, 31–2, 158–61
vulnerable persons:
  cybersecurity and, 34–5
  SIM cards and, 49
  social media and, 12
  workplace monitoring and, 124–6

Waema, TM, 207
weaponization of information, 150
Web 2.0, 62
Weiser, M, 15
WhatsApp, 28
whistleblowers, 47, 164
Wikipedia, 69, 149

Wildhaber, Isabelle, 9, 11, 117–34
Wissenschaftliche Dienste Deutscher Bundestag, 189
women:
  artificial intelligence and, 79–80
  digital divide, 208, 216
  domestic violence and, 208–9, 216
  health and safety and, 124
  #MeToo, 191, 208
  public sphere and, 153
  SDG 5, 214
  workplace monitoring and, 124–6
workplace:
  asymmetric power, 122
  'black box', 120
  Covid-19 and, 117, 118
  datafication, 117–18, 119–26
    collection, 119
    deletion, 119
    supervisors' data illiteracy, 121–2, 123
    use, 119
  health and safety, 124, 125–6
  human rights due diligence, 127–8, 131
  monitoring, 11
    accountability, 132–3
    biases, 124–6
    data protection, 121–2
    design-based protection, 121
    employees' low bargaining power, 122
    impact assessments, 127, 128–30
    opaque governance, 120–1
    oversight, 132–3
    privacy, 118, 119–33
    remedies, 131–2
    risks, 123–4
    Ruggie Principles, 118, 126–33
    stakeholder engagement, 129, 130
    tools, 119
    vendor lock-in, 124
    vulnerable and marginalised people, 124–6
World Summit on the Information Society, 1

Yik Yak, 71
YouTube, 69, 70, 82, 97, 162

Zeliger, Barbie, 193
Zimbabwe, 47
Zuckerberg, Mark, 82, 94, 101, 241

Lightning Source UK Ltd.
Milton Keynes UK
UKHW020700171221
395726UK00003B/182